This book consisting of more than 7,000 names is a most useful source of information for scholars, general readers and those who wish to name their children. All the major Sanskrit sources are searched for the compilation of this book. This reference work will be invaluable for all those seeking to learn more about the fascinating heritage of Hindu names.

ABOUT THE AUTHORS

Ramesh C. Dogra received his M.Phil. at the University of London and has written eight books and at 24 articles on many South Asian topics, particularly in the fields of Indology and Sikhism. He currently holds the position of Principal Assistant Librarian as Head of South Asia Department, at the School of Oriental and African Studies, University of London.

Mrs. Urmila Dogra, a Civil Servant in London, has been associated with the Research Projects of Mr. Dogra since 1986. She is the co-author of this book.

Published by :
STAR PUBLICATIONS (P) LTD.
NEW DELHI-110002 (INDIA)

R.C. DOGRA
U. DOGRA

Thought Provoking HINDU NAMES

with meanings and explanation in English
and
translation into Hindi

A REFERENCE BOOK, EQUALLY USEFUL FOR SCHOLARS AND GENERAL READERS WHO WISH TO SELECT MEANINGFUL NAMES FOR THEIR CHILDREN.

South Asian Librarian
School of Oriental & African Studies
University of London, LONDON WC1H OXG

ISBN 81-7650-013-5

Published by : **STAR PUBLICATIONS (PVT.) LTD.**
4/5, Asaf Ali Road, New Delhi-110002 (India)

Sec

Price : (Paperback Edition): Rs.195/-

Pice in U.K.: Pounds 11.95(PB)

Sole distributors in the U.K. :
STAR PUBLISHERS DISTRIBUTORS,
112, Whitfield St., LONDON W1T 5EE.
(Ph. (020) 7380 0622, E-mail: indbooks@aol.com)

Typesetting by PULLSHOPPE, 236 Kamla Market, Asaf Ali Road, New Delhi-2

Dedicated to

HINDUISM, the oldest heritage

in the history of mankind.

Introduction

This is a completely revised edition of our book 'A Dictionary of Hindu Names', published by Aditya Prakashan, New Delhi, in 1992. Upon this foundation we have superadded at least three thousand five hundred names from Sanskrit sources. According to F. Max Muller, Sanskrit is not the mother of Greek and Latin, as Latin is of French and Italian, but Sanskrit, Greek and Latin are sister tongues, though Sanskrit is the elder sister. All the Indo-Aryan languages are derived from Sanskrit.

Hindu names is a vast subject that would really need at least ten volumes to give it a justice. It is a big subject both in time and quantity. In time and quantity, because our earliest texts (Rig Veda) are dated earlier than c.1500 BC, and for all of the 1652 or so languages, we have taken names from Sanskrit sources only. All of the religious works, the drama, the lyrics, the sentimental and philosophical kavya, the Bhagvad Gita, Mahabharata, Ramayana, the fables, Hitopadesa, Vedas, and works on sciences were originally written in Sanskrit.

In this work, an effort has been made to meet the long-felt need for a dictionary of Hindu names. These names in Roman and Devanagari characters, together with their meanings and explanations, are given. The main portion of this work consists of names from Vedas, Puranas, Mahabharata, Ramayana and other Sanskrit sources and dictionaries. Following the world tradition of celebrating the Holy names of Gods and Goddesses, we have included in this book one thousand names of Lord Vishnu, and one hundred and eight names of each of the following Gods and Goddesses, significant of the one hundred and eight beads in a rosary which is used during prayers :

Lord Ganesha, Hanuman, Krishna, Ram, Shiva,
Goddess Durga and Lakshmi.

Ever since men evolved a language, they tried to give names to things of daily use in their life. With the progress of social consciousness, men were also named, as without particular names of individuals it was impossible to carry on the business of a cultured society. According to the general rules of the *Grihasutras*, the naming ceremony in Hindus is performed on the tenth or the twelfth or the hundredth day, or at the expiry of the first year, after the birth of the child. This wide option was due to the convenience of the family and health of the mother and the child.

Throughout the Vedic period, the name given to a person was his own secular name and one or more name derived from a variety of sources including either from his father's, grandfather's, mother's, or from his Gotra name (derived from Vedic Rishis), or from a locality. The Vedic people avoided personal names drawn from the Hindu gods or religion. The custom of giving names of divinity was popular among non-Aryans, i.e. South Indian people. The names of stars and planets were also avoided by the Aryans during the Vedic times, as they would use names taken from nature e.g. of mountains, hills, rivers, forests etc. The popular river names during Vedic times were Narmada/Narbuda (daughter of Mekala Rishi), Sarasvati (river goddess), Ganga (holy river, wife of Santanu and mother of Bhishmas).

During the Vedic period some Hindu families, and even some schools of Vedic study, were called after some animals, plants, or inanimate objects with which they were held to be totemically related. From Aja (goat) comes the name of Aja (a tribe mentioned in the Rig Veda); Ashva (horse) is the root of such names as Ashvapati (Lord of horses, an appellation of many kings), Asvatthama (son of Drona and Kripa), Aswins, Aswinau (dual), Aswini Kumaras (horseman, two Vedic deities, twin sons of the sun and the sky).

From Gautama/Gotama (bull) came the name of the sage Saradwat (son of Gotama and father of Kripa). There was another person called Gotama who was the founder of the Nyaya school of philosophy. Kaushik/Kaushak (owl) father of Vishwamitra, Kachchapa/ Kashyap (tortoise) is the name of a sage, the son of Marichi, and one of the prajapatis or progenitors of created things. Mudgal (a kind of fish), a Vedic Rishi from whom the Mudgal Brahmans sprang. Nakul (an animal of the mongooses genus) was the name of the fourth of the Pandu princes. He was the twin son of Madri, the second wife of Pandu, from Pipal (tree) comes the name of Pippalada a name of a sage who founded the school of Atharva Veda. From Shunak/Shaunak (dog) came the name of a sage, the son of Sunaka and grandson of Gritsa-mada (Atharva-Veda teacher). Bhardwaj (sky-lark, a well known bird that flies high as it sings) is the totemic name of a sage to whom many Vedic hymns are attributed.

Kukkura (dogs) were a tribe associated with the Virishnis along the Yamuna. Sometimes names were used as part of a name because of some association e.g. (Vyas, compiler of Mahabharata), was born on an island called Dvipa and he was known as Vyas Dvaipayan.

Hindus believe that there exists a link between the name and deeds or course of life of the divine or human being. Therefore a good name represents goodness e.g. Shiva's name is said to inspire respect because of its inherent energy, and this means that energetic and respect inspiring side of the God's character is expressed and transmitted by his name so as to impress those who know or hear it.

Modern Hindu names are aesthetic in sense, and tend to be neither too long nor too short. These may be a family's expression of gratitude to a deity for the blessings received or wishes fulfilled, or may show an association with an event, time, place or person. The name Dukhi Ram (miserable) was used to keep away the evil eye The name Sukhi Das (prosperous devotee) was used to show prosperity. When Chaitanya Mahaprabhu (a modern Vaishnava reformer, accounted as an incarnation of Lord Krishna) was born, some people proposed to give him the name of a tree with bitter leaves (Nimai), as they believed that this is not liked by the God of death.

In some villages, a pregnant woman who is afraid that her child would die will usually sell it to a friend before its birth for four or five cowries.* After birth the baby will be named Char cowries or Panch cowries, and it is believed that an evil eye, or God who is jealous of some child, will overlook one whose name be worthless. Similarly some children are named Kāla (black), Gunga (dumb), Bola (deaf). It does not mean that the child Bola is actually deaf. Such names were usually used by orthodox people, but now these names are not popular. A name usually serves to indicate or signify a person and does not impute a person. It is a matter of common knowledge that the name is regarded as an essential part of its bearer or its true existence. The connection between a name and its bearer is so intimate that there is for all practial purposes a question of identity, and it should be given in a well considered way and should denote the personality of its bearer.

At present name are not always derived from pure Sanskrit words, though mostly they do not differ from those used 500 years ago, either in form or derivation. Hindi, Prakrit and corrupted forms of dialectical variants, and even words of Persian and Arabic origin have crept into Hindu's personal names, like the Arabic word 'Jawahar' meaning "jewel", the Persian word 'Gulab' meaning "rose". Persian and Arabic influence is more dominant in Northern India than is other parts of India.

According to Hindu mythology, everything in the world is a manifestation of God, therefore the name of any entity can be used as a given name. A name is the primary mean of social intercourse. It brings realisation, merits and is also considered as the root of good fortune. The naming ceremony is very important in Hinduism, but in cities many people usually do not conduct the ceremony.

The following directions were laid down by the early law givers regarding the naming of children. A boy's name should begin with a consonant and have an even number of syllables. A girl's name should have an odd number of syllables and end with long 'a' or 'i'. The adoption of a second name (Ram Das) is assumed for success and distinction in life, or to show their patronymic or metronymic reasons like Mohandas Karamchand. A name should be easy to pronounce, not hard to hear. of clear meanings, charming, auspicious, or should contains some blessings.

In the olden days it was considered that the name of a Brahman should be auspicious; Kshatriya should denote power; Vaishya, wealth and that of Sudra, devotion. Secret names were also given and were considered a sort

---

* a currency denomination of ancient times.

of charm which may drive off evil and should not be used except in emergencies, lest its power should wear out. Hindus used to recite secret names only in prayers and during religious ceremonies. These days Hindus do not believe in such things and any one may choose any name he/she like.

Children were also given nakshatra (a lunar asterism under which the child was born, or from the presiding deity). For example, if a child was born under the constellation Asyini/Asvini, he was named Asvini Kumar, or if under Rohini, Rohini Kumar etc. etc. Some people also gave name to children according to their family deity i.e. Indra, Rama, Shiva, Ganesha, Lakshmi, etc. A good name should have good meaning, signify glory, fame and suggest the sex of the bearer.

A good and meaningful name is a symbol of cultural heritage and it should be able to focus the image of the person within a few words. Hindu culture, with its Sanskrit literature, has been famous in developing such a taste which is found illustrated in every walk of life. There is not a single Hindu name which does not speak of its heritage, ancestry, character and personality in detail. This is what we have tried to demonstrate in this book. Having considered the vastness of the field of personal names, and the fabulous nature of the wealth of Sanskrit literature, we had to confine ourselves, in our efforts, to some exemplary works of not a specific period, but from the Vedic times to the present day.

Amongst the Hindus and Sikhs in Northern India (Panjab, Haryana), Lord Indra's name (God of thunder, a personification of the sky, the chief of Devatas) has become very popular, e.g. Indra Singh, Indra Kumar, Narindra, Satyendra, Surindra, Devindra. Many Hindus and Sikhs use the name Indra as a suffix. The attributes of Indra correspond to those of the Jupiter Pluvius and Jupiter Tonans of the Greeks and Romans, and the Thor of Scandinavia, and as such he is the impersonation of the skies.

Names in this book have not been transliterated according to some specific style. Strictly speaking, transliteration means letter-by-letter transription from one alphabet into another, and some libraries and scholars favour this, as they are concerned with reversibility - that is reconstruction of the original - for the sake of identification. Other research scholars and libraries favour phonetic transcription and do not believe in the necessity of reversibility in transliteration. In this work we have used phonetic transcription without any diacritics, except for the long letter 'a' or 'i'.

The vowels a, i, e, ai, o, au, used in the text, are long, and have approximately the same pronunciation as the vowels in the English calm. A, i, u are short, and equivalent to the vowels in the English words. The reader should avoid pronuncing them as in English sat. Thus Sanskrit Sama is pronounced as English Sum. The letter 'b' and 'v' are occasionally interchanged, so that words not found under the one letter should be sought for under the other.

The words and their meanings in any dictionary can scarcely be proved by its compilers to belong to themselves. The aggregation and arrangements of words with correct definitions give any dictionary as the best right to be called an original work. The knowledge which has been stored here is quite useful for the new generation of Hindus and Sikhs, who wish to name their children according to their ancient traditions.

We are thankful to our son Rahul Dogra for going through the manuscript and offering his opinion and comments. Thanks are also due to for including this volume as a part of their prestigious publications, and our particular thanks to Shri Amar Nath Varma (Chairman and Managing Director) for his unfailing courtesy and welcome help, encouragement and willingness to publish the volume.

The idea of including names in Devanagari characters was the brain child of Mr. Amar Nath Varma, and we are thankful to him for all the help he has given us in this regard.

The abbreviations used in the parenthesis are as follows : a-adjective; f-feminine; m-masculine; n-neutral. D-Durga; G-Ganesh; H-Hanuman; K-Krishna; L-Lakshmi; R-Rama; S-Shiva; V-Vishnu.

SOAS
London (U.K.)
December 1998

U. Dogra
R. C. Dogra

A (अ, आ)

Ābādh (अबाध) (*m/f*) Free from any problem, unrestrained.

Abaj (अबज) (*m*) The moon, the physician of Gods, the conch.

Abālendū (अबालेन्दु) (*m*) Full moon.

Ābhā (आभा) (*f*) Light, splendour, colour, a reflection.

Ābhās/Abhāsā (अभास/अभासा) (*m,f*) Splendour, light, Vedantas, coloure, appearance.

Ābhāsanā (आभासना) (*n*) Illumination, making apparent or clear.

Abhāswaras (अभास्वरस) (*m*) A class of deities, sixty-four in number, of whose nature little is known.

Abhaya (अभय) (*m*) assurance of safety or protection, fearlessness. Name of a son of Dharma and Daya (a sage).

Abheri (अभेरी) (*f*) Name of one of the regions or modes of classical music (personified as a female).

Abhibhav (अभिभव) (*m*) Victorious, powerful.

Abhibhū (अभिभू) (*m/f*) One who surpasses, a superior person.

Abhichaksha (अभिचक्ष) (*m*) Gracious look, view, perceive.

Ābhidā (आभिदा) (*n*) Literal meaning. In poetics Abhida is used to distinguish what is seen as the basic words or signs.

Abhigit/Abhigita (अभिगीत/अभिगीता) (*m/f/n*) Addressed or praised in song (From Rig Veda)..

Abhigri (अभिग्री) (*n/f*) To welcome, praise, to approve of, accept propitiously.

Abhigupta (अभिगुप्त) (*m*) Guarding, protecting.

Abhigupti (अभिगुप्ती) (*f*) Same as Abhigupta.

Abhijan (अभिजन) (*m,f,n*) Relating to good descent, loftiness of birth. Noble descent, family, race.

Abhijāt (अभिजात) (*m*) A well-born, learned, faultless, aristocratic, noble.

Abhijāti (अभिजाति) (*f*) Same as Abhijāt.

Abhijātya (अभिजात्य) (*m*) Graceful, dignified.

Abhijay (अभिजय) (*m*) Complete victory.

Abhiji (अभिजी) (*n*) Noble birth, nobility, learning scholarship, beauty.

Abhijit (अभिजीत) (*m*) Victiorious name of a nakshatra (planet), Vishnu.

Abhijiti (अभिजीति) (*f*) Same as Abhijit.

Abhikāmika (अभिकामिका) (*m,f,n*) Wished for agreeable.

Abhikānkshā (अभिकांक्षा) (*f*) Longing for, desire.

Abhikham (अभिखम) (*m*) To desire, love.

Abhikram (अभिक्रम) To go near, beginning, undertaking a work.

Abhilakshya (अभिलक्ष्य) (*m/f*) To be fixed or indicated towards a mark of good fortune.

Abhilāp (अभिलाप) (*m*) Expression, declaration (as the object of vow)

Abhilāshā (अभिलाषा) (*f*) Desire, longing, craving wish.

Abhilīn (अभिलीन) (*m/f*) Adhering to, clinging to.

Abhim (अभिम) (*m*) One who causes no fear. Another name of Vishnu (V)

Abhimānyav (अभिमानयव) (*m*) Descendant of Abhimanyu. See also Abhimanyu.

Abhimanyu (अभिमन्यु) Son of Arjuna and Subhadra, Conqueror and famous for valour even as a boy.

Abhimāt (अभिमात) (*m*) Favourite, desirous.

Abhimāti (अभिमाती) (*f*) Favourite or desired.

Abhimukh (अभिमुख) (*m/f*) Friendly, going near, approaching. One of the ten Bhumi's (the earth, wide world) to be passed by a Buddhisattva before becoming a Buddha.

Abhinand (अभिनन्द) (*a*) To please, rejoice, salute, welcome, greet.

Abhinandana (अभिनन्दन) (*m*) Method of greeting, welcome, great, praise, applaud, delight.

Abhinandita (अभिनन्दित) (*m/f*) Same as Abhinand.

Abhinav (अभिनव) (*m*) Novel, new or recent.

Abhinaya (अभिनय) (*n*) Acting, dramatic performance, professonal actor.

Abhinetri (अभिनेत्री) (*m/f*) One who brings near to eyes (from Rig Veda).

Abhinila (अभिनील) (*m*) Intensely blue or dark blue (attribution to Buddha).

Abhinishchit (अभिनिश्चित) (*m/f*) Quite/convinced, settled or fixed with regard.

Abhinīti (अभिनीति) (*f*) Gesture, expressive, gesticulation in a dance. Friendship.

Abhinivesh (अभिनिवेश) (*m*) Application, intentness, affection, devotion, determination.

Abhinn (अभिन्न) (*m*) Identical, not different, close.

Abhipa (अभिपा) (*n*) Behold with attention, to protect, assist.

Abhipād (अभिपाद) (*n*) To approach a deity for help, mastr, to assist, to catch.

Abhipāl (अभिपाल) (*m*) Protector (from Mahabharata).

Abhipatin (अभिपतीन) (*m/f/n*) Hastening near, running to help (from Mahabharata).

Abhiprakāsh (अभिप्रकाश) (*n*) To become visible (from Mahabharata).

Abhiprayah (अभिप्राय) (*m*) To ultimate meaning (V).

Abhipriti (अभिप्रीति) (*f*) Full of love, pleasure.

Abhipujita (अभिपूजिता) (*m/f/n*) Honoured, approved, worshipped, assented to.

Abhir (अभिर) (*m*) A cowherd; according to Manu the offspring of a Brahman by a woman of the Ambashtha (medical tribe). Also name of an ancient rural region of India and its inhabitants.

Abhirā (अभिरा) (*m*) Beautiful, lovely, delightful.

Abhiraksh (अभिरक्ष) (*n*) To guard, protect, preserve (from Rig Veda).

Abhirām (अभिराम) (*m/f*) Beautiful like Lord Ram, pleasing, delightful. Name of Lord Shiva.

Abhirāma-Mani (अभिरामा-मणी) A drama in seven acts on the history of Rama, written by Sundara Mishra in AD 1599.

Abhirāmata (अभिरमाता) (*f*) Beauty, loveliness, delightful. (See also Abhiram).

Abhiranjana (अभिरंजना) (*f*) Entertainment from an artist by singing or acting.

Abhranjana-Kalā (अभिरंजन-काला) (*f*) The art of entertainment by skilled artist.

Abhirat (अभिरात) (*m/f*) Pleased, beauty, contented, satisfied.

Abhirati (अभिराति) (*m*) Same as Abhirat.

Abhiruchi (अभिरूचि) (*f*) Liking, taste.

Abhirup (अभिरूप) (*m/f*) Comfortable, pleasing, handsome, beautiful, wise, learned.

Abhirūpak (अभिरूपक) (*n*) Suitableness, beauty.

Abhiruptā (अभिरूपता) (*f*) Same as Abhirup.

Abhishek (अभिषेक) (*m*) Inaugurating or consecrating by sprinkling water; Also inauguration of a king, royal function. Anointing ceremony.

Abhishri (अभिश्री) (*m/f*) Attached to each other, keep in order, to prepare. See also Shri.

Abhishu (अभिशु) (*m/f*) Ray of light.

Abhishubh (अभिशुभ) (*m/f*) To adorn one self.

Abhishun (अभिशुन) (*m/f*) Successful, having an advantage over.

Abhivād (अभिवाद) (*m*) To address or salute with reverence. (From Mahabharata).

Abhivādan (अभिवादन) (*m*) Respectful salutation.

Abhivayakti (अभिव्यक्ति) (*f*) Manifestation, intimation, revelation, body language, facial expression by an artist.

Abhivīta (अभिविता) (*m/f*) Desired, driven, impelled by.

Abhranti (अभ्राँति) (*f*) Absence of error. Same as Abhrant.

Abhu (अभु) (*m*) Unborn (V).

Abjā (अबज) (*f*) A pearl or oyster. Also means lotus born or produced from water.

Abjabāndhav (अबजबन्धव) (*m*) The sun. Friend of the lotus.

Abjahast (अबजाहसत) (*m*) The sun represented as holding lotus in one hand.

Acchyuta (अच्चयुता) (*m*) Infallible. (V)

Achaksh/Achaksha (अचाक्ष/अचाक्षा) (*n*) To tell, inspect, relate, make communication about, acquaint, introduce (from Rig Veda).

Achal (अचल) (*a*) Immovable, stationery, firm.

Achalā (अचला) (*f*) The good earth.

Achaltā (अचलता) (*f*) Immovability, firmness.

Achamana (अचमना) (*m/f*) Water for religious ceremony. Sipping the water from the palm of the hand for plurification. (From Rig Veda).

Acharin (अचारिन) (*m/f*) Following established practice of good behaviour, actrin, conduct, custom.

Adbhut/Adbhutah (अद्भुत/अद्भुता) (*m*) Amazing (V) Surprise, making gifts. In a dance a sentiments of astonishment, saying ha ha waving the hand, mouth and movement of fingers and the like.

Achyut (अचयुत) (*m*) Imperishable, unfallen. Name of Vishnu.

Adesh (आदेश) (*m*) Advice, instructions, information, declaration, rule, command.

Adarsh (आदर्श) (*m*) An ideal, a model. A mirror, the original manuscript.

Adashyanti (आदेशयन्ती) (*f*) Mother of Parashara and wife of Shakti, son of celebrated sage Vasishtha.

Adbhut (अद्भूत) (*m*) Miracles. The Brahmin of miracles, in Sama-Veda.

Adarnilaya (अद्रानिलया) (*m*) The support of the Earth and all the beings.(V)

Adeshika (आदेशिका) (*f*) Precept. a rule of action, a commandment.

Adhata (अधता) (*m*) He who cvould snot be carried (created by any one. (V)

Adhibhu (अधिभु) (*m*) A master or superior.

Adhiga (अधिग) (*n*) In Atharveda it means to remember, notice, learn, read, study, to resolve, to teach.

Adhigun (अधिगुण) (*m/f/n*) Possessing of superior qualities.

Adhija (अधिजा) (*m/f*) Noble birth. Superior by birth.

Adhilokam (अधिलोकम) (*n*) On the universe (Mentioned in Upanishad).

Adhimukti (अधिमुक्ति) (*f*) Prosperity, confidence.

Adhip/Adhipā (अधिप/अधिपा) (*m*) King, ruler, commander.

Adhirath (अधिरथ) (*m*) A charioteer, the foster father of Karn. According to some he was the king of Anga, and according to others he was the charioteer of King Dhritrashtra; perhaps he was both.

Adhishri (अधिश्री) (*n*) Very beautiful, very rich.

Adhistri (अधिस्त्री) (*f*) Superior woman.

Adhit (अधित) (*m/f*) Well read, learned.

Adhiti (अधिती) (*f*) Perusal, study, desire, recollection.

Adhiyāsita (अधियासिता) (*m/f*) Scented or perfumed.

Adhiyan (अधियन) (*m/f/n*) Reading, studying, student, one who studies Vedas or teaches Vedas.

Adhih (अधिह) (*m*) Lord or master over others.

Adhishta (अधिश्ता) (*m/f/n*) Solicited, asked for instruction (as a teacher) instruction given by a teacher, announced, advised, instruction.

Adhokshaja (अधोक्षजा) (*m*) Of undecayable form. (V)

Adhri (अधरी) (*m/f*) Unrestrained, irresistible.

Adhrita (अधरिता) (*m*) Whom no one could carry or possess. (V)

Adhyātam (अधियात्म) (*m/f*) The supreme spirit, individual personality.

Adilakshmi (आदिलक्ष्मी) (*f*) The primal Lakshmi-goddess.

Adip/Adipa (अदीप/अदीपा) (*m/f*) Kindled, illuminating.

Adipāl (आदिपाल) (*m*) A name of Vishnu.

Adipana (आदिपना) (*n*) Embellishing, whitening a floor or wall on festival occasion.

Adipati (आदिपति) (*m*) Lord of mountains, the Himalayas.

Adirāj (आदिराज) (*m*) The king of mountains.

Adishtin (आदिश्तीन) (*m*) One who received religious instructions, a student. one who gives instructions.

Āditah (आदिता) (*adv.*) New, fresh, denovo.

Āditi (आदिती) (*f*) The mother of gods, the earth, speech, bundless. Also a name of the wife of Kashyap and of Brahmā.

Āditya (आदित्य) (*m*) Descendent of Aditi, or epithet of several gods who are regarded as sun gods. Aditya is also the epithet of Surya (sun god). (V)

Adivāch (आदिवाच) (*n*) From Rig Veda - to speak in favour of, to advocate.

Adhyatam (अध्यात्म) (*n*) Supreme spirit, concerning self or individaul personality.

Adhyatam Vidya (अध्यात्म विद्या) (*f*) Adhyatam as above and Vidya means Knowledge, education.

Adirjā (अधीरजा) (*f*) Belonging to mountains. Another name of Parvati.

Adrikā (अदरिका) (*f*) Name of an Apsara (heavenly nymph).

Adrinandini (अदरिनन्दिनी) (*f*) Goddess Parvati. See Devi.

Advaidha (अदवैद्य) (*m/f/n*) United, not divided into two parts, free from malice.

Advaita (अदवैता) (*m/f/n*) Unique, epithet of Lord Vishnu, having no duplicate, the unltimate truh, name of an ancient Hindu philosophy, title of an Upanishad (esoteric dotrine, the third division of Vedas-5th centruy B.C.)

Advitya (अदवित्या) (*m*) Unique or unparalleled.

Agastya or Agasti (अगस्ता/अगस्ती) (*m*) A Rishi, the reputed author of several hymns in the Rig Veda.

Agat (अगत) (*m/f/n*) Come, arrived, born, come into existence (from Rig Veda).

Āggyā (अगगया) (*f*) Order, command.

Agharm (अघारम) (*n*) Moon, cool, having cool splendour.

Aghmarshana (अघमारशना) (*m/f/n*) Name of a Vedic hymn. Removing sins. The rite of driving out sin. It consist in taking water in the right hand formed in the shape of cow's ear, holding it near one's nose and breathing out from the nose on the water with the idea of driving away sins from oneself.

Aghor (अघोर) (*m/f*) A title of Shiva. A worshipper of Shiva and Parvati.

Agneya (अगनिया) (*m*) Son of Agni, a name of Karttikeya (Mars); also an appelationof Rishi Agastya and others.

Agnivesh (अगनिवेश) (*m*) A sage, the son of Agni (the deity of fire), and an early writer on medicine.

Agrani (अगरानी) (*m*) One who moves in the venguard and take the aspirant to final release. (V)

Āgrapuja (अगरपूजा) (*f*) Highest act of reverence.

Āgratas (अगरतास) (*m/f/n*) Going in front, taking the lead.

Ahalya (अहल्या) (*f*) Wife of Rishi. Gautama and a very beautiful woman according to Ramayana. She was the first woman made by Brahma and he gave her to Gautama.

Ahut (अहूत) (*m*) Invited, summoned.

Ahuti (अहूति) (*f*) Daughter of Manu and Shatrupa. An oblation or offering.

Ailaukik or Adhlokik (ऐलौकिक/अधलोकिक) (*m/f*) Worldly, earthly, or secular.

Aindri (ऐन्दरी) (*m*) Son of Indra. Also an application of Arjuna.

Aishwarya (ऐश्वर्य) (*n*) Power or supremacy.

Aitarya (ऐतरया) (*m*) The name of a Brahmana (works composed by Brahmans) in the use of Rig Vedic hymns).

Aja (अजा) (*m*) To drive, propel, mover, beam of the sun. In Atharveda Aja means Brahma, Vishnu, Shiva, Ram. Mythical ruler. (V&S)

Aja Mudra (अजा मुद्रा) (*n*) Gesture of Aja (Aja Means the same as above.) Mudra-any instrument used for sealing.

Ajagav (अजागव) (*m*) The primitive bow of Shiva which fell from heaven at the birth of Prithu (a Rishi).

Ajamukhi (अजमुखी) (*f*) Wife of sage Durvasa.

Ajāta-Shatru (अजात-शत्रु) One whose enemy is unborn.

Ajay or Ajayā (अजय या अजया) (*m/f*) Unconquered, invincible.

Ajaya-Pāl (अजय-पाल) (*m*) Author of a Sanskrit vocabulary of great repute.

Ajey (अजेय) (*a*) invincible, unconquerable.

Ajir (अजीर) (*m/f*) Quick, rapid.

Ajit (अजीत) (*m*) A name of Shiva; or of Vishnu (unconquered). (V)

Ajit-bālā (अजीत-बाला) (*f*) unconquered power.

Ajjit (अज्जित) (*m*) Handsome or honoured.

Ajur (अजुर) (*m/f*) Not subject to old age or decay.

Ajya (अजय) (*m/f*) Good to be seen first after rising from one's bed.

Akadama Chakra (अकदमा चक्र) (*n*) One of the tables for the determination of suitability of a Mantra for the Sadhak (disciple). Tantrik diagram.

Akadavāda (अकदवाद) (*n*) Applauding in speech/body language. Tantric diagram.

Akalmesh (अकलमेश) (*m/f*) Spotless.

Akalpa (अकलप) (*f*) Adornment, dress, ornament.

Akalpani (अकलपनी) (*f*) Unimaginable, unthinkable, inconceivable.

Akalush (अकलुश) (*m*) Unblemished.

Akampan (अकम्पन) (*m*) A great king who lived during prehistoric times. His story was told to Yudhishtra by Vyas in Mahabharata war.

Akampit (अकम्पित) (*m/f*) Unshaken, firm.

Akan (अकन) (*n*) To be pleased with. (From Rig Veda)

Ākānkshā (आकांक्षा) (*f*) wish, inquiry.

Akantak (अकंटक) (*m/f*) Free from troubles or difficulties.

Akār (अकार) (*m*) A mine; source; storehouse, treasury.

Akarsh (अकरष) (*m/f*) Not hard, tender, gentle.

Ākarshak (आकर्षक) (*m*) Attractive, charming, alluring.

Akarshana (आकर्षण) (*f*) Attraction.

Akarshi (अकर्षी) (*m/f*) Attractive; alluring.

Ākāsh (आकाश) (*m*) The sky, the space.

Ākash (आकश) (*m*) A touch-stone.

Akāshgāmini (आकाशगामिनी) (*f*) Goddess Durga is described as clothed in space, sky-clad and She flies in the Sky. (D)

Akhil (अखिल) (*m*) A complete thing, all entire.

Akhilātmā (अखिलात्मा) (*m/f*) The universal spirit, the Brama.

Akhilesh (अखिलेश) (*m*) The supreme measter, the master of the universe.

Akhurta (अखुरत) (*m*) One with mouse as his charioteer. (G)

Akka (अका) (*f*) **Mother.** Respectful term for older sister or any older woman.

Ākriti (आकृति) (*f*) Form, figure, appearance, shape.

Ākroshti (आक्रोष्टी) (*f*) Attraction.

Akrur (अकरूर) (*m*) Yadava and uncle of Krishna. It was he who took Krishna to Mathura, who broke the great bow. He is chiefly noted as being the holder of Syamantaka gem. (V)

Aksha (अक्ष) (*m*) A name of Garuda (a mythical bird on which Vishnu rides). Also a name given to a son of Satyabhama and Krishna.

Akshaj (अक्षज) (*m*) A diamond, Vishnu.

Akshalā (अक्षला) (*m*) Whole, unbroken. (S)

Akshamālā (अक्षमाला) (*f*) A name of Arundhatī. The morning star, personified as the wife of Rishi Vasishtha.

Aksha Mālin (अक्ष मालिन) (*f*) Wearing a rosary of beads.

Akshara (अक्षर) (*m*) A term for a great soul. An epithet of Brahma. (V)

Aksharam (अक्षरम) (*m*) Making things imperishable. (V)

Akshasutra (अक्षसुत्र) (*f*) Rosary of Rudraksha (sacred tree) or loeocarpus. A string of beads carried by saints and others for chanting Mantras. Usually 108 beads in a rosary.

Akshat (अक्षत) (*m*) Unimpaired, intact, whole grain of rice.

Akshāvali (अक्षावाली) (*f*) Rosary of beads.

Akshay (अक्षय) (*m*) Imperishable, undecaying; perennial.

Akshayin (अक्षाइन) (*f*) Undecaying. Name of Shiva's wife.

Akshi (अक्षी) (*f*) An eye, the eye-ball, the pupil, a daughter of Rohini (the favourite wife of the moon).

Akshinitārā (अक्षिनीतारा) (*f*) The pupil of the eye.

Akshi Samparak (अक्षी संपर्क) (*m*) Eye contact in body language or dancing.

Akshita (अक्षिता) (*m/f*) Permanent, undecaying.

Akshobhaya (अक्षोभय) (*m*) He who cannot be disturbed or agitated. (V)

Akunth (अकुंथ) (*m/f*) Ever fresh, eternal abode, heaven.

Akuta (अकुत) (*f*) Intention, purpose, gesture in a dance.

Akuti (अकुती) (*f*) A beautiful daughter of Manu Swambhuva and Sata-Rupa.

Alakā (अलका) (*f*) The capital of Kuvera and abode of the gandharvas on Mount Meru. Gandharva-deity who knew and revealed the secrets of heaven and divine truth in general. It is also called Vasu-dhārā, Vāsu-sthāli, and Prabhā. Alakā also means "curl lock."

Alaka-Nanda (अलक-नन्दा) (*f*) One of the four branches of the river Ganges. This is terrestrial Gangā which Shiva received upon his head.

Ālakshi (आलक्षी) (*m/f*) Beholding, seeing.

Ālakshita (आलक्षीता) (*f*) Beheld, seeing, perceived (from Brahmanas)

Alampata (अलम्पत) (*m*) The eternal (G)

Alāp (अलाप) (*m*) Speak, address, speech, conversation, communication melody.

Alankār (अलंकार) (*n*) Poetic ornament, figure of speech.

Alāpanā (अलापना) (*v&f*) To tune the voice.

Alark (अर्लक) (*m*) A mighty king who left his kingdom for the sake of truth and righteousness. His story is mentioned in Mahabharata.

Alaukik (अलौकिक) (*m/f*) Uncommon, unusual.

Ālekhya (आलेख्य) (*m/f/n*) To be written or painted, a picture portrait.

Ālokana (अलोकन) (*m/f/n*) Looking at, contemplating, seeing, sight, beholding.

Alhād (अलहाद) (*m*) Joy, delight.

Ālok (आलोक) (*m*) Sight, light, lustre, enlightenment.

Ālokavat (अलोकवत) (*m/f*) Having light or lustre.

Ālokin (आलोकिन) (*m/f/n*) Seeing, beholding, contemplating.

Ālokya (आलोक्य) (*m/f*) Unusual, (From Brahmana).

Ālola (आलोल) (*m/f*) Firm, steady, unagitated.

Amal (अमल) (*m/f*) Spotless, stainless, clean, pure, shining. (L)

Amalya (अमल्य) (*n*) To make spotless, brilliant.

Amani (अमनी) (*m*) Not caring for his individual honour. (V)

Amar (अमर) (*m*) Immortal, eternal, undying.

Amarāvati (अमरावती) (*f*) The capital of Indra's heaven. It is sometimes called Deva-pura (city of gods). It is situated somewhere in the vicinity of mount Meru.

Amaresh (अमरेश) (*m*) Lord of the gods. (S)

Amareshwara (अमरेश्वर) (*m*) Lord of the immortals. A title of Vishnu, Shiva and Indra.

Amar-Kantak (अमर-कंटक) (*m*) Peak of immortals.

Amar-mālā (अमर-माला) (*f*) Immortal rosary. (See also Amar and Mala) Also title of a dictionary called Amar Kosh).

Amarnāth/Amar Nāth (अमरनाथ) (*m*) Immortal Lord. Lord of gods. A name of Shiva. In Kashmir, Amarnath is also a mountain peak (17,321 feet) the mountain of the pilgrim, very beautiful in the evening sun.

Amar-rāj (अमर-राज) (*m*) Immortal King. King of the Gods.

Amarapā (अमरपा) (*m*) Lord of Gods. Name of Lord Indra. (See also Amar).

Amarprabhu (अमरप्रभु) (*m*) The Master of the celestials. (V)

Amar-ratna (अमर-रत्न) (*n*) Jewel of the Gods.

Amar-rupam (अमर-रूपम) (*m*) God like.

Amarta (अमरत) (*f*) Immortality.

Amar-Savitā (अमर-सविता) (*f*) River of the Gods. (See also Amar and Savita).

Amar-Shakti (अमर-शक्ति) (*n*) Immortal power. See also Amar and Shakti.

Amar-Shri (अमर श्री) (*m*) Eternally divine (Vishnu, Mahesh and Indra).

Amartya (अमरत्य) (*m*) Immortal, divine, god.

Amar-uttam (अमर-उत्तम) (*m*) The best of gods.

Amaryad (अमरयद) (*n*) Having no limits. Transgressing every bound.

Amatra (अमत्र) (*m/f/n*) Without measure, boundless (as Lord Indra).

Ambā (अम्बा) (*f*) A name of Durga, Parvati (saviour of the world). Also the name of the eldest daughter of the king of Kashi.

Ambak (अम्बक) (*m*) The eye.

Ambālikā (अम्बालिका) (*f*) The daughter of the king of Kashi and wife of Vichitra-Virya and mother of Pandu.

Ambar (अंबर) (*m*) The sky; clothes, garment.

Ambārisha (अंबारिश) (*m*) A king of Ayodhya, twenty-eighth in descent from Ikshwaku. An applellation of Shiva.

Ambas (अंबस) (*n*) Fruitfulness. Celestial water.

Ambhiji (अंभीजी) (*f*) Name of a preceptress who transmitted the white Yajurveda to the goddess of speech.

Ambhonidhi (अंभोनिधी) (*m*) Huge like the sea, the store.

Ambhojā (अंभोजा) (*f*) Water-born, lotus.

Ambhojini/Ambojini (अंभोजीनी/अंबाजीनी) (*f*) The lotus plants.

Ambikā (अंविका) (*f*) Wife of Shiva, daughter of Daksha. Also known as Parvati.

She is often identified with Ambā. Ambika, together with Parvati, Durga and Kali forms the central object of the Shakti cult. In later times Ambika is identifed with Umā (light)-A name of the consort of Shiva.

Ambrish (अंबरीश) (*m*) The sun; a name of Vishnu and Shiva.

Ambu (अंबु) (*m*) The water, a lotus flower, a cloud.

Ambuj (अंबुज) (*m/f*) A lotus, the thunderbolt of Indra, the moon, the conch, camphor.

Amey (अमेय) (*a*) Unlimited, boundless, limitless.

Amisha (अमीश) (*f*) Free from guile or deceit.

Amit (अमित) (*m/f*) Boundless, infinite, immense, enormous.

Amitābh (अमिताभ) (*m*) A name of Lord Buddha. Unlimited brilliance.

Amitābhās (अमिताभास) (*m*) A group of gods.

Amitāshan (अमिताशन) (*m*) One who devours all world. (V)

Amitvaj (अमित्वज) (*m*) A Panchala chief who fought in the Mahabharata war on the side of Pandavas.

Amitāvikrama (अमिताविक्रम) (*m*) Of infinite valour. (V)

Amiti (अमिती) (*f*) Boundlessness (as Lord Indra).

Amlān (अमलान) (*m/f*) Clean, clear, bright.

Amnāya (आमनाय) (*m/f*) Sacred tradition. The Vedas in the aggregate.

Amod (अमोद) (*m*) Joy, perfume.

Amodini (अमोदिनी) (*f*) Famous, fragrant.

Amogh (अमोघ) (*m*) Uttering. One who does not make futile attempts. (V)

Amritma (अमृतम) (*f*) Food obtained from chrning of he ocean of milk.

Amrāvati (अमरावती) (*f*) Name of the abode of Lord Indra.

Amri (अमरी) (*f*) A goddess.

Amrit (अमृत) (*m*) Immortal. The water of life produced at the churning of ocean by the gods and demons.

Amritā (अमृता) (*f*) Meaning more or less the same as Amrit.

Amritā Devi (अमृता देवी) (*f*) Goddess enshrined in Vindhyan cave.

Amritah (अमृताह) (*m*) Immortal. (V)

Amritānsh (अमृतांश) (*m*) He whose hope is never belied. (V)

Amritānshubhāva (अमृतांशुभाव) (*m*) The origin of the moon, the sea, at the time of churning. (V)

Amritapah (अमृतपह) (*m*) He who drinks nectar and make other gods also drink it. (V)

Amritavāpu (अमृतवापू) (*m*) Of imperishable body. (V)

Amrita-prabhā (अमृत-प्रभा) (*f*) Light of nector, wise, intelligent.

Amritesh (अमृतेष) (*m*) Lord of the immortals. (S)

Amriteshvari (अमृतेश्वरी) (*f*) Lady of nector (an epithe of Varuni-wife of Varuna, one of the oldest of Vedic deities.)'

Amritikā (अमृतिका) (*n*) The nector of immortality.

Amritānshu (अमृतांशु) (*m*) The moon.

Amritdhārā (अमृतधारा) (*f*) Stream of Amrit (See Amrit).

Amritshin (अमृतशीन) (*m*) Living on Amrit (See also Amrit).

Amrityu (अमृत्यु) (*m*) The one without death. (V)

Amulya (अमूल्य) (*n*) Priceless, valuable, precious.

Amurti (अमूर्ति) (*m*) Formless. (V)

Anādi (अनादि) (*m*) Having no beginning, ever-existent, eternal.

Anal (अनल) (*m*) Fire.

Anāmikā (अनामिका) (*f*) The ring finger.

Anand (आनन्द) (*m*) Joy, happiness, supreme spirit. An appelation of Shiva and also of Balrama.

Anandagiri (अनान्दगिरि) (*m*) A follower of Sankaracharya and a teacher and expositor of his doctrines. He was the author of a Sankara-vijaya and lived about the tenth century.

Anandamrita (अनन्दामृता) (*n*) Joy-nectar, happiness, consisting of happiness.

Anagha (अनघा) (*f*) Sinless. Goddess Lakshmi is untained, pure consciousness. (L)

Analah (अनलह) (*m*) Endowed with immense power and wealth. (V)

Anamayah (अनमयह) (*m*) Free from any kind of affliction. (V)

Ānandan (आनन्दन) (*m*) Delighting, making happy.

Ānandi (आनन्दी) (*m*) Happiness, enjoyment, pleasure. (V)

Ānandin (आनन्दीन) (*m/f*) Delightful, blissful, happy, cheerful.

Ānanditā (आनंदिता) (*f*) Same as Ānandi.

Ānandmālā (आनन्दमाला) (*f*) Garland of happiness, Name of a work. See also Anand and Mala.

Ānandrup/Ānandrupa (आनन्दरूप) (*m/f/n*) Consisting of happiness. (See also the meaning of Anand

Ananga (अनगं) (*m*) Bodiless. An epithet of Kāma. Having disturbed Shiva's life of austerity by filling him with love for Pravati, he was made bodiless by a flashing glance from the third eye of Shiva.

Anant (अनन्त) (*m*) Endless, eternal, infinite. Also a name of Vishnu, Shiva and Krishna.

Anantā (अनन्ता) (*f*) Wife of Svayambhuva Manu.

Anantamatī (अनन्तमत्ती) (*f*) Of endless thought.

Anantamukhi (अनन्तमुखी) (*f*) Having face of Anant.

Anantachidrūpayam (अनन्ताचिद्रूपयम) (*m*) Infinite and consciousness personified. (G)

Anantadevi (अनन्तदेवी) (*f*) Having no other Godderss.

Anantadrishti (अनन्तदृष्टि) (*m*) Of infinite vision. The invincible Lord is infinite, impersishable and omniscient. (S)

Anantah (अनन्तह) (*m*) Infinite. He who is endless. (V)

Anantarup (अनन्तरूप) (*m*) Infinite forms. (V)

Anantashri (अनन्तश्री) (*m*) He who has immense psychic powers. (V)

Anantātmā (अनन्तात्मा) (*m*) The soul infinite. (V)

Anantesha (अनन्तेष) (*m*) Lord of Anant.

Anantga (अनन्तगा) (*m/f/n*) Going or moving for ever or indefinitely.

Anantgun (अनन्तगुन) (*m/f/n*) Having boundless excellencies.

Anantkar (अनन्तकर) (*m/f/n*) Rendering endless, magnifying endlessly.

Anantrasi (अनन्त्रसी) (*m*) An infinite quantity.

Anantrūp (अनन्तरूप) (*m/f/n*) Having innumerable forms or shapes. (From Vedas).

Anantshakti (अनन्तशक्ति) (*m/f/n*) Omnipotent. Name of an ancient king. Mighty power.

Anantsushmā (अनन्तसुषमा) (*m/f/n*) Possessing boundless energy, strength.

Anantvat (अनन्तवत) (*m/f/n*) Eternal, infinite. In the Upanishads one of Lord Brahma's four feet (earth, intermediate space, heaven & ocean).

Anantyā (अनन्तया) (*f*) Divine, eternal, endless.

Ananyā (अनन्या) (*m/f*) No other, not different, unique, not more than one.

Ananyabhāv (अनन्यभाव) (*m/f/n*) In Vedas it means - thinking of the only one of the supreme spirit.

Ananyadev (अनन्यदेव) (*m*) Having no other God.

Ananyagati (अनन्यगति) (*f*) Sole resort or resource.

Anapār (अनपार) (*m/f/n*) Name of Lord Brahma. Without another, single.

Anapāy (अनपाय) (*m/f/n*) Prosperous, without obstacle, freedom from mischief.

Anapet (अनपेट) (*m/f/n*) Faithful to, possessed of, not gone off.

Anaranya (अनरण्य) (*m*) A descendant of Ikshwaku and king of Ayodhya.

Aneshvar (अनेश्वर) (*m*) Immortal, eternal, imperishable.

Anāvarat (अनावरत) (*m*) Continuous, incessant, unremitting.

Anayāh (अनयाह) (*m*) Totally free, liberated. (V)

Anāyu (अनायु) (*f*) A daughter of Daksa, a consort of Kashyap, and a mother goddess.

Anchal (अंचल) (*m*) A region, frontier territory. The outward fringe or portion of a Sari.

Anchit (अंचित) (*a*) Loved and respected.

Anekmurti (अनेकमुर्ति) (*m*) Having many forms. (V)

Anga (अंग) (*m*) The country of Bengal proper. A Mlechha king.

Angabhāv (अंगभाव) (*m*) Correlation between parts of the body. A stylized form of communication suggested by the receiprocal arrangement of the parts of body in a gesture etc. in a dance.

Angad (अंगद) (*m*) One of the generals in the army of Lord Ram and the son of monkey-king Bāli. Also son of Lakshmana and king of Angadi-country near the Himalaya.

Angaj (अंगज) A son.

Angajā (अंगजा) A daughter.

Angamudra (अंगमुद्रा) (*f*) Position of the body in a dance (both the fists are upstretched and got released and bound up again). Mudra means seal-ring.

Anganā (अंगना) (*f*) Another name of Chitrangadā the princess of Manipur.

Angarachanā/Anga Rachanā (अंग रचना) (*n*) Make up. Bharata in his *Natya Sastra* has discussed the technique of make up before dancing.

Angarāj (अंगराज) (*m*) Application of scented cosmetics to the body after bath. Karna, son of Pritha of Kunti by Surya (Sun God) was also known as Anga-Raja, King of Anga.

Angavaikrita (अंगवॅकृत) (*n*) In a dance it is an expression of the face leading to a knowledge of internal thoughts. We learn to manipulate our bodies to convey emotions and this is called Angavaikrita.

Angavidyā (अंगविद्या) (*f*) The knowledge of all the marks on the body. Kinetic art. It is the study of how body language is related to communication.

Angiras (अंगीरस) A Rishi to whom many hymns of the Rig Veda are attributed.

Angurī (अंगूरी) (*f*) Appertaining to grapes. Colour of grapes.

Anika (अनिका) (*n*) Face, front, army. In a dance the face conveys more information about the nature of an emotion.

Anil (अनिल) (*m*) The god of wind. In Vedas he is often associated with Indra, and rides in the same car with him.

Anilāh (अनिलाह) (*m*) Ever awake, vital air. (V)

Anilas (अनिलास) A class of deities, forty-nine in number, connected with Anil (the wind god).

Animā (अनिमा) (*f*) Atomism, Infinite. The first of the eight Siddhis (perfections).

Animān (अनिमान) (*m*) Limitless, immense, divine.

Animisha (अनिमीष) (*m*) Who does not wink: a general epithet of all gods.

Anirdeshyavapu (अनीदेश्यवापू) (*m*) Of undefinable image. Whose divine form is ineffable. (V)

Aniruddh (अनिरूद्ध) (*m*) Uncontrolled, unopposed; an aspect of Vishnu.

Anirvannah (अनेरवन्नः) (*m*) One who is never bored by any activity. (V)

Anirvinna (अनीरविन) (*m*) Free from the surfeit or boredom. (V)

Anish (अनीष) (*m*) Having no one above nom. (V)

Anit/Anitā (अनीत/अनीता) (*m/f*) Not having obtained, not gone to.

Anivarti (अनीवर्ती) (*m*) Indomitable in war or in the protection of Dharma. (V)

Aniyām (अनीयाम) (*m*) Above any regulations. (V)

Anjali (अंजली) (*f*) The cup shaped hallow formed by joining of the two palms together. A mode of worship by joining both hands.

Anjali mudra (अंजली मुद्रा) (*f*) A gesture in a dance, worship and sculpture where both open hands are folded and joined to form a slight hollow or cavity to mark a reverential attitude or supplication.

Anjanā (अंजना) (*f*) Mother of Hanumat/Hanuman by Vayu (god of the wind).

Añjaneya (अंजनेय) (*m*) Son of Anjani (Hanuman). (H)

Anjanī (अंजनी) (*f*) Mother of Hanuman.

Ankamma or Ankālammar (अंकामा/अंकालामार) A popular goddess worshipped in Nellore. The goddess of house and family.

Ankana (अंकन) (*n*) The act of marking, branding, ciphering and writing.

Ankati (अंकति) (*n*) Wind, fire, Lord Brahma. A Brahman who maintains the sacred fire.

Ankin (अंकिन) (*m/f/n*) In Rig Veda it means possessing a book (knowledge).

Ankit (अंकित) (*a*) Marked, spottled, counted, approved, written.

Ankitā (अंकिता) (*f*) Auspicious signs.

Ank-Mālikā (अंक-मालिका) (*f*) Necklace, an embrace, a chaplet, a corcle of gold.

Ankur (अंकुर) (*m*) A sprout; an offshoot, a seed bud.

Ankurit (अंकुरित) (*adj.*) Sprouting, budding.

Ankush (अंकुश) (*m*) A hook, elephant driver's iron hook.

Ankushi (अंकुशी) (*f*) One who exercises restraint. One of the twenty-four Jaina goddesses.

Anmol (अनमोल) (*m*) Invalauable, precious, priceless.

Annād (अन्नाद) (*m*) Son of Krishna.

Annām (अन्नाम) (*m*) The bestower of food for every being. (V)

Anna-Purnā (अन्न-पूर्णा) Full of food. A form of Durga worshipped for her power of giving food. Mother of plenty.

Annishvari (अन्निश्वरी) (*f*) Goddess of food. (D)

Anpeksha (अनपेक्ष) (*m/f/n*) Regardless, careless, indifferent, impartial.

Ansh (अंश) (*m*) Part, share, division.

Anshak (अंशक) (*m*) A sharer, in incarnation.

Ansh-āvtār (अंश-अवतार) (*m*) A partial incarnation.

Anshu (अंशु) (*m*) Ray of light, sunbeam.

Anshudhar (अंशुधर) (*m*) Bearer of sun rays. Another name of the sun.

Anshuk (अंशुक) (*m*) Fine cloth, fine silk.

Anshul (अंशुल) (*m*) Radiant, splendid. A name of Chanakya (a celebrated Brahmin).

Anshumālī (अंशुमाली) (*m*) The Sun.

Anshumān (अंशुमान) (*m*) The Sun, an epithet of the Sun.

Anshumati Mudrā (अंशुमती मुद्रा) (*f*) Radiant gesture in a dance.

Ansuyā (अनसुया) (*f*) Charity. Wife of the Rishi Atri. She was the mother of sage Durvasa and she had miraculous powers.

Antag (अंतग) (*m*) One who knows every thing. A competent person.

Antakāh (अंतकाह) (*m*) Death is the realaity which ends beings' life. (V)

Antarā (अंतरा) (*n*) Middle, inside, within, between.

Antarbhāvanā (अंतरभावना) (*f*) Inner feeling, conscience.

Antasār (अंतसार) (*m/f/n*) Having internal essence, internal treasure, inner store or contents.

Antarvira (अंतरवीर) (*m*) Intermission, intermittence.

Antikā (अंतिका) (*m/f/n*) Near, approximate, vicinity, nearness.

Anu (अनु) (*m/f*) A prefix meaning after, afterwards, like, alongwith. Also it means measurement of time. A molecule, atom, minute particle.

Anubhaj (अनुभज) (*n*) To worship.

Anubhav (अनुभव) (*m*) Perception, understanding, knowledge from personal experience.

Anubhāvana (अनुभावना) (*m*) Same as Anubhav.

Anubhraj (अनुभ्रज) (*n*) To illuminate.

Anubhu (अनुभु) (*m/f/n*) Perceiving, understanding.

Anubudh (अनुबुध) (*m*) To recollect, to learn, to communicate, to remind.

Anubhuti (अनुभूति) (*f*) Perception knowledge.

Anuchar (अनुचर) (*m/f*) In Rig Veda it means; adhere to, attendant, to behave, seek after, continuing following.

Anudit (अनुदित) (*n*) In Rig Vedas it means: unsaid, unuttered.

Anudruta (अनुद्रुत) (*m/f/n*) Followed, pursued, accompanied, a measure of time in music.

Anug (अनुग) (*m*) Companion, a follower.

Anugitā (अनुगीता) (*f*) An after song. Name of part of the fourteenth book of Mahabharata.

Anugiti (अनुगीति) (*f*) Name of a metre of two verses.

Anugrah-pradā (अनुग्रह-प्रदा) (*f*) Granter of good wishes Goddess Lakshmi. (L)

Anugunika (अनुगुणिका) (*m/f/n*) Human merits, knowing or studying the Anuguna (i.e. according to the art of keeping within the bounds of one's faculties).

Anugun (अनुगुण) (*m/f*) Having similar qualities, congenial to, sutiable, according to one's merits.

Anuh (अनुह) (*m*) The molecule. (V)

Anuj (अनुज) (*m*) A younger brother.

Anujā (अनुजा) (*f*) A younger sister.

Anukal (अनुकल) (*m*) Favourable, agrreable, befitting.

Anukām (अनुकाम) (*m*) To desire, fulfilling one's desire, agreeable. (From Rig Veda).

Anukampā (अनुकम्पा) (*f*) Kindness, compassion.

Anukānkshā (अनुकांक्षा) (*f*) Desire, wish.

Anukār (अनुकार) (*m/f*) Imitating, assistant, resembling.

Anukari/Anukri (अनुकारी/अनुकरी) (*n*) To follow in doing, to imitate, to equal, to become filled.

Anukariti/Anukriti (अनुकृति/अनुकृति) (*f*) Imitation in drama in several places (from *Natya sastra*).

Anukarsh (अनुक्रश) (*m*) Attraction, drawing.

Anukāsh (अनुकाश) (*m*) Clearness, reflection of light.

Anukirat (अनुकीर्त) (*n*) To relate, proclaiming.

Anukramani/Anukramanikā (अनुक्रमणी/अनुक्रमणिका) (*f*) An index or table of contents particularly of a Veda. The Anukramani's of the Vedas follow the order of each Samhitā and assign a poet, a metre, and a deity to each hymn or prayer, (Samhita or Sanhita is the portion of a Veda which comprises the hymns).

Anukriti (अनुकृति) (*f*) Imitation, copy.

Anukta (अनुकक्त) (*m/f/n*) Recited after from the Vedas. Study, spoken after. Unsaid, extraordinary, unuttered.

Anukti (अनुकक्ति) (*f*) Meaning the same as Anukta. Study of Veda, repeating, mentioning after.

Anukul (अनुकुल) (*m/f*) In Atharveda it means favourable, agreeable, comfortable, friendly, kind, obliging. (V)

Anukuj (अनुकुज) (*n*) To follow in cooing or singing or groaning.

Anulā (अनुला) (*f*) Pious person, gentle, name of a Buddhist saint, also name of a queen of Ceylon.

Anuli (अनुली) (*f*) Respectful, respected, homage.

Anulok (अनुलोक) (*m*) A person to whom every one is attached. Liked by every one.

Anumā (अनुमा) (*f*) Inference, conclusion from given premises, to be unable to equal, conclude. (From Rig Veda).

Anumān (अनुमान) (*m/f*) To approve, assent to, permit, grant, to honour.

Anumat (अनुमत) (*m/f*) Approved, aggreable, pleasant, loved, beloved.

Anumati (अनुमति) (*f*) Same as Anumat. Also personified as a goddess.

Anumoditā (अनुमोदिता) (*f*) Applauded, delighted, pleased.

Anumud (अनुमुद) (*n*) To join in rejoicing, to sympathise with, to allow with pleasure, express approval. (From Rig Veda).

Anun (अनु) (*m/f*) Not less, not inferior, having full power.

Anunand (अनुनन्द) (*n*) To enjoy.

Anunita (अनुनीता) (*m/f*) Disciplined, taught, obtained, respected, pleased.

Anuniti (अनुनिति) (*f*) Respectful, conciliation, courtesy, supplication.

Anunu (अनुनु) (*m*) In Rig Veda it means to follow with acclamations of praise.

Anunya (अनुन्य) (*n*) Form of speech and thought, request, courtesy. (from Natya Sastra).

Anup (अनूप) (*m*) Unequalled, unparalleled, singular, unique.

Anupech (अनुपैच) (*n*) To make or become ripe by degrees (from Mahabharata).

Anupalav (अनुपलव) (*m*) A companion, a follower.

Anupam (अनुपम) (*m*) matchless, unparalled, excellent, incomparable.

Anupamitā (अनुपमिता) (*m/f*) Uncompared, matchless.

Anupamyā (अनुपाम्य) (*f*) The wife of Bānāsura. Ill treated by mother-in-law and sister-in-law. She was initiated into a mantra by Nārada to control them and to be ever pleasing to her husband.

Anupāsh (**अनुपाश**) (*m/f/n*) Perceiving, seeing, Yoga, discover, notice, to show, to look upon.

Anupatī (**अनुपति**) (*m*) Lord of the atom, lord of the subtle.

Anuprabhā (**अनुप्रभा**) (*f*) To shine upon.

Anupreksh (**अनुप्रेक्ष**) (*n*) To follow with eyes.

Anupurnā (**अनुपूर्णा**) (*f*) A form of Durga (goddess).

Anupush (**अनुपुश**) (*m*) To go on prospering, extremely fortunate.

Anupushi (**अनुपुशी**) (*f*) Same as Anupush.

Anurādh (**अनुराध**) (*m*) A request, entreaty.

Anurādhā (**अनुराधा**) (*f*) Causing welfare. Name of a nakshatra-its influence is good. Nakshatras-mansions of the moon, lunar asterisms.

Anurāg (**अनुराग**) (*m*) Affection, fondness, love attachment.

Anurāj (**अनुराज**) (*m/f*) Brilliant, shine, the best.

Anuranjan (**अनुरंजन**) (*m*) Recreation, amusement.

Anuraksh (**अनुरक्ष**) (*n*) To guard, take care of.

Anurakt/Anurakta (**अनुरक्त/अनुरक्ता**) (*m/f/n*) Fond of, attached, pleased, beloved.

Anurati (**अनुरती**) (*f*) Love, attachment.

Anurodh (**अनुरोध**) (*m*) Obliging, respectful.

Anurodhan (**अनुरोधन**) (*m*) Same as Anurodh.

Anurodhitā (**अनुरोधिता**) (*f*) Same as Anurodh.

Anurohini (**अनुरोहिनी**) (*m/f*) Belonging to the constellation Rohini. See also Rohini.

Anuru (**अनुरू**) A son of Tarkshya and Kadru charioteer of the sun.

Anurudh (**अनुरूद्ध**) (*m*) One of the four forms of Hari (god) the supreme ruler of the senses.

Anurup (**अनुरूप**) (*a*) Comfortable, fit, like, according to.

Anurupak (**अनुरूपक**) (*m*) Resembling, counter part.

Anurupamaya (**अनुरूपमय**) A Vasu. The Vasus are a class of deities, eight in number-personifications of natural phenomena (Apa-water; Dhruvapole-star; Soma-moon; Dhara-earth; Anil-wind; Anala-fire; Prabhās-dawn; and Pratyusha-light).

Anurupya (**अनुरूपया**) (*m/f*) confirmity, suitableness.

Anush/Anushā (**अनुष/अनुषा**) (*m/f*) To desire something.

Anushak or Anushat (**अनुशक/अनुशत**) (*m*) In continuous order, one after the other, uninterruptedly (from Rig Veda).

Anushakta (अनुशक्त) (*m/f/n*) Closely connected with, supplied from something preceding.

Anushās (अनुशास) (*n*) To rule, govern, to order, to teach, direct, advise, correct.

Anushat see Anushak

Anushatya (अनुशत्य) (*m/f/n*) Being comfortable to truth, honesty, truthfulness.

Anushikh/Anushikhā (अनुशिख/अनुशिखा) (*m/f*) Crested, decorated, respected.

Anushobhin (अनुशोभिन) (*m*) Shining, illuminating, bright, dignified.

Anushobhini (अनुशोभिनी) (*f*) Shining, illuminating, bright, dignified.

Anushrav (अनुश्रव) (*m/f*) According to hearing, resting on tradition.

Anushtup (अनुशतुप) (*m/f*) Hymn, invocation, metre, praise.

Anushuk (अनुशूक) (*m/f/n*) Being with or within the awns (as rice). After shoot of rice.

Anusriti (अनूससृति) (*f*) Confirming, going after.

Anutam/Anutamah (अनुत्तम/अनुत्मा) (*m*) To extend along, to carry on, to continue, to develop. Peerless (V)

Anuttam (अनुत्तम) (*m/f*) Excellent, the best, chief.

Anuvāch (अनुवाच) (*f*) To recite the sacred formulas from the sacred Rig Veda. To recite for religious ceremony.

Anvadhi (अनवधी) (*f*) To remember, think of, to recollect. (From Atharva Veda)

Anvalabh (अनवलभ) (*n*) Grasp, take in hand, to hold. (From Rig Veda)

Anuvesh (अनुवेष) (*n*) Obedience to the will of God.

Anvesh/Anveshā (अनवेष/अनवेषा) (*m/f*) Desire, seek, searching, inquiring.

Anuvidha (अनुविध) (*n*) To regulate, lay down a rule, to follow rules.

Anviksha (अनविक्ष) (*f*) Meditation, examining, inquiry.

Anuvinda (अनुविंद) A king of Ujjayini.

Anuvishnu (अनुविष्णु) (*n*) After Lord Vishnu (See also **Vishnu**).

Anuyām (अनुयाम) (*f*) Guide, to direct, to give direction (from Rig Veda).

Anuyukta (अनुयुक्त) (*m/f/n*) Enjoined, asked, enquired, examined, questioned. Anvita.

Anvita (अनवित) (*m/f/n*) Gone along with, joined, attended, accompanied by, linked with, reached by the mind.

Anuvittī (अनुवित्ती) (*f*) Finding something (from Brahmanas).

Anuvrat (अनुव्रत) (*m/f/n*) Devoted to, faithful to.

Anyā (अन्या) (*n/f*) Other than, different from, another person, inexhaustible (as the milk of a cow).

Anyādevtā (अन्यादेवता) *(m/f/n)* Having another divinity, different characteristic.

Anyaka (अन्यक) *(m/f/n)* Another person (from Rig Veda).

Anyatā (अन्यता) *(f)* Difference. Also see the meaning of Anya.

Apādev (अपादेव) *(m)* Name of the God of water (Varuna).

Apāla (अपाल) *(f)* Undefeated, unguarded (R.V.).

Apanajey (अपनजेय) *(m)* Invincible, unconquerable.

Apāpati (अपापती) *(m)* Lord of waters. Name of Varuna.

Apār/Aparā (अपार/अपारा) *(m/f/n)* Unbound, not having an opposite shore, boundless, divine, (applicable to earth or heaven).

Aparāhna (अपराह्ं) *(n)* When the sun passes three Muhurtta (a measure of time_ from the mdhyāhna (middle).

Aparājit (अपराजित) A son of Krishna and Mādri. An elephant at one of the four cardinal points to maintain the balance of the world. (V)

Aparājitā (अपराजिता) *(f)* A mindborn mother; following Māyā. Unconquered. Name of Durga (goddess).

Aparanta (अपरांत) *(n)* On the western border. A country which is named in Vishnu Puran.

Apāra-Shivā (अपार-शिवा) Apara means having no rival or superior. Shiva (god)-the unrivalled or the great Shiva.

Aparitā (अपरिता) *(f)* Glanddened, joyous.

Apārmeyah (अपारमे) *(m)* Not proveable by evidence etc. (V)

Aparnā (अपर्णा) *(f)* According to Hari-Vansa, the eldest daughter of Himavat and Menā, the wife of Shiva also known as Uma, Parvati etc.

Aparnesh (अपर्णेश) *(m)* A nother name of Shiva. Lord of Parvati. (S)

Aparoksh (अपरोक्ष) *(m)* Direct, visible, tangible.

Aparyant (अपर्यंत) *(m/f/n)* Unlimited, unbounded.

Apastamba (अपासतम्ब) *(m)* A wise man. An ancient writer on ritual and law, author of sutras connected with the Black Yajur-Veda and of a Dharma Sastra.

Āpava (अपव) *(m)* Who sports in the waters. According to Mahabharata, Apava is a name of the Prajapati Vashishtha.

Apayayana (अपय्यन्) *(m/f/n)* Causing fulness, increasing welfare, gladdening, refreshing, satisfying.

Apdān (अपदान) *(n)* A great or noble work, In Buddhism (Avdan) former and future births of men/women exhibiting the consequences of their good and bad actions.

Apdosh/Apdoshā (अपदोष/अपदोषा) (*m/f/n*) Faultless, super.

Api (अपी) (*m*) An ally, a friend, an acquaaintance, to obtain wealth. (R.V.)

Apigun (अपीगुण) (*m/f/n*) Excellent, full of merits, virtue, quality.

Apindra (अपीन्द्र) (*m*) Resembling Indra. Virtuous, divine, beautiful.

Aplāshin (अपलाशिन) (*m/f/n*) Free from desire.

Aplava (अपलव) (*m*) Ablution, bathing, sprinkling with water on auspicious occasions.

Apmanyu (अपमन्यु) (*m/f/n*) Free from grief.

Aprājeya (अप्राजेय) (*m*) Invincible.

Aprameyatma (अप्राम्यात्म) (*m*) Immeasurable by any scale. (V)

Aprati (अप्रती) (*m*) Unequalled. Without any opponent.

Apratatirath (अप्रततीर्थ) (*m*) Having no opposition. (V)

Apratima (अप्रतिमा) (*m/f*) Unequalled, incomparable.

Apratul (अप्रतुल) (*m*) Unequal, unparallel.

Apratunān (अप्रतुनान) (*m/f*) Same as Apratima.

Apritā (अप्रीता) (*m/f/n*) Occupied, engaged, gladdened, joyous.

Apsara (अप्सरा) (*f*) The celebrated nymphs of Indira's heaven.

Apta (अपत) (*m/f/n*) Reached, overtaken, gained, obtained, full, true, clever, trustworthy, abundant, complete

Aptakam (अप्तकम) (*m/f/n*) One who has gained his wish, satisfied. One who knows the identity of Brahman (Supreme Soul).

Apti (अप्ति) (*f*) Reaching, meeting with, gain, obtaining, fortune.

Apu (अपु) (*m*) Pure, virtuous, divine.

Apura (अपुर) (*m*) Excess, abundance, flooding, filling up.

Apuranā (अपूर्णा) (*m/f/n*) Making full, filling up, satiating.

Apurv (अपूर्व) (*m*) Not having existed before, unparalleled, extraordinary.

Apuravā (अपूर्वा) (*f*) Unparalleled, extraordinary, new.

Apuran (अपूर्ण) (*m/f*) Modern, fresh.

Apurvatā/A-purvatā (अपूर्वता/अ-पूर्वता) (*f*) Incomparable, unparalleled (same as Apurva).

Apurit (अपूरित) (*m*) Full, full to the brim.

Apurv (अपूर्व) (*m*) Unprecedented, novel, unique.

Apyā (अप्या) (*m/f/n*) To be reached, obtainable, alliance, relationship, friendship.

Apyāha (अप्याह) (*m*) The point of final coalescence. (V)

Ārādhak (आराधक) (*m*) A worshipper adoration.

Arādhanā (आराधना) (*f*) Worship, adoration of dieties.

Arādhy (अराध्य) (*m*) Adorable, worthy of worship.

Araja (अराज) (*f*) Clean, pure, virtuous. Name of the daughter of Rishi Bhargava.

Aranyani (अरण्यनी) (*f*) In the Rig Veda, the goddess of woods and forests.

Arātaki (अरात्की) (*f*) Name of a plant in Atharva-veda.

Araudrā (अरौद्रा) (*m*) The embodiment of peace. (V)

Arbudā (अरबुदा) Mount Abu Name of the people living in the vicinity of that mountain.

Archā (अर्चा) (*f*) Worship.

Archaka (अर्चक) (*m/f/n*) Honouring, worshipping, worshipper, respected

Archanā (अर्चना) (*f*) Worship, honouring, praising.

Archaniyā (अर्चनिया) (*m/f*) To be worshipped, adoration.

Archat (अर्चत) (*m*) Brilliant, praising, glorious, shining. Name of a Rishi.

Archatri (अर्चतरी) (*m/f/n*) Wind God (Marut), roarin (from Rig Veda).

Archi (अर्ची) (*n*) Ray, flame (from Rig Veda).

Archishman (अर्चिषमन) (*m*) The source of brightness of all luminaries. (V)

Archishmat (अर्चीष्मत) (*m*) Brilliant, resplendant. Another name Agni, Vishnu and the Sun. (V)

Archishmatī (अर्चीष्मती) (*f*) Brilliant, resplendant. Name of the daughter of Angiras (from Mahabharata).

Archit/Architā (अर्चित/अर्चिता) (*m/f/n*) Honoured, worshipped, respected, saluted, offered with reverence.

Architāh (अर्चिताह) (*m*) Worshipped by all. (V)

Architin (अर्चितिन) (*m/f/n*) Honouring with, honoured.

Architri (अर्चितरी) (*m*) Worshipper (from Rig Veda).

Ardit (अरदित) (*m/f*) Asked, requested, begged.

Arenu (अरेणु) (*m*) Pure, celestial, a god.

Arghā (अर्गहा) (*m/f*) Worth, value, price, flowers, pearls.

Arghadan (अर्घधन) (*n*) A presentation of a respectful offering.

Arghya (अर्घय) (*m/f/n*) Valuable. Respectful offering of water flowers, rice grains to God or venerable person.

Arhah (अर्हाह) (*m*) Supremely adorable for all. (V)

Arhanā (अर्हना) (*m/f/n*) Deserving, meriting, honouring, worshiping, having a claim to being entitled to.

Arjit (अर्जीत) (*m*) A son of Krishna and Bhadrā.

Arishtā (अरिष्टा) (*f*) Safe, secure. A daughter of Daksha, wife of sage Kashyapa. Another name of goddess Durga. (D)

Arishtanemi (अरिष्टनेमी) Son of Rishi Kashyap. His story is told in Mahabharata.

Arishtut (अरिष्तुत) (*m*) Full of praise. Another name of Lord Indra.

Arisudan (अरीसुदन) (*m*) Slayer of foes. Lord Krishna slew dreaded demons like Narakasura, Panchajana, Banasura etc. and was the cause for the death of Kansa. (K)

Arj (अर्ज) (*n*) To procure, acquire.

Arjaka (अर्जक) (*m/f/n*) Procuring, acquiring, the plant Ocimum Gratisrimum.

Arjana (अर्जन) (*m*) Procuring, acquiring, gaining, earning.

Arjit (अर्जित) (*m/f/n*) Acquired, gained, earned.

Arjun (अर्जुन) (*m*) White, clear. A name of the third Pandava prince. All the five Pandav brothers were of divine paternity, and Arjun's father was Indra, hence he is called Aindri.

Arjuni (अर्जुनी) (*m/f*) A descendant of Arjun.

Arjunsakhi (अर्जुनसखी) (*m*) Friend of Arjuna. Another name of Krishna. (K)

Arka (अर्क) (*m*) A ray, flash of ligtning, the Sun (from Rig Veda), one who praises, a singer, name of Lord Indra, learned person. The plant Calotropis Gigantea (the larger leaves are used for religious ceremonies).

Arkah (अर्काह) (*m*) Adorable by the adored. (V)

Arkash (अर्कश) (*m*) Illuminated by the sun. Visible manifest.

Arkashmani (अर्कशमणि) (*m*) Jewel of the sun crystal, sunstone, ruby.

Arka Suta (अर्क सुत) (*m/f*) Name of the sacred river Yamuna. See also Arka.

Arkaj (अर्कज) (*m*) Son of the Sun. Another name of Karna.

Arki (अर्की) (*m*) Descendant of the sun. Another name of Karna.

Arkin (अर्कीन) (*m/f/n*) Radiant with light, shining, bright. (R.V.)

Arkya (अर्क्य) (*m/f/n*) Belonging to Arka (See also Arka

Arna (अर्ना) (*n*) Wave, flood, stream, river (from Rig Veda)

Arnapati (अर्णपती) (*m*) Lord of the seas.

Arnās (अर्नास) (*n*) Meaning the same as Arna. The ocean of river (from Rig Veda).

Arochanā (अरोचना) (*m/f*) Bright, shining, glorious.

Arpan (अर्पण) (*m*) An offering, surrendering.

Arpitā (अर्पिता) (*m/f*) Fixed upon (as the eyes on mind), concentration, offered, engraved, entrusted. (From Rig Veda)

Arpya (अर्प्य) (*m/f/n*) To be delivered, consignable.

Arsha (अर्शा) (*m/f*) Relating to or belonging to Rishis

Arshodhā (अर्शोधा) (*f*) Female Marriage according to Arsha form (a form of marriage according to Rishis who composed Vedic hymns)

Artha (अर्थ) (*n*) Aim, purpose, meaning, cause, wealth, property, money, benefit (from Rig Veda) Adorable by all owing to His being bestower of happiness (V)

Arthanā (अर्थना) (*f*) Money, desire, wealth, profitable, request, entreaty.

Arthadrisā (अर्थद्रिषा) (*f*) An eye on (i.e. consideration of) the truth

Artharashi (अर्थाशी) (*m/f*) Great wealth.

Arthdrishti (अर्थदृष्टि) (*f*) Seeing profit..

Arthin (अर्थीन) (*m/f/n*) Active, industrious, longing for.

Arthita (अर्थित) (*m/f/n*) Asked, desired, requested.

Arthvat (अर्थवत्) (*m/f/n*) Wealth, full of sense, significant.

Arthvidyā (अर्थविद्या) (*f*) Knowledge of practical life.

Arthyas (अर्थ्यस) (*m/f/n*) Highly significant.

Arthyukti (अर्थायुक्ती) (*f*) Gain, profit, highly significant.

Ārti (आरती) (*f*) A ceremony performed in adoration of a deity by circular movement of lighted lamp before the deity.

Arukshitā (अरुक्षिता) (*f*) Young, tender soft.

Arulamani (अरुलामणि) (*f*) Jewel of the sun

Arun (अरुण) (*.n*) reddish, brown, the dawn (personified as the charioteer of the sun). In South India Arun means Surya (sun god) himself.

Arunā (अरुणा) (*f*) Red, gold, passionate. the saffron plant, name of a daughter of Kashyap Rishi.

Arunābhā (अरुणाभा) (*f*) Life giving sun light, passonate.

Arunākar (अरुणाकर) (*m*) Red rays. Another name of the sun.

Arundati (अरुणदती) (*f*) the morning star, personified as the wife of the Rishi Vashishtha. Name of a goddess (a personification of the morning star) belonging to the Great Bear.

Arunesh (अरुणेश) (*m*) Lord of Arun, another name of the sun.

Arunimā (अरुणिमा) (*f*) Reddish brown tinge colour.

Arunodaya (अरुणोदय) (*m*) Break of day, dawn.

Arunopāl (अरुणोपाल) (*m*) A Ruby.

Arunkamal (अरुणकमल) (*n*) Red lotus, having red rays.

Arunpriya (अरुणप्रिया) (*m/f/n*) Name of an Aspra (heavenly nymph), most beautiful. See also Arun and Priya.

Arunpushpa (अरुणपुष्प) (*m/f/n*) Having red flowers.

Arunta (अरुणता) (*f*) Red colour. See also Arun

Arvachana/Arvachinā (अर्वचन/अर्वचना) (*m/f*) Turned towards, favouring, being on this side (from Rig Veda)

Arusha/Arushi (अरुश/अरुशी) (*f*) Red. In the Rig Veda the red horses or mares of the sun of fire, the rising sun.

Arushi (अरुशी) (*f*) Wife of Aurva grandson of Bhrigu.

Arvan/Arvā (अर्वन/अर्वा) (*m*) A horse. One of the horses of the moon. A fabulous animal, half horse, half bird, on which the aityas (god) are supposed to ride.

Arvavasu (अर्ववसू) A son of a great Vedic scholar Raibhya. Like his father he was also a great scholar of Vedas.

Arvind (अरविंद) (*m*) A lotus flower.

Arvindakshā (अरविन्दक्षा) (*m*) Having lotus like eyes (V)

Arvindra (अरविंद्र) (*m*) Lord of the priests, horses and wheels.

Arvindini (अरविंदनी) (*f*) An assemblage of lotus flowers.

Aryā-Bhat (अर्या-भट) (*m*) The earliest known Hindu writer on Algebra born in Patna in AD 476. Aryan means loyal or faithful. The name of the immigrant race from which all that is Hindu originated. The Rig-vedic people.

Aryachetas (आर्यचेतस) (*m*) Noble mind.

Āryadev (आर्यदेव) (*m*) Lord of the nobles. Name of a Buddhist Philosopher.

Āryakā (आर्यका) (*m/f*) Honourable, respectable.

Aryāman (आर्यमान) (*m*) A bosom firiend. One of the Adityas (celestial deities); chief of the Pitris (sons of gods).

Aryavrat (आर्यव्रत) (*m*) The land of the Aryans.

Asamanjas (असमंजस) (*m*) Son of Sāgara (king of Ayodhya, son of king Bahu).

Asammita (असम्मीता) (*m*) Immeasurable (V)

Asang (असंग) (*m/f*) Independently, free from ties

Asankhya (असंख्य) (*m/f*) Innumerable, exceedingly numerous.

Asat (असत) (*m*) The false worldly form. (V)

Āshā (आशा) (*f*) Hope, desire, a region. ray, promise, prospect, trust.

Āshākrit (आशाकृत) (*m/f/n/*) Formed into expectation, hopeful of expectation being gratified

Āshanā (आशना) (*f*) The queen of Bali and mother of Bān. Friend, acquaintance.

Āshani (अशनी) (*m/f*) Indra, fire, a missile, the thunderbolt, a flash of lighting. Ashani is also an epithet of Shiva. Also a mother goddess.

Ashāpāl (आशापाल) (*m*) Guardian or Lord of the regions.

Ashapāra (आशपरा) (*f*) Name of a Goddess.

Ashāprāpt (अशप्राप्त) (*m/f/n*) Formed into expectation, hope of success.

Ashavari (आशावारी) (*f*) Celestial spirit.

Ashechānā (असीचाना) (*m/f*) Charming, lovely, beautiful.

Ashesh (अशेष) (*e*) Complete, entire.

Ashirdaya (अशीरदय) (*f*) Fulfilling of a benediction or wish.

Āshish (आशीष) (*f*) blessings, benediction.

Ashit (अशित) A very learned and wise sage whose story is mentioned in the Mahabharata.

Āshman (अशमन) A very learned brahman who advised king Janak. His story was told by Vyas Rishi to Yudhishtra.

Ashmati (अशमती) (*m/f*) Supreme, divine, unequal.

Ashok (अशोक) (*m*) A celebrated king of the Maurya dynasty who spread Buddhism. He reigned thirty-six years, from about 234 to 198 BC and exercised authority from Afghanistan to Ceylon. Not feeling Sorrow.

Ashok-kāntā (अशोक-कांत) (*f*) Very dear to Ashok. Colour yellow or golden.

Ashrama (अश्राम) (*m*) the resting place for all. (V)

Āshu (आशु) (*a*) Prompt, quick, speedy, swift.

Ashutosh (आशुतोष) (*m/f/n*) Lord Shiva is extremely benevolent, gets easily pleased, and goes to any extent to bless His devotees. (S)

Ashvani Kumāra (अश्वनी कुमार) These twin gods were physicians to the gods.

Ashvin (अश्विन) (*m*) The seventh month of the Hindu calendar.

Ashvini (अश्विनी) (*f*) the first lunar mansion.

Ashwapati (अश्वपति) Father of Savitri. He ruled over his people in Madradesha benevolently and led a very religious life.

Ashwath (अश्वथ) (*m*) The Peepal tree belivedd to be the most pious. (V)

Asīm (असीम) (*a*) Limitless, boundless.

Askshobhya (अकशोभ्या) (*m*) He who cannot be frightened by anyone of anything. (V)

Asmaka (अस्मक) (*m*) Son of Madyanti, the wife of Kalmasha Pada or Saudasa (king of solar race.)

Asmitā (अस्मिता) (*f*) Ego, vanity, pride.

Asthita (अस्थिता) (*m/f/n*) Staying or sitting on, believing, acknowledging.

Astika (अस्तिक) (*m*) An ancient sage, son of Jarat-Karu by a sister of the great serpent Vasuki.

Asumat (असुमत) (*m/f*) Life, the principle of vitality.

Asusam (असुसम) (*m*) Dear as life, husband, lover.

Aswatthama (अश्वत्थामा) (*m*) Son of Drona and Kripa, and one of the generals of the Kaurvas.

Atal (अटल) (*a*) Firm, irrevocable, resolute, solid.

Atal (अटल) (*a*) Bottomless, fathomless. The first of the seven regions of Pātāl (below the earth). The soil of Atal is white and the place is embellished with magnificent palaces.

Atarva (अतर्व) (*m*) One of the fifteen teachers of the school of white Yajurveda.

Atharv (अथर्व) (*m*) The fourth and the last of the Vedas.

Atharvan (अथर्वन) (*m*) Name of the priest mentioned in the Rig Veda. He is mythologically represented as the eldest son of Brahma, to whom the God revealed Brahma Vidya (knowledge of God).

Atibhānu (अतिभानू) (*m*) A son of Krishna and Satyābhāmā.

Atibhāshā (अतिभाषा) (*m/f*) Language of the super human. In Sanskrit plays, Atibhasha is language of the Gods,

Atibhāv (अतिभाव) (*m*) Superior, many emotions.

Atideva (अतिदेवा) (*m*) Above gods. Surpassing the gods.

Atikānt (अतिकांत) (*m/f*) Excessively beloved.

Atimānitā (अतिमनीता) (*f*) Greatly respected. Very bold.

Atimodā (अतिमोदा) (*f*) Fragrant, jasmine flower, very happy.

Atimukt (अतिमुक्त) (*m*) Entirely liberated.

Atimukti (अतिमुक्ति) (*f*) Same as Atimukt.

Atindra (अतीन्द्र) (*m*) Virtuous, chaste, powerful, meritiorious. Excelling over India in the self knowledge (V)

Atindriya (अतीन्द्रीय) (*m*) Beyond the approach of senses (V)

Atiriya (अतीरीय) (*f*) Lovely, dear, rare.

Atirup (अतिरुप) (*m/f*) Very beautiful.

Atirupā (अतिरूपा) (*f*) Very beautiful. Another name of supreme being.

Atisav (अतिसव) (*m/f*) Superior to all. The supreme.

Atishakti (अतिशक्ति) (*m/f*) Very powerful.

Atishay (अतिशय) (*a*) Exceedingly excessive.

Atishreshth (अतिश्रेष्ठ) (*m/f*) Best of all.

Atishubh (अतिशुभ) (*m/f*) To be brilliant, adorn, to praise.

Atistuti (अतिस्तुति) (*f*) Excessive praise.

Atisuhit (अतीसुहित) (*m/f*) Very kind.

Ativ (अतीव) (*a*) Very much, too much.

Ātmā/Ātmān (आत्मा/आत्मन) (*m*) The soul, the principle of life the supreme soul.

Ātmabhū (आत्मभू) (*m*) Self createded. Another name of Brahma, Vishnu and Mahesh (V)

Ātmajā (आत्माजा) (*f*) Daughter of the soul. Another name of Parvati.

Ātmajyoti (आत्मज्योति) (*m/f*) Light of the soul. Supreme spirit.

Ātmā-Nand (आत्मा-नन्द) (*m*) The pleasure of, self-realisation.

Ātmā-Rām (आत्मा-राम) (*m*) Soul of Lord Ram; spiritual knowledge

Ātmavān (आत्मवान) (*m*) Reposed in His Own Glory (The knopwer of self). (V)

Atmayoni (आत्मायोनी) (*m*) Self created. (V)

Ātnu (अत्नू) (*m*) The sun.

Atreya (अत्रेय) (*m*) A patronymic from Atri, a son or descendent of Atri (a Rishi and author of many Vedic hymns).

Atri (अत्ररी) (*m*) A Rishi, and author of many Vedic hymns in paraise of Agni (fire), God Indra etc. As a Rishi he is one of the stars of Great Bear.

Atul (अतुल) (*a*) Unparalleled, unequalled, immense.

Atulya (अतुल्य) (*m*) Unequalled.

Auchiti (औचिती) (*f*) Appropriate, the soul of good poetry.

Auddhatty (औद्धत्य) (*m*) Impertinenee, rudeness, haughtiness.

Augadh (औगध) (*m*) Carefree reveller. Lord Shiva is frequently described as carefree, jovial and master of the art of dancing (S)

Aujasika (औजसिक) (*m/f*) energetic, vigorous.

Aujasya (औजस्य) (*n/f*) To increase vitality or energy.

Aurva (औरवा) (*m*) A Rishi, son of Urvad and grandson of Bhrigu Rishi. He is described in the Mahabharata as son of the sage Chyavana by his wife Arushi. From his race he is called Bhargava.

Aushadhim (औषधिं) (*n/f*) The medicine to cure all worldly ills. (V)

Aushija (औशिज) (*m*) Glorious, renowned, A name of a very powerful king who was as strong as Lord Indra. Name of a sage.

Avabhā (अवाभा) (*f*) Shining, brilliant, bright.

Avabhāsita (अवाभासिता) (*m/f*) Shining, brilliant, bright.

Avabhās (अवाभास) (*m*) Splendour, shine, brilliant, appear, to become manifest.

Avabhāsaka (अवाभासका) (*m/f/n*) In Vedanta philosophy it means-illuminting, making manifest.

Avadāt/Avadata (अवदात/अवदात) (*m/f/n*) Clean, clear, pure, blameless, excellent, white splendour. intelligent.

Avahān (आवाह्न) (*m*) Invocation.

Avakāsh (अवकाश) (*n*) To be visible, be manifest, to cause to look.

Avanī (अवनी) (*f*) The good earth.

Avanibhushan (अवनीभूषण) (*m*) Jewel of the earth.

Avanikānt (अवनीकांत) (*m*) A king, beloved of the earth.

Avanimohan (अवनीमोहन) (*m*) Attracting the world.

Avanindra (अवनीनदरा) (*m*) Lord/protector of the earth.

Avanipāl (अवनीपाल) (*m*) Lord/protector of the earth.

Avanish (अवनीश) (*m*) Lord/protector of the earth. (G)

Avanishvar (अवनीश्वर) (*m*) Lord/protector of the earth.

Avanti/Avantikā (अवंती/अवंतिका) A Name of Ujjayini, one of the seven sacred cities.

Avanthī (अवंथी) A mame of son of Arjuna.

Āvapāka (अवपाक) (*m/f*) A bracelet of gold.

Āvapika (अवपिका) (*m/f/n*) Additional, inserted, supplemented.

Avapta (अवप्त) (*m/f*) One who has obtained or reached his or her destination.

Avapti (अवप्ती) (*f*) Same as Avapta.

Avartan (अवर्तन) (*m*) One who keeps his global cycle moving. (V)

Avash (अवश) (*m*) Independent, free.

Avasyu (अवश्यु) (*m*) Keen to help. Another name of Lord Indra.

Avedin (अवेदिन) (*m/f/n*) Announcing, declaring.

Āvesh (अवेश) (*m*) Entrance, taking possession or being possessed of. Name of a less complete degree of incarnation of a god (especially of Vishnu) for a certain occasion; the incarnation of Parasurama is e.g. so regarded, as the incarnation of Vishnu as the Buddha.

Avidheyātmā (अविधेयत्म) (*m*) Whose real form is ineffable (V)

Avidosh (अविदोष) (*m*) Blameless, faultless.

Avighan (अविगहन) (*m*) Without obstacles. Lords Ganesh is responsible in keeping away obstacles from the path of His devotees. (G)

Avigyata (अविज्ञाता) (*m*) The supreme spirit. (V)

Avijit (अविजीत) (*m*) One who cannot be conquered.

Avikshin (अविक्षिन) (*m*) A true son of his father in virtuous qualities.

Avikshit (अविक्षित) (*m*) The son of Karamdham and father of Marutta.

Avimuktam (अविमुक्तम) (*m*) The name which Benaras city got after Shiva and Umā made it their residence in Kaliyuga. Also it means that city Benaras which is not left by Shiva at anytime.

Avimkuktesh (अविमकुकतेश) (*m*) A from of Shiva, very firm, auspicious.

Avināshi (अविनाशी) (*a*) Immortal, indestructable, imperishable.

Avish (अविश) (*m*) Nectar, life giving, sky, ocean, king. heaven, earth.

Avishi (अविशी) (*f*) Nectar, life giving, sky, ocean, king, heaven, earth.

Avit (अवित) (*m/f*) Protected, favoured.

Avitri (अवित्री) (*f*) Same as Avit.

Avsātri (अवसात्री) (*m*) A liberator.

Avtār (अवतार) (*m*) descent, name of a divine incarnation, the birth into the world. The incarnations of Vishnu are usually ten in number, each of them being assumed by Vishnu (the great preserver of power) to save the world from some great danger or trouble. The following are incarnation of Vishnu: 1. Matsya (the fish); 2. Kurma (the tortoise) 3. Varaha (the boar); 4. Nara-Simha (the man lion); 5. Vaman (the dwarf); 6. Parsu-Rama (Rama with the exe); 7. Rama (the hero of the Ramayana); 8. Krishna (the black or dark colour Krishna;) 9. Buddha (who spread Buddhism); 10. Kalki (the white horse for the restoration of purity).

Avyakta (अव्यक्त) (*m*) Unmanifest (V)

Avyangah (अव्यंगः) (*m*) Perfect in every sense. (V)

Avyayah (अवय्याह) (*m*) Impeerishable (V)

Avyayaprabhu (अवय्याप्रभु) (*m*) Imperishable Lord Shiva. He is without beginning, creater, sustainer, destroyer and is the ruler of time. (S)

Ayamah (अयाम) (*m*) Beyond the limit of death or any bondage. (V)

Ayusmat (आयुष्मत) (*n*) Long lived, honorific term of address.

Ayodhya (अयोध्या) (*m*) The modern Oude, the capital of lkshwaku—thefounder of solar race and afterwards the capital of rāma. It is one of the seven sacred *cities.* The exact site has not been discovered.

Ayus (आयूश) (*m*) The first born son of Pururavas and Urvashi.

Azād (आजाद) (*a*) Independent.

B (ब, बा)

Babhruha (**बभारूह**) (*m*) The nourisher of the realms. (V)

Badara (**बदारा**) (*m*) The Jujube tree

Badarī/Badarikāsram (**बदरी/बदरीकसराम**) A place sacred to Vishnu, near the Ganges in the Himalayas. Also a title of Vishnu as Badri Nath (Lord of Badri).

Badarikā (**बादरिका**) (*f*) A fruit or berry of the Jujube tree.

Badaryāna (**ब्दरयान**) (*m*) A name of Ved Vyas, especially used for him as the reputed author of the Vedanta philosophy.

Badrikā (**बदरिका**) (*f*) The fruit or berry of the jujube. Source of the Gạnges.

Bageshvari (**बागेश्वरी**) (*f*) Prosperity, beauty, one of the classical Ragas.

Bahlik (**बहलिक**) (*m*) Younger brother of king Shantanu. See Shantanu.

Bahu/Bahuka (**बहु/बहुका**) (*m*) A King of the solar race. He was the father of Sāgara.

Bahudevtiya (**बहुदेवतीया**) (*m/f*) Belonging to many deities.

Bahudhana (**बहुधन**) (*m/f*) Wealthy, possessing much wealth.

Bahugandhā (**वहुगन्ध**) (*f*) Strong, perfume, scent, Jasmine, sandalwood, musk.

Bahugunā (**बहुगुणा**) (*m*) Having many good qualities or virtues, multifarious, manifold.

Bahukalpa (**बहुकल्प**) (*m/f/n*) Manifold, multifarious.

Bahukalyān (**बहुकल्याण**) (*m/f*) Most noble, very illustrious.

Bahukāra (**बहुकार**) (*m/f*) Useful in many ways, doing much, busy.

Bahuli (**बहुली**) (*m/f*) manifold; the full moon in the month of Kartika, a versatile person.

Bahulikā (**बहुलिका**) (*f*) manifold, a versatile person.

Bahumātā (**बहुमाता**) (*m/f*) Possessing many necklaces.

Bahumānya (**बहुमान्य**) (*m*) Very honourable person-honoured by many.

Bahumati (**बहुमती**) (*f*) Intelligent, extremely knowledgeable.

Bahumitra (**बहुमित्र**) (*m*) Popular, famous with many friends.

Bahupriyā (**बहुप्रिया**) (*f*) Very dear to many.

Bahuras (**बहुरास**) (*m/f*) Having much juice.

Bahushakti (**बहुशक्ति**) (*f*) Possessing great strength. Very powerful.

Bahushira (**बहुशिरा**) (*m*) The one of many heads. (V)

Bahusvarna (**बहुस्वर्ण**) (*m*) Rich in gold.

Bahvricha (**बहव्रच**) (*m*) A priest or theologian of the Rig Veda.

Baka (बाक) (*m*) A great sage for whom Lord Indra had great respects.

Bakadalbhya (बकदालभय) A sage who visited the Pandavas in Dwaitya forest during their banishment to the forests and advised them to compliment Kshatriya strength with Brahmana wisdom.

Bāl (बाल) (*m*) Child carried in the arms of a mother.

Bālā (बाला) (*f*) Girl, young woman, Goddess. A daughter of Prajapati, fell down upon earth while going across the sky.

Balabhadra (बलभद्र) (*m*) Whose strength is good. An epithet of Balrām especially as companion of Krishna in his aspect as Jagannāth.

Balabhadrapriyā (बलभद्रप्रिया) (*m*) Lord Krishna fond of Balarama and his sister Subhadra (K)

Balabhrit (बालाभृत) (*m*) A name of god Indra.

Baladev (बलदेव) (*m*) The god of strength, an epithet of Balrām.

Baladhi (बलधि) (*m*) A sage who undertook severe penances to obtain a boon of immortality for his son Medhavi. Gods were pleased with his penances, but they could not grant such a boon.

Bāla Ganpati (बाल गणपति) (*m*) The child Ganesh. An epithet and aspect of god Ganesh as a child.

Bālagopāl (बालगोपाल) (*m*) The child-cowherd. An epithet of Krishna as a youthful cowherd.

Balāgra (बलअग्र) (*n*) Utmost strength, extreme force.

Bālāji (बालाजी) (*m*) The dear child. In *south* Indian an epithet of Venkatesha.

Bālaka (बालक) (*m/f*) Young, childish.

Bālakrām (बालकराम) (*m*) Child Rām.

Bālakrishna (बालकृष्ण) (the child Krishna) An epither of Krishna especially in his form as Damodara, Makhanchor (butter stealer).

Balamohini (बालमोहिनी) (*f*) A mother goddess.

Bālandharā (बालन्धार) (*f*) Wife of Bhim and daughter of Kashirāja.

Balarāma/Balrām (बलराम) (*m*) (Balabhadra and Baladeva are other forms of this name) The elder brother of Krishna. Extremely powerful. Strength of Ram. Balarāma was the son of Vasudeva and Devaki together with Rohini, (as a result of the transfer of the embryo in the womb of Devaki to that of Rohini). Thus Balarāma had two mothers. Balaram/Balram is often regarded as a particular avtār of Vishnu.

Balchakra (बलचक्र) (*n*) Circle of power, dominion, sovereignty, pretty woman, earth.

Bālchandra (बालचन्द्र) (*m*) Sporting the moon crest. The moon being the symbol of mind and peace-it denotes a pot of nectar, providing divine coolness to the wearer. (G)

Baldev (बलदेव) (*m*) Gof of strength. The elder brother of Krishna.

Baldhāra (बलधारा) (*n*) Very strong.

Baldvish (बालद्विश) (*m*) Name of Indra.

Balesh (बालेश) (*m*) Lor of strength. The commander of an army.

Bālgopāl (बालगोपाल) (*m*) Lord Krishna as a young herdsman. (K)

Baleshvara (बलेश्वर) (*m*) Lord of children. Another name of Lord Krishna. (K)

Balganpati (बलगणपति) (*m*) Beloved child. G)

Bāli (बाली) (*m*) A good and virtuous Daitya king. He was son of Virochana, son of Prahlād, son of Himaya-Kashipu.

Bālikā (बालिका) (*f*) The goddess following Revati.

Balimān (बलीमान) (*m*) Power, strength.

Bālirāj (बलिराज) (*m*) A very wise and righteous king who saved sage Dirghatma who was drowning in the river Ganges.

Balishtha (बलिष्ठ) (*m/f/n*) Most powerful, very strong, mighty

Bālihan (बलिहान) (*m*) Name of Vishnu, slayer of Bali.

Baliyas (बलियश) (*m/f/n*) Most powerful or mighty.

Balkar (बलकर) (*m/f/n*) Inspiring strength, strengthening.

Balkeli (बलकेली) (*f/m*) Child's play or amusement.

Bālkrishna (बालकृष्ण) (*m*) Boy-Lord Krishna. See also Krishna.

Bālmati (बालमती) (*f*) Childish intellect.

Bālmohan (बालमोहन) (*m*) Child Krishna. Very attractive children.

Bālmukund (बालमुकुन्द) (*m*) Child Krtishna. a child, tender, soft as a young blossom.

Bālnuja (बलनुजा) (*m*) Younger brother of Balram (see Baladev/Balram)

Balprāna (बलप्राण) (*m*) Strength and spirit.

Ballav (बल्लव) (*m*) Another name of Bhim while employed as a cook in the household of king Virat of Matsya.

Bālrāj (बलराज) (*m*) Child king.

Balram (बलराम) (*m*) The elder brother of Krishna. Very powerful Lord of strength.

Balranjini (बालरंजिनी) (*f*) Pleasing children.

Bālsarasvati (बालसरस्वाती) (*f*) Goddess of Knowledge, learning and speech. See also Saraswati.

Balsen (बलसेन) (*m*) Strong leader

Bālsurya (बालसूर्य) (*m*) The rising sun.

Balula (बलुला) *(m/f/n)* Powerful, strong.

Balvirya (बलवीर्य) *(n)* Strength and heroism.

Balya (बल्या) *(m/f)* Giving strength, powerful, strong, vigorous.

Bambhari (बमभरी) *(m)* One of the tutelary deityies of the Soma plant.

Bāna (बान) *(m)* A deity, eldest son of Bālī. He was a great devotee of Shiva.

Bandhu (बंधु) *(m)* Connection, relation, association.

Bandhuka (बंधुक) *(n)* Pentapetes Phoenicea (name of its flower)

Bandhura (बंधुर) *(m/f/n)* Bent, wavy, lovely, charming

Bandi (बँदी) *(m)* A Vedic scholar in the court of king Janaka.

Bāni/Vāni (बानी/वानी) *(m/f)* Speech, orator.

Banshankara (बँशंकर) *(m)* Arrow of Lord Shiva. Tranquility and welfare.

Banvāri (बँवरी) *(m)* Another name of Lord Krishna. Dwelsler of the forest. (K)

Barendra (बरेन्द्र) *(m)* Lord Indra, the best.

Barhanā (बर्हना) *(m/f/n)* Strong, firm, realy, certainly. (R.V.)

Barhishmati (बरीशमती) *(f)* Pure, pious, worship, blazing.

Barhishtha (बर्हीश्था) *(m/f/n)* Mightiest, strongest, highest.

Batansiddhikar (ब्तंसिधिकर) *(m)* Granter of strength (H)

Bhadrā (भद्रा) *(f)* Auspicious of a goddess. Probably belonging to the circle of Shiva.

Bhadrabāhu (भद्रबाहु) *(m)* Auspicious armed. Name of a Jaina author.

Bhadrachāru (भद्रचारू) *(m)* A son of Krishna and Rukmini.

Bhadrachitra (भद्रचित्र) *(m)* A son of Jambvati and Krishna.

Bhadra-Kāti (भद्रा-काती) *(f)* Name of a goddess. In modern times it applies to Durga.

Bhadramana (भद्रमन) *(f)* Kind hearted, noble minded,

Bhadramukhi (भद्रमुखी) *(f)* Beautiful face Charming face.

Bhadra-nidhi (भद्र-निधी) *(m)* Treasure of fortune.

Bhadrapāla (भद्रपाल) *(m)* Protector of goodness.

Bhadrarupā (भद्ररुप) *(m)* Beautiful face.

Bhadrasana (भद्रासना) *(n)* A golden throne with cushions It is also a body posture in a dance or in a Yoga exercise.

Bhadrasara (भद्रसार) *(m)* Essence/ocean of goodness.

Bhadrasen (भद्रसेन) *(m)* Son of Rsabha. Also a son of Devaki and Vasudev killed by Kans.

Bhadravāc (भद्रवाच) *(n)* Speaking auspiciously.

Bhadravat (भद्रावत) *(m/f)* Auspicious, fortunate.

Bhadravatī (भद्रावती) (*f*) A daughter of Sambavati and Krishna. Also name of a branch of the Ganges river.

Bhadresh (भद्रेष) (*m*) Lord of nobles.

Bhāg (भाग) The inherited share. The gracious Lord. Epithet of several gods.

Bhāgānandā (भागानन्द) (*f*) Fortunate, bestower of happiness,

Bhāghā (भागा) (*m*) He who withdraws all opulence of his devotees in order to test the firmness of their devotion. (V)

Bhāgdatt (भागदत्त) (*m*) Given by gracious lord.

Bhagesh (भगेष) (*m*) The lord of fortune or prosperity.

Bhāgevita (भागेविता) (*m*) Satisfied with good fortune and prosperity.

Bhāgin (भागिन) (*m/f/n*) Fortune, good luck, share of good fortune, blessed with good fortune.

Bhāginī (भागिनी) (*f*) The sister who is very fortunate.

Bhāginikā (भागिनिका) (*f*) Fortunate little sister.

Bhāgirath (भागीरथ) (*m*) Having a golden chariot or the chariot of Bhagi (epithet of river Ganges. Bhagirath was an ancient king who caused the holy river Gangā to come down from heaven to earth, and hence was the instrument of descent).

Bhāgirathī (भागीरथी) (*f*) The river Ganges. The name is derived from Bhgiratha, a descendant of Sāgara, whose austerities induced Shiva to allow the sacred river to descend to earth for the purpose of bathing the ashes of Sagara's sons, who had been consumed by the wrath of sage Kapila.

Bhāg-mālinī (भाग-मालिनी) (*f*) A Shakti, goddes mother.

Bhagvān (भगवान) (*m*) The principal and eternal god. Bha-means cherisher and supporter of the universe. Ga-means the creator, Va-means elemental spirit in which all being exist, and which exists in all beings. Thus it is the name of Vasudev (Krishna)

Bhāgvat (भागवत) (*m*) The Bhagvat Purān (the most popular of the Purānas) in which the ample details of duty are described. Bhāgvat also means the glorification of Vishnu. The tenth book of Bhagvat Purān narrates in detail the history of Krishna.

Bhagvatī (भगवती) (*f*) Of good fortunes. The name of a gracious aspect of Parvati.

Bhāgyalakshmi (भाग्यलक्ष्मी) (*f*) Goddess of fortune, another name of Lakshmi

Bhairav (भैरव) (*m*) The terrible. LORD Shiva the dstroyer of evil. He despels gloom by a gresat flame from His third eye. (S)

Bhākosh (भाकोश) (*m*) Treasure of light, another name of the sun.

Bhaktā (भक्ता) (*m/f/n*) Worshipped, liked, served, distributed, assigned, loyal, faithful, honouring.

Bhaktajā (भक्तजा) (*f*) Nectar, devotedness, attachement, inclination.

Bhaktavatsal (भक्तवत्सल) (*m*) Kind of his devotees. (V)

Bhaktijanpriya (भक्तिजनप्रिय) (*m*) Lover of devotees.

Bhaktī (भक्ति) (*f*) Devotion of a mystical religious doctrine of faith, according to which the devotion attain the union with God.

Bhaktila (भक्तिला) (*m/f/n*) Attached, faithful, devoted, adorer, worshipper.

Bhaktri (भक्त्री) (*m/f/n*) Attached, faithful, devoted, adorer, worshiper.

Bhālanetra (भालनेत्र) (*m*) With eye in the forehead. His (Shiva's) three eyes have vision into past, present and future. The third eye in the middle of the forehead denotes His extreme visionary power. (S)

Bhālchandra (भालचन्द्र) (*m*) Having the moon on his forehead. Name of a form of Ganesh.

Bhālendra (भालेन्द्र) (*m*) Lord of fortune. Another name of Lord Shiva (S)

Bhāleshvari (भालेश्वरी) (*f*) Goddess of forehead.

Bhallavi (भाल्लवी) (*f*) Name of an Upanished. Esoteric doctrine. The third division of the Vedas attached to the Brahmana portion, and forming part of the Shruti or revealed word.

Bhāmā (भामा) (*m*) Light, brightness, splendour. (R.V.)

Bhāmin (भामिन) (*m/f/n*) Shining, splendid, beautiful. A beautiful woman.

Bhāmini (भामिनि) (*f*) A beautiful woman. Meaning the same as Bhamin

Bhānemi (भानेमी) (*m*) The sun.

Bhānu (भानू) (*n*) Light, ray of light. Epithet of Surya (sun).

Bānuchandra (भानूचन्द्र) (*m*) Ray-moon, name of a prince.

Bhānudev (भानूदेव) (*m*) A Panchala chief who fought on the side of Pandavas in the Mahabharata war.

Bhānuja (भानूज) (*m*) Son of the sun, the planet Saturn.

Bhānumat (भानूमत) (*m*) Luminous, splendid. beautiful (V)

Bhānumati (भानूमती) Daughter of Bhanu, a Yadava chief.

Bhānuta (भानूत) (*f*) The state or master. a friend, the moon, the sun.

Bharabhrita (भरभृत) (*m*) The carrier of the earth's load. (V)

Bharanya (भरण्य) (*m*) A protector or master, a friend, the moon, the sun.

Bharas (भरस) (*f*) Bearing, holding, cherishing. One who beabears or maintain.

Bharat (भारत) (*m*) The celebrated son of an ancient king Dushyant and his consort Shakuntala, whose name is said to have formed the basis for this (India) country's name. Bharat Varsh is also the mane of India as having been the kingdom of Bharat (ancient king of the first Manwantra). Bharat is also a name of many heroes. Rama's brother was also called Bharat.

Bhārati (भारती) (*f*) Speech, Saraswati (the goddes of speech), mother India, In the Vedas Saraswati is celebrated in the hymns both as a river and a deity. Also regarded as the wife of Ganesh.

Bhāravā (भारवा) (*f*) Pleasing sound, sacr ed basil plant (Tulsi)

Bhāravi (भारवी) (*f*) Shining sun. God's protection.

Bharatiyam (भारतीयम) (*n*) Indianness. The idea of national identity.

Bhargas (भारगस) (*n*) Radiance, lustre, splendour, glory (from Rig Veda).

Bhārgava (भार्गव) A descendant of Bhrigu Rishi. See also Aurva.

Bharta (भरता) (*m*) The sustainer of the world who gives food to all beings (V)

Bhartri (भरत्री) (*m*) Chief, Lord, protector, protection.

Bhās (भास) (*f*) Light or ray of light, Lord of rays or light.

Bhāsana (भासन) (*n*) Shining, glittering, brilliance, splendour.

Bhāsanta (भासन्त) (*m/f/n*) Splendid, the beautiful, the sun or the moon.

Bhāsin (भासिन) (*m/f/n*) Shining, brilliant.

Bhāskar (भास्कर) (*m*) The sun. Making light.

Bhāskarācharya (भास्कराचार्य) (*m*) A celebrated mathematician and astronomer who was born early in the eleventh century AD. He was the author of Bija-ganita (arithmetic), the Lilāvatī (Algebra), and the Siddhānta Siromani (astronomy).

Bhāskardyuti (भास्करद्युति) (*m*) Radiant like the sun (V)

Bhāskari (भास्करी) (*f*) Radiant like the sun-goddess Lakshmi. (L)

Bhāsura (भासुरा) (*m*) Shining, radiant, bright, splendid.

Bhāsvara (भास्वर) (*m/f*) The sun, shining, brilliant, bright, resplendent. Name of a satellsite of the god of the Sun.

Bhav (भव) (*m*) Existence. An epithet of Shiva, especially in the form in which he married Sati, a daughter of Daksha.

Bhāvah (भावा) (*m*) Eternal and self created (V)

Bhāva Karna (भावा करना) (*n*) Indication of intention through dance movement.

Bhāvukatā (भावुकता) (*n*) The first emotion of love. emotion, love.

Bhāvanā (भावना) (*f*) Sentiment, feeling, emotion.

Bhāvanah (भावनह) (*m*) The bestower of fruit of actions.

Bhavānī (भवानी) (*f*) An epithet of Parvati (wife of Shiva) She is said to be the Shakti of Shiva.

Bhāvartha/Bhav-artha (भावार्थ/भाव-अर्थ) (*n*) The obvious meaning of a word, the subject matter.

Bhāvastha/ Bhav-astha (भावास्था/भाव-आस्था) (*m/f/n*) Being in love.

Bhāvat (भावत) (*m/f*) Being, present (from Rig Veda). Your Lordshi, your honour, your worship.

Bhāvayarupa/Bhavya-rupa(n) (भाव्यरूप/भाव्य-रूपन) (*n*) A good figure or form, handsome, beautiful.

Bhāvayanā (भाव्यना) (*f*) Coming from Lord Shiva. Name of Ganges.

Bhāvbhuti (भावभूति) (*f*) Welfare, prosperity, name of a celebrated poet.

Bhāvesha (भावेश) (*m*) FLord of the world.

Bhavika (भविका) (*m/f*) Well-meaning, rightcous, pious.

Bhāvin (भाविन) (*m/f/n*) Living being, inevitable, pre-destined, manifesting, showing, blessing, beautiful, illustrious.

Bhāvishnu (भाविष्णु) (*m/f/n*) Imminent, future, faring well, thriving.

Bhāvita (भाविता) (*m/f/n*) Created, produced, obtained, manifested, displayed, cherished, promoted, in high spirit (from Mahabharata).

Bhavitātmā/Bhavit-ātman (भावितात्मा/भावित-आत्मा) (*m/f/n*) One whose sole is purified by meditating on the universal soul. One whose thoughts fixed on Supreme spirit, holy, a sage, saint.

Bhavitra (भावित्र) (*n*) The three worlds (the earth, heaven and the lower regions).

Bhāvmaya/Bhav-maya (भावमय/भाव-मया) (*m/f*) Consisting of Lord Shiva.

Bhāvpushpa/Bhav-pushpa (भावपुष्पा/भाव-पुष्पा) (*n*) The heart compared to the flower. See also Bhav.

Bhāvrupa (भावरूप) (*m/f/n*) Really existing, real, actual.

Bhāvuka (भावुक) (*n*) Appreciating beauty. Having a taste for poetry.

Bhavya (भव्य) (*a*) Existing, future, suitable, good happy. A name of King of Shakadvipa.

Bhayakritā (भयाकृता) (*m*) Frightening to the wicked (V)

Bhayanashan (भयानशन) (*m*) Destroyer of the fear and ignorance (for his devotees). (V)

Bhayanashini (भयानशिनी) (*f*) Destroyer of the fear and ignorance (for his devotees). (V)

Bhayapah (भयापा) (*m*) God who removes fear from His devotrees heart. (V)

Bhelā (भेला) (*m*) An ancient sage who wrote upon medicine.

Bheshaja (भेषज) (*m/f*) Curing, healing, remedy, medicine. Doctor. (From Rig Veda)

Bheshajam (बेषजम) (*m*) The medicine for mortal ills (V)

Bhim/Bhim Sen (भीम/भीम सेन) (*m*) The terrible. The strongest. The second of the five Pandva princes, and mythically the son of the wind god (Vāyu). As son of winds Bhim was brother of Hanuman, and was able tgo fly with great speed.

Bhimbal/Bhim-bal (भिंभल) (*m*) Possessing to much stength like Bhim.

Bhim-parakramah (भीम-परिक्रमा) (*m*) Performer of the terrifying feats for the wicked. (V)

Bhimeswara (भीमेश्वर) (*m*) Name of the twelve great Lingas (The symbol under which shiva is universally worshipped). The twelve names of Lingas are: 1. Som-nāth (lord or moon): 2. Mallikarjuna or Sri Saila (The mountain of Shri); 3. Mahā Kal; 4. Omkār; 5. Amareswara (Gid if gids); 6. Vaidyanāth (Lord of physicians); 7. Rāmesa or Rāmeswara (Lord of Ram); 8. Bhim Shankar; 9. Vishweshra (Kird of all); 10. Tryambaka or Tryaksha (/tru-ocular); 11. Gautamesa (Lord of Gautama) 12. Kedar-nāth or Kedaresa (the deity is represented as a shapeless mass of rock.)

Bhishma (भीष्म) (*m*) Son of king Santanu by holy river goddess Gangā, hence called Santanuva, Gāgeya and Nadija (the river born). He is famous for self denial, devotion, fidelity and determination, Name of the patriarch of the Kauravas and Pandavas who fought in the great war of mahabharat and led the armies of the Kaurvas.

Bhishamaka (भीष्मका) (*m*) An appelation of Shiv. Also king of Vidarbha, father of Rukamani (wife of Krishna).

Bhogvat (भोगवत) (*m/f/n*) Delightful, happy, prosperous.

Bhoj (भोज) (*m*) A name borne by many kings. Feast, entertainment, festivity. a banquet.

Bhojanam (भोजनाम) (*m*) The nourishment provider to the devotees. (V)

Bhojaraja (भोजराज) (*m*) God of genorisity. Another name of king Bhojadeva. Bhojarāja

Bhokta (भोक्ता) (*m*) The one who enjoy eternal Bliss. Enjoyer of all natural bounties. The sufferere in the form of human being and enjoyer of all the rewards. (V)

Bhrāj (भ्राज) (*f*) Ligt, lustre, splendour.

Bhrājaka (भ्राजक) (*m/f*) Causing to shine, making bright.

Bhrājat (भ्राजत) (*m/f*) Shining, glittering (from Rig Veda).

Bhrājin (भ्राजीन) (*m/f*) Shining, glittering (from Rig Veda).

Bhrājishnu (भ्रजीष्णु) (*m*) Uniformly radiant form. (V)

Bhrigu (भृगु) A vedic sage. He is one of the Prajapatis and great Rishis, and is regarded as founder of the race of the Bhrigus or Bhargavas.

Bhruvilāsa (भ्रुविलास) (*n*) Graceful movment of the eyebrow in a dance. The eyebrows of the Gopis are raised to attact Lord Krishna.

Bhudev (भूदेव) (*m*) Gof of earth. The creater, sustainer and destroyer of the world, he bestows happiness and prosperity on his noble devotees. (S)

Bhugarbh (भूर्गभ) (*m*) The sustainer of earth in its embryonic stage. (V)

Bhuiyu (भूयो) (*m/f*) Wealthy, rich.

Bhujagottam (भूजगौतम) (*m*) The best among the serpents. Sheshnag (V)

Bhuji (भूजी) (*f*) One who grants favour, a protector, favour, the granting of enjoyment (from Rig Veda).

Bhujyu (भूज्यु) (*m/f/n*) Wealthy, rich (from Rig Veda)

Bhukand (भूखंड) (*m*) A medicinal plant.

Bhukta (भुक्त) (*m/f*) Enjoy, possess.

Bhukti (भुक्ति) (*f*) Enjoyment.

Bhumanyu (भूमन्नयु) (*m*) Name of a son of Bharat and Dhritrashtra.

Bhumātri (भूमात्री) (*f*) Name of Durga. See Devi.

Bhumi (भूमि) (*f*) The earth. In the Vedas the earth is personified as the mother of all beings, and is invoked together with the sky.

Bhumijā (भूमिजा) (*m/f/n*) Produced from the earth. Earthly being. Another name of Sita.

Bhumindra (भूमिन्द्र) (*m*) King, price, earth-chief, king of earth.

Bhumipāl (भूमिप्राल) (*m*) Lord/guardian of the earth.

Bhumijaya/Bhumi-jaya (भूमीजया) (*m*) Earth conquering.

Bhumitra (भूमित्र) (*m*) Earth friend.

Bhunetri (भूनेत्री) (*m*) King, prince, earth protector.

Bhupālan/Bhu-pālan (भूपालेन) (*n*) Sovereignty, dominion, earth protection, Lord Vishnu.

Bhupati (भूपति) (*m*) Lord of the earth. Lord of Lords. Worshipped by Brahma and in all the three world (G)

Bhupendra (भूपेन्द्रा) (*m*) A King, an emperor.

Bhurbhuvah (भूरभूवाह) (*m*) The support of this earth (V)

Bhuri (भूरी) (*m/f/n*) Much, abundant, frequent, strong, mighty (from Rig Veda)

Bhuribala/Bhuri-bala (भूरीवाला/भरी-वाला) (*m*) Having much strength.

Bhuridakshana (भूरीदक्षना) (*m*) One who give fees to the priests liberally. (V)

Bhuridhara/Bhuri-dhara (भूरीधारा/भरी-धारा) *(m/f)* Yielding, abundant, rays of light.

Bhuriguna/Bhuri-guna (भूरीगुणा) *(m/f/n)* Multiplying greatly, bearing manifold front.

Bhurishravā (भूरीश्रव) *(m)* A mighty and powerful king. grandosn of Shantanu's brother Bahlika.

Bhurivasu/Bhuri-vasu (भूरीवसु) *(m)* Having much wealth.

Bhusha (भूषा) *(n)* Ornaments.

Bhushana (भूषण) *(m)* An ornament, decoration, anything decorative.

Bhushayah (भूशैय्या) *(m)* He who came and slept on earth in the form of Lord Ram (V)

Bhushin (भूशिन) *(m)* World-ruler, king, prince.

Bhushnu (भूषणू) *(m/f/n)* Desiring prosperity or happiness, growing, thriving.

Bhutabhavan (भूतभावन) *(m)* The creator and sustainer of the physical world (V)

Bhutabhavya Bhavannath (भूतभाव्य भावनाथ) *(m)* The lord of the past, present, and future of all beings. (V)

Bhutabhavya Bhavatprabhu (भूतभव्य भवतप्रभु) *(m)* The lord of the past, present, and future of all beings. (V)

Bhutabhrita (भूतभृत) *(m)* The sustainer of the world (V)

Bhutadi (भूतदी) *(m)* The root causee of all beings. (V)

Bhutakritah (भूतकृत) *(m)* The creator of the physical world. (V)

Bhutātma (भूतात्मा) *(m)* The dwelling spirit in every being's soul. (V)

Bhutamaheshwar (भूतमहेश्वर) *(m)* Lord of all mortal creation (V)

Bhutavas (भूतवास) *(m)* The ultimate abode of all mortals (V)

Bhutesh (भुतेश) *(m)* Lord of baser beings. Anothre name of Brahma, Vishnu and the Sun. (V)

Bhuteshwar (भूतेश्वर) *(m)* A Lord of beings or of created things. A name applied to Vishnu, Brahma, and Krishna and Shiva.

Bhuti (भूती) *(f/m)* Existing, well-being, thriving, prosperity, power, wealth, fortune, welfare. The support of all existence (V)

Bhutikrit (भूतकृत) *(m)* Causing welfare, Name of Lord Shiva, prosperity, happiness.

Bhuvan (भुवन) *(m)* The world, the earth.

Bhuvanchandra (भूवनचन्द्र) Moon of the world.

Bhuvanesh (भुवनेश) *(m)* Lord of the world, Shiva. See Shiva.

Bhuvaneshvarī (भुवनेश्वरी) *(f)* Mame of various goddesses. Good luck.

Bhuvaneshvarya (भूवनेश्वरया) (*f*) Name of goddess Lakshmi as supreme deity. She holds a pitcher of nectar in one hand, and in the other, a bell constantly ringing-these proclaim Her victory. (L)

Bhuvanpati (भूवनपति) (*m*) Lord of Lords. Brahma, Vishnu and Mahesh pays obeisance and propitiate Him to save the world from evil. (G)

Bhuvaneshi (भूवनेशी) (*f*) Goddess of the earth.

Bhuvari (भूवरी) (*f*) Good luck. Name of Goddess.

Bhuvas (भूवास) (*m/f*) The air, atmosphere. A sacred word in the Vedas.

Bhuvshasin (भूवशसिन) (*m*) King, prince, world ruler.

Bhuvis (भूविस) (*m*) The sea, ocean.

Bibhatsu (बीभत्सु) Loathing. An appelation of Arjuna.

Bijamavyam (बीजमव्यम) (*m*) The imperishable entity of the world (V)

Bilvā (बिलवा) (*m*) Wood-apple tree. Its fruit when unripe is used for medicine and leaves are employed in the ceremonial of the worship of Lord Shiva.

Bimba (बिम्ब) (*m/f*) The disk of the sun or moon. Name of a wife of Balditya (king of Kashmir).

Bimbaka (बिम्बक) (*f*) The pupil of the eye. The disk of the sun or moon.

Bimbaki (बिंबकी) (*f*) Same as Bimbak.

Bimbini (बिम्बनी) (*f*) The pupil of the eye.

Bimbisāt (बिम्बीसात) (*m*) Name of a king of Magadha (contemporary and patron of Buddha).

Bindi/Bindiya (बिन्दी/बिन्दया) (*f*) A point, dot, zero, cipher, spot.

Bindu (बिन्दू) (*m*) A point, dot, zero, cipher, spot.

Bindudev (बिन्दुदेव) (*m*) Buddhist deity.

Bindumati (बिन्दुमती) (*f*) The queen of Marici and mother of Bindumat.

Binduphal (बिन्दुफल) (*n*) Name of a pearl.

Bindurekhā (बिन्दुरेखा) (*f*) A row or line of points or dots.

Bindusār (बिन्दुसार) (*m*) A king (son of Chandragupta)

Bipinchandra (बीपिनचन्द्र) (*m*) Moon of the forest. Another name of Lord Krishna (K)

Birendra (बीरेन्द्र) (*m*) Lord of warriors.

Bireshvar (बीरेश्वर) (*m*) Lord of warriors.

Birju (बीरजू) (*m*) Powerful.

Bishan (बिशन) (*m*) Corrupted form of the sanskrit Bisan/Vishnu. One of the Hindu triad, the god in the character of a preserver. See Vishnu.

Bodh (बोध) (*m/f*) knowing, understanding.

Bodhak (बोधक) (*m/f*) Awakening, teaching.

Bodhan (बोधन) (*m/f*) Intellect, knowing, understanding.

Bodhendra (बोधेन्द्र) (*m*) Lord of the intelligence

Bodhi (बोधी) (*m/f*) Prefect knowledge, wisdom.

Bodhimaya (बोधीमय) (*m/f/b*) Consisting of knowledge.

Bodhin (बोधिन) (*m/f/n*) Enlightening, awakening, perceive, intent upon, careful of, knowing, familiar with.

Bodhisattva (बोधिसत्व) (*m*) One whose essence is perfect knowledge.

Bodhitā (बोधिता) (*m/f*) Good knowledge, intellect, instructed.

Bodhkār (बोधकार) (*m/f*) One who awakens, teaches or informs.

Brahamatā (ब्राह्मता) (*f*) Learned woman. The state of a learned person.

Brahm (ब्रह्म) (*m*) The supreme soul of the universe, self-existent, absolute, eternal, from which all things emanate, and to which all return.

Brahmā (ब्रह्मा) (*m*) The first member of the Hindu triad, the supreme spirit manifested as the active creator of the universe. He is of a red colour and has four hands. Hence he is called Chatur-Anāna or Chatur-Mukh (four faced). The Mahabharata represents Brahma as springing from the navel of Vishnu; hence he is called Nābhi-ja (navel born); Kanj (the lotus), Sarojin (having a lotus), Abja-ja, Abja-yoni, and Kanj-ja (lotus born). Brahma is also called Vidhi, Vedhās, Druhina, and Srashtri (creator); Dh¯ atri, Vidhātri (sustainer); Pitāmah (the great father); Ādi-kavi (the first poet; and Dru ghana (the axe or mallet.)

Brahmabhāv (ब्राह्मभाव) (*m*) Same as Brahmā

Brahmabhuti (ब्राह्मभूति) (*f*) Twilight. Brahma. See Brahma.

Brahmadas (ब्रह्मदास) (*m*) Devotee of Brahma. See brahma.

Brahmadatta (ब्रह्मदात) (*m*) Given by Brahma.

Brahmadev (ब्रह्मदेव) (*m*) God. See Brahma.

Brahma-Gupta (ब्रह्म-गुप्त) (*m*) An astronomer who composed the Brahma-Gupta Siddhntā in AD 628.

Brahmagya (ब्रह्माग्य) (*m*) He who knows Brahm and scriptures (V)

Brahma-Gita (ब्रह्म-गीत) (*f*) Verses attributed to Brahma.

Brahmajyoti (ब्रह्मज्योति) The light of Brahma. See Brahma.

Brahmakalā (ब्रह्मकला) (*f*) The goddess enshrined in wisdom.

Brahmakrita (ब्रह्माकृत) (*m*) Who created order for Breahmans (V)

Brahma-kuta (ब्रह्म-कुते) (*m*) Thoroughly learned Brahman.

Brahma-lekha (ब्रह्म-लेख) (*m*) Brahma's writing.

Brahma-Mālā (ब्रह्म-माला) (*f*) Necklace of Brahmā.

Brahma-murti (ब्रेह्म-मूर्ति) (*m/f*) Having the figure or form of Brahma. See also Brahma

Brahmanah (ब्रह्माण) (*m*) Looking at all without prejudice (V)

Brahmanidā (ब्रह्मनिधा) (*n*) The resting place of Brahma or holy people.

Brāhmanikā (ब्रह्मानिका) (*m/f*) Derived from or relating to the Brahmins.

Brahma-prajāpti (ब्रह्म-प्रजापति) (*m*) Brahma and Prajapati see Brahma and Prajapati.

Brahmanpriya (ब्रह्मणप्रिया) (*m*) Very dear to Brahmins (V)

Brahamanya (ब्रह्मणय) (*m*) Protector of the Brahman, the noble and of knowledge. (V)

Brahma-putra (ब्रह्मपुत्र) (*m*) Son of Lord Brahma. See also Brahma.

Brahma-rāj (ब्रह्म-राज) (*m*) Kingdom of Brahma.

Brahma-ratna (ब्रह्म-रत्न) (*n*) Jewel of Brahma, any valuable present made to Brahmans.

Brahma-rishi (ब्रह्म-ऋषि) (*m*) A sage like Brahma.

Brahma-rup (ब्रह्म-रूप) (*m*) Name of Vishnu

Brahm-stuti (ब्रह्म-स्तुति) (*f*) Praise of the Brahma.

Brahmasut (ब्रह्मसुत) (*m*) Brahma's son.

Brahmavartta (ब्रह्मवरत्त) Between the two divine rivers (Sarasvati and Drishadwati),—visited by gods.

brahma-vidya (ब्रह्म-विद्या) (*f*) Sacred knowledge.

Brahma-vinā (ब्रह्म-वीणा) (*f*) Sacred divine stringerd instrument.

Brahvivardhanah (ब्रविवर्धना) (*m*) Enhancer of the Brahm or its manifestation (V)

Brahmi (ब्रह्मी) (*f*) Brahma's consort is Brahmi also known as Saraswati (goddess of learning).

Brahmya (ब्रम्य) (*m/f*) Relating to Brahma.

Brajrāj (बृजराज) (*m*) Lord of Braj. Another name of Lord Krishna (K)

Brajbhushan (बृजभूषण) (*m*) Ornament of nature. Another name of Krishna (K)

Brihadashwa (बृहदश्व) (*m*) A sage who visited Pandavas during their thirteen years of banishment from Hastinapur and told them the story of Nal and Damyanti.

Brihadya (बृहद्य) (*m*) A Jayādev and son of Brahmā.

Brihajjan (बृहज़्न) (*m*) A great or illustrious man.

Brihajyotis (बृहज्योतिश) (*m/f*) Bright, shining, Name of grandson of Brahma.

Brihatejas (बृहतेजस) (*m/f*) Very powerful or energetic. Name of planet Jupiter.

Brihatkirti (बृहतकीर्ति) (*m/f*) Very famous person. Name of a grandson of Brahma.

Brihatsena (बृहतसेना) (*m*) A son of Krishna and Bhadrā.

Brihatvan (बृहतवन) (*m*) Name of Dev-gandharv.

Brijbālā (बृजबाला) (*f*) Daughter of nature and Braj, and also another name of Radha.

Brindavananta (बृन्दावनन्त) (*m*) Inhabiter of Brindavan Orchard (K)

Bruhanella (ब्रुहनेल) Another name of Arjuna when he was employed in the court of king Virat of Matsya, teaching dance and music to his daughter Uttara.

Budbudā (बुदबुदा) (*f*) An Apsara who danced in joy to entertain Arjuna when he reached heaven to meet Indra to obtain divine weapons.

Bubhuksha (बुभुक्ष) (*f*) Desire of enjoying anything, appetite, hunger.

Buddha (बुद्ध) (*m*) The ninth incarnation of Vishnu. Vishnu is said to have appeared as Buddha to reject caste system. Buddha was the founder of Buddhism.

Buddhi (बुद्धि) (*f*) Meaning the same as Budh

Budh (बुद्ध) (*m*) Wise, intelligent, te planet Mercury.

Budhar (बुद्धर) (*m/f*) Earth supporting.

Budhātri (बुद्धात्री) (*f*) Earth mother. A scholarly person.

Budhdās (बुद्धदास) (*m*) A devotee of Buddha.

Buddhidevi (बुद्धिदेवी) (*f*) Goddess of wisdom

Buddhividhātā (बुद्धिविधाता) (*m*) God of wisdom (G)

Budhkāri (बुद्धकारी) (*f*) Name of the princess.

Budhmātikā (बुद्धमातिका) (*f*) Name of a woman. Intellect, wisdom.

Budhrāj (बुद्धराज) (*m*) Name of a king. Kingdom of Buddha.

Budhsāgar (बुद्धसागर) (*m*) Ocean of wisdom.

Budhshudhi (बुद्धशुद्धि) (*f*) Purification of the mind in Vedas.

Budhvridhi (बुद्धवृद्धि) (*f*) Development of intellect. Intellectual.

C (च, चा)

Chaitanya (चैतन्य) (*a/m*) Conscious, sensitive. alert and awake, consciousness, spirit

Chaityaka (चैत्यक) (*m*) Monument, above of consciousness, a sacred mountain Magadha.

Chakās (चकास) (*m/f*) Shining.

Chakāsit (चकासित) (*m/f*) Illuminated, splendid.

Chakradhar (चक्रधर) (*m*) Vishnu, a sovereign or governor.

Chakragadadharam (चक्रगदधर्म) (*m*) The weilder of the disc and the mace. (V)

Chakrapāni (चक्रापाणी) (*m*) Vishnu, a sovereign or governor.

Chakravarti (चक्रवर्ती) (*m*) A universal emperor.

Chakri (चक्री) (*m*) The welder of the discus called Sudarshan Chakra. (V)

Chakshani (चक्षनी) (*m/f*) An illuminator.

Chakshas (चक्षस) (*n*) Radiance, clearness, look, sight, eye, spiritual teacher, teacher of the Gods.

Chakshu (चक्षु) (*m*) An eye. Name of a prince.

Chakshushia/Chakshushya (चकक्षुष्य) (*m*) Beautiful, pleasing to the eye, another name of the sun god.

Chakshuh Priti (चक्षु-प्रीति) (*f*) Delight of the eyes.

Chakshurag (चक्षुराग) (*n*) Love as manifested by exchange of glances. Eye love, love at first sight.

Chakshus (चक्षुस) (*m/f/n*) Light, clearance, seeing (from Rig Veda).

Chakshushya (चक्षुष्य) (*m/f/n*) Pleasing to the eyes, wholesome for the eyes. Good looking, beautiful.

Chala (चला) (*m*) Everywhere like wind. moveable. (V)

Champakali (चम्पाकली) (*f*) Bud of the Champaka tree (Michelia champaka)

Chaman (चम्मन) (*m*) A small garden, bed of garden, a place of life and luxury.

Chameli (चमेली) (*f*) A King of jasmine plant and its flower.

Chāmikar (चामिकर) (*m*) Gold

Champā (चम्पा) (*m*) The tree Michelia Champace and its pleasant fragrant light yellow or yellowish white flower.

Champak (चम्पक) (*m*) A tree bearing yellow fragrant flowers or its flowers. See Champā

Chamundā (चमुण्ड) (*f*) A name of the consort of Shiva.

Chana (चना) (*m/f/n*) Renowned, famous.

Chanakya (चाणक्य) (*m*) A celebrated Brahmin, the Minister of Chandra-Gupta (emperor of Hindustan). He was a great master of artifice, and has been called the Machieavelli of India. He is the author of Chanakya Sutra (on morals and polity). He is also known by the names of Vishnu-Gupta and Kautilya.

Chanchalā (चँचला) (*f*) An epithet of Lakshmi (the goddes of wealth.)

Chanchal (चँचल) (*a*) Agile, restless, energetic, lively, playful.

Chanchu (चँचू) (*m/f/n*) Renowned or famous for, a beak, bill.

Chanchutna (चँचुटना) (*n*) Being famous for.

Chānd (चान्द) (*m*) the moon.

Chandā (चन्दा) (*f*) The moon, subscription, contribution, donation.

Chandak (चन्दक) (*m/f*) Pleasing, moon, moonlight.

Chandan (चन्दन) (*m*) Sandalwood. The moon.

Chandanangadi (चंन्दनांगद्दी) (*m*) Having His body anointed with sandal paste. (V)

Chandan-giri (चन्दन-गिरी) (*m*) Sandal mountain.

Chāndanī (चांदनी) (*f*) The moonlight.

Chandānin (चंदनिन) (*m/f*) Anointed with Sandal. Name of Shiva.

Chandayi (चंदइ) (*f*) Cool like the moon. Another name of moon-faced goddess Lakshmi (L)

Chandeshvara (चन्देश्वर) (*m*) Lord of the Moon. Lord Shiva.

Chandī (चंडी) (*f*) The Goddess Durga, especially in the form she assumed for the destruction of the Asura called Mahisha.

Chandikā (चंडिका) (*f*) Name of Durga. See Durga and Devi.

Chandilā (चंडिला) (*m/f*) Name of Lord Shiva. Name of river.

Chandipati (चंडपति) (*m*) Husband of Chandi. See Shiva.

Chandodevi (चंदोदेवी) (*f*) Goddess of metre. Another name of Gayatri.

Chandoga (चंदोगा) (*m*) A priest or chanter of the Sama Veda.

Chandorga (चंदोर्गा) (*f*) Name of one of the eight Shaktis of Goddess Durga.

Chandra (चन्द्र) (*m*) The moon, crescent.

Chandrabālā (चन्द्रबाला) (*f*) Daughter of the moon. Very beautiful like the moon.

Chandrabhanu (चन्द्रभानू) (*m*) Radiant as the moon. Sun and moon conjoined. Illuminating, enlightening.

Chandra Bimb (चन्द्र विम्ब) (*n*) The moon disc. Consisting of moon disc.

Chandra-bindu (चन्द्र-बिन्दू) (*m/f*) Moon like spot.

Chandra-datt (चन्द्र-दत्त) (*m*) Moon-given.

Chandra-dev (चन्द्र-देव) (*m*) Moon god.

Chandra Dipikā (चन्द्र दीपिका) (*f*) Light of the moon. Name of an astrological work.

Chandra Golika (चन्द्र गोलिका) (*f*) Moonlight.

Chandrajā (चन्द्रजा) (*f*) Daughter of the moon

Chandrak (चन्द्रक) (*m*) The moon. Like the moon.

Chandra-kalā (चन्द्र-कला) (*f*) A digit of the moon.

Chandrakānt (चन्द्रकांत) (*m*) The brilliance or lustre of the moonlight.

Chandrakānti (चन्द्रकांती) (*f*) The same as Chandrakānti.

Chandra Kāntiyā (चन्द्र कांतीया) (*f*) Resemble the moon.

Chandra-ketu (चन्द्र केतू) (*m*) A son of Lakshman. A king of the city of Chakora (a country near the Himalayas).

Chandra Kitā (चन्द्र किता) (*m/f/n*) Furnished with brilliant moon-like spots.

Chandra Lochan (चन्द्र लोचन) (*n*) Moon eyed. Beautiful like moon.

Chandralok (चन्द्रलोक) (*m*) The worlds or spheres of the moon.

Chandra Mālā (चन्द्र माला) (*f*) Moon rosary.

Chandra-mata (चन्द्र माता) (*n*) Doctrine of moon worshippers.

Chandramauli (चन्द्रमौली) (*m*) With moon for crest jewel. The crescen momon is an adornment in Lord Shsiva's matted haiora. The moon was given refuge in Lord Shiva's matted hair when the former was under a curse. (S)

Chandra Mukh (चन्द्र मुख) (*n*) Moon faced.

Chandramani (चन्द्रमणी) (*m*) Same as Chandrakānt.

Chandranshu (चन्द्रांशु) (*m*) Like cool moonlight to the those distressed with heat

Chandra-mātā (चन्द्र-माता) (*n*) Doctrine of moon worshippers.

Chandra Mukh (चन्द्र मुख) (*n*) Moon faced.

Chandra Mukhi (चन्द्र मुखी) (*f*) Moon faced. Most beautiful.

Chandra Muktā (चन्द्र मुक्ता) (*m*) Lord Shiva. Moon crested.

Chandrapād (चन्द्रपाद) (*m*) Moon-beam.

Chandra-prabhā (चन्द्र-प्रभा) (*f*) Moon Light.

Chandra Ratan (चन्द्र रत्न) (*n*) Pearl of the moon.

Chandra-rekhā (चन्द्र-रेखा) (*f*) The streak of the moon.

Chandrarupa (चन्द्ररूपा) (*f*) Moon faced-goddess Lakshmi. (L)

Chandrasahodri (चन्द्रासहोद्री) (*f*) Sister of the moon (L)

Chandresh (चन्द्रेश) (*m*) Lord of the moon. another name of Lord Shiva (S)

Chandra Surya (चन्द्र सूर्य) (*m*) Moon and the sun.

Chandra Taraka (चन्द्र तारक) (*m*) The moon and the stars.

Chandra-vadana (चन्द्र-वदन) (*f*) Moon-faced (goddess Lakshmi) (L)

Chandra Vimal (चन्द्र विमल) (*n*) Pure as the moon. See also Chandra and Vimal.

Chandra-Vispardimukhā (चन्द्र-विशपरदीमुखा) (*f*) Beautiful like the moon (D)

Chandrikā (चन्द्रिका) (*f*) The moonlight, moon shine.

Chandrimā (चन्द्रिमा) (*f*) Moonlight.

Chandrin (चन्द्रिन) (*m/f*) Golden, possessing gold.

Chandrudrilā/Chand-rudrilā (चन्दरूद्रिला/चन्द-रूद्रिला) (*f*) Knowledge of mythical nature acquired for worship.

Chandrupā/Chand-rupā (चन्दरूपा/चन्द-रूपा) (*f*) Most beautiful like moon. Name of Goddess Brahma.

Chandra Shakti (चन्द्र शक्ति) (*m*) Great strength of impetuous valour.

Chantan (चंतन) (*m/f*) Renowned, famous.

Chantav (चंतव) (*n*) Being famous for.

Chaplā (चापला) (*f*) The goddess Lakshmi, lightning—a feminine form of Chapal.

Charaka (चरक) (*m*) A wanderer, religious student, ascetic, medical plant, a physician and Muni for alleviating disease.

Charanjivi (चंरजीवी) (*f*) Blessed

Charitarthatā (चरितार्थता) (*m/f/n*) Satisfied.

Chantav (चन्तव) (*n*) Being famous for.

Charmunda (चरमुण्ड) (*f*) A form of Durga. See Durga and Devi.

Charubālā (चारुबाला) (*f*) Beautiful girl.

Charitarthatā (चरितार्थता) (*m/f/n*) Satisfied.

Charu Darshana (चारु दर्शन) (*f*) Good looking women. A posture in dance.

Chāru-hasini (चारु-हसिनी) (*f*) Sweet smiler. This epithetis used for Rukmini (wife of Krishna.)

Charumat (चारुमत) (*m/f*) Lovely.

Chāru-mati (चारुमती) (*f*) Daughter of Krishna and Rukmini.

Charunetra/Charu-Netra (चारुनेत्रा) (*m/f*) Beautiful-eyed.

Chārutā (चारूता) (*f*) Loveliness, beauty.

Chāruvi (चारूवी) (*n*) Splendour, beautiful.

Chasha (चश) (*n*) A blue jay bird, The sight of a bird when starting journey is a sign of good luck and prosperity.

Chātak (चातक) (*m*) An Indian bird-cuckoo who is supposed to drink only drops of rain.

Chātan (चातन) (*m*) Name of the Rishi of the Chātan verses in Atharvaveda.

Chatu (चतु) (*n*) Flattering words, agreeable speech, amorous chattering.

Chaturāji (चेतुरजी) (*f*) Very fortunate who obtains four thrones.

Chaturandrishta (चतुरनहष्टा) (*m*) The four jawed form (Lord Narasimha) (V)

Chaturbhuja (चतुर्भुजा) (*m*) The four armed Lord Vishnu. (V)

Chaturbhujeti (चतुर्भुजेती) (*m*) Four armed. The four arms represent the four castes (Brahmin, Kshatriya, Vaishya and Shudra) symoblically indicating his divinity. (G)

Chaturashtrah (चतुराष्ट) (*m*) The embodiment of all Vedic knowledge. (V)

Chaturvyuha (चतुरव्यूह) (*m*) The four arrays of life (creation, sustenance, destructioln and survival (V)

Chaudamani (चौदमणि) (*m*) The best or most excellent. A jewel worn by men and women.

Chekitān (चेकितान) (*m/f*) Intelligent.

Chekritān (चेक्रितान) (*m*) Shiva, name of a king.

Cheshtā (चेष्ट) (*f*) A gesture in a dance or produced by the movements of limbs representing some thought, feeling or intention.

Cheshtita (चेष्टित) (*f*) Gesture, manner of life activity, effort, any mental or phyiscal process.

Chetan (चेतन) (*f*) Life, soul, mind, animate.

Chetanā (चेतना) (*f*) Life, consciousness, awareness.

Chetas (चेतश) (*n*) Splendour, intellilgent thinking soul, heart, mind (from Rig Veda)

Chettri (चेत्तरी) (*m/f*) Attentive, guardian.

Chhathā (छथा) (*f*) Refulgence, splendour, lustre, beauty.

Chhavi (छवी) (*f*) Pretty, features, splendour, beauty, photograph

Chhāyā (छाया) (*f*) Shadow, shade, image, reflection, resemblance. A handmaid of the sun god.

Chidrupa (चिद्रूप) (*m/f*) Knowledge of incarnate.

Chikti (चिक्ती) (*m/f*) Shining.

Chinmaya (चिन्मय) (*m*) Supreme spirit, very intgelligent.

Chinnasamshya (चिन्नसमश्य) (*m*) He who removes all doubts (V)

Chintāmani (चिन्तामणी) (*f*) A fabulous mythological gem supposed to grant all desire. It is said to have belonged to Brahmā, who is himself called by this name. it is also called Divya-ratna.

Chiranjiv (चिरंजीवनी) (*m*) Eternal being. Another name of Vishnu (V)

Chiranjivī (चिरंजीवी) (*a/m*) One blessed with longevity, a benedictory epithet prefixed with the names of youngsters.

Chiranjivinī (चिरंजीवीं) (*m*) Eternal being. As long as Lord Rama's name survives on earth, He (Hanuman) too shall remain alive on earth. (H)

Chitrā (चित्रा) (*f*) Name of fourteenth lunar mansion. Also a corrupted form of the Sanskrit word Chitrak (leopard) Excellent, distinguished.

Chitrabhānu/Chitra-bhānu (चित्रभानू/चित्रा-भानू) (*m/f*) Shining with light.

Chitrabhiny (चित्राभिनय) (*f*) Representation of special objects and ideas through dance, picture etc.

Chitra Jivin (चित्रजीवन) (*m*) Long lived. Gods or deified mortals, who live for long periods.

Chitrag (चित्रग) (*m*) Affection, desire.

Chitrayoti (चित्रोती) (*m*) Shining, glorious, brilliant.

Chitrakala (चित्रकला) (*f*) The art of painting.

Chirtrakatha (चित्रकथा) (*f*) Charming or entertaining story.

Chitrakriti/Chitra-kriti (चित्रकृती/चित्र-कृती) (*f*) Portrait, picture, painted resemblance.

Chitraksha (चित्रक्ष) (*m*) Speckled eye. Name of a king. Also name of a son of Dhrit Rashtra.

Chitra-lekhā (चित्र-लेखा) (*f*) A picture. Name of a nymph who was skilled in painting and in the magic art.

Chitranetra (चित्रनेत्र) (*f*) A distinguished or excellent eyed person.

Chitrangad (चित्रांगद) (*m*) Elder son of king Shantanu and queen Satyavati.

Chitrarath (चित्रार्थ) (*m*) AGandharva chief who gave Arjuna some Gandharva knowledge on warfare and gave him divine horses which never tired.

Chitrarupa (चित्ररूपा) (*m/f*) With variegated form. An attendant of Lord Shiva.

Chitrasen (चित्रसेन) (*m*) A chief of Yakshas. One of the hundred sons of Dhritrashtra. Name of a son of Karna. Name of a Pandava king. Also a name of a Panchala chief.

Chitrashri (चित्रश्री) (*f*) Divine beauty

Chitrashwa (चित्रश्व) Another name of Satyavan, husband of Savitri.

Chitravāhan (चित्रवाहन) (*m*) A king of Manipur. Arjuna married his daughter Chitrangada during his travels. From their marriage a son was born who was known as Babruvahana.

Chitravasu/Chitra-Vasu (चित्रावसु/चित्रा-वसु) (*m/f/n*) Shining stars, rich in brilliant ornaments.

Chitravidya (चित्रविद्या) (*f*) The art of painting.

Chitrin (चित्रिन) (*f*) A woman endowed with various talents.

Chitrini (चित्रिनी) (*f*) Art lady (the lady who has good education, beautiful figure and well versed in various arts)

Chitriyā (चित्रीय) (*f*) Brilliant, to cause surprise.

Chitrokti (चित्रात्त) (*f*) A marvellous or heavenly voice.

Chitti (चिट्टी) (*f*) Wisdom, thinking, thought, a wise person (from Rig Veda)

Choksha (चोक्ष) (*m/f*) A pure and clean person, agreeable, pleasant.

Churā-mani (चूरा-माणी) (*m*) A jewel worn on the top of the head, best excellent.

Chushini (चूशिनी) (*f*) Brilliant. Name of a female attendant of Durga.

Chyavana (च्यवन) (*m*) A sage, son of the Rishi Bhrigu, and author of some hymns.

D (द, दा)

Dadhasyu (दधस्यू) (*m*) Son of sge Agastya and Lopamudra. He was a great scholar and a poet.

Dadhich/Dadhynch (दधीच/दध्यच) (*m*) A Vedic Rishi, son of Atharvan, whose name frequently occurs in Vedas.

Daiksh (दैक्ष) (*m/f*) Relating to initiation or inauguration.

Divya (दिव्या) (*m*) Divine—in a special sense. The art or knowledge of divination or portents.

Daivaita (दैवैत) (*m*) Relating to God's

Daksha (दक्ष) (*m*) Able, competent, intelligent. This name generally carries with it the idea of creative power. Daksha is the son of Brahma.

Daksha (दक्षा) (*m*) The expert or efficient in every art (V)

Dakshajā (दक्षजा) (*f*) Born of Daksha. Epithet of Parvati (wife of Shiva).

Dakshakālikā (दक्षकालिका) (*f*) A form of Durga. See Durga.

Dakshakanya (दक्षकन्या) (*f*) Intelligent girl. Another name of Durga.

Dakshayanin (दक्षायनिन) (*m/f/n*) Wearing golden ornaments. Brahman student.

Dakshapati (दक्षपति) (*m*) Lord of the faculties.

Dakshatā (दक्षता) (*f*) A name of Aditi (Infinity, the boundless heaven as compared with the finite earth) as daughter of Daksha.

Dakshāyani (दक्षयानि) (*f*) Any one of the twenty-seven lunar mansions. Name of Aditi, mother of gods, Pārvati.

Dakshesh (दक्षेश) (*m*) Lord of Daksha. another name of Lord Shiva.

Dākshi (दक्षी) (*m*) A son of daksha.

Dakshinā (दक्षिणा) (*f*) A daughter of Ruchi and Akuti (a daughter of Manu and Satarupā, whom he gave to the patriarch Ruchi).

Dakshinah (दक्षिणा) (*m*) The destroyer (V.)

Dakshya (दक्षया) (*n*) Skilful, clever, fitness, capable.

Dalip (दलीप) See Dilip.

Damah (दमाह) (*m*) Reforming the wicked by adequate punishment (V)

Daman (दमन) (*m/f*) Self-control, overpowering. A sage by whose kindness king Bhim of Bidarbha was able to have a daughter Damayanti and three sons (Dama, Danta and Daman).

Damayanti (दमयन्ती) (*f*) Virtuous and beautiful daughter of king Bhima of Vidarbha who married the famous & righteous king Nala. Also it means subduing and self control. A kind of Jasmine.

Damayit (दमयित) (*m*) The Ruler like Yama to keep vice forces in control (V)

Dambhodabhav (दमभोदभव) (*m*) A mighty and powerful king who took the advice of Nara Rishi and became righteous and respectful towards others and ruled benevolently over his subjects.

Dambholi (दमभोली) (*m*) Indra's thunderbolt.

Dāminī (दामीनि) (*f*) Lightning.

Damodara (दामोद्रा) (*m*) A name given to Krishna because his foster mother tried to tie him up with a rope round his belly.

Dampati Hasta (दम्पति हस्त) (*f*) In dance - gesture indicatimg a couple standing and taking hands of each other. Dhampati means couple.

Dandah (दन्दः) (*m*) The staff for punishment of the wicked. (V)

Dandak (दण्ड) (*n*) The aranya (forest), lying between the Godavari and Narmada. This forest is the scene of many of Rama and Sita's adventures.

Dant (दंत) (*m*) Brother of Damyanti (wife of Nala).

Danta/Dantaya (दंत/दंतया) (*m*) Unpereturebed Calm. Another name of Lord Ram and Lord Hanuman. (R&H)

Danvendra (दनवेन्द्र) (*m*) Granter of boons (K)

Darpadah (दर्पदा) (*m*) Bestower of the glory (V)

Darpaha (दर्पाह) (*m*) Browbeater of the arrogant (V)

Darpana (दर्पण) (*f*) Causing vanity. Hand-mirror held in one of the hands of feminine deities.

Darsha (दर्श) (*m*) A son of Brahma and Mantrasarira. Also a name of a son of Krishna and Kālindi.

Darshaka (दर्शक) (*m/f/n*) Seeing, looking, showing, examining, a skilful man.

Darshamya (दर्शम्य) (*m/f/n*) Visible, good looking, beautiful

Darshan (दर्शन) (*m*) Sight, view, appearance, demonstration, becoming visible.

Darshanā (दर्शना) (*f*) To show, to display, to exhibit.

Darshanika (दर्शानिक) (*m/f*) Connected with Darshana, the six school of Hindu philosophy.

Darshaniya (दर्शनीय) (*m/f/n*) Visible, good looking, beautiful.

Darshita (दर्शिता) (*m/f/n*) Shown, displayed, explained.

Daruka (दरूक) (*m*) A wise, devoted and skilful charioteer of Lord Krishna.

Darunah (दरूनाः) (*m*) Terrible (for those treading un-righteous path) (V)

Dasanu (दशानू) (*m*) Name of a Semi-divine being

Dasbal (दसबल) (*m*) Possessing ten powers. Very strong.

Dashajyoti (दशज्योति) (*f*) Whose glory spread in ten directions. Ten flames.

Dasharha (दशरहा) (*m*) Appearing in the Dasharha family (V)

Dashrāj (दशराज) (*m*) Leader of a fishing community along Yamuna. Father of Satyavati wife of king Shantanu.

Dasmālā (दशमाला) (*f*) Having ten garlands

Dāspati (दशपती) (*m*) Lord of oblations. Lord of devotees.

Dasrath (दशरथ) A prince of the solar race—son of Aja, a descendant of Ikshwaku, and king of Ayodhyā. Father of Rām.

Dasrathi (दशरथी) (*m*) A descendant of Dasrath (i.e. Ram, Lakshman, Bharat, Shatrughan.)

Dastra (दशत्र) One of the twin gods Ashwanikumaras—the other being Nasatya.

Dāsu (दासु) (*m/f*) Worshipping.

Dasvas (दशवश) (*n*) Honouring or serving the gods, gracious, giving, granting.

Dātri (दात्ररी) (*m*) Giver, liberality.

Dātritā (दात्रित) (*f*) Same as Dātri.

Dattātreya (दत्तात्रेय) (*m*) Given by Atri. Another name of trinity (Brahma, Vishnu and Shiva)

Daulmi (दौलमी) (*m*) Name of Lord Indra.

Dausyant (दूशन्त) See Dushmanta, Dushyanta.

Dayā (दया) (*f*) Pity, mercy, compassion, sympathy.

Dayākar (दयाकर) (*m/f/n*) Showing pity, merciful. Remover of obstacles, worries and troubles (S)

Dayānidhi (दयानिधि) (*m*) Treasure of mercy, very compassionate person. Also the name of Lord Krishna. (K)

Dayāsāgar (दयासागर) (*m*) Ocean of compassion.

Dayāshankar (दयाशंकर) (*m*) Compassion from Lord Shiva.

Dayāsār (दयासार) (*m*) Essence of kindness. (R)

Dayāshil (दयाशील) (*m/f/n*) Compassionate person, treasure of mercy.

Dayāvati (दयावती) (*f*) Full of compassion.

Dayāvir (दयावीर) (*m*) Champion of compassion

Desh (देश) (*m*) Point, region, place, portion.

Dehadipā (देहदीपा) (*f*) Eye - the lamp in the body.

Deshadevatā (देशदेवता) (*m*) Tutelary deity of the region.

Deshkāri (देशकारी) (*f*) In music a name of a Rāgini

Deshmālā (देशमाला) (*m*) Garland of a place, or region.

Deshna (देशना) (*n*) Giving, a gift (from Rig Veda)

Deshnu (देशनू) (*m/f*) Giving, liberal.

Deshpāli (देशपाली) (*f*) In music a name of a rāgini (musical mode).

Deshrāj (देशराज) (*m*) King, ruler of a country.

Dev (देव) (*m*) A god, divine, a deity, a king.

Devabal (देवबल) (*m*) Having God's strength.

Devabhakti/Deva Bhakti (देवभक्ति) (*f*) Service of the Gods.

Devabhiti/Deva Bhiti (देवभीति/देव भीति) (*f*) Fear of the Gods.

Devabhridaguru (देवभ्रादगुरू) (*m*) Guru of the Gods who takes special care of them. (V)

Devabodhi/Deva Bodhi (देवबोद्धि/देवा-बोद्धि) (*m*) God inspired.

Devadant (देवदंत) (*m*) Name of the conch-shell of Arjuna.

Devadatta (देवदत्त) (*m*) God-given.

Devadev (देवदेव) (*m*) Lord of Lords worshipped in the three worlds (G)

Devadhani/Deva Dhani (देवधनी/देवा-धनी) (*f*) Divine abode. Name of India's city.

Devadvipa/Deva Dipa (देवद्वीप/देवा-दीप) (*n*) Divine lamp, eye.

Devadūta/Deva Dūta (देवदूत/ देव-दूत) (*m*) Divine messenger

Devagana/Deva Gana (देवगन/देव-गन) (*m*) A troop or class of Gods.

Devaganeshvar (देवगनेश्वर) (*m*) Lord of the divine. Another name of Lord Indra.

Devagayāna (देवगायन) (*m*) Celestial singer.

Devagiri (देवगिरी) (*f*) Divine knowledge.

Devagopa (देवगोपा) (*f*) Guardian, divine protectress (from Rig Veda)

Devaguru (देवगुरु) (*m*) Father of perceptor of the Gods.

Devgati (देवगती) (*f*) Fortune, course of destiny.

Devahuti (देवाहूति) (*f*) The wife of Pururavas (in the Vedas, a mythical personage connected with the sun and the dawn, and existing in the middle region of the universe).

Devaja (देवजा) (*n*) God-born (R.V.)

Devajanta (देवजनता) (*m/f*) God loved.

Devak (देवक) (*m*) Father of Devaki and maternal grandfather of Krishna.

Devakalpa (देवकल्प) (*m/f/n*) God like (from Mahabharata)

Devakanyā (देंवकन्या) (*f*) Celestial maiden.

Devakī (देवकी) (*f*) wife of Vasudev, mother of Krishna and cousin of Kans (king of Mathura) She is sometimes called and incarnation of Aditi (boundless heaven).

Devakiya (देवकी) (*f*) Divine.

Devakirtti (देवकीर्ति) (*f*) The first part is Deva (god) and the second part is Kirtti (fame). The whole expression means—having fame like that of the gods.

Devala (देवल) (*m*) A Vedic Rishi, to whom some hymns are attributed.

Devālā (देवला) (*f*) Music, personified as female

Devalatā (देवलता) (*n*) Divine creeper.

Devalaya (देवालय) (*m*) Heaven.

Devaloka (देवलोक) (*m*) Sphere of God's. Heaven, paradise.

Deva Madhu (देव मधु) (*n*) Divine honey.

Deva Mālā (देव माला) See Devmala

Devamani (देवमणी) (*m*) Divine amulet. jewel of Gods.

Devamitra (देवमित्र) (*n*) Having Gods' as friends.

Devamurti (देवमूर्ति) (*n*) Image of God.

Devan (देवन) (*m*) The younger brother.

Devānand (देवानन्द) (*m*) Delight of gods.

Devanāth/Deva Nāth (देवनाथ/देव-नाथ) (*m*) Lord of the Gods.

Devanayak (देवनायक) (*m*) Divine scholar.

Devānganā (देवांगना) (*f*) An apsara (the celebrated nymphs of Indir's heaven).

Devapalita/Deva Palita (देवपालिता/देव पालिता) (*n*) God protected.

Devapandit (देवपंडित) (*m*) Divine scholar.

Devāpi (देवापि) (*m*) A friend or favourite of gods.

Devaprabhā (देवप्रभा) (*m/f*) Divine splendour.

Devapratimā/Deva Pratimā (देवप्रतिमा/देव-प्रतिमा) (*f*) Image of a deity, idol.

Devapriya/Deva Priya (देवप्रिया/देव-प्रिया) (*f*) Dear to the Gods.

Devapujjit (देवापुज्जित) (*m*) Worshipped by Gods.

Devapushpa (देवपुष्प) (*n*) Divine flower.

Devarāja (देवराज) (*m*) King of gods. Usually signifies Indra.

Deva Rakshita (देव रक्षित) (*n*) God protected.

Devarat (देवरत) (*m*) Eldest son of sage Vishwamitra.

Devarātri (देवारात्रि) (*f*) A night long festival in honour of a deity.

Devarati/Deva Rati (देवरति/देव-रति) (*f*) Gods' delight.

Devarishi (देवऋषि) (*m*) Divine Rishi (holy man or sage).

Devarupa (देवरूप) (*f*) Divine form.

Devasarman (देवश्रमण) (*m*) The first part of word Deva (god), and the second part Sarman (means—a name ending, added to the name of Brahman as prescribed by the Dharmasastras)

Devashakti/Deva Shakti (देवशक्ति/देव-शक्ति) (*n*) Having divine power.

Devasharma (देवाश्रम) (*m*) Name of a sage and husband of Ruchi.

Deva-Shikhamani (देव-शिखमणि) (*m*) God supreme (K)

Devāt (देवात) (*m/f*) Agreeable to gods.

Devātmā (देवात्मा) (*f*) Mother of gods.

Devatva (देवत्व) (*m*) Divinity.

Devavanda/Deva Vanda (देववंद/देव-वंद) (*n*) Praising the Gods'

Devavata/Deva Vata (देववत/देव-वत) (*n*) Agreeable to the gods'.

Devavāni (देववाणी) (*f*) A daughter of Brihaspati (a deity).

Devavardhan (देववर्धन) (*m*) Supported by gods.

Devavata/Deva Vata (देववत/देव वत) (*n*) Agreeable to the Gods'.

Devavrata (देवव्रत) (*m*) A name of Bhisma who knew the yoga power of Vishnu. A son of Shantanu and Jahnavi (the Ganges). See also Bhishma.

Devaya (देव्या) (*n*) Loving or serving the Gods, pious.

Devayāni (देवयानी) (*f*) A daughter of Jayanti and a grand daughter of Indra. Also daughter of Shukracharya living at the court of Vrishaparva.

Devbhāg (देवभाग) (*m*) Uncle of Lord Krishna and younger borther of Vasudev and Prutha (Kunti).

Devāchāryā (देवाचार्य) (*f*) Devotee of god.

Devchit (देवचित) (*m/f*) The will of the gods.

Devdatta (देवदत्त) (*m/f*) God-given.

Devdeva (देवदेव) (*m*) Lord of the Gods. (S)

Devdhāni (देवदानी) (*f*) Divine abode.

Devdut (देवदूत) (*m*) Divine messenger.

Devdipa (देवदीपा) see Deva Dipa.

Devendra (देवेन्द्र) (*m*) God Indra. See Indra.

Devendrāshika (देवेन्द्राशिखा) (*m*) Prortector of the Gods. Lord Ganesha is the embodiment of peace and tranquility - the giver of peace to all. (G)

Devesh (देवेश) (*m*) Chief of the gods (Brahma, Vishnu, Mahesh or Indra).

Deveshi (देवेशी) (*f*) Chief of goddesses.

Deveshvar (देवेश्वर) (*m*) Lord of gods. (S)

Devguru (देवगुरु) (*m*) The father of preceptor of the gods.

Devhuti (देवहूती) (*f*) Invocation of the gods.

Devi (देवी) (*f*) The goddess or Mahadevi (the great goddess) wife of Shiva, and daughter of Himavat (Himalayan mountain. As the Shakti (female energy of Shiva)) she has two characters, one mild the other fierce. In her mild form she is Uma (light and a type of beauty); Gauri (the yellow or the brilliant); Parvati (the mountaineer) and Himavati from her parentage; Jagat-Mātā (mother of the world) and Bhavāni. In her terrible form she is Durga (the inaccessible); Kali and Shyama (black); Chandi and Chandika (the fierce); and Bhairvi (the terrible). The Chandi Mahatmya, which celebrated the victories of this goddess over the Asuras speaks of her under the following names:- 1. Durga (when she received messengers of the Asuras); 2. Das-bhuja when she destroyed part of their army; 3. Sinha-Vahini (riding on a lion when she fought Asura chief Rakta-vija; 4.Mahisha Mardini (destroyer of Asura Mahisha); 5. Jagad-dhatri (foster of the world); 6. Kali the black—she killed Rakta Vija); 7. Mukta-Kesi (with dishevelled hair who defeated Asuras again); 8. Tārā (star); 9. Chhinna-mastaka (the headless form in which she killed Nisumbha; 10. Jagad-gauri (World's fair one—as lauded by gods for her triumphs). The other names which obtains from her husband are: Bhagvati, Ishani, Ishwari, Kaushiki and Kirati etc.

Devibhāshā (देवीभाषा) (*f*) Language of Goddess

Devidās (देवीदास) (*m*) Devotee of Devi.

Devikā (देवीका) (*m/f*) Derived from god. Wife of Yudhishthira and mother of Yaudheya.

Devila (देविला) (*n*) Righteous, virtuous, divine. Appertaining to a deity.

Devirūp (देवीरूप) (*f*) Figure, from, beauty of Goddes.

Devjāmi (देवजामी) (*f*) Sister of the gods.

Devjot (देवजोत्) (*m/f*) God-sped, inspired by god.

Devkinandan (देवकीनन्दन) (*m*) Son of Devaki (Lord Krishna) (V)

Devlatā (देवलता) (*f*) Divine creeper.

Devmālā (देवमाला) (*f*) Divine garland.

Devnāth (देवनाथ) (*m*) Lord of the gods.

Dev-pālita (देव-प लेता) (*m*) God-protected.

Devrāt (देवरत्त) (*m*) God-given.

Devrishi (देवऋषि) (*m*) A Rishi (sage) as Nārad Rishi.

Devrupa (देवरूप) (*f*) Divine form.

Dev-samitā (देव-समिता) (*f*) Having a divine smile.

Devshakti (देवशक्ति) (*m*) Divine strength.

Devshri (देवश्री) (*m/f*) Worshipping, approaching the gods.

Dev-vrata (देव-व्रत) (*m*) Any religious observation or vow. Name of Bhishma.

Dhairya (धैर्य) (*f*) Self control, or a state of mind free from inconsistency and boastfulness. One of the natural graces of women.

Dhām (धाम) (*m*) The final refuge of all (V)

Dhananjaya (धनांजय) (*m*) Winner of wealth (V)

Dhanashri (धनश्री) (*f*) Goddess of wealth.

Dhanyamālā (धन्यमाला) (*f*) Garland of wealth, virtuous, meritorious.

Dhanetri (धनेत्री) (*m*) Prince, king, bringer of wealth.

Dhananjay (धनंजय) (*m*) Another name of Arjuna—meaning that he conquered large territories and brought back great wealth.

Dhanesha (धनेषा) (*f*) Longing after, desire for riches.

Dhaneshvar (धनेषवर) (*m*) Treasure Lord. Lord of all riches. (V)

Dhanika (धनिका) (*m/f/n*) Wealthy, opulent, virtuous or excellent women.

Dhanjit (धनजीत) (*m/f*) Victorious, wealth-acquiring.

Dhanshri (धनश्री) (*f*) In music it is a name of a Rag, See Ragini.

Dhanurdharah (धर्नुधर) (*m*) The bow weilde (Lord Ram). (V)

Dhanurvedah (धर्नुवेदा) (*m*) An expert in archery. (V)

Dhantripti (धनत्रिप्ति) (*f*) Sufficiency of money.

Dhanuketaki (धनुकेतकी) (*f*) King of flower.

Dhanushaksha (धनुशक्ष) (*m*) A very wise and famous sage.

Dhanvat (धनवत) (*m/f/n*) Wealthy, rich, rich man.

Dhanvi (धनवी) (*m*) Wielder of the bow Shranga. (V)

Dhanvine (धनवीन) (*m*) Of the solar race. Another name of Lord Rama. (R)

Dhanya (धन्या) (*m/f/n*) Auspicious, fortunate, bringing or bestowing wealth. Also the name of goddess Lakshmi who is most benevolent and compassionate. (V&L)

Dhanyamālā (धन्यमाला) (*f*) Garland of wealth, virtuous, meritorious.

Dhārā (धारा) (*f*) Steam or current of water, margin , a sharp edge especially of a sword or knife.

Dharādhar (धराधर) (*m*) The support of the earth. (V)

Dharamadhyaksha (धर्माध्यक्ष) (*m*) The head of the Dharma (righteousness) (V)

Dharam (धर्म) (*m*) Custom, piety, duty, justice, merit, character, religion.

Dharmah (धर्मा) (*m*) The Dharma or the conduct of living. (V)

Dharmakrita (धर्मकृता) (*m*) Showing by action how to uphold the righteousness.

Dharmaviduttam/ Dharma Viduttam (धर्मविदुत्तम) (*m*) He who knows the

Dharma best. (V)

Dharmayup (धर्मयुप) (*m*) The pillar of Dharma. (V)

Dharmgup (धर्मगुप) (*m*) The protector of Dharma. (V)

Dharmi (धर्मी) (*m*) The base of all Dharmic tenets. (V)

Dharamadhar (धर्माधार) (*m*) Supporter of law or religion.

Dharna (धरना) (*m/f*) Holding, bearing, keeping in memory.

Dharnidhar (धर्नीधार) (*m*) Suypporter of the earth. (V)

Dhārmik (धार्मिक) (*m*) One who favours charity (G)

Dhārmnilaya/Dharm-nilaya (धर्मनिलय) (*f*) Establisher of eternal law - goddess Lakshhmi (L)

Dharampāl (धर्मपाल) (*m*) The guardian of law or religion.

Dharamrāj (धर्मराज) (*m*) Law king. Also a name of Yudhishthira.

Dharamsil (धर्मशील) (*m/f*) Just, pious.

Dharamvir (धर्मवीर) (*m*) Sentiment of righteous heroism.

Dharanendra (धर्नेन्द्र) (*m*) The god Indra who supports.

Dharani (धर्नी) (*f*) The earth. The wife of Parasu-rāma. She is a personification of earth and regarded as an incarnation of Lakshmi.

Dharendra (धरनेन्द्र) (*m*) King of earth.

Dharmgup (धर्मगुप) (*m*) The creator of the best deeds and their effect (V)

Dharmishth (धर्मिष्ठ) Extremely devout, religious virtuous.

Dharmsvāmi (धर्मस्वामी) (*m*) Lord of duty.

Dhāta (धाता) (*f*) Sustainer of the world. An epithet of Durga. See also Devi.

Dhātri (धात्री) (*f*) Maker, creator. A deity operating in the production of life and the preservation of health. Promotes generation and presides over domestic life.

Dhaturuttamah (धातूरुत्तमा) (*m*) The creator of the best deeds and their effect (V)

Dhaumya (धौम्य) (*m*) The younger brother of Devala and family priest of the Pandavas. Author of a work on law.

Dhaval (धवल) (*a*) White, pure.

Dhavani (धवनी) (*f*) Earth as the wife of Dhruva and the mother of celestials.

Dhira (धीर) (*m/f*) Steady, constant, firm, brave, courageous calm.

Dhiraj (धीरज) (*m*) Patience, eloquent.

Dhirayā (धीरया) (*m*) Valiant. Lord Hanuman is known for His valour, intel ligence and determination and devotion to Lord Ram. Another name of Hanuman. (H)

Dhiroshani (धीरोशनी) (*m*) Brave and fiery. One of the Vishva Devas.

Dhirta (धीरता) (*f*) Courage, firmness, fortitute.

Dhirya (धीर्य) (*m/f/n*) Intelligence, prudence.

Dhishna (धीषन) (*m/f/n*) Intelligent, wise. Any Guru or spiritual preceptor.

Dhishnaya (धीश्नया) (*m/f/n*) Mindful, attentive, benevolent, liberal.

Dhita (धीत) (*m/f*) Satisfied, pleased.

Dhrishaj (धृषज) (*m/f*) Hero, bold, courageous.

Dhrishat (धृषट) (*m/f*) Same as Dhrishaj.

Dhrishni (धृश्नि) (*m/f*) Ray of light.

Dhrishtā (धृष्टा) (*m/f*) Bold, courageous, independent.

Dhrishtadyumna (धृष्टद्युमन) (*m*) Brother of Draupadi, and commander-in-chief of the Pandava armies. He was born as a fully armed adult warrior out of fire during a Yajna performed by Upayaja sage to please king Draupad. He and his sister Draupadi, also born out of the same fire, were considered to be the children of king Drupada.

Dhrishtaketu (धृष्टकेतू) (*m*) King of Chedi and son of Shishupal who was killed by Lord Krishna. In the Mahabharata war he was appointed as one of the seven commanders of the Pandava army.

Dhrishu (धृशु) (*m/f*) Clever, courageous.

Dhrita (धृता) (*m/f/n*) Supported, possessed, used, practised.

Dhritaka (धृतका) (*m*) Name of Budh, saint or patriarch.

Dhritashi (धृतषी) (*m*) Resolute with soft kindness to his votaries. (V)

Dhritātma (धृत्तम) (*m*) Beyond the cycle of life and death, the one who creates himself at will. (V)

Dhritavarama (धृतवरण) (*m*) Dhrit means borne, maintained, solemnly. Varma means having armour. A name of youngest son of Trigarta king Susharma.

Dhriti (धृती) (*f*) Supporting, command, content, firmness, to find pleasure.

Dhritvan (धृतवन) (*m/f*) Resolute, steadfast, the sky, then sea. (V)

Dhruti (ध्रुती) (*f*) Valiant. Most powerful goddess Durga destroyer of evil-saves Her devotees from evil and egoism. (D)

Dhruv (ध्रूव) (*m/f*) Firm, permanent, the polar star a celebrated boy devotee.

Dhruvaka (ध्रूवक) (*m*) The unchangeable longitude of fixed stars.

Dhruvdevi (ध्रूवदेवी) (*f*) Name of a princess. See also Dhruv and Devi.

Dhruvi (ध्रूवी) (*f*) Firmly fixed, firm like a mountain. (from Rig Veda) See also Dhruva.

Dhukkā (धूक्का) (*f*) A kind of flute in music.

Dhumatsena (धूमतसोना) (*m*) He was a king of Shalva and father of righteous Satyavan.

Dhumavati (धूमवती) (*f*) Name of a place of pilgrimage.

Dhupaka (धूपक) (*m/f*) Prefumer, prepare of incense.

Dhupaya (धूपय) (*f*) Perfume, to speak or to shine, to fumigate.

Dhupita (धूपिता) (*f*) Made fragrant or fumigated with incense.

Dhuriya/Dhurya (धूरीया/धूरय) (*m/f/n*) Eminently fit for important duties. Minister charge d'affaires. Leader, chief.

Dhurnika (धूर्निका) (*f*) Attendant of Devayani daughter of Shukracharya who was a wise Guru at the court of king Vrishaparva. The root word Dhur means at the head or chief.

Dhyāndhara (ध्याँधार) (*m*) Object of meditation. All human beings concentrate and meditate upon Lord Shiva. (S)

Dhira (धीर) (*m/f*) Steady, constant, firm, brave, courageous calm.

Dhiraya (धीर्य) (*m*) Valiant. Lord Hanuman is known for His valour, intelligence and determination and devotion to Lord Ram. Another name of Hanuman (H)

Dhiroshnin (धीरोशनीन) (*m*) Brave and fiery. One of the Vishva Devas.

Dhirta (धीरता) (*f*) Courage, firmness, fortitute.

Dhirya (धीर्य) (*m/f/n*) Intelligence, prudence.

Dhishna (धीशन) (*m/f/n*) Intelligent, wise. Any Guru or spiritual preceptor.

Dhishnaya (धिषनय) (*m/f/n*) Mindful, attentive, benevolent, liberal.

Dhita (धीत) (*m/f*) Satisfied, pleased.

Dhrishat (धृष्ट) (*m/f/n*) Bold, courageous, confident

Dhrita (धरीता) (*m/f/n*) Supported, possessed, used, practised.

Dhritaka (धृतका) (*m*) Name of Budh, saint or patriarch.

Dhritashi (धृतशी) (*m*) Resolute with soft kindness to his votaries (V)

Dhritātma (धृतात्मा) (*m*) Beyond the cycle of life and dedath, the one who creates himself at will (V)

Dhriti (धृरती) (*f*) Supporting, command, content, firmness, to find pleasure.

Dhritvan (धृतवन) (*m/f*) Resolute, steadfast, the sky, then sea (V)

Dhruti (ध्रूती) (*f*) Valiant. Most powerful goddess Durga destroyer of evil - saves Her devotees from evil and egoism. (D)

Dhruvaka (ध्रूवका) (*m*) The unchangeable longitude of fixed stars.

Dhruvdevi (ध्रूवदेवी) (*f*) Name of a princess. See also Dhruv and Devi

Dhruvi (ध्रूवी) (*f*) Firmly fixed, firm like a mountain. (from Rig Veda) See also Dhruva.

Dhukkā (धुक्का) (*f*) A kind of flute in music.

Dhumarvarna (धूमरवर्ण) (*m*) Smoke coloured body (G)

Dhumavati (धूमवती) (*f*) Name of a place of pilgrimage.

Dhupaka (धुपका) (*m/f*) Prefumer. prepare of incense.

Dhupaya (धुपय) (*f*) Perfume. to speak or to shine, to fumigate.

Dhupitā (धुपिता) (*f*) Made fragrant or fumigated with incense.

Dhuriyā/Dhuryā (धुरीया/धुरया) (*m/f/n*) Eminently fit for important duties. Minister charge d'affaires. Leader, chief.

Dhyutidhar (ध्युतीधर) (*m*) Having brilliance. The radiance of Lord Shiva, shines with a brilliance of billion sun, radiating rays of power and love upon everything. (S)

Didhiti (दीधीती) (*f*) Brightness, splendour, light, a ray, majestic power.

Didivi (दीदीवी) (*m*) The sky.

Digambara (दिगम्बर) A title of Shiva. Clothed with space. A naked mendicant.

Diganta (दिगंत) (*m*) End of the horizon, remote distance.

Dig-vijat (दिग-विजत) (*m*) A portion of Mahabharata describing the victorious of Pandu's

Dikkāl (दीक्काल) (*f*) Time and space

Dik-kanyā (दिक-कन्या) (*f*) A quarter of the sky deified as a young virgin. Dik Kanya is also known as Dikkanta and Dikkamini.

Dikpati (दिकपती) (*m*) A region or guardian of the sky.

Dikshā (दीक्षा) (*f*) Religious observation. Name of wife of Soma.

Dikshāpati (दीक्षापती) (*m*) Lord of Dikshā

Dikshita (दीक्षित) (*m/f*) Consecrated, initiated into. Instruct, performed

Dilip (दिलीप) (*m*) King of Hastinapur, an ancestor of Ram.

Dimbeshvari (दिम्बेश्वरी) (*f*) Goddess of creation (D)

Dinādi (दिनादी) (*m*) Dawn, day-break.

Dinakar (दिनकर) (*m/f*) The sun, making day or light.

Dinabandhave (दिनबन्धव) (*m*) Prortector of the downtrodden. Another name of Lord Hanuman. (H)

Dinabandhu (दीनाबन्धु) (*m*) Friend of the poor, supreme spirit.

Dinamani (दीनामनी) (*m*) Jewel of the day. Day jewel.

Dinanāth (दीनानाथ) (*n*) The sun, day-lord.

Dinaprabhā (दीनप्रभा) (*f*) Sunshine. day's splendour.

Dinbandhu (दीनबन्धु) (*m*) The sun, day-friend.

Dinansh (दिनेंश) (*n*) Day portion, day time.

Dinesh (दिनेश) (*m*) Son of the Sun, the planet Saturn.

Dinjyoti (दिनज्योति) (*n*) Daylight, sunshine.

Dinkartāri (दिनकरतारी) (*m*) The sun, day-maker.

Dinmani (दिनमनी) (*n*) Day jewel.

Dinmukha (दिनमुख) (*n*) Day face, day break.

Dinnis (दिनिस) (*n/f*) Day and night

Dinprāni (दीनप्राणी) (*m*) The sun, day-leader.

Dinrāj (दिनराज) (*m*) The sun day-king.

Dīp (दीप) (*m*) Light, lamp, shining, illustrious.

Dipā (दीपा) (*f*) Personification of the lamp or the goddes of light.

Dipada (दिपदा) (*n*) One who gives light.

Dipak (दीपक) (*m*) A lamp. Illumination.

Dipakarni (दीपकरणी) (*m*) With good ears, one who digest what one hears.

Dipākshi (दीपाक्षी) (*f*) With bright, shining eyes.

Dipalakshmi (दीपलक्ष्मी) (*f*) A lamp consisting of a tray for one wick, carried in the hands by Lakshmi (Goddess of wealth).

Dipāli/Dipāvali (दीपाली/दीपावली) (*f*) A row of lights, illumination.

Dipamudra/Dip Mudra (दीपमुद्रा) (*f*) Gesture of a lamp in a dance. One fore-finger is joined to another and the little finger is also joined to another. Two middle and ringfingers are raised touching their respective backs. This makes this gesture.

Dipamālā (दीपमाला) (*f*) A row of lights.

Dīpan (दीपन) (*m/f*) Kindling, illuminating, stimulating.

Dīpaniya (दीपनिया) (*m/f*) Kindled, lighted.

Dipānjali (दीपांजली) (*f*) Lamp for praying (held in hand and waved around the idol at the time of worship)

Dipāvali (दीपावली) (*f*) A row of lights.

Dīpdān (दीपदान) (*m/f*) Giving light.

Dīpdhārini (दीपधारिणी) (*f*) A female carrier of light.

Dipikā (दीपिका) (*f*) Light.

Dipit/Dipitā (दीपित/दीपिता) (*m/f*) Illuminated, manifested, enlightened.

Dīpmālika (दीपमालिका) (*f*) Feast of lights.

Dīp-pujā (दीप-पूजा) (*f*) Worship of lights.

Diprāj (दीपराज) (*m/f*) Flaming, shining, radiant.

Dīpta (दीप्त) (*m/f*) Shining, bright, brilliant, splendid.

Diptayi (दीपतयी) (*f*) Flame-like. Shine like thousand suns-goddess Lakshmi (L)

Dipti (दीप्ति) (*f*) Brightness. light, splendour, beauty

Diptimān'(दीप्तिमान) (*m*) Bright, shining, a seer of the 8th Manvantra.

Diptimurti (दीप्तिमूर्ति) (*m*) Having radiant image (V)

Dipyā (दीप्या) (*m/f*) To be illuminated or inflamed.

Dirghā (दीर्घा) (*m*) Lofty, long, beautiful. another name of Lord Shiva (S)

Dirghanetrā (दीर्घनेत्रा) (*f*) Beautiful woman with long eyes.

Dishā (दिशा) (*f*) Direction, region.

Dishāh (दिशाह) (*m*) Like the Vedas showing the right directions (V)

Dishāpāl (दिशापाल) (*m*) Guardian of direction, a part of the sky.

Ditsā (दित्शा) (*f*) Desire or intention of giving, wishing or willing to give.

Dishtā (दिश्ता) (*m/f*) Shown, pointed, assigned, directed.

Diti (दिती) (*f*) Boundless. A goddess or personification in the Vedas who is associated with Aditi, and seems to be intended as an antithesis or as a complement to her.

Dityā (दित्या) (*f*) Answer of prayers. Another name of goddess Lakshmi (L)

Diva/Divoja (दिव/दिवोज) (*m/f*) Born or descended from heaven.

Divāka (दिवाक) (*m*) Son of Bhanu and father of Sahadeva. Leader of an army.

Divākar (दिवाकर) (*m*) The sun, the sun flower.

Divāmani (दिवामणि) (*n*) Day jewel. The Sun.

Divas (दिवस) (*m*) Heavenly.

Divaskriya (दिवसक्रिया) (*f*) Religious performances of the day.

Divasprik (दिवसप्रीक) (*m*) Spreading upto heaven (V)

Divasu (दिवासु) (*m/f*) Beautiful by day.

Divi (दिवी) (*m*) The blue sky.

Divigat (दिवीगत) (*m/f*) God, being in heaven.

Divij (दिविज) (*m*) A god.

Divijā (दिविजा) (*m/f/n*) Sky-born, heavenly.

Divisha (दिवीश) (*m*) Heaven. Godly.

Divishti (दिविष्टि) (*f*) Heavenly, devotion, worship

Divit (दिवित) (*m/f*) Heavenly, going to the sky.

Divo-dāsa (दिवो-दास) A pious liberal king mentioned in the Rig Veda.

Divyā (दिव्या) (*m*) A superhuman being, divine, wonderful, the sky.

Divyābhārati (दिव्याभारती) (*f*) Divine, wonderful mother India, speech.

Divyā-Kumāri (दिव्या-कुमारी) Celestial maiden.

Divyāmanush (दिव्यामानुष) (*m*) A man from heaven, semi-god.

Divyām-bardharā (दिव्यां-बरधरा) (*f*) Beautifully robe-goddess Durga (D)

Divyadevi (दिव्यादेवी) (*f*) Devine goddess.

Divyajyoti (दिव्याज्योति) (*f*) Divine light.

Divyākriti (दिव्याकृति) (*f*) Divine form, most beautiful.

Divyā-nārī (दिव्या-नारी) (*f*) A female from heaven.

Divyānshu (दिव्यांशु) (*m*) The sun.

Divyaprabhāv (दिव्यप्रभाव) (*f*) Divine form, most beautiful.

Divyāprabhāv (दिव्यप्रभाव) (*m*) With divine power

Divyaratna (दिव्यरत्न) (*m*) Divine jewel.

Divyasarit (दिव्यसरित) (*f*) The Ganges.

Divyendu (दिव्येन्दु) (*f*) Moon light.

Draupad (द्रुपद) (*m*) King of Panchal and son of Parishata. Father of Draupadi, Dhristadyumna and Shikhandin. His father king Parishat and Drona or Dronacharya's father Bharadwaj were good friends. Both Draupad and Drona received their education from sage Agnivesha.

Draupadī (द्रोपदी) (*f*) Patronymic daughter of Draupad. Name of the common wife of five Pandu-princes in the epic Mahābharata. She is regarded as the spiritual daughter of Indrani.

Dravinahpradah (द्रविनप्रदा) (*m*) Bestower of riches to His devotees who want them (V)

Dridah (द्रिदाह) (*m*) Determined. (V)

Dridha (द्रिधा) (*m*) Firm, fixed, steady.

Dridhabhakti (द्रिधाभक्ति) (*m*) Firm in devotion.

Driptah (द्रिप्तह) (*m*) Immersed in the eternal bliss. (V)

Drisha (द्रिश) (*m*) Look, apearance.

Drishadwati (द्रिशदवती) (*f*) A common female queen. The wife of king divo-das. A name of a river.

Drishalu (द्रिशलू) (*m*) The sun.

Drishān (द्रिषान) (*m*) Spiritual teacher.

Drishāntā (द्रिशाँत) (*f*) Form of speech and thought (From Nyaya philosophy)

Drishati/Drishti (दृष्टि) (*f*) Look, appearance, seeing, viewing, beholding, wisdom, intelligence.

Drishi (द्रिशी) (*f*) Power of seeing (From Vedanta)

Drishikā (द्रिशिका) (*m/f*) Splendid, conspicious.

Drishtā (दृष्टा) (*m/f*) Seen, looked at, perceived, learnt,understood, acknowl-edged.

Drishyā (दृश्या) (*m/f*) Visible, conspicuous.

Dronā/Dronā Āchārya (द्रोण/द्रोणा अचार्य) (*m*) A bucket, A Brahman so named from his having been generated by his father, Bhardwāj, in a bucket. He got married to Kripu, half sister of Bhishma, and by her was father of Aswatthaman. He was teacher of the military art, both to the Kaurvas and Pandavas.

Drupad (द्रुपद) See Draupad

Dughdin (दुग्धीन) (*m/f*) Milky.

Duh-sālā (दु-शाला) (*f*) The only daughter of Dhrita-rashtra and wife of Jayadratha.

Duhitri (दुहित्री) (*f*) A daughter

Dushwapnanashan (दुशव्पंनेशन) (*m*) The destroyer of the nightmares. (V)

Dundu (दुंदु) (*m*) Flute player, a musician. Another name of Vasudeva.

Duradharsha (दुर्दषा) (*m*) Unassailable. (V)

Durariha (दुररीह) (*m*) Slayer of the demons who tread the unrighteous path. (V)

Duratikrama (दुर्तीक्रम) (*m*) He whose order is inviolable. (V)

Duravas (दुर्वास) (*m*) Difficult to hold (in one's heart). (V)

Durdhārā (दुरधारा) (*m*) In accessible (V)

Durgā (दुर्गा) (*f*) The spouse of Shiva, symbolising primeaval energy. See also Devi.

Durgāh (दुर्गा) (*m*) In accessible (V)

Durgama (दुर्गम) (*m*) In accessible (V)

Durgāvallabha (दुर्गावल्लभ) (*m*) Beloved of Durga

Durgi (दुर्गी) (*f*) Name of a deity. See Durga.

Durjaya (दुर्जय) (*m*) Difficult to subdue and conquer. (V&S)

Durjā (दुर्जा) (*m*) The invincible. (G)

Durjaniya (दुर्जनीय) (*m*) Difficult to be known. Eminent universal form of eternal bliss Lord Shiva. (S)

Durlabha (दुर्लभ) (*m*) Rare to perceive. (V)

Durmarshan (दुर्मरशन) (*m*) Whose dazzling radiance is unbearable (V)

Dur-vāsā (दूरवासा) (*m*) Ill clothed. A sage, the son of Atri and Anasuya. He blessed Kunti, so that she became a mother by the Sun.

Dushkritah (दुष्कृत:) (*m*) He who destroys the sin of sinner (V)

Dushmanta/Dushyanta (दुष्मंत/दुष्यंत) (*m*) A valiant king of the lunar race. He was the husband of Sakuntalā by whom he had a son Bharat. The loves of Dushyant and Shakuntala, her separation from him. and her restoration throught the discovery of his token ring in the belly of a fish form the plot of Kali-dāsa's celebrated play Shakuntalā.

Dvaimatur (द्वैमतुर) (*m*) Son of two mothers. Goddess Parvati created Lord Ganesha from the perspiration that came off her body. She lowered him into the River Ganga and he grew into a large being. Both Parvati and Ganga claimed to be his mother. (G)

Dvārkā (द्वारका) (*m*) Many gated. Name of capital founded by Krishna.

Dvārakānāth (द्वारकानाथ) (*m*) Lord of Dvārakā. (K)

Dvija (द्विज) (*m*) A son of Surasena.

Dwābhā (द्वाभा) (*f*) Twilight.

Dwāpara (द्वापर) The third age of the world, extending to 864,000 years,

Dwārkā (द्वारका) See Dvārā.

Dwipa (द्वीप) (*m*) An insular continent. It stretches out from the mountain Meru as their common centre, like the leaves of a lotus, and are separated from each other by distinct circumambient oceans.

Dyāsu (दयाशु) (*m*) The sky, heaven. In the Vedas, he is a masculine deity, and is Dyaus-pitri (heavenly father), the earth being regardless the mother.

Dyota (दयोत) (*n*) Light, brilliance, sunshine.

Dyotan/Dyotani (दयोतन/दयोतिनी) (*m/f*) Shining, glittering, illuminating, enlightening.

Dyudhuni (दयूधुनी) (*f*) Heavenly river, the Ganges.

Dyukash (दयक्ष) (*m/f*) Heavenly, celestial, light brilliant (from Rig Veda)

Dyumani (दयूमणी) (*m*) Sky jewel, the sun (S)

Dyumat (दयूमत) (*m*) Excellent, brilliant, bright, splendid.

Dyupati (दयूपति) (*m*) Sky Lord, God.

Dyupath (दयूपथ) (*m*) Sky path, upper part of the sky.

Dyutā (दयूता) (*f*) Shining, splendour, ray of light. Name of a Rishi-soem Vedic hymns ascribed to him.

Dyutaru (दयूतरू) (*m*) Tree of heaven.

Dyuti (दयूती) (*f*) Splendour as a goddess.

Dyutidhar (दयूतीधर) (*m*) Dazzling brlliance. (V)

Dyutimati (दयूतीमती) (*m/f*) Of brilliant understanding, clear minded.

Dyutita (दयूतित) (*m/f/n*) Enlightened, illuminated, shininmg.

Dyuvani (दयूवनी) (*f*) Heavenly grove.

E (ए, ऐ)

Edhas (एधस) (*m/f*) Prosperity, happiness.

Edhatu (एधातु) (*m*) Same as Edhas.

Ehad (एहद) (*m*) A pledge, commitment.

Ekadant (एकदन्त) (*m*) An epithet of Ganesh.

Ekadev (एकदेव) (*m*) Supreme being, one god.

Ekah (एकह) (*m*) Unique. (V)

Ekajyoti (एकज्योति) (*m*) The sole light. (S)

Ekākshar (एकाशार) (*m*) S

Ekaling (एकलिंग) (*m*) An epithet of Shiva.

Ekalvya (एकलव्य) (*m*) Son of Hiranyadhanu, king of Nishad. He was a great archer and wanted to be equivalent to Arjun in the art of warfare.

Ekam (एकम) (*m*) Unique, peerless.

Ekanishth (एकनिष्ठ) (*m*) Attached or devoted to a single individual or god.

Ekanishthi (एकनिष्ठी) (*f*) Meaning as Ekanishth.

Ekāntsidhi (एकांतसिद्धि) (*m/f*) Absolute success

Ekapat (एकपत) (*m*) He who measured the world by his one step. (V)

Ekarāj (एकराज) (*m*) One king

Ekardab (एकरदव) (*m*) An Epithet of Ganesh.

Ekāshtakā (एकाष्तका) (*f*) A deity mentioned in the Atharva-veda as having practised austere devotion and being the daughter of Prajapati and mother of Indra.

Ekatā (एकता) (*f*) Oneness, harmony, identity, union.

Ekātmah (एकातमह) (*m*) Unique, without a second. (V)

Ekāvali (एकावली) (*f*) A single string of pearls, beads or flowers.

Ekbāl/Iqbāl (एकबाल/इकबाल) (*m*) Eminence, power, good fortune, acceptance.

Ekarāj (एकराज) (*m*) One king

Ekdant (एकदंत) (*m*) Of a single tusk - Lord Ganesh. A single broken tusk of Lord Ganesh symbolises as beyond the rules of cosmic orderliness, as he is the cosmos itself. The broken tusk represents the shedding of the ego. The single tusk also represents the non-dualistic nature of reality.. (G)

Ekendra (एकीन्द्र) (*m*) One god.

Ekisha (एकिश) (*f*) One goddess.

Ekrishi (एकऋषि) (*m*) The only or chief Rishi (holy man) (from Atharva Veda)

Ekritu (एकऋतु) (*m/f*) The only season, the only time.

Ekshruti (एकश्रुति) (*f*) Only Shruti or Vedic passage.

Emush (एमुष) (*m*) In the Brahmana, a boar which raised up the earth, represented as black and with a hundred arms. This is the boar incarnation of Vishnu.

Eshāniya (एशनिय) (*a*) Coverable, worth desiring for.

Eshnā (एशना) (*f*) Wish, strong desire.

Eshanputra (एशनपुत्र) (*m*) Son of Shiva (G) See also Ishan.

Eshtā (एश्ता) (*m/f/n*) That which is desired or asked for (from Rig Veda).

Eshti (एश्ती) (*f*) Wish, desire. (R.V.)

Etā (एता) (*m/f*) Rushing, variegated colour, shining, brilliant. A kind of deer (from Rig Veda)

Etagav (एतगव) (*m/f*) Shining, brilliant.

Etānt (एताँत) (*m/f*) So great, too much.

Etasa (एतस) (*m/f/n*) That which is desired or asked for (from Rig Veda)

Evavad (एव्वद) (*m*) Honest, a singer (R.V.)

Evyavan (एव्यवन) (*m*) Very fast, granting desire. (V)

Evyamarut (एव्यमरूत) (*m*) A hymn of Rig Veda, a sage (R.V.)

F (फ, फा)

Falgun (फाल्गुन) Another name of Arjuna who was born under the sign of the Falguna constellation of stars.

G (ग, गा)

Gabhastinemi (गभस्तीनेमी) (*m*) Reposed like the sun among the rays. (V)

Gabhirātma (गभीरात्मा) (*m*) He who has depth in his character (V)

Gada (गद) (*m*) A sentence. Name of a son of Vasudev and a younger brother of Lord Krishna. He was greatly respected by Lord Krishna whom he accompanied to Rajasuya and Ashvamedha Yajna performed by Yudhishtra.

Gadādhar (गदाधर) (*m*) Wielder of the mace called Kaumudi (V&G)

Gadāgarja (गदागर्ज) (*m*) Elder to Gada (V)

Gadeli (गदेली) (*m/f*) The palm of the hand.

Gaddi (गद्दी) (*m*) One who seeks knowledge. Name of sage Vishvamitra.

Gaditā (गदिता) (*m/f/n*) Spoken, said, related, named, enumerated (from Mahabharata)

Gagan (गगन) (*m*) Empty, void, heavens, the sky.

Gaganchārin (गगनचारिन) (*m/f/n*) Coming from the sky (voice)

Gaganpriya/Gagan Priya (गगनप्रिय/गगन-प्रिय) (*n*) Fond of the sky.

Gahan (गहन) (*m*) Intense and mysterious. (V)

Gajakarna (गजकरण) (*m*) Elephant eyed. The small sys of Ganesh radiate wisdom and compassion, powerful, yet gentle. (G)

Gajanana (गजनन) (*m*) Elephant faced Lord Ganesha stands for power and strength. He is capable of destroying all evil. (G)

Gagansindhu (गगनसिन्धु) (*f*) The heavenly.

Gajavakra (गजवक्र) (*m*) Lord Ganesh - Elephant trunk which is twisted, is symbolic of his vast knoledge, spiritual progress and powers of discrimination. The curved trunk is shaped like "OM" - also symbolic of the life force energy. (G)

Gajendra (गजेन्द्र) (*m*) Elephant king. Avatāra of Vishnu.

Gajendra-Karuna (गजेन्द्र-करुण) (*m*) Gajendra's saviour when he cried out to him in distress. Devotees will be blessed if they concentrate on His name. (K)

Gajrā (गजरा) (*m*) A thick flower garland.

Gajrī (गजरी) (*f*) Meaning as Gajrā.

Gālava (गालव) (*m*) A pupil and son of Vishwamitra sage. The sage in a time of great distress tied a cord round his waist and offered him for sale. Prince Satyavrata gave him liberty and restored him to his father. From his having been bound with a cord (gala) he was called Gālava.

Gamati (गमती) (*f*) With a flexible mind.

Ganācharya (गनाचार्य) (*m*) Teacher common to all.

Gana-Devatā/Gana Devas (गण-देवता/गण देवस) (*m*) Troops of nine classes of deities.

Gnagopāla (गनगोपाल) (*m*) The singing shepherd. Epithet of Krishna, especially in his form as Venugopāla.

Gananath (गणनाथ) (*m*) Lord of Ganas (S,G)

Gananāyaka (गणनायक) (*f*) Consort of the Lord of the ganas (Parvati).

Ganapati (गणपति) (*m*) The Lord of Ganas. A name of Ganesha.

Ganata (गणत) (*f*) Forming a class or multitude, belonging to a party

Ganayag (गणयग) (*m*) Worship of troops or class of deities.

Gancharya (गणचार्य) (*m*) Teacher of Ganas i.e. Vishnu.

Gandhaja (गणधज) (*m/f*) Consisting of fragrant substances.

Gandhakshya (गणधक्षय) (*m*) Lord of the celestial hordes-Lord Ganesh is the first to be worshipped by the gods and mortals. (G)

Gandhalikā (गंधालिका) (*f*) Fragrance, perfumed.

Gandhalu (गंधालू) (*m/f*) Fragrant.

Gandhamālin (गधमालिन) (*f*) With fragrant garlands.

Gandhanā (गणधना) (*f*) Another name of Satyavati—because of smell coming form her body. See also Satyavati. Another mane of daughter of the king of Kashi whom Bhim married after the end of the great Mahabharata war.

Gandhapālin (गंधपालीन) (*m*) Protector of fragrance (S)

Gandhapushpā/Gandha pushpā (गन्धपुष्प/गन्ध-पुष्प) (*f*) A fragrant flower

Gandhāri (गंधारी) (*f*) Princess of Gandhar. The daughter of king of Gandhar, wife of Dhritarashtra and mother of his hundred sons. Her husband was blind, so she always wore a bandage over eyes to be like him.

Gandhārin (गंधारिन) (*m*) Possesing perfume. Name of Shiva.

Gandharv (गंधारव) (*m*) Mythological community of celestial musicians. The heavenly Gandharv of the Veda was a deity who knew and revealed the secrets of heaven and divine truth in general.

Gāndharvakalā (गांधरवकला) (*f*) Art of the Gandharvas, son, music.

Gandharvi (गंधर्वी) (*f*) Speech of Gandharva (celestial musicians) Another name of goddes Durga (D)

Gandhavā (गंधवा) (*f*) A plant full of fragrance.

Gāndhini (गांधिनी) (*f*) Name of a princess of Kashi. Leading lady.

Gandhīs (गंधीश) (*m*) Name of Shiv or Ganesh.

Gandhmādini (गंधमादिनी) (*f*) Strong-scented, perfume.

Gandhmātri (गंधमात्री) (*f*) Mother of fragrance, the earth.

Gandhpushpa (गंधपुष्प) (*m/f*) Flower full of fragrance.

Gandhsār (गंधसार) (*m*) Sandal wood. A kind of jasmine.

Gāndīva (गांडीव) (*m*) The bow of Arjuna, said to have been given by Soma to Varuna, by Varuna to Agni, and by Agni to Arjuna.

Ganendra (गनेन्द्र) (*m*) Lord of the troops.

Ganesh (गणेश) (*m*) A popular Hindu deity beloved to be the god of wisdom symbolising auspiciousness. Son of Shiva and Parvati, Lord of the Ganas or troops of inferior deities especially those attendant upon Shiva.

Ganeshagit (गणेशगीत) (*f*) Song of Ganesh.

Ganeshan (गणेशन) (*m*) The God Ganesh.

Gangā (गंगा) (*f*) The Ganges considered to be the most sacred river by the Hindus. It is said to be mentioned only twice in Rig Veda. Personified as a goddess, Ganga is the eldest daughter of Himavat and Mena and her sister was Uma. She became the wife of King Santhanu and bore him a son, Bhishama.

Ganeshvara (गणेश्वर) (*m*) Lord of Ganas. Lord Shiva is Lord of three world. The ganas or celestials pay obeisance to Him and meditate upon Him, seeking His blessings for self enlightenment. (S)

Gangādhar (गंगाधर) (*m*) an epithet of Shiva.

Gangahari (गंगहरी) (*f*) River ganges plus Hari. Waves of the ganges.

Gangastuti/Ganga Stuti (गंगस्तुति) (*f*) In praise of the river Ganges

Gangkā (गंगका) (*f*) Same as Ganga.

Ganratna (गणरत्न) (*m/f*) Pearls of troops of deities.

Ganyag (गणयग) (*m*) Worship of the classes of deities.

Gārgi (गार्गी) (*m*) Name of an astronomer.

Gargi (गर्गी) Also known as **Vidushi** (*f*) The most learned women who obtained Brahamvidya.

Garud (गरूड) (*m*) A mythical bird on which Vishnu rides.

Garudā Dhvaj (गरूडाध्वज) (*m*) He who has Garuda mark in his flag (V)

Gatashakti (गतशक्ति) (*f*) Power of motion (from Rig Veda)

Gāthā (गाथा) (*f*) A song, a verse. A religious verse, but one not taken from the Vedas.

Gathāni (गथानी) (*m/f*) Leading singer.

Gātri (गात्री) (*m*) A singer.

Gattisattam (गत्तीसत्ताम) (*m*) The noble's destination (V)

Gatu (गतुं) (*m*) Song (from Rig Ved) Gandharva of celestial chorister.

Gaurav (गौरव) (*m/f*) Importance, high value or respect shown to a person. Belonging to or relating to Guru.

Gaurī (गौरी) (*f*) The goddess Parvati, Shiva's spouse. It also means yellow or brilliant.

Gaurijā (गौरिजा) (*m*) Son of Parvati. See also Parvati

Gaurī-kānt/Gaurī-nāth (गौरी-कांत/गौरी-नाथ) (*m*) Lord Shiva.

Gauripujā (गौरीपूजा) (*f*) Adoration of Gauri. See Devi.

Gaurish (गौरिश) (*m*) Lord of Gauri (S)

Gaurisut (गौरीसुत) (*m*) son of Gauri, another name of Parvati (G)

Gautama (गौतम) (*m*) Patronymic from Gotama. Clan name of the historic Buddha. Also a name of the sage Saradwat as a son of Gotama. He was the husband of Ahalya.

Gautami (गौतमी) (*f*) An epithet of Durga. See also Devi.

Gaveshin (गवेशिन) (*m/f*) Seeking, searching.

Gavijat (गवीजत) (*m*) A great sage who helped king Nahusha from his difficult task of correctly evaluating the worth of Chayavan sage.

Gāvinda (गाविंद) (*m*) Name of a son of Krishna and Lakshman.

Gayā (गया) (*m*) What has been conquered or acquired. Name of a Rājarishi One of the greatest philonthropic kings of ancient times was also known as Gaya. Also a name of a town.

Gayāprasād (गयाप्रसाद) (*m*) The blessing of Gaya (sacred pilgrimage place - Gaya)

Gāyatri (गायत्री) (*f*) A most sacred verse of the Rig Veda, which it is duty of every Hindu to repeat mentally in his morning and evening devotions. It is addressed to the sun as Savitri, the generator, and so it is called also Sāvitri. Personified as a goddess, Savitri is the wife of Brahma, mother of the four Vedas. The approximate translation of Gayatri mantra is (the earth, sky, heaven—let us meditate on these, and on the most excellent light and power of that generous, sportive, and resplendent sun (praying that) it may guide our intellects.

Geshna/Gishnu (गेष्णा/गेष्णु) (*m*) A singer, One who chants Sama Veda.

Ghanāmud (घनामुद) (*m/f/n*) Highly pleased

Ghanarupa (घनरूप) (*f*) Compact ih shape. candied sugar.

Ghanshyām (घनश्याम) (*m*) black, clouds. an epithet of Lord Krishna.

Ghata-karpāra (घट-करपार) (*m*) A poet, who was one of the nine gems of the court of Vikramaditya.

Ghritāchi (घरिताची) (*f*) An apsara (heavenly nymph). Rishi Bhardwaj lost his composure on seeing her beauty and Dronacharya was born.

Girā (गीरा) (*m/f*) Delighting in or thriving by praise.

Gīrdevi (गिरदेवी) (*f*) The goddess of speech. Sarasvati.

Giribālā (गिरिबाला) (*f*) Daughter of mountain. Another name of Ganges and Parvati.

Giridhar (गिरिधर) (*m*) Holder of the mountain. Another name of Lord Krishna (K)

Girijā (गिरिजा) (*m*) Mountain born. A name of Parvati or Devi. See also Devi.

Girjāpati (गिरजापती) (*m*) Spouse of Girija or Parvati or Uma. She is the graceful daughter of the lofty mountains. (S)

Girikā (गिरिका) (*f*) Giri means the vehicle of speech. Girika was the beloved and most beautiful wife of Uparichara, king of Chedi. Girika means hearts of Gods.

Girikantak (गिरीकटंक) (*m*) Indra's thunderbolt.

Girigangā (गिरीगंगा) (*f*) The mountain Ganga. Pure and clean.

Giridhar (गिरीधर) (*m*) Holder of the mountain. another name of Lord Krishna (K)

Girikā (गिरीका) (*f*) Summit of the mountain. Daughter of river Suktimati.

Girikarni (गिरीकर्णी) (*f*) Lotus of the mountain.

Girilāl (गिरीलाल) (*m*) Son of the mountain. Another name of Gandsh (G)

Girjāpati (गिरजापती) (*m*) Spouse of Girija or Parvati or Uma. She is the graceful daughter of the lofty mountains. (S)

Girnandini (गिरनंदिनी) (*f*) Mountain daughter. name of Parvati

Girindra (गिरीन्द्र) (*m*) Lord of speech. (S)

Girirāj (गिरीराज) (*m*) King of the mountains.

Girish (गिरीश) (*m*) Lord of speech. another name of Brahaspati.

Girrupa (गिरि-रूप) (*m/f*) Mountain shaped. Beautiful like mountain.

Girtarā (गिरतरा) (*f*) Excellent speech or voice.

Gīsh (गिश) (*m*) A learned man.

Gīshpati (गिशपति) (*m*) Learned man.

Gishtarā (गिशतरा) (*f*) Excellent speech or voice.

Gita (गीता) (*f*) Sacred writings in verse, in the from of a dialogue and containing an exposition of certain religious doctrines. A term specially applied to Bhagvad-Gitā. It contains the celebrated discourse of Lord Krishna. Bhagvad-Gitā. The song of the divine one. A celebrated episode of the Mahabharata, in the form of a metrical dialogue, in which the divine Krishna is the chief speaker, and expounds to Arjuna his philosophical doctrines.

Gitā-Govinda (गीत-गोविंद) A lyrical poem by Jayadeva on the early life of Krishna as Govinda, the cow-keeper.

Gitāli (गीताली) (*f*) Lover of songs, music.

Gitapriya (गीतप्रिय) (*f*) Lover of music.

Gitikā (गीतिका) (*f*) Poetry, verse, vocal music, song.

Gitpriya (गीतप्रिय) (*f*) Fond of songs.

Gohitah (गोहित) (*m*) The well wisher of cows (V)

Gokarna (गोकरण) (*m/f*) The span from the tip of the thumb to that of ring finger. Name of Shiva's attendant. Shiva as worshipped in Gokarna. Also name of a wife of king Takshaka and mother of Ashwasena.

Gokul (गोकुल) (*m*) The country round Vrindavan plus a flock of cows. A name of a town where Krishna was brought up.

Gomati (गोमती) (*f*) A goddess. The name of a river in Oudh.

Gopāl (गोपाल) (*m*) Cow-keeper. Epithet of Krishna. A name of youthful Krishna, who lived among the cowherds in Vrindavan.

Gopālpriya (गोपालप्रिया) (*m*) Lover of cowherds (K)

Gopana (गोपान) (*n*) Guarding, protection, preservation

Gopati (गोपति) (*m*) Lord of protector of cows. (V)

Gopesh (गोपेश) (*m*) Krishna. Name of Nand (Krishan's foster father).

Gopeshvara (गापेश्घर) (*m*) A form of Lord Shiva

Gopi (गोपी) (*f*) A cowherd's wife. The milkmaids who were the companions of Krishna, and the principal of whom was Radha.

Gopichandra (गोपीचन्द्र) (*m*) Moon of the Gopis. (K)

Gopila (गोपिल) (*m/f*) One who preserves or protects.

Gopta (गोप्त) (*m*) Keeping himself enveloped by his creative illusion. He who protects and nourishes every being. (V)

Gopināth (गोपीनाथ) (*m*) Lord of Gopis. (K)

Gopishvara (गोपीश्वर) (*m*) Lord of the Gopis (K)

Goptri (गोपत्री) (*m/f*) One who preserves or protects.

Gopya (गोप्य) (*n*) To Guard, protect, preserve.

Gorakhnāth (गोरखनाथ) (*m*) An incarnation of Shiva, Worshipped in Nepal.

Gotama (गोतम) (*m*) The founder of the Nyāya school of philosophy. He is also called Satananda, and is the author of a Dharma Sāstrā. See also Gautama.

Gotamī (गोतमी) (*f*) Also called Ahalya wife of Gotama. See also Gautami.

Govardhana (गोवर्धन) (*m*) A mountain in Vrindavan, which Krishna induced cowherds and cowherdesses to worship instead of Indra. This enraged the god indra, who sent a deluge of rain to wash away the mountain and all the people of the country, but Krishna held up the mountain on his little finger for seven days to shelter the people of Vrindaban. Indra retired baffled, and afterwards did homage to Krishna.

Govardhana-dhar (गोवर्धन-धर) (*m*) Upholder of Govardhana. A title of Krishna.

Govinda (गोविंद) (*m*) Rescuer of the earth. Epithet of Krishna.

Govindah (गोविंदा) (*m*) He who is capable of reclaiming the sunken earth. Comprehensible through Vedic study. (V)

Govindampati (गोविंदमपति) (*m*) The master of all who knows the Vedas. (V)

Goral (गोरल) (*m*) Likeable.

Gorma (गोरम) (*f*) Worth considering. Another name of Parvati.

Govindadcatta (गोविंदद्कत्त) (*m*) Given by Krishna. Name of a Brahman known for his compassion.

Grahish (ग्रहिश) (*m*) Lord of the planets. Another name of sun and saturn.

Grāmani (ग्रामणी) (*m*) Leader of a group (V)

Granthika (ग्रंथिका) (*m*) A relater or narrator. One who understand the division of time. Name assumed by Nakul when he was appointed master of horses to king Virat.

Griddha (ग्रिध) (*m/f*) Desirous of, eagerly longing for.

Guhā (गुहा) (*m*) Secret. A name of the god of war. A name used in the Mahabharata for Krishna.

Guhyāh (गुह्या) (*m*) The occult who resides in every heart (V)

Guhyaka (गुह्यक) (*m*) Demi-gods who are attendants of the god of wealth.

Gulkesh (गुलकश) (*m*) Never fading flower. Emblem of immortality.

Gulnār (गुलनार) (*m*) Red colour which is like the flower of a pomegranate.

Gunābdhi (गुनाब्धी) (*m*) Full of merits. Name of Buddha.

Gunādhār (गुणाधार) (*m*) Virtuous person.

Gunadhya (गुनध्य) (*m/f*) Possessing very good qualities.

Gunagrahin (गुनग्रहीन) (*m*) Acceptor of Gunas (pure, active and inert) These gunas cause the emergence of newer forms of nature, and Lord Shiva controls them. (S)

Gundipika (गुनदीपिका) (*n*) Of very good qualities.

Gunakali (गुनकली) (*f*) Possessing virtues, a ragini (Rag Malkaus)

Gunakeshi (गुनकेशी) (*f*) Full of merits. Name of a daughter of Matali (the charioteer of Indra).

Gunang (गुणांग) (*m/f*) Action resulting from good Qualities. Having many good qualities.

Gunantra (गुनांत्र) (*m/f*) Endowed with different kind of qualities or merits. Superior person.

Gunarām (गुनराम) (*m*) Pleasure-grove of good qualities.

Gundhara (गुन्धर) (*m/f*) Possessing very good qualities.

Gundipika (गुनदीपिका) (*n*) Of very good qualities.

Gunesh (गुणेश) (*m*) The lord of the virtues.

Gunin (गुणिन) (*m*) Lord of all virtues - Lord Ganesh. Auspicious. (G)

Gunjan (गुंजन) (*m*) Buzzing, humming, sounding.

Gunjani (गूंजनी) (*f*) Female of Gunjan.

Gunkar (गुणकर) (*m/f/n*) Profitable, productive of good qualities

Gunkiri (गुनकिरी) (*f*) Full of merits.

Gunmaya (गुणमय) (*n*) Possesing merits.

Gunnidhi (गुण-निधि) (*m*) Treasury of good qualities.

Gunnikā (गुन्निका) (*f*) Full of virtues. Garland.

Gunapriya (गुणप्रिय) (*m/f*) Excellence or fond of merit.

Guna-rāshi (गुण-राशि) (*m/f*) Mine of virtues (S)

Gunratna (गुनरत्न) (*m*) Pearl of good qualities.

Gunsabhrita (गुणसभरित) (*m*) The mine of all virtues (V)

Gunsat (गुणसत) (*m/f*) Full of hundred excellent qualities.

Gunvat (गुणवत) (*m/f*) Full of good qualities.

Gupil (गुपिल) (*m*) Protector, king.

Guptah (गुपतह) (*m*) Secret, incomprehensible by description (V)

Gupah (गुपः) (*m*) Secret, incomprehensible by description (V)

Guru (गुरु) (*m*) Teacher of all (V)

Gurudatta (गुरुदत्त) (*m*) Given by the Guru

Gurukarman (गुरुकमर्ण) (*m*) Any affair of a spiritual teacher

Gurunāth (गुरुनाथ) (*m*) Lord of the spiritual teachers.

Gururāj (गुरुराज) (*m*) Lord of the spiritual teachers.

Gurutam (गुरुतम) (*m*) Greatest teacher (V)

Gururatan (गुरुरत्न) (*m*) jewel among spiritual teachers.

Gyān/Janān (ज्ञान/जनान्) (*m*) Knowledge, sacred knowledge, consciousness, sense, learning.

Gyangamaya (ज्ञानगमय) (*m*) Comprehensible by knowledge (V)

Gyanmuttamam (ज्ञानमुत्तमम) (*m*) The best knowledge of every thing (V)

H (ह, हा)

Haim/Haimā (हैम/हैमा) (*m/f*) Golden, pertaining to the winter season.

Haimi (हैमी) (*f*) Golden

Haimāvatī (हैमावती) (*m/f*) Relating to or connected with Ganesh.

Hajāri (हजारी) (*m*) A commander over one thousand soldiers.

Hakikat (हकीकत) (*f*) Truth, sincerity, reality.

Hans (हंस) (*m*) Swan, the sun, Brahma, god.

Hansak (हंसक) (*m*) Swan, an ornament worn on the toes.

Hansani (हंसनी) (*f*) AFemale swan.

Hansgāmini (हंसगामिनी) (*f*) Graceful woman, walking like a swan.

Hansi (हंसी) (*f*) Swan. Daughter of Phagirath and wife of sage Kautsa.

Hansin (हंसीं) (*m/f/n*) Containing the universal soul (said of Lord Krishna)

Hansmālā (हंसमाला) (*f*) Line or flight of Hansa.

Hanumadakshita (हनुमदक्षिता) (*m*) Dependent on Hanuman. Another name of Lord Ram (R)

Hanumān (हनुमान) (*m*) A celebrated monkey god. He was son of Pavan (the wind god). He was able to fly, and is a conspicuous figure in the Ramayana.

Hanumant (हनुमंत) (*m*) Same as Hanuman.

Hanumat/Hanumate (हनुमत/हनुमते) (*m*) Meaning the same as Hanuman (H)

Hara (हर) (*m*) Remover of sins. (S)

Haramala (हरमाला) (*f*) Garland of Lord Shiva.

Haramanas (हरमानस) (*f*) The soul of Shiva, the soul; of god.

Haramohan (हरमोहन) (*S*) Attrrracting Shiva.

Harchand/Harichand (हरचन्द/हरीचन्द) (*m*) Vishnu plus moon. Also a kind of sandal of yellow colour.

Harendra (हरेन्द्र) (*m*) Indra and Shiva conjoined

Hareshvar (हरेश्वर) (*m*) Shiva and Shiva conjoined

Hari (हरी) (*m*) Yellowish, reddish brown. Epithet used for several gods, e.g. Indra, Shiva, Vishnu, but Vishnu in particular is known by the name of Hari. (V)

Hariāksha (हरीअक्ष) (*m*) The eye of Vishnu.

Haribālā (हरिबाला) (*f*) Daughter of Vishnu.

Haribhadra (हरिभद्र) (*f*) Auspicious, beautiful and praiseworthy as Vishnu.

Haribhajan (हरिभजन) (*m*) A hymn to Vishnu.

Haribhakt (हरिभक्त) (*m*) Worshipper of Vishnu.

Haribhāvana (हरिभावना) (*f*) Choice of Vishnu, desire of Vishnu, preference of Vishnu.

Harichandan (हरिचन्दन) (*m*) Hari means Vishnu and Chandan means sandalwood.

Haridatta (हरिदत्त) (*m*) Given to Vishnu, blessed by Vishnu.

Haridhan (हरिधन) (*m/f*) Treasure of Vishnu.

Haridra (हरिद्र) (*m*) The Golden one. Lord Ganesh has a moon crest on his forehead, a sacred thread in the form of a serpent round his body, cheeks anointed with a vermilion paste, glowing golden like the rays of the sun. (G)

Haridev/Hari-devi (हरिदेव/हरि-देवी) (*m*) Lord Vishnu. See also the meaning of Hari and Dev

Haridish/Hari-dish (हरिदिश/हरि-दिश) (*f*) Indra's quarter.

Harigangā (हरिगंगा) (*f*) The Ganga (river ganges) of Vishnu.

Harigitā/Hari-gitā (हरिगीता/हरि-गीता) (*m*) Doctrine communicated by Narayan to narad (from Mahabharata)

Hari-har (हरि-हर) A combination of the names of Vishnu and Shiva, and representing the union of the two deities in one.

Harikā (हरिका) (*m/f/n*) Being like Hari. See also Hari (Lord Vishnu)

Harikāntā (हरिकांता) (*f*) Dear to Vishnu. Another name of Lakshmi.

Harikesh/Hari-kesh (हरिकेष) (*m*) Fair headed. Name of one of the 7 principal rays of sun. (R.V.)

Harikrishna (हरिकृष्ण) (*m*) Vishnu and Krishna conjoined.

Harilāl (हरिलाल) (*m*) Son of Vishnu.

Hari-mālā (हरि-माला) (*f*) Garland of Vishnu.

Harimani (हरिमनि) (*m*) Vishnu's gem.

Harimitra (हरिमित्र) (*m*) Vishnu's friends.

Harinā (हरिना) (*f*) Beautiful woman with beautiful eyes.

Harinetra (हरिनेत्र) (*m*) Eye of Vishnu.

Harinetra (हरिनेत्र) (*m*) Eye of Vishnu.

Hariom (हरिओम) (*m*) Lord of Om. See also Hari and Om.

Hariprasad (हरिप्रसाद) (*m*) The blessing of Vishnu.

Hariprit (हरिप्रीत) (*f*) Beloved of Vishnu (Lakshmi).

Hari-Priya (हरि-प्रिया) (*m/f*) Liked or loved by Vishnu or Krishna.

Harirāj (हरिराज) (*m*) King of Hari, king of lion.

Hari-rām (हरि-राम) (*m*) Vishnu plus Ram.

Hariratna/Hari-ratna (हरिरत्न/हरि-रत्न) (*m*) Jewel of Hari.

Hari-rup/Har-rup (हरि-रूप/हर-रूप) (*m*) Having the form of Vishnu or Shiva.

Hari-rupani (हरी-रुपनी) (*f*) Same as Hari-rup.

Harish (हरिश) (*m*) Vishnu and Shiva conjoined.

Harish Chandra (हरिश चन्द्र) (*m*) Twenty-eighth king of the Solar race, and son of Tri-sanku. He was celebrated for his piety and justice. There are several legends about him.

Harishankar (हरिशंकर) (*m*) Shiva and Vishnu conjoined.

Harishmani (हरीशमणि) (*m*) Gem of Vishnu.

Hari-shri (हरि-श्री) (*m/f*) Gold coloured, Vishnu.

Haristuti/Hari-stuti (हरीस्तुति/हरि-स्तुति) (*f*) Hymns in praise of Lord Vishnu

Harisut (हरिसुत) (*m*) Son of Vishnu. Another name of Arjuna.

Harita (हरिता) (*m/f*) Yellowish, pale yellow. Yellow colour is a sign of prosperity. See also the meaning of Hari.

Hari-vallabh (हरि-वल्लभ) (*m*) Loved by Vishnu.

Harivallabhi (हरिवल्लाभि) (*f*) Consort of Lord Hari - godess Lakshmi (L)

Hari-vansha (हरि-वंश) (*m*) The genealogy of Hari (Vishnu); a long poem of 16,374 verses. It purports to be a part of the Mahabharata.

Harivarna (हरिवर्ण) (*m*) Same as Vishnu's coloiur, green, name of a sage who wrote some hymns.

Harivatsa (हरिवत्स) (*m*) Belonging to Vishnu. Another name of Arjuna.

Harivir (हरिवीर) (*m*) Warrior of god.

Harshālā (हर्षाला) (*f*) Happy, glad.

Harmushtā (हरमुश्ता) (*m/f*) Robust, strong, healthy.

Harmushti (हरमुश्ति) (*f*) Same as Harmushta.

Harsh (हर्ष) (*m*) joy, jubilation, mirth, delight, happiness.

Harshālā (हर्षाला) (*f*) Happy, glad.

Harshaman (हर्षमन) (*m/f*) Full of joy.

Harshan (हर्षन) (*f*) Causing happiness.

Harshanya (हर्षनय) (*m/f*) Pleasant, delightful.

Harshavinā (हर्षावीणा) (*f*) A flute that delights.

Harsh Dev (हर्ष देव) (*m*) A king of Kashmir who reigned between AD 1113 and 1125, and the reputed author of the play called *Ratnavali.*

Harshi (हर्षि) (*f*) Very happy, joyful.

Harshitā (हर्षिता) (*m/f*) Full of joy.

Harshuka (हरर्षुक) (*m/f*) Delighting, gladdening.

Harshumati (हर्षुमती) (*f*) Full of joy.

Harshvardhan (हर्षवर्धन) (*m*) name of a Buddhist king of India. A prince, the son of Yajnakrit, one of the descendants of Ksheattravriddha.

Harvind (हरविंद) (*m*) Name of various authors. A form of Vishnu.

Hasamukha (हसमुख) (*m*) Smiling.

Hasamukhi (हसमुखी) (*f*) Smiling.

Hasini (हसीनी) (*f*) Delightful.

Hasitā/,Harshitā (हसीता/हर्षीता) (*f*) Smile, laugh, smiling is a sign of happiness.

Hastkamal/Hast Kamal (हस्तकमल) (*m/f*) Lotus in hands. Symbol of prosperity (from Garuda Purana).

Havi (हैवी) (*m*) The supreme offering (of the Yagya) (V)

Hem/Hema (हेम/हेमा) (*m*) Snow, hale, gold.

Hemā (हेमा) (*f*) Apsaras (nymphs of heaven).

Hemachandra (हेमचन्द्र) (*m*) Golden moon. A name of a celebrated Jain author (AD 1078-1172) He belonged to the Svetambara sect.

Hemāgandhini/Hemā Gandhini (हेमागंधिनी/हेमा-गांधिनी) (*f*) Perfume.

Hemaka (हेमक) (*n*) A piece of gold.

Hemā-Kānti (हेमा-कान्ती) (*m*) Gold, glittering like gold.

Hemākshi (हेमक्षी) (*f*) Golden eyed.

Hemakut (हेमकुट) (*m*) Golden peak. A chain of mountains represented as lying north of the Himalayas, between them and mount Meru.

Hemalatā (हेमलता) (*f*) Golden creeper.

Hema-mālā (हेम-माला) (*f*) Golden garland.

Hemā-Mālini (हेमा-मालिनी) (*f*) *Hema* means sun or gold or nymphs of heaven and *Malini* means wife of a garland-maker Hema also means a beautiful woman.

Hemānāth (हेमानाथ) (*m*) Lord of gold.

Hemang (हेमंग) (*m*) Having golden body or organs (V)

Hemant (हेमन्त) (*m*) The winter season. A mind-born son of Brahmā in the 16th Kalpa. Kalpa means a day and night of Brahma, 4,320,000,000 years.

Hemanth-nāth (हेमनथ-नाथ) (*m*) Lord of winter.

Hemāprabhā (हेमाप्रभा) (*f*) Golden light.

Hemāpushpaka (हेमापुष्पक) (*f*) With golden flowers.

Hema-rāgini (हेम-रागिनी) (*f*) Gold coloured, golden melody.

Hemāvarna (हेमावर्ण) (*f*) Golden complexion

Hemavati (हेमावती) (*f*) River ganges. An epithet of Parvati. See Devi.

Hemendra (हेमेन्द्र) (*m*) Lord of gold, another name of Indra.

Heramba (हेरम्ब) (*m*) Beloved of the mother and her protector - Lord Ganesh (G)

Hesha (हेश) (*m/f*) Quick, strong, powerful.

Hetu (हेतु) (*m*) The purpose of the world (V)

Hetupmā (हेतुपमा) (*f*) Illustration, the figure of speech

Hevant (हेवंत) (*m*) Same as Hemant.

Himā (हिमा) (*f*) Snow, winter, night,

Himabjā (हिमब्जा) (*n*) Blue lotus.

Himādri (हिमाद्रि) The golden mountain i.e. Meru.

Himagu (हिमगु) (*m/f*) The moon, cold-rayed.

Himājyoti (हिमज्योति) (*m*) Like snow. Another name of moon.

Himāni (हिमानी) (*f*) A mass of snow. A glacier.

Himānshu (हिमांशु) (*m*) An epithet of the moon.

Himāvan (हिमावन) (*m*) He is regarded as the father of parvati (Himavati) and Gangā.

Himāvat (हिमावत्) (*m*) The personification of the Himalayan mountains, husband of Mena or Menaka, and father of Uma and Ganga.

Himnā (हिमना) (*m*) The planet Mercury.

Hirā (हीरा) (*m*) Diamond. Epithet of Lakshmi.

Hirāk (हिराक) (*m*) Diamond.

Hirang (हिरंग) (*m*) A person who has a body like a gem.

Hirānmayi (हीरण्मयी) (*f*) Golden appearance - goddess Lakshmi (L)

Hirānya (हिरंय) (*m*) Gold, silver.

Hiranyagarbha (हिरण्यगर्भ) (*m*) Holding in his belly the golden ovam. Having aureate navel for the creation of the world. (V)

Hiranya-kashipu (हिरण्य-कशिपु) (*m*) Golden dress.

Hiranyaksha (हिरण्याक्ष) (*f*) Golden eye.

Hiranyaprakā (हिरण्यप्रका) (*f*) Amidst gold. Goddess Lakshmi stands out amidst the glittering gold-like rays of a thousand suns (L)

Hirārām (हीराराम) (*m*) Diamond plus Rām. A name of apoet in ancient times.

Hiren (हीरे) (*m*) Lord of gems. beautiful pearls.

Hiresh (हीरेश) (*m*) King of gems.

Hiri (हीरी) (*m/f*) Golden, yellow.

Hiteshvara (हितेश्वर) (*m*) God of welfare. Caring for others. Glad, delighted.

Hitkām (हितकाम) (*m/f*) Wishing well, to benefit.

Hitkāmya (हितकाम्य) (*f*) Desiring every ones welfare

Hitokti (हितोकती) (*f*) Kind or good advice.

Hitprāni (हितप्राणी) (*m*) Executing what is advantageous.

Hitvata/Hitvati (हितवत/हितवती) (*m/f*) Useful, favourable.

Holaka (होलक) (*n*) Spring festival. From Holi

Homadhenu (होमधेनु) (*m*) An ascetic whose calf was accidentally killed by Karna when practicing archery in the forest. Karna was cursed by him that at the crucial moment in this battle for life and death, the wheel of his chariot would get stuck in mud. Homa means a sort of burnt offering which can be made by Brahmans only.

Hotri (होत्री) (*m*) A priest who recites the prayers from the Rig Veda.

Hridaya (हृदया) (*m*) The heart, the chest, essence, science.

Hridayeshwar (हृदयेश्वर) (*m*) The lord of one's heart, dear one, dear husband.

Hrideshawari (हरीदेश्वरी) (*f*) The beloved of one's heart, beloved, beautiful lady.

Hrishikesh (हृषीकेश) (*m*) A name of Krishna or Vishnu.

Hrishta (हृष्ट) (*m/f/n*) Rejoiced, pleased, glad, merry.

Hrishti (हृषति) (*f*) Delight, joy, rapture.

Hrishu (हृषु) (*m/f/n*) Glad, happy, the sun, the moon.

Hulsi (हुलसी) (*f*) Happiness.

Humā (हुमा) (*f*) A bird of paradise.

Humel (हुमेल) (*f*) A necklace made of threaded gold.

Hutābhuk (हुताभुक) (*m*) The consumer of all offerings. (V)

Huti (हुती) (*f*) Invocation, calling.

I (इ, ई)

Idā (इदा) (*f*) In the Rig Veda Idā is primarily food, refreshment, or a libation of milk; thence a stream of praise, personified as the goddess of speech.

Idikā (इदिका) (*f*) The good earth.

Ijyah (ईज्याह) (*m*) Adorable (V)

Ikrām (इकराम) (*m*) Reward, prize, honour, respect (From Rig Veda)

Ikshā (इक्षा) (*f*) Viewing, sight.

Ikshanā (इक्षणा) (*n*) A look, view, aspect, sight, eye (from Mahabharata)

Ikshu (इक्षु) (*m*) Sugar-cane, sweetness, eye-lash.

Ikshuda (इक्षुदा) (*m*) Sweet tongue. Pleasant. Granting wishes.

Ikshulatā (इक्षुलता) (*m*) Creeper of sweetness.

Ilā (इला) (*f*) The earth, speech. One of Vasudev's wives. Mother earth, worshipped for gain of bodily strength. Also a name of a daughter of Manu and Shradha born through Yajna performed by sage Vasishtha. She married Chandra's son Buddha and their son was Pururava, an ancestor of the Pandavas.

Ilākshi (इलाक्षि) (*f*) Centre of the earth, eye of the earth.

Ilāpati (इलापति) (*m*) A surname of Krishna.

Ilinā (इलीना) (*f*) Possessing high intelligence.

Ināksh (इनाक्ष) (*m*) To obtain, to reach, (used in Rig Veda.)

Inākshā (इनाक्षा) (*n*) To try to reach, strive to obtain (from Rig Veda)

Ināni (इनामी) (*f*) Name of a plant (=Vattapttri).

Inda (इंदा) (*m*) To be powerful. Same as Indra.

Indambar (इंदम्बर) (*m*) Blue lotus.

Indar/Indra (इंदर/इंद्र) (*m*) The king of gods. The god of rains.

Indhā (इंधा) (*m/f*) Lighting, kindling. Name of a Rishi (sage).

Indirā (इंदिरा) (*f*) A surname of Lakshmi (goddes of wealth and prosperity).

Indirālaya (इंदिरालय) (*m/f*) Abode of Indira, blue lotus from which Lakshmi emerges at the time of creation.

Indirāni (इंदिरानी) See Indrāni.

Indivar (इंदीवर) (*m*) The blue lotus.

Indra (इंद्र) (*m*) See Indar.

Indrabālā (इंद्रबाला) (*f*) Daughter of Indra.

Indra-bhāgini (इंद्र-भागिनी) (*f*) Name of Indra's sister.

Indrabhuti (इंद्रभूति) (*m*) Image of Indra

Indra-Chandan (इंद्र-चन्दन) (*m/f*) Indra's bow, the rainbow.

Indradatta (इंद्रदत्त) (*m*) Gift of Indra

Indra-jit (इंद्र-जीत) (*m*) Son of Rāvana called Megha Nath. In a battle with Lord Indra, he fought most valiantly and won. Brahma went to obtain the release of Indra and gave to Megha Nath the name of Indra-jit.

Indrakarma (इंद्रकर्मा) (*m*) Performing Lord Indra like deeds (V)

Indraketu (इंद्रकेतु) (*m*) Indra's banner. name of a banner which is erected during a spring festival and dedicated to Indra.

Indrākshi (इंद्राक्षी) (*f*) Indra's eye. Name of a goddess.

Indra-loka (इंद्र-लोक) (*m*) Indra's heaven.

Indrāni (इंद्राणी) (*m*) The wife of Lord Indra, and mother of Jayanta and Jayanti. She is also called Sachi and Aindri. She is mentioned a few times in the Rig Veda, and is said to be most fortunate of females.

Indra-nalī (इंद्र-नली) (*m*) Sapphire.

Indrapriya (इंद्रप्रिया) (*m/f*) Dear to Indra.

Indra-pushpi (इंद्र-पुष्पी) (*f*) A medicinal plant.

Indra-rājan (इंद्र-राजन्) (*m*) Having Indra as a king.

Indrasen (इंद्रसेन) (*m*) Son of nala and Damayanti. Also name of a charioteer of king Yudhishthira.

Indrasenā (इंद्रसेना) (*m*) Daughter of Nala and Damayanti.

Indra-shakti (इंद्र-शक्ति) (*f*) Wife of Indra. Same as Indrani.

Indratā (इंद्रता) (*f*) Power and dignity of Indra.

Indratam (इंद्रतम) (*m/f*) Like Indra. Any one having the qualities of Indra.

Indrapālita (इंद्रपालिता) (*m/f*) Protected by Indra. One who has blessings of Indra.

Indravarāj (इंद्रवराज) (*m*) The name of Vishnu.

Indravarmā (इंद्रवर्मा) (*m*) King of Malava whose elephant Ashwatthama was killed by Bhim during the Mahabharata war.

Indravishnu (इंद्रविष्णु) (*m*) Indra and Vishnu conjoined.

Indraya (इंद्रया) (*n*) To behave like Lord Indra (From Rig Veda)

Indrāyani (इंद्रायणी) (*f*) Wife of Indra, the feminine form of Indra's energy.

Indreshvar (इंद्रेश्वर) (*m*) Lord of senses, a form of Shivalinga.

Indriya (इंद्रिय) (*m/f*) Belonging to or agreeable to Indra.

Indriyāni (इंद्रीयाणी) (*f*) Senses; five under the control of Buddhi (knowledge) and five under Karma (action, deeds).

Indrotā (इंद्रोता) (*m*) Upheld or promoted by Indra

Indu (इंदु) (*m*) The moon. The king of gods, the best. See also Soma.

Indubha (इंदुभ) (*f*) Light of the moon.

Induka (इंदुक) (*n*) Name of a plant, = Ashmantaka

Indu-kakshā (इंदु-कक्षा) (*f*) Radiating circle all around the moon.

Indukalā (इंदुकला) (*f*) Digit of the moon. Name of several plants.

Indu-kamal (इंदु-कमल) (*n*) the blossom of the white lotus.

Indukānt (इंदुकांत) (*m*) The moon-stone.

Indulekhā (इंदुलेखा) (*f*) A digit of the moon.

Indumani (इंदुमणि) (*m*) The moon gem. See also Chandrakānt.

Indumati (इंदुमती) (*f*) The full moon day. Also the name of sister of Bhoja (king of Vidarbha). Also the name of the mother of Dashrath.

Indumauli (इंदुमौलि) (*m*) Another name of Shiva.

Indumukhi (इंदुमुखी) (*f*) Face - beautiful like moon.

Indu-ratna (इंदु-रत्न) (*n*) A pearl.

Indurekhā (इंदुरेखा) (*f*) A digit of the moon.

Indushikhar (इंदुशिखर) (*m*) Another name of Shiva.

Indushital (इंदुशीतल) (*f*) Cool like the moon (L)

Ingita (इंगित) (*n*) Gesture of the motion of various limbs indicating one's intentions. Movement of the limbs in a dance.

Inguda (इंगुदा) (*f*) Medicinal tree.

Ipsā (इप्सा) (*f*) Asking, desire or wish to obtain (from Mahabharata)

Ipsana (इप्सन) (*n*) Desiring or wishing to obtain (from Mahabharata).

Ipsita (इप्सिता) (*m/f/n*) Same as Ipsana.

Irā (इरा) (*f*) The earth, water, speech. The name of goddess Sarasvati.

Irāvan (इरावन) (*m*) Son of Arjuna by his wife Ulupi.

Irāvat (इरावत) (*m*) A son of Arjuna.

Irāvati (इरावती) (*f*) One of the wives of Rudra. Also a name of river Ravi.

Iresha (इंरेष) (*m*) Name of Vishnu. A king, sovereign.

Isha (ईषा) (*m*) Powerful, supreme, god. A title of Shiva.

Ishāh (ईशाह) (*m*) Omnipotent Lord (V)

Ishān (ईशान) A name of Shiva or Rudra.

Ishānah (ईशानह) (*m*) The controller of all spirits. (V)

Ishānam (ईषानाम्) (*m/f*) Light, splendour.

Ishāni (ईषानी) (*f*) A name of Yoga Māyā: a Shakti. An epithet of Durga.

Ishaya (ईषय) (*a*) to be fresh, or active or powerful.

Ishāyu (ईषायु) (*m/f/n*) Fresh, strong, powerful (from Rig Veda)

Ishi (ईषी) (*f*) Same as Ishaya (R.V.)

Ishir (इषिर) (*m/f*) Refreshing, fresh, flourishing.

Ishirā (ईषिरा) (*f*) Refreshing, fresh, flourishing, vigorous, active.

Ishitā (ईषिता) (*f*) A Siddhi devi.

Ishkrita (ईषक्रीता) (*m/f/n*) Arranged, set in order (from Rig Veda)

Ishma (ईश्म) (*m*) Spring, name of Kam Dv (God of love)

Ishrupa (ईश्रूप) (*m/f*) The first manifestation of divine power.

Ishta (ईष्ट) (*m/f*) Sought, wished, desired, cherished.

Ishtadev (इष्टदेव) (*m*) A favourite god, a chosen deity.

Ishtadevi (इष्टदेवी) (*f*) A favourite goddess, a chosen deity.

Ishtajan (इष्टजन) (*m*) A beloved person, man or woman

Ishtaka (ईष्टक) (*f*) Desirous, beloved, reverenced.

Ishtani (ईष्टाणि) (*m/f*) To be worshipped (R.V.).

Ishtātamā (ईष्टात्मा) (*m/f/n*) Dearest, most desired, beloved

Ishti (इष्टि) (*f*) Seeking, going after, wish, request, desird object. An oblation consisting of butter and fruit.

Ishtu (इष्टु) (*f*) Wish, desire.

Ishtva (इष्टवा) (*n*) Worshipped.

Ishudā (ईषुदा) (*f*) Name of a river.

Ishumati (ईषुमती) (*f*) Name of a river in Kurukshetra.

Ishurasa (ईशुरस) (*n*) The juice of the sugarcane, molasses

Ishuya (ईशुया) (*n*) To strive for, endeavour to obtain.

Ishva (ईश्व) (*m*) Spiritual teacher.

Ishvaku (इक्ष्वाकु) (*m*) Eldest son of Manu and founder of the Ishvaku dynasty.

Ishvar (ईश्वर) (*m*) God. A title of Shiva. Lord who rules the universe.

Ishvarchandra (ईश्वरचन्द्र) (*m*) The moon among gods. The suspreme Lord.

Ishvargita (ईश्वरगीता) (*f*) Song of the Lord. Kurma Puran which is devoted to Shiva as a supreme deity.

Ishwar (ईश्वर) (*m*) the same as Ishvar.

Ishya (ईष्य) (*m/f*) The spring season, effecting wishes.

Issakī (ईसाकी) (*f*) Name of a goddess in Kerala.

Itham (ईथम) (*v*) Endowed with such good qualities (Atharva Veda).

Ithimikā (ईथिमिका) (*f*) Name of a section of Kāthak recension of the Yajurveda.

Itkilā (इत्किला) (*f*) Name of a perfume.

J (ज, जा)

Jabāli/Javali (जबाली/जवाली) (*m*) A Brahman, priest of king Dasrath, who held sceptical philosophical opinion. He was a logician, belonging to Nyaya school of philosophy.

Jadorāy/Yadorāy (जदोराय/यदोराय) (*m*) An epithet of Lord Krishna.

Jagachandra (जगचन्द्रा) (*m*) The moon of the universe.

Jagaḍambā (जगदम्बा) (*f*) Mother of the world. Epithet of Durga emphasising her aspect as *the great mother.*

Jagad-dhātri (जगद्-धात्री) (*f*) Goddess Sarasvati. See Durga.

Jagadadijah (जगदादिजः) (*m*) The root of the world (V)

Jagad-dīp/Jagdip (जगद्-दीप/जगदीप) (*m*) World-illuminator.

Jagad-dīpā/Jagdipā (जगद्-दीपा/जगदीपा) (*m*) World-illuminator.

Jagadev (जगदेव) (*m*) Lord of the world.

Jagad-gaurī (जगत-गौरी) (*f*) Name of Mansā Devi (goddess)

Jagadgirī (जगतगिरि) (*f*) An epithet of goddess Durga.

Jagadguru (जगतगुरु) (*m*) An epithet of Shiva. The most holy and respectable person.

Jagadguruve (जगद्गुरुवे) (*m*) Spiritual teacher of the universe (R)

Jagadish (जगदीश) (*m*) Lord of the universe. (S)

Jagadishvar (जगदीश्वर) (*m*) Lord of the universe. (S)

Jagamohan (जगमोहन) (*m*) One who attracts the world. (K)

Jagan (जगन) (*m*) World, univers.

Jagan-mātṛi (जगन-मात्रि) (*f*) World mother. See Durga.

Jagan-nāth (जगन्-नाथ) (*m*) World-lord (Vishnu or Krishna).

Jagarati (जागरती) (*f*) Waking, vigilance

Jagat (जगत) (*m/f*) That which moves and alive.

Jagatahsetu/Jagatah-Setu (जगतःसेतु/जगतः-सेतु) (*m*) The bridge to go across this world. (V)

Jagati (जगती) (*f*) A living person of this earth.

Jagatpati (जगत्पति) (*m*) Lord of the world, a king, earth-lord.

Jagdambā (जगदम्बा) (*f*) The mother of the world. See Durga.

Jagdhātā (जगधाता) (*m*) An epithet of three gods (Brahma, Vishnu ans Shiva).

Jagdhoni (जगधोणि) (*f*) An epithet of of goddess, the earth.

Jagdish (जगदीश) (*m*) Lord of the universe.

Jagdishvar (जगदीश्वर) (*m*) Same as Jagdish.

Jagdishvari (जगदीश्वरी) (*f*) The supreme goddess.

Jagesh (जगेश) (*m*) Lord of the world (V)

Jagish (जगीश) (*m*) Lord of the world (V)

Jagjivan (जगजीवन) (*m*) A living person of this world.

Jagjoni (जगजोनि) (*m/f*) Creator of the world, the earth.

Jaguri (जगुरी) (*m/f*) Leading, conducting.

Jāhi (जाही) (*f*) A kind of fragrant flower like Jasmine.

Jahnavī (जाह्नवी) (*f*) An epithet of the river Ganges.

Jahnu (जह्नु) (*m*) A sage descended from Pururavas. He was disturbed in his devotion by the passage of the river Ganga, and consequently drank up its waters. He afterwards relented, and allowed the stream to issue from his ear, hence Gasnga is called Jāhnavi, daughter of Jahnu.

Jai (जय) (*m*) Conqueror. Another name of Indra.

Jaibhushan (जयभूषण) (*m*) Ornament of victory.

Jaichandra (जयचन्द्रा) (*m*) Moon of victory.

Jaidev (जयदेव) (*m*) Lord of victory.

Jaidurgā (जयदुर्गा) (*f*) Victorious Durga.

Jaigopāl (जयगोपाल) (*m*) Victorious Krishna.

Jailekhā (जयलेखा) (*f*) Garland of victory.

Jailekhā (जयलेखा) (*f*) Record of victory.

Jaikirti (जयकीर्ति) (*f*) Glory of victory.

Jaimālā (जयमाला) (*f*) Garland of victory.

Jaimini (जैमिनी) (*m*) A celebrated sage, a disciple of Vyas. He was also the founder or the Purva Mimansa Philosophy.

Jaiminiya (जैमिनीय) (*m/f/n*) Relating to or composed by Jaimini. See also Jaimini.

Jaiprabhā (जयप्रभा) (*f*) Light of victory.

Jaipriyā (जयप्रिया) (*f*) Beloved of victory.

Jairāj (जयराज) (*m*) Victorious king.

Jairām (जयराम) (*m*) Victorious Ram.

Jaisudhā (जयसुधा) (*f*) Nectar of victory.

Jaitra (जयत्र) (*m*) Symbolising victory. Lord Rama personifies victory in every respect. (R)

Jaivant (जयवंत) (*m*) Victorious, long lived.

Jaivanti (जयवंती) (*m*) Victorious, long lived.

Jalbhushan (जलभूषण) (*m*) Ornament of the water, Lotus.

Jaljāt (जलजात) (*m*) A lotus.

Jalpushpa (जलपुष्प) (*m*) Water lily.

Jalshāy (जलशाय) (*m*) An epithet of Lord Vishnu.

Jamadagani (जमदग्नि) A Brahman and a descendant of Brigu. He was the son of Richika and Satyavati, and was the father of five sons, the youngest and most renowned of whom was Parsu Ram.

Jambālinī (जम्बालिनी) (*f*) A river, lotus flower of a small size.

Jambhāri (जमभारी) (*f*) The thunderbolt, Indra, fire, the god Vishnu.

Jambvati (जंबवती) (*f*) Daughter of Jambvan married to Lord Krishna.

Jamunā (जमुना) (*f*) The river Jamuna.

Janak (जनक) (*m*) Father, procteator, originator. The King of Mithila of the Solar race and father of Sita.

Jānaki (जानकी) (*f*) A patronymic of Sita. (Wife of Rām)

Jānakivallabh (जानकीवल्लभ) (*m*) Consort of Jānaki (Sita). Sita who is born wombless, found by her father Janak while ploughing his field. (R)

Janamejya (जनमेजय) (*m*) A great king who was son of Parikshit, and great-grandson of Arjuna. It was to this king that Mahabharata was recited by Vaisampāyana.

Janana (जनान) (*m/f*) Creator, progenitor, coming into existence, race lineage.

Jananah (जनानह) (*m*) The origin of all beings (V)

Janārdana (जनार्दन) (*m*) Name of an aspect of Vishnu. Also epithet of Krishna. To whom one worship. The adored of mankind.

Jan-bāndhav (जन-बांधव) (*m*) Friend of mankind.

Janchakshu (जनचक्षु) (*m*) The sun.

Janchandra (जनचन्द्र) (*m*) Moon among men.

Jan-dev (जन-देव) (*m*) King, man-god.

Janeshwar (जनेश्वर) (*m*) Lord of all beings (V)

Janmajanmadi (जन्मजन्मदी) (*m*) The root cause of all beings' birth (V)

Janmālā (जनमाला) (*f*) Garland of men.

Janmamrityu-jaratigah (जन्ममृत्यु-जरातिगह) (*m*) Beyond life and death (V)

Janman (जनमन) (*m*) Lotus, water born

Jan-mohini (जन-मोहिनी) (*f*) Beloved of mankind.

Janpadi (जनपदी) (*f*) An apsara (heavenly nymph).

Janpriya (जनप्रिया) (*m/f*) Generally loved, loving to all, favourite of mankind.

Janrāj (जनराज) (*m*) King of mankind. Name of a man.

Jantu (जन्तु) (*m*) The eldest of the hundred sons of Somaka. Also the name of a son of Sudanwan.

Japani (जपनी) (*f*) Arosary for counting mantras (hymns).

Japmālā (जपमाला) (*f*) A rosary for counting prayers.

Jaradhishamanā (जरधीशमना) (*m*) Redeemer from afflictions. Lord Shiva redeems his devotees from decay and sorrow. (S)

Jaratkāru (जरत्कारु) (*m*) The Vyasa of the twenty-seventh Dwapara. An ancient sage who married a sister of the great Vasuki and was father of the sage Astika.

Jaritā (जरिता) (*f*) A certain female bird of the species called Sāringikā, whose story is told in the Mahabharata.

Jartār (जरतार) (*m*) Wire of gold or silver.

Jathārāgin (जथाराग्नि) (*m*) The name in a previous birth of the sage Agastya.

Jatilā (जतिला) (*f*) daughter of Gotama, who is mentioned in the Mahabharata as a virtuous woman. Gotama was the founder of the Nyaya school of philosophy.

Jatin (जतिन) (*m*) Having matted hair. The waters of river Ganga, flowing from Vishnu's feet, are intercepted by Lord Shiva, using His tendril locks to break the force of flow (S)

Japesh (जपेश) (*m*) Lord of recters. (S)

Jauhar (जौहर) (*m*) Precious stone, jewel, self sacrifice.

Javā (जवा) (*m/f/n*) Swiftness, speed, velocity

Javādhikā (जवाधिका) (*m/f/n*) Very fast

Javaki (जवाकि) (*f*) A kind of sweet singing bird.

Javishtha (जविस्ठा) (*m/f*) Very fast.

Jay (जै) (*f*) Conquest, victory, triumph. Jay is also a name of son of Indra, Yudhishthira and attendant of Vishnu and Arjuna.

Jayadev (जयदेव) (*m*) A poet and author of Gita Govinda (a lyrical poem on the early life of Krishna as Govinda the cowherd.).

Jayanta (जयन्त) (*m*) Name of a son of Indra

Jayanti (जयन्ती) (*f*) Victorious. Name of a goddess probably epithet of Durga. Also it means a flag. Birth anniversary, jubilee.

Jayāti (जयाति) (*f*) The metre created from the western mouth of Brahma along with the Sama Veda, the collection of hymns termed Saptadasa and the Aitaratra sacrifice.

Jayāye (जयायी) (*f*) Victorious. Goddess Durga represents the triumph of spirit over its obstacles. She is Shakti who destroys the variopus forcses of bondage. (D)

Jayadevi (जयदेवी) (*f*) Goddess of victory

Jayānandani (जयाननदनी) (*f*) Daughter of victory, daughter of Lakshmi.

Jayāni (जयानी) (*m/f*) Conqueror. Also name of a daighter of Indra (K)

Jayāntah (जयानतः) (*m*) The victor of the enemy (V)

Jay-Durgā (जय-दुर्गा) (*f*) Victorious Durga.

Jayendra (जयेन्द्र) (*m*) Lord of victory

Jayeshvar (जयेश्वर) (*m*) Lord of victory. (S)

Jayi (जयी) (*a*) Winner, victorious, conqueror.

Jayishnu (जयीष्णु) (*a*) One who conquers/achieves victory, ever victorious.

Jayishnu (जयीष्णु) (*m/f*) Victorious.

Jay-jay-vanti (जय-जय-वन्ति) (*f*) A musical note played in honour of victory.

Jaykārin (जयकारिण) (*m/f*) Gaining a victory.

Jay-lakshmi (जय-लक्ष्मी) (*f*) Goddess of victory.

Jaypāl (जयपाल) (*m*) Name of Brahma, Vishnu, a king.

Jay-shri-Jai-shri/Jai-sri (जय-श्री-जय-श्री/जय-श्री) (*f*) The goddess of victory.

Jeman (जेमन) (*m*) Victoriousness

Jenya (जेन्य) (*m/f*) Genuine person, noble orgin, true.

Jeta (जेत) (*m*) A natural victor (V)

Jetri (जीत्रि) (*m/f*) Conqueror, victorious, triumphant, gaining.

Jigishā (जिगिसा) (*f*) Desire of obtaining or gaining.

Jigīshti (जिगिष्ति) (*m/f*) Wishning to obtain or gain.

Jigishu (जिगीषु) (*m/f/n*) To obtain or gain (from Mahabharata)

Jigishutā (जिगिषुता) (*f*) Desire of excelling, ambition.

Jīmut (जीमूत) (*m*) sun, cloud, mountain.

Jinabhadra (जिनभद्र) (*m*) Rightly victorious.

Jinadev (जिनदेव) (*m*) Lord of victory.

Jināharsh (जिनाहर्ष) (*m*) Pleasure of victory.

Jinākirti (जिनाकीर्ति) (*m*) Fame of victory. A Jaina Suri.

Jināshā (जिनाशा) (*m/f*) Desire to know. Jinasha is the process of finding both source and object of knowledge.

Jinendra (जिनेन्द्र) (*m*) Name of Budha, a Jain saint.

Jinesh (जिनेश) (*m*) Lord of victory. Jaina Suri.

Jishnu (जिष्णु) (*m*) A name of Arjuna, victorious, the Sun, Indra, Vishnu.

Jit (जीत) (*f*) Victory, success.

Jitakrodha (जितक्रोध) (*m*) He who has subdued his anger (V&R)

Jitamanyu (जितमन्यु) (*m*) He who has subdued anger (V)

Jitamitrah (जितमित्रः) (*m*) Friend of the wicked's enemies (the gods) (V)

Jitavarshaye (जितवर्षये) (*m*) Conqueror of the ocean. (R)

Jitawati (जितवती) (*f*) Daughter of sage Ushinara.

Jitendra/Jitendriya (जितेन्द्र/जितेन्द्रिय) (*m*) in full control of one's senses, ascetic, virtuous person, Virtuous Indra.

Jiti (जीती) (*f*) Victory, gaining, obtaining.

Jitvan (जीतवन) (*m/f*) Victorious.

Jityā (जीत्या) (*m*) Victorious.

Jiv/Jivā (जीव/जीवा) (*m/f*) Living, existing, anything living in this world.

Jivaka (जीवक) (*m/n/f*) Living, alive, making a livelihood

Jivala (जीवल) (*m*) One of the charioteers of king Rituparna. He served under king nala.

Jivāditya (जीवादित्य) (*m*) The living sun.

Jival (जीवल) (*m/f*) Full of life.

Jivan (जीवन) (*m/f*) Giving life, enlivening.

Jivanah (जीवनाः) (*m*) The very life of all existences (V)

Jivapushpa (जीवपुष्प) (*f*) Flower of life.

Jivant (जीवन्त) (*m/f*) Long-lived, medicinal and edible plant.

Jivantā (जीवंता) (*f*) Life, mode of life.

Jivanti (जीवंति) (*f*) A medicinal creeper.

Jivantikā (जीवन्तिका) (*f*) Bestower of long life. Flower (Tinospora corolifolia)

Jivānuj (जीवानुज) (*m*) Name of the sage Gargacharya.

Jivapriya (जीवप्रिया) (*f*) Beloved of living beings.

Jivarāj (जीवराज) (*f*) Lord of life.

Jivaratna (जीवरत्न) (*f*) Gem of life.

Jivat (जीवत) (*m*) Spirit, courage, bravery, boldness.

Jivātu (जीवातु) (*f*) Life, life giving medicine.

Jiv-dātri (जीव-दात्री) (*f*) Life giver.

Jivikā (जीविका) (*f*) Living, life, maintenance, support.

Jiv-priya (जीव-प्रिया) (*m/f*) Dear as life.

Jivrā (जीवरा) (*m*) Life, souL

Jivri (जीवरी) (*f*) Same as Jivrā

Jiyāri (जीयारि) (*f*) Life, livelihood, courage, firmness of mind.

Jiyati (जीयति) (*f*) Life, spirit.

Jnārdan (जनार्दन) (*m*) An epithet of Lord Vishnu.

Jogeshvar (जोगेश्वर) (*m*) Lord Shiva, a devout yogi.

Jogindar (जोगिन्द्र) (*m*) An epithet of god Indra.

Jogu (जोगु) (*m/f*) Praising.

Johār (जोहार) (*f*) Salutation, obeisance.

Jojangandha (जोजनगन्ध) (*f*) Pleasing fragrance which can be sensed from nine miles. Another name of Satyavati, King Shantanu's second wife.

Josh (जोश) (*m/f*) Satisfaction, approval, pleasure.

Joshanā (जोशना) (*n*) Liking, choosing, approval, expression of satisfaction.

Joshikā (जोशिका) (*f*) A cluster of buds.

Joshya (जोश्य) (*f*) Delightful.

Joshitā (जोशिता) (*f*) Delightful, pleased.

Jugal (जुगल) (*m*) A pair. Same as Yugal.

Juhī (जूही) (*f*) A kind of Jasmine.

Juhoti (जुहोति) (*m/f*) Technical name of Hindu religious ceremonies.

Juhu (जुहू) (*f*) Goddess of speech and wife of Brahma.

Jumnotri (जुमनोत्री) (*f*) A sacred spot in the Himalaya mountains, near a junction of three streams.

Jush (जुश) (*m/f*) Liking, fond of.

Jushta (जुश्त) (*m*) Loved, liked, wished, worshipped propitious.

Jushti (जुश्ति) (*f*) Same as Jushta.

Jvālā (ज्वाला) (*f*) Flame, light, torch, shining brilliantly.

Jvālādevi (ज्वालादेवी) (*f*) A goddess whose place of worship is in Kangra (H.P.)

Juvas (जुवस) (*m/f*) Quickness (from Rig Veda)

Jvālitā (ज्वालिता) (*f*) Lighted, blazing, shining.

Jyeshtha (ज्येष्ठ) (*m*) The eldest among all (V)

Jyokti (ज्योक्ति) (*f*) Long life.

Jyoti (ज्योति) (*f*) Light, brilliance, splendour, sun sight.

Jyotih (ज्योतिः) (*m*) The supreme radiance (V)

Jyotindra (ज्यातीन्द्र) (*m*) Lord of light.

Jyotiprakāsh (ज्योतिप्रकाश) (*m*) Light of the flame.

Jyotirāditya (ज्योतिरादित्य) (*m*) The brilliant sun (V)

Jyotirganeshvar (ज्योतिरर्गणेश्वर) (*m*) Lord of luminaries (V)

Jyotis (ज्योतिष) (*n*) Light of the sun, brightness of the sky, light appearing in three worlds. Light as divine principle of life or source of intellegence.

Jyotishmati (ज्योतिष्मती) (*f*) The night illuminated by stars. Peaceful state of mind in Yoga philosophy.

Jyotishprabhā (ज्योतिषप्रभा) (*m/f*) Brilliant with light.

Jyotsnāpriyā (ज्योत्सनाप्रिया) (*f*) Beloved of the moon.

Jyotsnā/Jyotshna (ज्यात्सना/ज्योत्सना) (*f*) Moonlight.

Jyotsnākāli (ज्योतसनाकाली) (*f*) Daughter of chandra. She married Aditi's eldest son Surya.

Jyotsni (ज्योत्सनी) (*f*) Moonlight.

K (क, का)

Kabalikruta (कबलीक्राता) (*m*) Swallower of the Sun. Lord Hanuman, unaware of His stength, flew up to the sun and swallowed it till, at the request of the gods, He brought it out. (H)

Kabandhā (कबन्धा) (*m*) A pupil of the Muni Sumanta who became a teacher of the Samhitas of the Atharvaveda.

Kabir (कबीर) (*m*) A saint who tried to unite the Hindus and Muslims into a single monotheistic faith.

Kacha (कचा) (*m*) A son of Brihaspati. According to the Mahabharata he became a disciple of Shukra or Usanas, with the object of obtaining from him the mystic power of restoring the dead to life, a charm which Shukra alone possessed.

Kadali (कदली) (*m/f*) Plantation, banana - regarded as lucky fruit/tree and believed to be abode of Devi in North India.

Kādamba (कादम्ब) (*m/f*) The name of the tree that grows on Mount Mandara, the flowers of which are said to yield a spirit on distillation, whence Kadambari is one of the synonyms of spirituous liquor.

Kādambari (कादम्बरी) (*f*) A spirituous liquor, the goddess of learning, a female cuckoo. Name of a daughter of Chitra-ratha and Madirā. Her name has been given to a well known prose work, written by Van or Banbhatta in the seventieth century.

Kah (कह) (*m*) Embodiment of bliss (V)

Kāhan (काहन) (*n*) A Jay of Brahma (one thousand yugas). A yuga equivalent to 8,640 million years.

Kailāsh (कैलाश) (*m*) Name of amountain and residence of Shiva.

Kailāshdhipati (कैलाशधिपति) (*m*) Lord of Kailash (Mount Kailash) (S)

Kailashpati (कैलाशपति) (*m*) Lord of Kailash (Mount Kailash) (S)

Kaileshvari (कैलेश्वरी) (*f*) Goddess of water. Another name of Durga. (D)

Kaimshuka (कैमशुक) (*m/f*) Belonging to or coming from Kimshuka tree (Butea Frondosa).

Kaishav (कैशव) See Keshav

Kaivalya (कैवल्य) (*m/f*) The fourth chapter of the Yoga Sutras, being a treatise on the extatic abstraction or isolation of the soul.

Kajali (कजली) (*f*) A typical folk song sung during the rainy season.

Kajjal (कज्जल) (*m*) A cloud, lamp, black, collyrium.

Kākali (काकली) (*f*) A soft sweet sound, musical instrument, name of an Apsara (heavenly nymph).

Kakand (**ककन्द**) (*m*) Gold, Name of a king

Kākil (**काकिल**) (*m*) jewel worn upon the neck.

Kakkolika (**ककोलिका**) (*f*) A psecies of plant.

Kākshi (**काक्षि**) (*f*) Perfume, fragrant earth, of jungle.

Kakubhā (**ककुभा**) (*m/f*) Lofty, distinguished.

Kakud (**ककुद**) (*f*) One of the daughters of Daksha who was married to Dharma.

Kakuha (**ककुह**) (*m/f/n*) Lofty, high, great, eminent (from Rig Veda).

Kakummati/Kakumm-Mati (**ककुम्मती/ककुम्म-मती**) (*f*) Name of a metre in poetry.

Kāl (**काल**) (*m*) The measurem of all (V)

Kalā (**कला**) (*f*) A small part, a digit of the moon, an art, a division of time, craft, skill.

Kalakā (**कलका**) (*f*) A wife of Kashyap. Also a daughter of Daksha (creator).

Kalā-nāth (**कला-नाथ**) (*m*) The moon, lord of the digits, husband of Kalā.

Kalānāth (**कलानाथ**) (*m*) The moon, lord of the digit.

Kālanbha (**कालंभा**) (*m*) Controller of time. Another name of Lord Hanuman - illustrious son of Wind-God. (H)

Kalānidhi (**कलानिधि**) (*m*) Treasure of digits, arts, skills. Moon.

Kalanjra (**कलंजर**) (*m*) Name of a sacred mountain - to practice austere and devotion. Name of Shiva and Durga.

Kalāpriya (**कलाप्रिया**) (*m/f*) Lover of arts.

Kalāpurna (**कलापूर्ण**) (*m/f*) Prefect in arts. Moon.

Kalendu (**कलेन्दू**) (*m*) Digit of the moon.

Kalhan/Kahlan (**कलहन**) (*m*) Name of the illustrious scholar of Rajtarangini i.e. the history of Kashmir.

Kalī (**कली**) (*f*) a bud, a maiden who has yet to attain youth, an unblossomed maiden.

Kālicharan (**कालीचरन**) (*m*) Devotee of Kali.

Kālidās (**कालिदास**) (*m*) The greatest Sanskrit poet and dramatist of India. He was one of the 'nine gems' that adored the court of King Vikramaditya at Ujjain.

Kālikā (**कालिका**) (*f*) An epithet of Durga. A Kind of musical instrument. a bud.

Kalind (**कलिन्द**) (*m*) The sun, a mountain from which the Jamuna flows.

Kālindī (**कालिन्दी**) (*f*) A name of the river Yamuna as daughter of Kalind.

Kālinemiha (कालिनेमिः) (*m*) The slayer of the demon Kāli-nemi (V)

Kalinī (कालिनी) (*f*) Carrier of blossoms, watermelon, a vessel, red flower. Another name of river Yamnuna, wife of Krishna and daughter of Surya.

Kalki (कल्कि) (*m*) The tenth and last incarnation of Vishnu, which is yet to come. The white horse.

Kallālesh (कलालेश) (*m*) Name fo a God (Lakshmi-kant)

Kalmali (कल्मलि) (*m*) Splendour, brightness, sparkling.

Kalp/Kalpā (कल्प/कल्पा) (*m/f*) A day and night of Brahma. Also it means a ceremonial directory or rubric expressed in the form of Sutras.

Kalpalatā (कल्पलता) (*f*) A fabulous creeper granting all desires.

Kalpana (कल्पना) (*f*) Imagination, fiction, supposition, assumption.

Kalpesh (कल्पेष) (*m*) Lord of perfection

Kalya (कल्य) (*m/f*) Timely, reasonable, auspsicious, agreeable, pleasant.

Kalyān (कल्यान) (*m/f*) Beautiful, agreeable, noble, generous, virtuous, excellent, fortunate, lucky.

Kalyān-chār (कल्यान-चार) (*m/f*) Following virtuous courses.

Kalyān-Devī (कल्यान-देवी) (*f*) Virtuous Devi. Same as Kalyan and Devi.

Kalyānī (कल्याणी) (*f*) Excellent, prosperous, virtuous and lucky person.

Kalyānkā (कल्यानका) (*m/f*) Auspicious, prosperous, happy, efficacious.

Kalyānin (कल्याणीं) (*m/f*) Happy, lucky, auspicious, prosperous, virtuous.

Kalyāni-priya (कल्याणी-प्रिया) (*f*) An excellent woman, wife or beloved worthy of honour.

Kalyān-kirti (कल्याण-कीर्ति) (*m/f*) Having excellent reputation. See also Kalyān.

Kāmākshi (कामाक्षी) (*f*) Whose looks are amorous. Name of goddess who is regarded as a form of Shiva's Shakti.

Kamal (कमल) (*m*) A lotus flower and its plant.

Kamalā (कमला) (*f*) An excellent woman. An epithet of Lakshmi.

Kamlakānt (कमलकांत) (*m*) Beloved of Kamala (Lakshmi) (V)

Kamal-ākshan (कमल-अक्षण) (*m*) Lotus eyed. (S)

Kamalākshi (कमलक्ष्मी) (*f*) Lotus eyed.

Kamalesh (कमलेश) (*m*) Lord of Kamala (Lakshmi) (V)

Kamaldev (कमलदेव) (*m*) Lord of the lotus. (V)

Kamalesh (कमलेश) (*m*) Lord of Kamala (Lakshmi) (V)

Kamalinī (कमलिनी) (*f*) Small lotus.

Kamalnāth (कमलनाथ) (*m*) Lord of Kamala (another name of godess Lakshmi) (K)

Kamal-nayan (कमल-नयन) (*f*) Lotus eyes, i.e. having eyes, i.e. having eyes like the petals of lotus flower.

Kamal-netra (कमल-नेत्र) (*m/f/n*) Lotus eyed.

Kamalāpati (कमलापति) (*f*) Lord of Kamala. (V)

Kamalpatraksha (कमलपत्रक्ष) (*m*) Lotus eyed extremely beautiful Lord Krishna (K)

Kamalsambhavā (कमलसम्भव) (*f*) Emanating from the lotus - goddess Lakshmi (L)

Kāmam (कामं) (*m/f*) According to wish or desire. Freely, willingly (from Rig Veda)

Kāmaniya (कामनीया) (*m/f/n*) To be desired or wishes for. Lovely, pleasing, beautiful.

Kāmanī (कामनी) (*f*) The fine of passion, excessive passion. Loving woman.

Kamcharini (कामचारिनी) (*f*) Acting on one's own accord. Supreme omnipresence - goddss Durga. (D)

Kāmdev (कामदेव) (*m*) The god who fulfills all desires (V)

Kāmeshvari (कामेश्वरी) (*f*) One of the five idols of the goddess at Kamkhya.

Kāmi (कामी) (*m*) Whose desires are ever fulfilled (V)

Kāmika (कामिक) (*m/f*) Desired, wished.

Kāmin (कामिन) (*m/f*) Desirous, loving, wanton, amorous.

Kāminī (कामिनी) (*f*) Same as Kamin.

Kāmitā (कामिता) (*m/f*) Wished, desired, longing.

Kāmkrita (कामकृत) (*m*) Granter of his devotees wishes. (V)

Kamlā (कमला) (*f*) Same as Kamalā.

Kamlini (कमलिनी) (*f*) An assemblage of lotuses, a lotus plant.

Kāmnā (कामना) (*f*) Inclination, desire, lust, wish.

Kampal (कम्पल) (*m*) Satiator of all desires. (V)

Kāmpradāh (कामप्रदाह) (*m*) Bestower to his devotees their desired objects. (V)

Kāmrupine (कामरूपिनी) (*m*) Changing forms at will. Another name of Lord Hanuman. (H)

Kamsu (कम्सु) (*f*) Grantifying wishes, Another name of Rukimini.

Kāmuka (कामुक) (*m/f*) Desiring, wishing, loving.

Kāmya (काम्य) (*m/f*) Wish, desire, longing for or striving after, intention.

Kanād (कनाद) (*m*) The founder of the Vaisheshika system of Hindu philosophy.

Kanaka (कनक) (*n*) Gold (from Mahabharata) wheat, several other plants.

Kanakāngadi (कनकांगदी) (*m*) He who has a golden armlet (V)

Kanak-mālā (कनक-माला) (*f*) Garland of gold

Kanak-māyā (कनक-माया) (*f*) Made of gold, golden.

Kanak-muni (कनक-मुनि) (*m*) Name of Buddha

Kanak-prabhā (कनक-प्रभा) (*m/f/n*) Bright as gold

Kanak-pushpi (कनक-पुष्पी) (*f*) A species of Pandanus with yellow blossoms.

Kanak-sthali (कनक-स्थली) (*f*) A gold mine.

Kanankā (कनंका) (*f*) The pupil of the eye.

Kanchani (कंचनी) (*f*) Dancing girl.

Kanchān (कंचन) (*m*) Gold.

Kanchanbhā (कंचंभा) (*m*) Golden - hued body. Another name of Lord Hanuman (H)

Kanchanmālā (कंचनमाला) (*f*) Garland of gold.

Kanchanprabhā (कंचनप्रभा) (*f*) Shining or bright like gold.

Kanchar (कंचर) (*m*) The sun.

Kānchī (कांची) (*f*) one of the seven sacred cities (Kanjeveram).

Kandārshi (कंदार्शि) (*m*) A Rishi (sage) who teaches one particular kind or part of the Veda.

Kandurā (कंदुरा) (*f*) A kind of plant.

Kanganī (कंगनी) (*m*) A small bracelet.

Kāṇha (कान्हा) (*m*) Name of Lord Krishna

Kanhaiyā (कन्हैया) (*m*) A corrupt form of Krishna. Also it means a charming child or boy.

Kānī (कानी) (*f*) A girl, maiden.

Kanikā (कनिका) (*f*) An atom, a particle of (as of sand); grain, granule.

Kānīn (कानिन) (*m/f*) Young, youthful.

Kanishka (कनिष्क) (*m*) Name of a king of Kushana empire of Mathura in the 2nd century AD.

Kanishth (कनिष्ठ) (*a*) The youngest, junior most.

Kanishthikā (कनिष्ठिका) (*m*) The youngest, the little finger.

Kaniyās (कनियास) (*m/f/n*) Younger brother of sister.

Kanj (कंज) (*m*) A lotus, nector, the food of gods, name of Brahma.

Kanjaja (कंजज) (*m*) Lotus born. An epithet of Brahma.

Kanjana (कंजन) (*f*) God of love

Kanjlochan (कंजलोचन) (*m*) Lotus-eyed (K)

Kankara (कंकर) (*m*) Buttermilk mixed with water.

Kānkshā (कांक्षा) (*f*) Desire, longing, prosperity.

Kānkshi (कांक्षी) (*f*) A kind of fragrant earth.

Kānkshin (कांक्षिन) (m/*f*) Desiring, longing, expecting.

Kānnanā (कान्ना) (*m*) Name of Krishna in South India. A forest.

Kānt (कांत) (*m*) A loved, dear, pleasing, husband, the moon, spring, precious stone.

Kāntā (कांता) (*f*) Wife, sweetheart, beloved, lovely.

Kantair (कंतैर) (*m*) The creator, the master

Kāntāh (कांताः) (*m*) Very enchanting person, very beautiful (V)

Kāntāmani (कांतामणी) (*m*) Beauty incarnate. Lord Krishna stands out as one who has no comparison in beauty and form. (K)

Kanthaka (व.ठक) (*f*) An ornament for the neck.

Kanthdhara (कंठधर) (*f*) Holder of Shiva's neck. Goddess Durga held Lord Shiva's nech when He swallowed the poison, arresting the poison from descending further into His body. (D)

Kanthlatā (कंठलता) (*f*) Necklace, a collar.

Kanthmālā (कंठमाला) (*f*) Garland worn round throat. (F)

Kanthmani (कंठमणी) (*n*) A jewel worn on throat, dear or beloved object.

Kanth-nika (कंठ-निक) (*f*) Vina or Indian lute.

Kānth-shruti (कांथ-श्रुति) (*f*) Name of an Upanishad belonging to Atharva Veda.

Kānti (कांति) (*f*) Brilliance, charm, grace, loveliness, additional charm caused by love, desire, wish.

Kāntida (कांतिदा) (*m/f*) Giving beauty, beautifying, adoring.

Kantu (कंतु) (*m/f/n*) Love, the gold of love, the mind, heart.

Kantva (कंतव) (*n*) Happiness, prosperity.

Kanupriyā (कंनुप्रिया) (*f*) Beloved of Krishna (Radha)

Kanvaka (कंवक) (*m/f/n*) Pertaining to Kanwa/Kanva Rishi.

Kanvāyan (कन्वायन) (*m*) Descendant of Kanva Rishi

Kanviyā (कन्वया) (*m/f*) Relating to Kanva Rishi (sage).

Kanwā (कंवा) (*m*) Name of a Rishi to whom some hymns of the Rig Veda are ascribed, he is sometimes counted as one of the seven great Rishis. The sage who brought up Shakuntala as his daughter.

Kanyā (कन्या) (*f*) A girl, virgin, daughter.

Kanyābhāv (कन्याभाव) (*f*) Maidenhood, virginity.

Kanyakā (कन्यका) (*f*) Girl, virgin, maiden, daughter, smallest.

Kanyana (कन्यन) (*f*) Maiden, girl.

Kanya-shri (कन्या-श्री) (*n*) Maiden's fortune. See also Shri and Kanya.

Kanyā-Kumāri (कन्या-कुमारी) (*f*) The virgin damsel. A name of Durga

Kapali (कपलि) (*m*) Name of Shiva

Kapih (कपिह) (*m*) The Sun God. (V)

Kapil (कपिल) (*m*) Tawny-coloured Lord Ganesh is the god of wisdom and through wisdom alone can one reach salvation (G)

Kapilā (कपिला) (*f*) A gentle woman, white or grey, coloured cow.

Kapilah (कपिलाः) (*m*) The sage Kapil (V)

Kapildev (कपिलदेव) (*m*) Kapil means ancient sage (founder of Sankhya system of philosophy and Dev means God).

Kapindra (कपिन्द्रा) (*m*) Lord of monkeys (Shri Ram). (V)

Kapiratha (कपिरथ) (*m*) Name of Lord Ram and Arjuna.

Kapolā (कपोला) (*f*) Cheecks. There are six types of Kapola gestures in a dance.

Karadhuni (करधुनि) (*f*) A kind of musical instrusment.

Karam (करम) (*m*) Deed, action, any religious action or rites.

Karambhumī (करमभूमि) (*f*) The land of religious actions, i.e. Bharat-varsh (India).

Karambudhi (करमबुद्धि) (*f*) The mental organ of action.

Karam-chand (करम-चन्द) (*m*) Fate, destiny, luck. Chand means moon.

Karan (करन) (*m*) Doing, making, clever, skilful, a helper, companion.

Karanam (करनम) (*m*) The greatest means of creation (V)

Karavya (करव्या) (*m/f*) Relating to the singer. Name of certain verses of Atharva Veda.

Karanjīt (करनजीत) (*m*) The conqueror of Karan (name of Arjuna).

Karbhushan (करभूषण) (*n*) A hand ornament, bracelet.

Karikrata (करिकरत) (*m*) Name of one of the author's of Rig Veda.

Karira (करिर) (*m/f*) The shoot of a bamboo.

Karishma (करिश्मा) (*f*) Miracle.

Karkari (करकरी) (*f*) A kind of lute (from Rig Veda)

Karmālā (करमाला) (*f*) The hand used as a rosary in a dance.

Karmāli (करमाली) (*f*) An epithet of the Sun, full of rays.

Karmana (कर्मणा) (*m/f*) Action, performance (from Mahabharata) Action consisting in motion (Nyaya philosophy)

Karmānny (कर्मान्नी) (*a*) Industrious, hard working, active.

Karmatha (कर्मठ) (*m/f/n*) Capable of work, skilful or clever in work.

Karmika (कर्मिका) (*m/f*) Engaged in action. Name of a Buddhist philosophy school. Any variegated texture.

Karmodara (कर्मोदर) *(m/f)* Any honourable or valiant act.

Karmuka (कर्मुक) *(m/f)* Kind of honey. Efficacious as a medicine, a bamboo.

Karn (कर्ण) *(m)* An ear, helm, a name of a hero in the Mahabharata. He was regarded as a son Surya and Kunti, hence he was half-brother of Pandvas.

Karnikā (कर्णका) *(f)* Heart of a lotus. Creeper,

Karnphul (कर्णफूल) *(m)* An ornament worn in ear.

Karpāni (कर्पाणि) *(f)* Gladness

Kārshan (कर्षण) *(m/f)* Consisting of pearls or mother of pearls

Karta (कर्त) *(m)* One who is totally free to act (V)

Kartala (कर्तल) *(f)* Palm of the hand. There many palm gestures in a dance. Palm itching in India means that some money is coming to hand (a superstition in India).

Kartār (कर्तार) *(m)* The creator, the master.

Kartāri (कर्तारि) *(f)* Godly, righteous.

Karu (करु) *(m)* One who sings or praise, a poet (from Rig Veda). Name of a family of Rishis (holy men)

Karun (करुण) *(f)* Compassion, pity, pathos, tenderness of feelings.

Karunā (करुणा) *(f)* Pity, compassion, mercy, tenderness of feeling.

Karunāpursh (करुणापुरुष) *(m)* Giver of grace (K)

Karunesh (करुणेश) *(m)* Lord of mercy, another name of the moon.

Karuneshvar (करुणेश्वर) *(m)* Lord of mercy, another name of the moon.

Karunika (करुनीक) *(m/f)* Compassionate (from Mahabharata).

Karunikta (करुनीकत) *(f)* Compassion.

Karunya (करुण) *(m/f)* Compassion, kindness (from Mahabharata).

Karvi (कर्वी) *(f)* The leaf of the plant Asa foetida.

Kash (कश) *(m/f)* To shine, brilliant, to see clearly, visible, appearance.

Kāshi (काशी) *(f)* The modern Benares, shining, the sun.

Kashika (कशिक) *(m/f)* Coming from Kashi

Kashinath (काशीनाथ) *(m)* Lord of Kashi. (S)

Kashipati (काशीपति) *(m)* Lord of Kashi. (S)

Kashvi (कश्वि) *(f)* Shining, beautiful.

Kashyap (कश्यप) *(m)* Name of a celebrated sage to whom some Vedic hymns are attributed.

Kasturi (कस्तूरी) *(f)* Musk.

Katamb (कतम्ब) *(m)* A kind of musical instrument.

Kathā (कथा) (*f*) Speech, story, poetical composition.

Kathaka (कथक) (*m/f/n*) Relating, reciting, one who recites a st ory.

Katyayāna (कत्ययान) (*m*) An ancient writer of great celebrity, who came after panini, whose grammar he completed and corrected in what he called Varttika, (supplementary rules and annotations).

Katyayāni (कात्यायनी) (*f*) A name of goddess Durga.

Kaumudā (कुमुदा) (*f*) Moonlight, moonnshine (from its causing Kumudas to blossom)

Kaumodaki (कौमोदकि) The mace of Krishna, presented to him by Agni when engaged in fighting against Indira.

Kaumudi (कौमुदी) (*f*) Moonlight. Personified as wife of Chandra (moon).

Kaumudika (कौमुदिक) (*m/f/n*) Relating to water lilies.

Kauncha (कौंछ) (*m*) Name of a mountain (part of Himalayan range).

Kaunkuma (कौकुम) (*f*) Consisting of saffron

Kausambi (कौशाम्बी) (*f*) The capital of Vatsa (king of Udayan) near the junction of Ganges and Jamuna.

Kausuma (कौसुम) (*m/f*) Coming from or belonging to flowerws.

Kaushal (कौशल) (*f*) Skill, dexterity.

Kaushalyā (कौशल्य) (*f*) Belonging to the Kosala nation. There are several women known by this name. The wife of Dasrath and mother of Ram.

Kaushik (कौशिक) (*m*) An epithet of Indra. See Indra.

Kaustubha (कौस्तुभ) (*m*) A celebrated jewel obtained at the churning of the ocean and worn by Vishnu or Krishna. It represents consciousness, which manifests itself in all that shines, the sun, the moon, fire and speech.

Kautalya/Kautilya (कौटल्य/कौटिल्य) See Chanakya.

Kautiryā (कौटिर्य) (*f*) Name of goddess Durga - living in a hut (from Harivansh)

Kautuk (कौतुक) (*n*) Vehement desire, anything causing interest or admiration, festivity, festival, pleasure, happiness, prosperity. It is also a gesture in a dance.

Kautukitā (कौतुकिता) (*f*) Curiosity, desire, eagerness.

Kavash (कवश) (*m*) Son of ilusha and the author of several hymns in the tenth book of the Rig-Veda.

Kāveri (कावेरी) (*f*) A river in South India.

Kavi (कवि) (*m*) The poet who knows every thing (V)

Kavikā (कविका) (*f*) Poetess.

Kavindra (कविन्द्र) (*m*) Lord among poets.

Kavindu (कवीन्दु) (*m*) Moon among poets. Name of Valmiki

Kavi-Raj (कवि-राज) (*m*) Poet king. Author of the poem called Raghav-Pandaviyam.

Kavish (कवीश) (*m*) Lord of poets (G)

Kavishvar (कवीश्वर) (*m*) Lord of poets.

Kavita (कविता) (*f*) Poetry, a poem.

Kavitva (कवीत्व) (*n*) Intelligence (from Rig Veda)

Kāvya (काव्य) (*m/f*) Wise, poem. A class of deities associated with Angiras and Rikvan.

Kāvytā (काव्यता) (*f*) The wisdom of a sage.

Kayastha (कयस्थ) (*f*) A medicinal plant

Kedār (केदार) (*m*) A mountain, a meadow, a bason for water.

Kedār-nāth (केदार-नाथ) (*m*) A name of Shiva, Name of one of the twelve geat Lingas. It is a shapeless mass of stones at Kedār-nāth in the Himalayās

Keli (केली) (*m/f*) Play, sport, amorous sport, pastime, amusement.

Kelika (केलीक) (*m/f/n*) Sporting, sportive.

Keli-kamal (केली-कमल) (*n*) Lotus flower. Playing with:

Kesarisuta (केसरीसुता) (*m*) Son of Kesari. Lord Hanuman is the immensely powerful son of Kesari and Anjani (H)

Keshav (केशव) (*m*) Long haired. name of an aspect of Vishnu. Also an epithet of Krishna.

Keshiha (केशिहा) (*m*) Slayer of Keshi (V)

Ket (केत) (*m*) Desire, will, wealth.

Ketak (केतक) A name of a tree (Pandanus).

Ketaki (केतकी) (*f*) A tree, screw pine.

Ketan (केतन) (*m*) A house, a flag, a sign, an indispensable act.

Ketu (केतु) (*m*) Bright appearance, clearness, brightness, rays of light, flame.

Ketumālā (केतुमाला) (*m/f*) Name of son of Agnidhar. One of the nine great diviions of the known world. Garland of brightness.

Ketupriya (केतुप्रिय) (*f*) Beloved of brightness.

Ketya (केत्य) (*m/f*) To summon, call , invite.

Kevā (केवा) (*m*) Lotus, water, lily.

Keval (केवल) (*a*) Peculiar, sole, pure, alone, whole, absolute.

Kevalātman (केवलात्मन) (*m/f/n*) One whose nature is absolute unity.

Keval-gyan (केवल-ज्ञान) (*m*) Highest possible knowledge.

Kevalin (केवलिन) (*m/f*) Alone, one only, devoted to the doctrine of absolute unity of spirit.

Kevilā (केविला) (*f*) Name of a flower (commonly Kevera).

Keyur (केयुर) (*n*) Bracelet won on upper arm.

Khadhup (खधुप) (*n*) Air pervading perfume.

Khaganga (खगंगा) (*f*) Ganges of the heaven.

Khagola (खगोल) (*n*) Circle of heaven.

Khajal (खजल) (*n*) Air-water.

Khamurti (खमूर्ति) (*f*) A celestial body or person.

Khanak (खनक) (*f*) A jingle, click.

Khanda Parashu (खंदा परशु) (*m*) In the form of Parashuram, the exe holder (V)

Khatilaka (खतिलक) (*m*) Sky ornament, the sun.

Khushbu (खुशबू) (*f*) Fragrance, aroma, perfume, scent.

Khyāti (ख्याति) (*f*) Declaration, opinion, view, perception, knowledge (from Mahabharata)

Kim (किम) (*m*) Who is he - the question. Lord's (V)

Kimpal/Kimpala (किमपल/किमपल) (*m/f*) A kind of musical instrument.

Kimshukā (किमसुका) (*f*) Intellect tree (Celastrus paniculata). Small parrotg, parrot shaped.

Kinjal (किंजल) (*n*) The blossom.

Kinkani (किंकनि) (*f*) A small bell.

Kinshuk (किंशुक) (*m*) The tree Butea frondosa which bears beautiful flowers.

Kiran (किरन) (*m*) A ray or beam.

Kirat (किरत) (*m/f*) Scattering, spreading, pouring out.

Kirikā (किरिका) (*m/f*) Sparkling, beaming.

Kirit (किरित) (*m*) Shining like a sun. Very famous. Another name of Arjuna on whose head Indra had put a crown (Kirita) shining like the sun when he went to defend the Devas against the demons.

Kirnamaya (किरनमय) (*m*) Full of rays, consisting of rays, bnrilliant, enlightening.

Kirnamayi (किरनमयी) (*f*) Full of rays, consisting of rays, bnrilliant, enlightening.

Kirtan (कीर्तन) (*m*) Devotional singing, song.

Kirti (कीर्ति) (*f*) Reputation, fame, renown, glory.

Kirti-mālini (कीर्ति-मालिनी) (*f*) Garlanded with fame

Kirtimati (कीर्तिमती) Very famous, glory. wife of Anuha, daughter of Shuka, father of Brahmadatta.

Kirti-maya (कीर्ति-मय) (*m/f*) Consisting of fame

Kirtin (कीर्तिन) Crowned with a diadem. A title of Indra and also of Arjuna.

Kisalya (किसलय) (*m*) A sprout a young shoot, a side bud.

Kishalya (किशलय) The same as Kisalya.

Kishor (किशोर) (*a*) Adolescent, youthful, the sun.

Kishoraka (किशोरक) (*m/f*) Youthful, youths and girls.

Kishori (किशोरी) (*f*) A maiden, a young woman.

Kohal (कोहल) (*n*) Name of a Muni (seer) - inventor of drama. Speaking indistinctly, a sort of spirituous liquor, a kind of musical instrument.

Kohaliya (कोहलीय) (*n*) Name of Kohla's work on music. see also Kohala.

Kojagar (कोजगर) (*m*) A kind of festival on full moon night - celebrated in september - October with various games. Night is spent in honour of Goddess who promises. wealth to all those who were awake.

Kokil (कोकिल) (*f*) Indian Cuckoo, its cry is supposed to inspire love.

Kokila-devi (कोकिला-देवी) (*f*) Name of Goddess.

Kolaka (कोलक) (*n*) A kind of perfume. Alangium hexapetalum, Cordia Myxa.

Kolambaka (कोलम्बक) (*m/f*) The body of a lute.

Kolambi (कोलम्बी) (*f*) Lord Shiva's lute.

Koli (कोलि) (*f*) Jujube tree (Zizyphus jujuba)

Komal (कोमल) (*a*) Soft, tender, delicate, slender.

Komalāngā (कोमलांगा) (*f*) Having tender body.

Komalka (कोमल्क) (*m/f*) Fibrers of the stalk of lotus.

Komal-mālā (कोमल-माला) (*f*) Tender, charming, and pleasing garland.

Komaltā (कोमलता) (*f*) Softness, deliicacy, gently, tenderness.

Komasikā (कोमसिका) (*f*) Budding fruit.

Komya (कोम्य) (*m/f/n*) Polished, lovely (from Rig Veda).

Konalak (कोनलक) (*m*) A kind of aquatic bird.

Koraka (कोरक) (*m/f*) A bud, perfume, A berry containing a resinous and fragrant substance.

Korangi (कोरंगी) (*f*) Small cardmoms.

Koshansha (कोशंश) (*m*) A part of treasure, a portion of wealth.

Koshl (कोशल) See kaushil.

Koshpāl (कोशपाल) (*m*) A treasure garden.

Kotisuryaprabhā (कोटिसूर्यप्रभा) (*m*) Radiance of a crore suns. Lord Krishna is the splendour which is in the sun, and which illumines the whole world. (K)

Kramah (क्रमः) (*m*) The order setter (V)

Krānti (क्रांति) (*f*) A revolutionary.

Kratu (क्रत) (*m*) One of the Prajapatis (creator), and sometimes reckoned among the great rishis and spiritual sons of Brahma.

Kramah (क्रमः) (*m*) The order setter (V)

Kratuman (क्रतुमन) (*n*) Secrificial ceremony (from Rig Veda).

Kratumat (क्रतुमत) (*m/f*) Intelligent, prudent, wise, having power, vigorous.

Kratumaya (क्रमय) (*f*) Endowed with intelligence. (R.V)

Kripa (कृपा) (*m*) Son of sage Saradwat, and the adopted son of King Shantanu. He became one of the privy council at Hastinapur, and was also a teacher of Kauravas and Pandavas.

Kripajalnidhi/Kripa-Jalnidhi (कृपाजलनिधी/कृपा-जलनिधी) (*m*) Ocean of grace. (K)

Kripākaram (कृपाकर्म) (*m*) Who is merciful-Lord Ganesh. (G)

Kripālu (कृपालु) (*m/f/n*) Pitiful, compassionate.

Kripānil (कृपनील) (*m/f*) Pitiful, merciful, compassionate.

Kripā-sāgār (कृपा-सागर) (*m/f/n*) Ocean of compassion.

Kripi (कृपि) (*f*) Wife of Drona and mother of Aswathaman. Sister of Kripa or Kripacharya. The sage Saradwat or Gotama so alarmed Indra by his austerities that the god sent a nymph to tempt him. Though she was unsuccessful, two children were born to the sage in a tuft of grass. King Shantanu found them and brought up out of compassion (Kripā), whence their names, Kripa and Kripi. The children passed as Shantanu's own. The Vishnu Puran represents them as children of Satya-dhriti, grandson of Saradwat by the nymph Urvashi, and as being exposed in a clump of long grass.

Krishah (कृशाह) (*m*) Very light and thin (V)

Krishi (कृषि) (*f*) Harvest, agriculture.

Krishna/Krishan (कृष्ण/कृषण) Black. The name occurs in the Rig Veda, but without any relation to the great deity of later times. The earliest mention of Krishna, the son of Devaki, is in the Chhandogya Upanishad. The modern deity Krishna is the eighth Avatar or incarnation of Vishnu. He appears prominently in the Mahabharata and delivered the celebrated song, Bhagvad-gitā. In this work he distinctly declares himself to be the Supreme Being. He says:- "All this universe has been created by me; all things exist in me;" and Arjuna addresses Him as "the supreme universal spirit, the supreme dwelling, the eternal person, divine, prior to the gods, omnipresent. Krishna was of the Yadav race, being descended from Yadu, one of the sons of Yayāti. The history of Krishna's birth, as given in the Mahabharata is that Vishnu plucked out two of his own hairs, one white, the other black. These tow hairs entered the wombs of Rohini and Devaki; the white hair became blarām and the black (Krishna) hair (Kesh) became Krishna or Keshav. His reputed father, Vasudev, was brother of Kunti, the wife of Pandu, and so Krishna was cousin of the three elder Pandava princes. Krishna is an another name of Arjuna who was born of the same complexion as Krishna.

Krishna-Bhāgini (कृष्ण-भागिनी) *(f)* Auspicious, Lord Krishna's sister. Name of Goddess Durga.

Krishnadās (कृष्णदास) *(m)* Devotee of Lord Krishna.

Krishnagangā (कृष्णगंगा) *(f)* River of Lord Krishna

Krishnagata (कृष्णगेट) *(m/f/n)* Devoted to Lord Krishna.

Krishnakānt (कृष्णकांत) *(m)* Beloved of Krishna.

Krishnamitra (कृष्णमित्र) *(m/f)* Friends of Lord Krishna.

Krishnapinga (कृष्णपिंग) *(f)* Name of Goddess Durga.

Krishnapingaksha (कृष्णपिंगक्षा) *(m)* Black-yellowish-brown-eyed. The small eyes of Lord Ganesha radiate power, compassion, wisdom and love, is omnipotent and infinite. (G)

Krishnapushpa (कृष्णपुष्पा) *(m/f)* Lord Krishna's flower. Black-blossom.

Krishnashraya (कृष्णआश्रय) *(m)* Devotion to Lord Krishna.

Kritagam/Kritagamah (कृतगम/कृतगमह) *(m)* The creator of the Vedas. Author of all scriptures. (V)

Kritagya (कृतज्ञ) *(m)* Greateful to his devotees for devotion. (V)

Kritakarma (कृतकरम) *(m)* He who has done all that was due. (V)

Kritakrita (कृतकृत) *(m)* He who does action without cause. (V)

Kritanakrita (कृतन्नकृत) *(m)* He liberatesz when worshipped. (V)

Kritartha (कृर्तांथ) *(m/f)* One who has attained an object or end, successfu., satisfied. contented.

Kritatman (कृतत्मन) *(m/f)* One whose spirit was disciplined.

Kritbudhi (कृतबुद्धि) *(m/f/n)* Learned. wise. or formed mind.

Kriti (कृति) *(f)* A work of art, an artistic creation, The act of doing, performing, manufacturing, composing.

Kritiha (कृतिहा) *(m)* The motivating force in the being's efforts. (V)

Kritin (कृतिन) *(m/f/n)* expert, active, clever. skilful., learned, good, virtuous.

Kritindev (कृतिनदेव) *(m)* Supreme God.

Kritindevi (कृतिनदेवी) *(f)* Clever, skilful goddess.

Kritinmālā (कृतिनमाला) *(f)* Good garland.

Kritinmāntā (कृतिनमानता) *(f)* Clever, honourable. virtuous, learned opinion.

Kritinmohani (कृतिनमोहनी) (*f*) Clever, virtuous woman.

Kritkarij/Kritharija (कृतकरीज/कृतकरीज) (*m/f*) One who has obitained his object.

Kritmangal (कृतमंगल) (*n*) Blessed, consecratd.

Kritomkār (कृतोमकार) (*m/f*) One who has pronounced a holy syllable OM.

Kritnu (कृत्नु) (*m/f*) Skiful, clever, artist, artificer, mechanic.

Kritpriya (कृतप्रिया) (*m/f/n*) One who has been favoured or pleased.

Kritya (कृतय) (*m/f/n*) Performed, practicable, feasible.

Kriya (क्रिया) (*f*) Work, performance, action.

Kshama (क्षमा) (*f*) Forgiveness. Embodimentment of gorgiveness-goddess Durga. (D)

Kshamah (क्षमाह) (*m*) Competent, capable of quelling all disorders. (V)

Kshamakaram (क्षमाकर्म) (*m*) Abode of forgiveness. (G)

Kshama Mandal (क्षमा मंडल) (*m/f*) The whole earth.

Kshaminah Varah (क्षामिनाः वराह) (*m*) Best among those who forgives. (V)

Kshantā (क्षांता) (*f*) The earth.

Ksharām (क्षराम) (*m*) Causing decay in physical entities or the decadent (V)

Kshema (क्षेम) (*f*) Safety, welfare, peace,

Kshemkrita (क्षेमकृत) (*m*) The protector of the shelter seekers. (V)

Kshetragya (क्षेत्रग्य) (*m*) He who knows all about the body and its nature (V)

Kshipra (क्षिप्र) (*m*) Quick acting (G)

Kshirjā (क्षिरजा) (*f*) An epithet of the goddess Lakshmi.

Kshirod (क्षिरोद) (*m*) The sea of milk.

Kshitesha (क्षितेश) (*m*) Master of earth (V)

Kshobhan (क्षोभन) (*m*) On who agitates being and nature before creation (V)

Kubera (कुबेर) (*n*) Treasure of the gods. As the chief of the Yakshas, he lived on the top of Gandhamadana mountain which was prohibited to humans. Bhim in search of a divine lotus flower to please Draupadi reached there and Kubera blessed him and all the Pandavas.

Kuchaka (कुचक) (*f*) The milky juice of a bulbous plant.

Kukubh (कुकुभ) (*f*) Peak, summit, region or quarter of the heaven.

Kukud (कुकुद) (*m/f*) Peak, summit, chief, head.

Kukut (कुकुत) (*m*) Same as Kukud.

Kulāmbā (कुलांबा) (*f*) Family deity. See also Amba

Kulānand (कुलानन्द) (*m*) The joy of his family.

Kulānandi (कुलानन्दी) (*f*) The joy of his family.

Kulānganā (कुलांगना) (*f*) A respectable or virtuopus woman.

Kulapida (कुलपीद) (*m*) The glory of a family.

Kulbālikā (कुलबालिका) (*f*) A virtuous high-born woman.

Kulbhāva (कुलभाव) (*m/f/n*) Born in a noble family.

Kuldipak (कुलदीपक) (*m*) Glory of the whole world.

Kuleshvar (कुलेश्वर) (*m*) The Lord or chief of a family.

Kulbhushan (कुलभूषण) (*m/f*) Family-adoring, family-ornament.

Kulika (कुलिक) (*m/f*) Of good family. Chief or head person of a guild.

Kulin (कुलीन) (*m/f*) Belonging to a noble family, eminent descent.

Kulnandan (कुलनन्दन) A gladdening or doing honour to a family.

Kulpāli (कुलपालि) (*f*) Virtuous woman, family protectress.

Kul-pradip (कुल-प्रदीप) (*m*) Lamp, light or glory of a family.

Kulvant/Kulwant (कुलवंत/कुलवंत) (*a*) A noble birth, of a noble family.

Kulvardhini (कुलवर्धिनी) (*f*) Developer of the race. Goddess Durga as ultimate power and ruler of the universe - is the progenitor, the sustainer and protector of all the races.

Kulyā (कुल्या) (*f*) Virtuous, well born, respectable.

Kulyoshit (कुल्योशित) (*f*) A virtuous high born woman.

Kumārī (कुमारी) The damsel. An epithet of Sita, also of Durga.

Kumarikā (कुमारिका) (*f*) Maiden, the Jasmine flower. Another name of Durga and Sita.

Kumbha (कुम्भ) (*m*) The pitcher of existence (V)

Kumkum (कुमकुम) (*f*) Saffron or turmeric or turmeric red powder.

Kumud (कुमुद) (*m*) The white water lily, red lotus, a name of Vishnu.

Kumudah (कुमुदह) (*m*) The delighter of the earth. (V)

Kumudesh (कुमुदेश) (*m*) Lord of the white water lily. Another name of the moon.

Kumudinī (कुमुदिनी) (*f*) A lily flower as Kumud. A place full of lotuses.

Kumud-maya (कुमुद-मय) (*m/f*) Consisting of white lotus flowers.

Kumudnāth (कुमुदनाथ) (*m*) The moon.

Kumudpati (कुमुदपति) (*m*) The moon.

Kumud-vati (कुमुद-वती) (*f*) An assemblage of white lotus flowers.

Kunāl (कुनाल) (*m*) A kind of bird, sweet, elegant, graceful. name of a son of Ashok (Emperor of India).

Kunchika (कुंचिक) (*m/f*) Bamboo shoots. Lord Shiva used Kunchika as an adornment on his body (from Skanda Puran)

Kunda (कुन्द) (*m/f*) A kind of Jasmine (fragrent oleander)

Kundah (कुंदः) (*m*) The donor of the earth to sage Kashyapa (V)

Kundali (कुण्डली) (*m*) The wearer of the ear rings as bright as the sun (V)

Kundalin (कुण्डलीं) (*m*) Having earrings. The eternal being, Lord Shiva. (S)

Kundan (कुन्दन) (*m/f*) Purified and glittering gold.

Kundarah (कुनदराह) (*m*) Penetrator of the earth to kill Hirnyaksha (V)

Kundini (कुन्दिनी) (*f*) An assemblage of Jasmine.

Kundīr (कुन्दीर) (*m/f*) Strong, powerful.

Kundmālā (कुन्दमाला) (*f*) Garland of Jasmine (fragrant oleander)

Kuni (कुनी) (*m*) Name of a tree; author of a Dharmashastra. Name of a son of Satyaki—a great Yadav who was a long life friend of Krishna and Arjuna.

Kunj (कुंज) (*m*) A bower, an armour, ivory.

Kunsha (कुंश) (*m*) Shining, speaking.

Kunshi (कुंशी) (*f*) Shining, speaking.

Kuntal (कुंतल) (*m*) The hair, plough. A particular head-dress. Goddess Lakshmi.

Kuntī (कुंती) (*f*) Also called Prithā and Pārshnī. Daughter of the Yādavaprince Sura, king of Surasenas, whose capital was Mathura. She was a wife of Pandu, and the mother of Yudhishthira, Bhima and Arjuna and who were called Pandavas.

Kunti-bhoj (कुन्ती-भोज) (*m*) King of the people called Kuntis. the adoptive father of Kunti. Kuntibhoj had no children of his own and received Sura/Shura's first born child Prutha (Kunti) whom he brought up as Kunti.

Kush (कुश) (*m*) One of the twin sons of Rama and Sita. After the death of Ram, his two sons Kush and Lav became kings of the southern and northern Koshalas and Kush built Kush-sthali or Kushavati in the Vindhyas and made it his capital. Kush also means a sort of sacrificial grass.

Kushal (कुशल) (*m/f*) Right, proper, suitable, good, healthy, prosperous.

Kushali (कुशली) (*f*) To make right or proper arrangement.

Kushalin (कुशलीन) (*m/f*) Healthy, well, prosperous, auspicious, favourable, virtuous, clever.

Kushaltā (कुशलता) (*f*) Cleverness, ability, skilful, friendly.

Kushikā (कुशिका) (*m*) A king who, according to some, was the father of Vishvamitra, or according to others, the first of the race of Kusikas from the Gadhi, the father of Vishvamitra, descended.

Kushilvā (कुशिल्वा) (*m*) A poet, actor, singer, an epithet of Valmiki (original writer of Ramayana in Sanskrit).

Kush-ketu (कुश-केतु) (*m*) Name of god Brahma.

Kuslai (कुसलाई) (*f*) Skilful, expertness, welfare.

Kustum (कुस्तुम) (*m*) An epithet of Vishnu. The ocean.

Kustumbari (कुस्तुम्बरी) (*f*) The plant coriander.

Kusum (कुशुम) (*f*) Bloom, a plant with yellow flowers, a fruit.

Kusumanjali (कुसुमंजली) (*f*) A handful of flowers offered by Hindus to gods in worship.

Kusumb (कुसुम्ब) (*m*) A large Indian tree.

Kusumbhi (कुसुम्भि) (*a*) Of red colour.

Kusumlatā (कुसुमलता) (*f*) A creeper in blossom.

Kusumavali (कुसुमवली) (*m/f*) Name of a medicinal work.

Kusumaya (कुसुमय) (*n*) To produce flowers, to furnish with flowers.

Kusum-vichitra (कुसुम-विचित्र) (*m/f*) Having various flowers.

Kutuhal (कुतूहल) (*n*) Eagerness, curiosity. In a dance to be impatient to see a thing of beauty is called Kutuhal.

Kuval (कुवल) (*m*) The water lily, a pearl.

Kuvalayinī (कुवलयिनी) (*f*) The lotus plant.

Kuvaleshya (कुवलेश्य) (*m*) He who reposes on the serpent's coil in water (V)

Kuvalya (कुवलय) (*m*) The blue water lily, the earth.

Kuvam (कुवम) (*m*) Producer of the earth. Another name of the sun.

L (ल, ला)

Labuki (लबुकि) (*f*) A kind of lute.

Lāghav (लाघव) (*m/f*) Swiftness, rapidity, speed.

Lājvantī (लाजवन्ती) (*f*) A typical sensitive plant, bashful, shy, blushing woman.

Lajjā (लज्जा) (*f*) A shakti (the wife or the female energy of a deity, but especially of Shiva.) Shame, modesty, bashfulness.

Lakini (लेकिनी) (*f*) Name of a Tantra goddess.

Laksh (लक्ष) (*m*) Perceive, observe, mark, sign target, aim.

Lakshak (लक्षक) (*m/f*) Indicating, hinting, expressing.

Lakshaki (लक्षकि) (*f*) Name of Sitā (wife of Ram)

Lakshan (लक्षन) (*m/f*) Same as lakshak.

Lakshanā (लक्षणा) (*f*) Aim, object, view. Name of an\ Apsara (nymph of heaven).

Lakshī (लक्षि) (*m/f*) To make a mark or object, aim or point or look at.

Lakshin (लक्षिन) (*m/f*) Auspicious mark.

Lakshman (लक्षमन) (*m*) Son of King Dasrath by his wife Sumitra. He was the twin brother of Shatrugan, and the half brother and especial friend of Rāma Chandra or Lord Rāma. Under the peculiar circumstances of his birth, one-eghth part of the divinity of Vishnu became manifest in him. But according to Adhyatma Ramayana, he was an incarnation of Sesha/ Sesha Nag (king of serpent race or Nagas, and of the infernal regions called Pātāla.)

Lakshmi (लक्ष्मी) (*f*) Goddess of wealth and prosperity and spouse of Lord Vishnu. Name of women symbolising prosperity. The word occurs in the Rig Veda with the sense of good fortune. Other names of lakshmi are Hira, Indira, Jaladhijā (ocean born), Chanchalā or Lolā, (the fickle) as goddess of fortune, Loka-māta (mother of the world). The Vishnu Purana says that her first birth was the daughter of Bhrigu and Khyati. It was at a subsequent period that she was produced from the sea at the churning of the ocean. When Hari was born as dwarf, Lakshmi appeared from a lotus (as Padma or Kamla). When he was born as dwarf, Lakshmi appeared from a lotus (as Padma or Kamla). When he was born as Parsu Ram, she was Dharani. When he was Ram Chandra, she was Sita. And when he was Krishna she became **Rukmini**.

Lakshmichandra (लक्ष्मीचन्द्र) (*m*) The moon of Lakshmi (V)

Lakshmidev (लक्ष्मीदेव) (*m*) Lord of Lakshmi (V)

Lakshmikānt (लक्ष्मीकांत) (*m*) Another name of Vishnu. A beloved of lakshmi

Lakshmipati (लक्ष्मीपति) (*m*) Another name of Vishnu.

Lakshmivān (लक्ष्मीवान) (*m*) Trasure of wealth, or Goddess of Lakshmi (V)

Lakshmi-vasati (लक्ष्मी-वसति) (*f*) Abode of Lakshmi. Name of the lotus flower

Lalān (ललां) (*m/f*) Sporting, playing, coruscating (as light or colour).

Lālimā (लालिमा) (*f*) Redness, ruddiness, lipstick, rouge.

Lalit (ललित) (*a*) Pretty, sweet, elegant, graceful.

Lalitā (ललिता) (*f*) Name of goddess Durga. Graceful amorous gestures of a woman.

Lalitmohan (ललितमोहन) (*m*) Handsome, attractive. (K)

Lalitya (ललित्य) (*f*) Loveliness, charm, beauty

Lambodra (लमबोदर) (*m*) Huge-bellied Ganesh is the symbol of the three worlds (G)

Lapita (लपित) (*f*) A female bird in whose favour sage Mandapala was reborn as a male bird.

Lashva (लश्व) (*m*) Actor, dancer.

Lāsya (लास्य) (*f*) Dance (especially accompanied with instrumental music and singing).

Latā (लता) (*f*) A creeper, vine, name of a daughter of Meru and wife of Ilāvrtā.

Latikā (लतिका) (*f*) A creeper, vine.

Lauhit (लौहित) (*m*) Trident of Shiva.

Lav (लव) (*m*) A very small division of time, particle: A name of one of the twin sons of Rama and Sita. He reigned at Sarāsvatī.

Lavali (लवली) (*f*) A kind of metre. Name of a woman.

Lavalina (लवलिन) (*f*) Absorbed, engrossed.

Lavanika (लवणिका) (*m/f*) Charming, lovely, dealing in salt.

Lavanya (लावण्य) (*m*) Charm, beauty, loveliness, pleasing, graceful.

Lavalina (लवलिना) (*m*) A smallest particle imaginable. Very small quantity.

Layputri (लयपुत्री) (*f*) Daughter of musical time, actress, dancer.

Lekhā (लेखा) (*f*) A line, a stroke, painting, border, calculation, an estimation.

Lekhrāj (लेखराज) (*m*) Supreme being. Lord of the gods.

Lilā (लीला) (*f*) Sport, manner, amorous sport.

Lilākamal (लीलाकंमल) (*m/f*) Women's toy-lotus.

Lilārati (लीलारती) (*f*) Sportive amusement

Lilāvatī (लीलावत्ती) (*f*) Charming, most beautiful.

Limni (लीमनी) (*f*) Manuscript of the gods.

Linā (लीना) (*a*) Absorbed, devoted, grace.

Lipikā (लिपिका) (*f*) Alphabet, manuscript, writing, anointing.

Lipkar (लिपकर) (*m*) A writer.

Lipsā (लिप्सा) (*f*) The desire to gain, wishing to acquire or obtain, longing for.

Lochan (लोचन) (*m*) Eye illuminating, brightening.

Lochanā (लोचना) (*f*) Illuminating, brightening, Buddhist goddess.

Lohitāksha (लोहताक्ष) (*m*) The red-eyed (V)

Lohmukti (लोहमुक्ति) (*f*) A kind of precious stone.

Lohmuktikā (लोहमुक्तिका) (*f*) A Ared pearl

Lohpushpā (लोहपुष्पा) (*m/f*) Bearing red flowers, flowering.

Lokabandhu (लोकबन्धु) (*m*) Friend of the people (V).

Lokandhipā (लोकन्धिपा) (*m*) Lord of the world.

Lokadhipati (लोधिपति) (*m*) Lord of the world

Lokādi (लोकादि) (*m*) Creator of the world. Another name of Brahma.

Lokādhyaksha (लोकाध्यक्ष) (*m*) Master of all realms (V)

Lokakriti (लोककृति) (*m*) Creator of the three worlds. (S)

Lokana (लोकन) (*m/f*) The act of looking, seeing, viewing.

Lokanāth (लोकनाथ) (*m*) Master of the people (V)

Lokaniya (लोकनीय) (*m/f*) To be seen or perceived, visible, worthy of being looked at.

Lokankarā (लोकंकरा) (*m*) Creator of the world. Lord Shiva for creation, maintenance and dissolution, manifests Himself in the three forms of Brahma, Vishnu and Mahesh. (S)

Lokasaranga (लोकसरंग) (*m*) He who's the essence of the world. (V)

Lokaswāmi (लोकस्वामी) (*m*) Master of all realms (V)

Lokata (लोकता) (*m*) Being possessed of one's world.

Lokatryashraya (लोकत्रयश्रय) (*m*) The support for all the three realms (V)

Lokdhārini (लोकधारिनी) (*f*) Name of earth.

Lokdhātri (लोकधात्री) (*m*) Creator of the world (Name of Lord Shiva from Mahabharata)

Lokesh (लोकेश) (*m*) Lord of the world

Lokgāthā (लोकगाथा) (*f*) A verse of song.

Lokin (लोकिन) (*m/f/n*) Possessing a world, possessing the best world. Inhabaitants of the universe.

Lokitā (लोकिता) (*m/f/n*) Seen, beheld, viewed.

Lokjit (लोकजीत) (*m/f/n*) Winning or conquering the world.

Lokkānt (लोककांत) (*m/f*) Loved, liked by every one, pleasing to all (from Mahabharata)

Lokkārtarī/Lok-Kārtari (लोककार्तरी/लोक-कार्तरी) (*f*) World creator.

Lok-mātrī (लोक-मात्री) (*f*) Mother of universe - goddess Lakshmi (L)

Loknāth (लोकनाथ) (*m*) Lord of the world (Brahma, Vishnu, Mahesh)

Lokokti (लोकोक्ति) (*f*) People's talk, proverbs

Lokpāl (लोकपाल) (*m*) A world protector, guardian of the world.

Lokpujya (लोकपूज्य) (*m*) Worshipped by the universe. Another name of Lord Hanuman (H)

Lokshokvinashan/Lok-shok-vinashan (लोकशोविनाषन/लोक-शोक-विनाषन) (*f*) Remover of universal agonies-goddess Lakshmi. (L)

Lokya (लोकय) (*m/f*) Granting a free sphere of action, bestowing freedom, heavenly.

Lokyn (लोकय्न) (*m/f*) Granting a free sphere of action, bestowing freedom, heavenly.

Lolākshi (लोलाक्षि) (*f*) A shakti (wife or female energy of a deity, but especially of Shiva).

Loma Harshana/Roma Harshana (लोमा हर्षन/रोम हर्षन) (*m*) A bard or panegyrist who first gave forth the Puranas.

Lomash (लोमेश) (*m*) A great sage who was a great friend of Pandavas. He accompanied five Pandavas to various places of pilgrimage and at each place he told them about the great sages who had lived earlier.

Lushāti (लुशती) (*f*) To adore, decorate.

M (म, मा)

Machukunda (मचुकुन्द) (*m*) A great king of ancient time whose story is mentioned in the Mahabharata.

Madan (मदन) (*m*) The god of love, the spring season, the Indian cuckoo.

Madanmohan (मदनमोहन) (*m*) An epithet of Lord Ram. Also a name of Krishna.

Madanpāl (मदनपाल) (*m*) Lord of love.

Madanripu (मदनरिपु) (*m*) An epithet of Lord Shiva.

Madayanti (मदयन्ती) (*f*) Wife of king of Saudasa (King of Solar race).

Mādhava (माधव) (*m*) Descendant of madhu, the Lord of knowledge. A name of an aspect of Vishnu. Also an epithet of Krishna. The spring Season.

Mādhavdās (माधवदास) (*m*) Devotee of Krishna.

Mādhavdeva (माधवदेव) (*m*) Divine Krishna

Mādhavi (माधवी) (*f*) A name of Lakshmi (goddes of wealth and prosperity). A sacred basil, a kind of spirituous liquor.

Madhu (मधु) (*m/f*) Sweet, charming, pleasant, delightful, the juice or nector of flowers.

Madhubālā (मधुवाला) (*m*) Sweet and beautiful maiden.

Madhubhuj (मधुभुज) (*m/f*) Enjoying sweetness or gladness.

Madhudān (मधुदान) (*m/f*) Pouring out sweetness.

Madhudhārā (मधुधारा) (*f*) A stream of honey or sweet intoxicating drink.

Madhujā (मधुजा) (*f*) The earth.

Madhuji (मधुजी) (*m*) Vishnu. See Vishnu

Madhujit (मधुजीत) (*m*) Conqueror of honey (Madhu (V&K)

Madhuka (मधुक) (*m/f*) Honey coloured, sweet, melodious.

Madhukulyā (मधुकुल्या) (*f*) A stream of honey.

Madhulā (मधुला) (*m/f*) Spirituous liquour, a mango tree.

Madhumādhavi (मधुमाधवी) (*f*) Spring flower abounding in honey.

Madhumālā (मधुमाला) (*f*) A string of honey, a garland of sweet things.

madhumati (मधुमती) (*f*) Charming worship. See also Madhu and Mati.

Madhumita (मधुमित) (*f*) Sweet/honest friend

Madhupa (मधुप) (*m/f*) Drinking sweetness, honey drinker.

Madhupriyā (मधुप्रिया) (*m*) Fond of nectar/honey.

Madhupushpa (मधुपुंष्प) (*f*) Spring flower, sweet flower. The Ashoka/tree.

Madhur (मधुर) (*a*) Sweet, melodious, pleasant, agreeable.

Madhurākriti/Madhur-ākriti (मधुरआकृति/मधुर-आकृति) (*m*) Pleasant looking (K)

Madhuratā (मधुरता) (*f*) Sweetness, pleasantness, softness, amiability.

Mādhuri (माधुरी) (*f*) Sweetness, pleasantness, most beautiful.

Madhurilatā (माधुरीलता) (*f*) Vine of sweetness.

Madhurimā (मधुरिमा) (*f*) Sweetness, harmoniousness, melodiousness,

Madhuripu (मधुरिपु) (*m*) An epithet of Krishna.

Mādhury (माधुर्य) (*f*) Meaning the same as mādhurī.

Madhushā (मधुशा) (*m/f*) Dropping of sweetness, abounding in sweetness.

Madhushrī (मधुश्री) (*f*) Queen of vasant ritu (spring season). Vernal beauty.

Madhusudan (मधुसूदन) (*m*) Slayer of madhu.A name of Krishna.

Madhuvanti (मधुवन्ती) (*f*) Endowed with hney/nectar. Name of a classical Raga.

Mādhvī (माधवी) (*f*) Meaning the same as mādhavī

Madhuvidyā (मधुविद्या) (*f*) Endowed with great knowledge.

Mādhvikā (माधविका) (*f*) A creeper which yields fragrant flowers.

Madhyatapini/Madhya-Tapini (मध्यतापिनी/मध्य-तापिनी) (*f*) Name of an Upanishad.

Madravati (मद्रावती) (*f*) Wife of king Parikshit. Mother of king Janmejaya.

Mādri (माद्री) (*f*) A sister of the king of Madras and second wife of Pandu, to whom she bore twin-sons (Nakul and Sahdev). A species of plant.

Madrikā (मद्रिका) (*f*) Madrā (woman of Madras).

Madrivijay (माद्रिविजय) (*f*) Wife of Sahadeva. Mother of Suhotra.

Madugha (मदुघा) (*m*) Name of a plant yielding honey or a species of liquorice (from Atharva Veda)

Madvan (मादवन) (*m/f*) Addicted to joy, gladdening, intoxicating.

Mahābal (महाबल) (*n*) Very strong. Name of Lord Shiva's attendants and Ganesh (G)

Mahābalah (महाबलः) (*m*) Supremely powerful (V)

Mahābali (महाबली) (*m*) Very strong. Bālī is also called mahābali. during his reign the world was like a heaven and every one was praising him in all the three worlds. People in Kerala state of India still celebrate the reign of Mahābali by a celebration named Onam.

Mahābhāg (महाभाग) (*m*) Extremely fortunate (V)

Mahābhav/Mahābhava (महाभव/महाभवा) (*m/f*) Great might, mighty, high, minded, noble, generous.

Mahābhog (महाभोग) (*m*) The great enjoyer. (V)

Mahābhish (महाभिष) (*m*) A great king of the Ishwaku dynasty who had attained heaven. In his second birth he was king Shantanu who married Ganga who gave birth to Bhishma.

Mahābhog (महाभोग) (*m*) The great enjoyer (V)

Mahāchandra (महाचन्द्र) (*m*) Great moon.

Mahāchārya (महाचार्य) (*m*) Great teacher, instructor.

Mahāchit (महाचित) (*f*) Great intelligence

Mahādev (महादेव) (*m*) The great god. An epithet os Shiva.

Mahādevi (महादेवी) (*f*) A mother goddess; a name of Lalitā (goddess Durga).

Mahādhana (महाधन) (*m*) Extremely rich (V)

Madadyut (महादयुत) (*m*) Most radiant. Another name of Lord Hanuman. (H)

Mahadyuti (महादयुती) (*m*) Supremely radiant. (V&S)

Mahaganpati (महागणपती) (*m*) The omnipotent and all powerful. (G)

Mahāgartā (महाग्रता) (*m*) A great reacess (of illusion or Maya) (V)

Mahāgauri (महागौरी) (*f*) One of the nine forms of goddess Durga. See Devi.

Mahagit (महागीत) (*m*) Great singer (V)

Mahajyoti (महाज्योति) (*f*) Great light, splendou, sun light.

Mahājyotish (महाज्योतिष) (*m*) Great light, sun light, splendour. (S)

Mahākalā (महाकला) (*f*) The night of the new moon.

Mahākānt (महाकांत) (*m*) Very pleasing, name of Shiva.

Mahākratu (महाक्रतु) (*m*) Embodiment of great sacrifice. (V)

Mahākarma (महाकर्म) (*m*) Performer of great deeds. (V)

Mahākaya (महाकय) (*m*) Gigantic. Another name of hanuman (H)

Mahākirti (महाकीर्ति) (*m/f*) Of illustrious fame.

Mahākosha (महाकोश) (*m*) One with great treasure. (V)

Mahākrama (मह्राकर्मा) (*m*) Performer of great feats (V)

Mahāksha (महाक्षा) (*m*) The wide eyed (V)

Mahāmakha (महामखा) (*m*) Making great sacrifice in which offering is made to Him (V)

Mahālakshmi (महालक्ष्मी) (*f*) Great goddess. Mother of Brahma, Vishnu and Shiva.

Mahāmālā (महामाला) (*f*) Wearing a great garland.

Mahāmanah (महामनाः) (*m*) he who accomplaished anything by merely thinking about it. (V0

Mahāmani (महामणि) (*m*) Costly gem (S)

Mahāmati (महामती) (*m/f/n*) Very clever, great understanding, planet jupiter.

Mahāmāyah (महामायाः) (*m*) The great illusor (V&S)

Mahāmukshi (महामुक्षी) (*f*) A devi. See Devi.

Mahāmukhi (महामुखी) (*f*) a mind-born mother.

Mahān (महान्) (*m*) The great (V)

Mahānidhi (महानिधि) (*m*) The grand abode of all (V&S)

Mahāniya (महानिया) (*n*) Honoured, praiseworthy, illustrious, glorious.

Mahāpadam (महापदम) (*m*) The great lotus, Indian lotus. Another name of Narada

Mahāpunya (महापुन्य) (*f*) Extremely auspicious, purifying, beautiful.

Mahārāja (महाराजा) (*m*) The great king. Buddhist divine being.

Mahārājni (महाराजनी) (*f*) A name of Lalitā (godd.·; Durga)

Mahāratn (महारत्न) (*m/f*) Most precious jewel. .

Maharhah (महारहाह) (*m*) Adorable (V)

Mahāridhi (महारिद्धि) (*m*) Having great glory (V)

Maharishi Kapilacharya (महाऋषि कपिलाचार्य) (*m*) The propounder of the Sankhya philosophy (the sage Kapil) (V)

Mahārūp (महारुप) (*m*) Extremely beautiful, great in form (S)

Maharūpā (महारूपा) (*f*) Extremely beautiful, great in form

Mahās (महास) (*n*) Greatness, might, power, glory.

Mahāsaukhya (महासौख्य) (*m/f/n*) He who has a great thorn (as the boar) (V)

Mahāshakti (महाशक्ति) (*m*) Supremely powerful (V&S)

Mahāsuri (महासुरी) (*f*) A mind-born mothe.

Mahāsvanah (महाश्वनाः) (*m*) One with great voice (V)

Mahat (महत) (*n*) The great intellect produced at the creation.

Mahātapase (महातपसे) (*m*) Great meditator - another name of Lord Hanuman (H)

Mahātejah (महातेज) (*m*) The radiance of the radiant (V)

Mahātejas/Mahatejase (महातेजस/महातेजसे) (*m/f/n*) Of great splendour, of great majesty, (said of Gods and men). Full of fire. Most radiant./ Another name of Lord hanuman (H)

Mahātmane (महात्मने) (*m*) Supreme being. Another name of Lord Hanuman (H)

Mahāvāni (महावाणी) (*f*) Great voice. Epithet of Saraswati (the river goddess—bestower of fertility, power and wealth).

Mahāvidyā (महाविद्या) (*f*) A name of Lalitā; symbolical of Devi. See lalitā and Devi.

Mahāvir (महावीर) (*a*) Having tremendous valour, extemely valorous, gallant. Lord Mahavir (the twenty-fourth Tirthankara of the Jains).

Mahāvirya (महावीर्य) (*m*) Supremely valorous (V)

Mahejyah (महेजयः) (*m*) Most adorable (among all deities) (V)

Mahendra (महेन्द्र) (*m*) The great Indra or Vishnu. Name of a younger brother of Ashok (who carried the Buddhist doctrine into Sri Lanka. One of the seven mountain ranges which runs from Gondwana to Orissa in India).

Mahendrapāl (महेन्द्रपाल) (*m*) Protected by Lord of Lords

Mahesh (महेश) (*m*) Lord Shiva.

Maheshān (महेशान) (*m*) Name of Shiva.

Maheshvar/Maheshwar (महेश्वर/महेश्वर) (*m*) A name of Lord Shiva.

Maheshvaram (महेशवरम्) (*m*) Lord of the Universe (G)

Maheshvari (महेश्वरी) (*f*) A Shakti and a mother goddess Lalita (Goddess Durga)

Maheshvasa (महेश्वसा) (*m*) Wielder of a great bow (V)

Mahi (मही) (*f*) The earth, the great world.

Mahibharata (महिभारत) (*m*) The giver of food to earth (V)

Mahikā (महिका) (*f*) Mist, frost

Mahimā (महिमा) (*f*) Exaltation, greatness, dignity, majesty, imporance.

Mahin (महिन) (*m/f*) Great, mighty, sovereignty.

Māhin (माहिन) (*a*) respected, advanced

Mahināth (महिनाथ) (*m*) The earth lord. Earth protector, a king.

Mahiputri (महिपुत्री) (*f*) Daughter of the earth. Another name of Sita.

Mahir (माहिर) (*m*) The Sun.

Mahish (महिश) (*m/f*) Great, powerful, the Sun.

Mahishī (महिशी) (*f*) The chief queen. Same as Mahish.

Mahitra (महित्र) (*m/m*) Name of a hymn in Rig Veda.

Mahiyā (महिया) (*f*) To be joyous or happy, to prosper, to be exalted

Mahiyu (महियु) (*m/f/n*) Joyous, happy (from Rig Veda)

Mahodadhishaya (महोदधिशय) (*m*) He who reposes in the grand ocean even during the paralay-time agitation and disturbance (V)

Mahodara (महोदर) (*m*) Mighty powerful. Very generous. (R)

Mahodaya (महोदय) (*m*) Great fortune or prosperity

Mahonnati (महोन्नती) (*f*) High rank or position, great elevation.

Mahorāga (महोरागा) (*m*) The Great Serpent (Vasuki) (V)

Mahotsaha (महोत्साह) (*m*) Ever enthusiastic to create, sustain and dissolute the world. (V)

Maina (मैना) (*m*) Gana (messengers of god).

Maināk (मैनाक) (*m*) A son of Himāvat and Menā;the brother of Ganga and Parvati.

Mairāl (मैराल) (*m*) Name of a mythical being.

Maithali (मैथली) (*f*) Sita (wife of Lord Ram)

Maitrata (मैत्रता) (*m/f*) Friendship, benevolence.

Maitraka (मैत्रक) (*m/f*) Friendship. Also a person who worships in a Buddhist temple.

Maitreyi (मित्रेयि) (*f*) Wife of Rishi Yajnawalkya, who was indoctrinated by her husband in the mysteries of religion and philosophy.

Maitri (मैत्री) (*f*) A daughter of Daksha and a wife of Dharm; mother of Prasāda. Friendship, good will, benevolence, equality.

Maitribālā (मैत्रीबाला) (*m/f*) Whose strength is benevolence. Name of a king regarded as an incarnation of Lord Buddha.

Makil (मकिल) (*m*) The moon.

Makrand (मक्रन्द) (*m*) Honey, the juice of flowers.

Makshu (मक्षु) (*m/f*) Name of a man in Vedas. Very quick and prompt in everything.

Makul (मकुल) (*m*) A bud.

Makur (मकुर) (*m*) A mirror.

Mālā (माला) (*f*) Garland symbolic of triumph; garland put by the bride round the neck of the bride-groom.

Mālādevi (मालादेवी) (*f*) Goddess of garland. A form of Lakshmi worshipped in Madhyapradesh (India).

Mālati (मालती) (*m*) The queen of Ashvapati and mother of Savitri.

Mālāvat (मालावत) (*m/f*) Garlanded, crowned, having a garland.

Malaya (मलय) (*m*) Sandalwood tree, fragrance. A mountain in South India.

Malaydhvaj (मलयध्वज) (*m*) A great king who fought on the side of Pandavas in the Mahabharata war.

Mālini (मालिनी) (*f*) Surrounded with a garland (mālā) of champā tree. A Shakti, a mind born mother

Mallikā (मल्लिका) (*f*) Fragrant, flower recembling the Jasmine.

Mālopamā (मालोपमा) (*f*) Garlands of smiles.

Mālti (मालती) (*f*) A kind of creeper that yields very sweet smelling flowers.

Maltika (मलतिका) (*f*) Made of Jasmine bud.

Mamta (ममता) (*f*) Self-interest; pride, affection, attachment. The sense of owing or being one with something or somebody.

Mamti (मम्ती) (*f*) Affectionate, loving, name of a disciple of Gautama and a devotee of Shiva.

Manad (मनद) (*m*) A great warrior, son of Dhrishtadyumna. He fought on the side of Pandavas in the Mahabharata war.

Manadah (मानदाह) (*m*) Bestowing honour to His devotees (V)

Manavdev (मानवदेव) (*m*) God among men. King, prince.

Manan (मानां) (*m*) Meditation, contemplation, brooding, pondering.

Manas (मानस) (*m*) Name of a Rishi. Intellect, intelligence, perception, charity.

Manasā (मनसा) (*f*) Name of a goddess.

Mānav (मानव) (*m*) A man (of Manu). See Manu.

Manavas (मानवास) (*m*) Twelve sons of Brahmā

Manavdev (मानवदेव) (*m*) God among men. King, prince.

Manavendra (मानवेन्द्र) (*m*) A king, great man.

Mānāvi (मानावी) (*m*) Manu'swife. See Manu,

Mānaviya (मानवीय) (*m/f/n*) Descended or derived from Manu. See also Manu.

Manayitri (मनयित्री) (*m/n/f*) One who honours or respects.

Manchitā (मन्चिता) (*m/f*) Desired, thought of.

Mandāk (मंदक) (*m/f*) Praising, praise, a strearn, current.

Mandākini (मंदाकिनी) (*f*) The Ganges; celestial Ganges which flows through Kedarnath.

Mandār (मंदार) (*m*) The coral tree, (etythrina Indica). Name of a fine heavenly tree. Also a name of a mountain used by gods for churning the ocean.

Māndavi (मांडवी) (*f*) A goddess enshrined at māndavya. Also a name of Sita and wife of Ram's brother Bharat.

Mandita (मंदित) (*m/f*) Adomed, decorated.

Manditri (मंदित्री) (*m/f*) Adorning, one who adorns.

Mandu (मंदु) (*m/f*) Pleasant, agreeable, charming, cheerful.

Mandukeya (मंदुकेय) (*m*) A teacher of the Rig Veda, who derived his knowledge from his father Indra-Paramati.

Mandukya (मंदुक्य) (*n*) Name of Upanishad (esoteric doctrine). The third division of the Vedas attached to the Brahmana portion. They are of later date than the Brahmanas and are about 150 of these works. Brahmans are works composed by the Brahmans for the use of Vedic hymns.

Mangal (मंगल) (*m*) The planet Mars, identified with Kartikeya, the god of war. Mangal also means lucky, bliss, festivity.

Mangalā (मंगला) (*f*) A servant Maid of Parvati (wife of god Shiva)

Mangalchandidi/Mangal-Chandidi (मंगलचांदीदी/मंगल-चांदीदी) (*f*) Name of Goddess Durga.

Mangalgiri (मंगलगिरी) (*m*) Mountain of fortune.

Mangaliya (मंगलिया) (*m/f/n*) Meaning the same as Mangalaya.

Mangalam Param (मंगलम् परम) (*m*) Supremely auspicious (V)

Mangalpradā/Mangal-Pradā (मंगलप्रदा/मंगल-प्ररदा) (*m/f*) Bestowing welfare

Manhan (मन्हन्) (*m/f*) Gift, present, promptly, readily, willingly.

Manhāyu (मंहायु) (*m/f*) Liberal, wishing to give.

Manhishtha (मंहिश्थ) (*m/f/n*) Granting most abundantly, liberal, generous, very rich or bountiful. One whose gifts are bountiful.

Mani/Maniva (मनि/मनिव) (*m*) Jewel, gem, pearl.

Manibhā (मनिभा) (*f*) Jewel-splendour.

Manibhu (मणिभु) (*f*) A floor inlaid with jewels.

Manichā (मनिचा) (*m/f*) A flower, pearl

Manidip (मनिदीप) (*m*) A lamp having jewels instead of a wick

Manijalā (मनिजला) (*f*) Having jewel like water.

Mānik (मानिक) (*m*) A ruby. A jewel, jem.

Mānikā (मानिका) (*f*) A ruby.

Manikanth (मणिकंठ) (*m*) The blu jade.

Manikya (मणिकय) (*n*) A ruby.

Manimanjari (मणिमंजरी) (*f*) Rows of jewels

Manimāla (मणिमाला) (*f*) Necklace of jewels, lustre, beauty.

Manimat (मणिमत्) (*m/f*) Adorned with Jewels. The Sun.

Manimaya (मणिमय) (*m/f*) Formed or consisting of jewels.

Manindra (मणीन्द्र) (*m*) Tje diamond. Chief of jewels.

Manirāj (मणिराज) (*m*) King of jewels.

Maniratna (मणिरत्न) (*m/f*) Jewel, jem, garland of jewels.

Manisar (मनिसर) (*m*) String or ornament of jewels.

Manishankar (मनिशंकर) (*m*) Lord Shiva with jewels.

Manishi (मनीषी) (*f*) Beloved of heart or desired by heart.

Manivar (मणिवार) (*m/f*) Best jewel.

Manishā (मनरषा) (*f*) Wisdom, intelligence, conception, thought, consideration. A wise and thoughtful person.

Manita (मनिता) (*m/f/n*) Honoured, respected, showing honour or resperect.

Manivek (मनिवेक) (*m*) A most excellent jewel.

Manjari (मंजरी) (*f*) Flower, a new shoot, a creeper, a cluster of flowers.

Manjiman (मंजिमन) (*m*) Beauty, elegance.

Manju (मंजु) (*a*) Beautiful, pretty, comely, lovely.

Manjudev (मंजुदेव) (*m*) Lord of beauty.

Manjugir (मंजुगीर) (*m/f/n*) Sweet voiced.

Manojava (मनोजव) (*m*) Traveller with the speed of mind (V)

Manjukeshi (मनजुकिशी) (*m*) An epithet of Lord Krishna.

Manjul (मंजुल) (*a*) The same meaning as Manju.

Manjulatā (मंजुलता) (*f*) Vine of beauty.

Manjumani (मंजुमणि) (*m/f*) Beautiful gem, a topaz.

Manjulata (मंजुलता) (*f*) Vine of beauty.

Manjumani (मंजुमणि) (*m/f*) Beautiful gem.

Manjumati (मंजुमती) (*m*) A beautiful princess.

Manjunāsī (मंजुनासी) (*f*) A beautiful woman. Name of Indra's wife or goddess Durga.

Manjusha (मंजूषा) (*f*) A casket, box, chest.

Manjutra (मंजुत्र) (*f*) Most beautiful or charming.

Mankanaka (मंकनक) (*m*) A sage who lived at the confluence of seven tributaries of Sarasvati river. His story is mentioned in Mahabharata.

Mankush (मंकुश) (*m*) A person who knows singing and dancing.

Manmath (मनमैथ) (*m*) The god of love.

Manmohini (मनमोहिनी) (*f*) Attracting the heart.

Manobhavā (मनोभवा) (*f*) Apsaras (the name given to the nymphs of heaven created by Brahma).

Manogavi (मनोगवी) (*f*) Wish, desire.

Manohar (मनोहर) (*a*) Lovely, comely, charming, alluring, captivating.

Manohartā (मनोहर्ता) (*f*) Same as Manohar.

Manoj (मनोज) (*a*) Lovely, handsome, beautiful. An epithet of love-god.

Manojava (मनोजव) (*m*) Treaveller with the speed of mind. (V)

Manojavaya (मनोजवय) (*m*) Speed like wind - Hanuman (H)

Manoju (मनोजु) (*m/f*) Swift as thought.

Manojyoti (मनोज्योति) (*m/f*) One whose light is the intellect.

Manomaya (मनोमय) (*m*) Conqueror of one's heart - Lord Ganesh (G)

Manomohini (मनोमोहिनी) (*f*) Attracting the heart.

Manorāg (मनोराग) (*m*) Affection, passion of the heart.

Manoramā (मनोरमा) (*f*) Lovely, pretty, charming attractive.

Manosiddhi (मनोसिद्धि) (*f*) One who controls mind and attains desires. A goddess.

Manotri (मनोत्री) (*m*) An inventor, discoverer, disposer, manager.

Manpriya (मनप्रिया) (*m/f*) Dear to the heart.

Mānsi (मानसी) Mental, spiritual.

Māntā (मानता) (*f*) Opinion, respect, honour, honouring one's Dharma or principles.

Mantra (मंत्र) (*m*) Comprehended by hymns of Rig, Sam and Yajur Vedas (V)

Mantu (मन्तु) (*m/f*) Adviser, manager, disposer, ruler, advice, counsel, intellect,.

Manu (मनु) (*m*) Thinking, wise,, intelligent, man par excellence and father of the human race.
Manu (From the root man, to think). This name belongs to fourteen mythological progenitors of manking and rulers of the earth, each of whom holds sway for the period called a Manwantara, (the age of Manu). Manu is also a name of a sage, the author of Dharmasastra (code of Hindu laws).

Manuj (मनुज) (*m*) A man.

Manujā (मनुजा) (*f*) Daughter of man.

Manukal (मनुकल) (*n*) The whole period of fourteen Manus.

Manurāj (मनुराज) (*m*) King of men

Mānushi (मानुषी) (*f*) woman or a human pertaining or befitting a human being.

Manuti/Manoti (मनुति/मनोति) (*f*) An assurance, a vow, to worship a deity after the fulfilment of a desire.

Mānvi (मानवी) (*f*) Descended from Manu.

Mānya (मान्य) (*m*) Respectable for every one. (v)

Manyanti (मन्यती) (*f*) Honourable, the daughter of Agni Manyu.

Mārg/Margah (मार्ग/मार्गः) (*m*) The ultimate path of salvation (V)

Māricha (मारिचा) (*m*) The author of a Purāna (an ancient legend of a tale of olden times according to Hindu mythology).

Mārichi (मारिची) (*m*) Chief of the Maruts (storm gods, who hold a very prominent position in the Veads and are represented as friends of Indra.) Name of one of the Prajapatis (Lord of creatures). He married Kala. the daughter of Kardama Rishi. He was father of Kashyapa—one of seven great Rishis.

Mārishā (मारिषा) (*f*) Daughter of sage Kandu, and wife of Prachectasas (ancient sage and law giver). She is also known as the daughter of wind and moon.

Mārkandeya (मारकंडेया) (*m*) A sage, the son of Mrikanda, and reputed author of the Mārkandeya Purāna. He was remarkable for his austerities and is called 'the long lived'

Mārkat (मारकाट) (*n*) An emerald.

Mārtand (मार्तण्ड) (*m*) The sun. Also a place of pilgrimage in Kashmir.

Mārut (मारुत) (*m*) the air-god, air, wind.

Marutātmaja/Marut-ātmaja (मरुतात्मजा/मरुतं-आत्मजा) (*m*) Most beloved like gems - Hanuman. (H)

Māruti (मारुती) (*m*) A name of Hanuman and Bhim. See also Hanumān and Bhim.

Marutta (मरुत्त) (*m*) A descendant of Manu. He was a Chakravarti, or universal monarch.

Maryādā (मर्यादा) (*f*) Limit exclusive, boundary mark. It is of two kinds relating to time and space.

Mātali (मातली) (*m*) Name of the charioteer of Indra. A divine being. He also drove Arjuna's chariot and showed him various celestial places.

Mati (मति) (*f*) Devotion, prayer, worship, hymn, sacred, utterance, resolution, wish, desire, thought.

Matimālā (मातिमाला) (*f*) Prayer string/garland

Matimānd (मतिमान्द) (*a*) Wise, intelligent.

Matipriya (मतिप्रिया) (*f*) Dear to talent, prayer. See also Mati and Priya.

Matsya (मत्स्य) (*m*) The fish. The fifth incarnation of Vishnu. The object of the incarnation was to save, the seventh Manu, and progenitor of the human race from destruction by deluge.

Mauli (मौलि) (*m*) The crown of the head, diadem, summit, best, foremost, most outstanding.

Māyā (माया) (*f*) Illusion personified as a female from of celestial origin, created for the purpose of beguiling some individual. Sometimes identified with Durgā as the source of spells. In this character she is Māyā-devī or Mahāmāyā.

Māyāni (मायाणि) (*m*) llusion. Veiled by His divine Maya, He is not revealed to all. (K)

Māyank (मयंक) (*m*) The moon.

Māyāvati (मायावती) (*f*) See Māyā.

Māyil (मायिल) (*m*) Peacock.

Mayuri (मयूरी) (*f*) Female peacock.

Medanipati (मेदनीपति) (*m*) The Lord of Earth (V)

Medhā (मेधा) (*f*) Wisdom, intelligence, very good memory.

Medhajah (मेधजाः) (*m*) He who Manifests Himself through Yagya (V)

Medhāvi (मेधावी) (*m*) Son of sage Baladhi. His story is mentioned in the Mahabharata.

Medhir (मेधिर) (*f*) Intelligence, prudence, wisdom.

Medin (मेडिन) (*m/f/n*) Possessing vigour or energy. A friend. companion.

Medini/Maidini (मेदिनी/मैदिनी) (*f*) The earth, a kind of musical instrument.

Medur (मेदुर) (*m/f*) Smooth, soft, a medicinal plant.

Meghashyāmal/Megha-shyāmal (मेघश्यामल/मेघा-श्यामल) (*m*) Cloud tinted (K)

Meghrāj (मेघराज) (*m*) Lord of the clouds (V)

Melā (मेला) (*f*) An association, assembly, societh, fair, a musical scale.

Melāpaka (मेलापक) (*m*) Uniting, bringing together. Conjunction of planets.

Menā/Menakā (मेना/मेनका) (*f*) In the Rig Veda, a daughter of a great king. In the Puranas, wife of Himavat and mother of Uma and Gangā. Also a name of an Apsara sent to seduce the sage Vishwamitra from his devotions, and succecing in this object, she became the mother of the nymph

Menajā (मेनजा) (*f*) Daughter f Mena. Another name of Parvati. See also Mena.

Meru (मेरु) (*m*) A fabulous mountain in the centre of the earth, on which is situated the heaven of Indra, containing the city of gods and the habitation of celestial spirits.

Meru Prabhā (मेरु प्रभा) (*n*) Shining like Meru mountain.

Mikikā (मिकीका) (*f*) Mist, snow, fragrance.

Minā (मीना) (*f*) A gem, a goblet of wine, a fish.

Mimānsā (मीमांसा) (*f*) Profound through, consideration, examination, discussion.

Mitā (मीता) (*m/f/n*) Fixed, founded, established (from Rig Veda).

Mitābhashini (मीताभषिनी) (*m*) Seldom speaks. Another name of Lord Rama. (R)

Mitī (मीति) (*f*) Fixing, erecting, establishing (from Rig Veda).

Modak (मोदक) (*m/f*) Gladdening, exhilarating, sweetmeat, gratifying.

Modakī (मोदकी) (*f*) Pleasing, delighting, a sweetmeat

Minākshī (मीनाक्षी) (*f*) Species of soma plant. Name of a daughter of Kubera. A deity worshipped in Madura slso called Mināchī.

Mīrā (मीरा) (*m*) the sea, ocean, a limit, boundary, drink, beverage, chieftan.

Mirābāi (मीराबाई) (*f*) Hindi poetic and mystic (AD 1450-1447). A Rajput princess of Chitor and to have married the Rānā of Udaipur. Her devotional lyric mainly about Krishna, are very popular in India.

Mīrāmirā (मीरामीरा) (*f*) A name of a woman.

Mitā (मीता) (*m/f/n*) Fixed, founded, established (from Rig Veda)

Mitābhashini (मिताभाषिनी) (*m*) Seldom speaks. Another name of Lord Rama (R)

Mithun (मिथुन) (*m/f*) In the Rig Veda it means paired, forming a pair, any couple. In later times it means pairing or copulation.

Miti (मिति) (*f*) Fixing, erecting, establishing (from Rig Veda)

Modak (मोदक) (*m/f*) Gladdening, exhilarating, sweetmeat, gratifying.

Modakī (मोदकी) (*f*) Pleasing, delighting, a sweetmeat

Modan (मोदन) (*m/f*) Same as Modak.

Modin (मोदिन) (*m/f*) Glad, cheerful, happy, rejoicing.

Modini (मोदिनी) (*m/f*) A Devi, goddess. See Devi.

Mohak (मोहक) (*a*) Charming, fascinating, casting a spell, causing illusion.

Mohan (मोहन) (*m*) Charming, attractive, tempting, enchantment, charm, epithet of Lord Krishna.

Mohanā (मोहना) (*f*) A mindborn mother.

Mohani (मोहनी) (*f*) Vishnu in the form of a fascinating woman. One who tempts, charm, attracts, the form of a woman assumed by god while distributing nectar after the churning of the ocean.

Mohini (मोहिनी) (*f*) See Mohani.

Mohit (मोहित) (*m/f*) Bewildered, infatuated by love, charmed, attracted.

Mohni (मोहनी) (*f*) See Mohani

Mridu (मृदु) (*a*) Soft, sweet, tender, gentle, mellow, mild.

Mridul (मृदुल) (*a*) Meaning the same as Mridu.

Mrigākshi (मृगाकक्षी) (*a*) Dear-eyed and most beautiful woman.

Mrida (मृदा) (*m/f/n*) Showing compassion or mercy. Gracious

Mrijā (मृजा) (*f*) Cleansing, washing, purification, purity, cleanliness (from Mahabharata)

Mrināl (मृणाल) (*m*) Root of a lotus plant: lotus-stalk

Mrinalinī (मृणालिनी) (*f*) Lotus plant, lotus.

Mrishta (मृष्ट) (*m/f/n*) Washed, claned, polished, pure.

Mrityunjaya (मृत्युंजय) (*n*) Bravo, Hurrah, applause, cheering.

Muchira (मुचिर) (*m/f*) Liberal, charity, virtue.

Muchukund (मुचुकुन्द) (*m*) In the Puranas, son of mandhatri, and called 'king of men'. He rendered assistance to the Gods in their wars with the Asuras (demons).

Mudā (मुदा) (*f*) To be merry, happy, delight, enjoy (R.V)

Mudākaram (मुदाकर्म) (*m*) Abode of joy - Lord Ganesh (G)

Mudgala (मुद्गल) (*m*) A Vedic Rishi from whom the Maudgalya Brahmans sprang. There were several other Brahmans named Mudgala. A sage of this mane is recorded in the Mahabharata who has lived a life of poverty, piety, and self-restraint, offering hospitality to thousands of Brahmans.

Muditā (**मुदिता**) (*f*) Glad, rejoiced, happy, Joyful.

Mukchandra (**मुकचन्द्र**) (*m*) Moon-like face.

Mukh Kamal (**मुख कमल**) (*n*) Lotus like face.

Mukt (**मुक्त**) (*m/f*) Set free, open, liberated, emancipated.

Mukitā (**मुकिता**) (*f*) Joy.

Muktā (**मुक्ता**) (*f*) A pearl. See also Mukt.

Muktak/Muktakā (**मुक्तक/मुक्तका**) (*n*) A stray or independent verse. Also the meaning as Mukti.

Muktalatā (**मुक्तलता**) (*f*) String of pearls.

Muktamālā (**मुक्तमाला**) (*f*) String of pearls

Muktātmān (**मुक्तात्मान्**) (*m*) Emancipated soul.

Muktānanda (**मुक्तानन्द**) (*m*) Joy of liberation.

Muktānām (**मुक्तानाम**) (*m*) The ultimate stage of the libereated Prama Gatih (Soul) (V)

Muktbudhu (**मुक्तबुधु**) (*m/f/n*) One whose soul is liberated.

Mukteshvar (**मुक्तेश्वर**) (*m*) Lord of the crown.

Mukteshvari (**मुक्तेश्वरी**) (*m*) Queen of the crown.

Mukti (**मुक्ति**) (*f*) Salvation, emancipation, deliverance, liberation, freedom.

Muktiday (**मुक्तिदय**) (*m*) Giver of eternal peace (G)

Mukul (**मुकुल**) (*m*) A bud, blossom.

Mukuldrishti (**मुकुलदृष्टि**) (*f*) A bud like glance in a dance

Mukulit (**मुकुलित**) (*a*) Semi blossomed, budded, blinking.

Mukulmudrā (**मुकुलमुद्रा**) (*f*) A gesture of a bud in a dance.

Mukund (**मुकुन्द**) (*m*) Lord Krishna, Lord Vishnu (deliverer).

Mukundah (**मुकुन्दः**) (*m*) The Bestower of Liberation (V)

Mukund-mālā (**मुकुन्द-माला**) (*f*) Name of a stotra (in 22 verses, addressed to Vishnu) by Kul-Shekhara.

Mumukshā (**मुमुक्षा**) (*f*) Desire of liberation from or final emancipation.

Munduka (**मुन्दुक**) (*f*) Name of an Upanishad (philosophical doctrines—third division of the Vedas attached to the Brahmana portion, and forming part of the Sruti (revealed word)).

Muni (**मुनि**) (*m*) A holy sage, a pious and learned person of divine nature. The title is applied to the Rishis or persons distinguished for their writings.

Munilakshmi (**मुनिलक्ष्मी**) (*f*) Treasure of ascetice or knowledge.

Muniratan (**मुनिरतन**) (*m*) Jewel among ascetics. Chaste, pious.

Munish (मुनीष) (*m*) Chief of Munis (sages). Name of Buddha, Jina, and Valmiki. Full of ascetics. A great ascetic, hermit, saint.

Munisha (मुनिषा) (*m/f/n*) Full of ascetics.

Munishvara (मुनीश्वर) (*m*) Name of Vishnu or Lord Buddha

Murāri (मुरारी) (*m*) An appellation of Lord Krishna.

Murli (मुरली) (*f*) Flute, pipe.

Murli-manohar (मुरली-मनोहर) (*m*) An epithet of Lord Krishna.

Murti (मूर्ति) (*f*) Idol, form, image, picture. Also a name of a daughter of Daksha and wife of Dharma.

Murtidevi (मूर्तिदेवी) (*f*) image of Devi. See also Devi.

Murti-punit (मूर्ति-पुनीत) (*f*) Image of sacredness.

Murti-taruni (मूर्ति-तरूणी) (*f*) Image of youthful woman.

Murti-Surupā (मूर्ति-सुरूपा) (*f*) Image of most beautiful.

Murti-svarn (मूर्ति-स्वर्ण) (*f*) Image of Gold of beauty.

Murti-tijilā (मूर्ति-तिजीला) (*f*) Image of moon.

Murtikalā (मूर्तिकला) (*f*) Art of image making.

Murti-saroj (मूर्ति-सरोज) (*m*) Image of lotus flower.

Mutya (मूत्य) (*m/f*) Pearl

N (न, ना)

Nabhakānti (नभाकांति) (*m*) Splendour of the sky.

Nabhaketan (नभकेतन) (*m*) Sky banner, another name of the sun.

Nabhgāmi (नभगामी) (*m*) The moon, a bird, the Sun, a star.

Nābhija (नाभिज) (*m*) Navel-born, epithet of Brahmā

Nabhit (नभित) (*m/f*) Not afraid, fearless.

Nabhomanī (नभोमणी) (*m*) Jewel of the sky.

Nabhonadī (नभोनदी) (*f*) The heavenly Ganges.

Nabhrāj (नभराज) (*m/f*) Name of a divine soma-keeper.

Nachiket (नाचिकेत) (*m*) Son of sage Udalaka. His story is told in the Taittiriya Brahmana and Katha Upanishad. He refused to be contented with anything but a true knowledge of the soul.

Nadīdhar (नदीधार) (*m*) Name of Lord Shiva, Mahadev.

Nādini (नादिनी) (*f*) A Shakti (goddess Durga)

Nadīsh (नदीष) (*m*) The ocean, sea.

Nadpratitishtha (नदप्रतिष्ठ) (*m*) Lover of Music (G)

Nagendra (नगेद्रा) (*m*) Mountain Lord. Himalayas.

Nagendri (नगेद्री) (*f*) Daughter of the mountains.

Nagesh (नगेश) (*m*) Lord of the mountain Kailash (S)

Nahusha (नहुष) (*m*) Son of Ayus the eldest son of Pururavas, and father of Yayati. This king is mentioned by Manu as having come into conflict with the Brahmans and his story is repeated several times in the Mahabharata. The object and aim of the story is to exhibit the retribution awaiting any man who derogates from the power of Brahmanan and the respect due to them.

Naikah (नैकः) (*m*) Owing to many forms. He is multi-faceted (V)

Naikakarmakrita (नैककर्मकृत) (*m*) Indulging in various activities (like creation, destructione etc.) for people's welfare. (V)

Naikarupha (नैकरूपा) (*m*) In Myriad forms. (V)

Naikashringa (नैकशृंग) (*m*) Having many media for His Resounding word. (V)

Naikātma (नैकात्म) (*m*) Adopting various forms in every age according to the need of time. (V)

Nakshatri (नक्षत्री) (*m*) Moon-like (V)

Nakul (नकुल) (*m*) The fourth of the Pandu princes. He was the twin son of Mādri (wife of Pandu).

Nal/Nala (नल/नाला) (*m*) King of Nishadha and husband of Damayanti. The story of Nala and Damayanti is one of the episodes of the Mahabharata. Nala was brave and handsome, virtuous, and learned in the Vedas, skilled in arms and in the management of horses, Nala and Damayanti loved each other upon the mere fame of their respective virtues and beauty. They got married and faced a lot of difficulties in their lives and eventually lived happily as king and queen.

Nalakini (नलकिनी) (*f*) A multitude of lotus flowers, a lotus lake.

Nalami (नालामी) (*f*) Fragrant nectar, the lute of Lord Shiva.

Nalayani (नलयनी) (*f*) Wife of the great sage Mudagalya.

Nalesh (नलेष) (*m*) King of flowers.

Nalikā (नलिका) (*m*) A measure of time and space

Nalin (नलिन) (*m*) The Indian crane, a lotus flower, water, indigo plant.

Nalinī (नलिनी) (*f*) Alotus, lily. Also a name of Ganges.

Naman (नमन) (*m*) Salutation, bowing, obeissance, bending, sloping.

Namanā (नमना) (*f*) Same as Naman.

Namas (नमस) (*n*) Reverence salutation. Bending, bowing.

Namasthetu (नमसथीतु) (*m*) Destroyer of all sins. (G)

Namasya (नमस्य) (*m/f*) To pay homage, worship. Reverence.

Nāmdev (नामदेव) (*m*) A famous devotee of Lord Krishna (famous Maratha poet).

Nāmit (नामित) (*m*) Named, nominated.

Namit-anugraha (नमित-अनुग्रह) (*m*) Blesser of devotees. (K)

Namritā (नम्रिता) (*a*) Modest, humble, polite, meek, modesty, humility, politeness.

Nāmvar (नामवर) (*a*) Famous, renowned.

Nāmvari (नाम्वरी) (*f*) famous, renowned.

Namya (नमय) (*m/f*) Venerable, to bend to bowed down to.

Nana (नन) (*m*) Differently, variously.

Nanadevata (ननदेवता) (*m*) Different Gods.

Nanvirya (ननविर्य) (*m*) Different powers.

Nand (नंद) (*m*) The cowherd by whom Lord Krishna was brought up. A king, or dynasty of kings, of Magadh, that reigned at Pātliputra. An epithet of Lord Krishna.

Nandā (नंदा) (*f*) Happiness, pleasure, name of a nymph, an epithet of Durga. See Devi.

Nandah (नन्दाः) (*m*) Prosperous with all comforts and luxuries (V)

Nandak (नन्दक) (*m*) Rejoicing, the sword of Vishnu.

Nandaki (नन्दकि) (*m*) The Wielder of the Sword called Nandak (V)

Nandan (नंदन) (*m*) Delighting, a son, Vishnu, Shiva, the garden of Indra.

Nandanah (नंदनाः) (*m*) The delighter of all (V)

Nandani (नंदनी) (*f*) One who delights, a daughter.

Nandvrāj (नंदवराज) (*m*) Son of the Vraj dynasty (K)

Nandi (नंदी) (*m*) The sacred bull of Shiva. His image, of milky white colour, is always conspicuous before the temples of Shiva.

Nāndi (नान्दी) (*f*) Benedictory verse or verses recited as a sort of prologue at the beginning of drama.

Nandini (नंदिनी) (*f*) The cow of plenty belonging to the sage Vashishtha, produced at the churning of the ocean, who granted every desire, and is reverenced as "the fountain of milk and curd". Another name of Nandini is Surabhi. Also a name of goddess Parvati.

Nandisa/Nandisha/Nandiswara (नंदिस/नंदिश/नंदीश्वर) (*m*) Lord of Nandi, a title of Lord Shiva.

Nandit (नंदित) (*a*) delighted, pleased.

Nand-kishor (नन्द-किशोर) (*m*) An epithet of Lord Krishna – being the adopted son of Nand.

Nānd-kumār (नान्द-कुमार) (*m*) An epithet of Lord Krishna.

Nand-lāl (नन्द-लाल) (*m*) Meaning the same as Nand-Kishor.

Nantra (नन्त्रा) (*n*) Praise, eulogy

Nārad (नारद) (*m*) A Rishi (saint) to whom some hymns of the Rig-Veda are ascribed. He is one of the seven great Rishis.

Naradeva (नरदेव) (*m*) Another name of Lord Rām. According to Bhagvat Puran, he is the eighteenth incarnation of Vishnu.

Nārah (नारः) (*m*) One who guides the noble (V)

Narasimha (नरसिम्हा) (*m*) According to Bhagvat Puran, he is the fourteenth incarnation of Vishnu.

Narasimhavapuh (नरसिम्हवपुः) (*m*) Man lion bodied (V)

Nārāyan (नारायण) (*m*) God, Lord Vishnu. Also a name of an ancient sage, who taught Bhagvat Puran to Nārad, who in turn taught it to Vyās.

Nārāyanah (नारायणः) (*m*) One who reposes in water, or water is whose home or abode. (V)

Nārāyanavarapriya (नारायणवरप्रिया) (*f*) Found of Narayana's boons. (D)

Nārāyani (नारायणी) (*f*) Lakshmi, the goddes of wealth, or the goddess Durga.

Narendra (नरेन्द्र) (*m*) Lord, king, prince, a physician, master of charms or antidotes.

Naresh (नरेश) (*m*) A king, lord.

Nareshwar (नरेश्वर) (*m*) A king, lord.

Naretra (नरेत्र) (*m*) Different from men, a God.

Nargis (नर्गिस) (*f*) The narcissus plant and its flowers. As beautiful as a narcissus flower.

Narhari (नरहरि) (*m*) Usually the fourth incarnation of Vishnu. See Narasimha.

Narma (नर्म) (*m*) Sport, pastime.

Narmadā (नर्मदा) (*f*) A name of a river which is esteemed holy. The personified river is variously represented as being daughter of a Rishi named mekala.

Narman (नर्मण) (*n*) Sport, play, amusement, pleasure, pastime.

Narotam (नरोत्तम) (*m*) The foremost best of men, an excellent man.

Narpāl (नरपाल) (*m*) Men protector, king.

Nartaka (नर्तक) (*m/f/n*) Dancer, actor, causing to dance. Dancing master.

Nartita (नर्तिता) (*m/f/n*) Made to dance, dandled.

Narma (नर्म) (*m*) Sport, pastime.

Narmān (नरमान) (*m*) Sport, play, amusement, pleasure, pastime.

Naruna (नरुन) (*m*) A leader.

Natesh (नटेश) (*m*) Lord of dance, Lord Shiva.

Nateshvar (नटेश्वर) (*m*) Lord of dancers (S)

Nāth (नाथ) (*n*) Refuge or help, proterctor, possessor, owner, lord.

Nāthvindu (नाथविन्दु) (*m/f*) Posesessing or granting protection.

Nāthman (नाथमन) (*m/f*) Seeking help, suppliant (from Mahabharata)

Nāti (नाटी) (*f*) Female dancer. The term applied to Shakti when Goddess dances out of delight at the performance of her rituals.

Natrāj (नटराज) (*m*) King of dance. Lord Shiva dances in the cremation ground, respresenting the principle of destruction. The Thandava dance represents the frenzic throes of extreme grief and annoyance, and the Lasya dance, of calmness and bliss. He is king of all dances. (S)

Natvar (नटवर) (*m*) A good actor, competent person, very clever, Lord Krishna.

Nava/Nāv (नवा-नाव) (*m/f*) Recent, young, moddrn, new.

Navajā (नवजा) (*f*) Daughter of wisdom.

Navadurgā (नवदुर्गा) (*f*) All nine forms of goddess Durga. Another name of goddess Lakshmi. (L)

Navambu (नवम्बु) (*n*) Fresh water

Navak (नवक) (*m/f*) New, fresh, young.

Naval (नवल) (*a*) fresh, young, recent, an epithet of Lord Krishna.

Navanā (नवना) (*f*) The ceremony of the first fruits. Literally it means new rice, it is performed in the month of November-December after the harvest.

Navanit (नवनीत) (*m*) Fond of butter - Lord Krishna (K)

Navnitānta (नवनितान्त) (*m*) Dancer with butter (K)

Navatā (नवता) (*m/f*) Novelty, freshness.

Navateja (नवतेज) (*m*) New energy.

Navatrā (नवत्रा) (*m/f*) Newer, younger, fresher

Navdal (नवदल) (*f*) Fresh leaf of a lotus or any fresh leaf.

Navdurgā (नवदुर्गा) (*f*) Goddess Durga in her nine forms.

Navelī (नवेली) (*f*) A young and beautiful woman.

Navendra (नवेन्द्र) (*m*) New/young Indra. See Also Indra.

Navibhu (नविभु) (*f*) To become new.

Navīn (नवीन) (*a*) New, modern, recent, fresh, youthful, young.

Navishtha (नविष्ठ) (*m/f*) The newest, youngest.

Navishti (नविष्टि) (*f*) Song of praise, a hymn in Rig Veda.

Naviyā (नवीया) (*f*) New, fresh, young (from Rig Veda)

Navkhand (नवखंड) (*m*) The nine portions of the world.

Navnit (नवनीत) (*n*) Fresh butter, butter like soft, gentle.

Nav-ratan (नव-रतन) The nine gems of the court of Vikramaditya, whose era begins in 56 BC. The nine gems are: pearl, ruby, topaz, diamond, emerald, lapis, lazuli, coral, sapphire, go-meda.

Navshakti (नवशक्ति) (*m*) Having nine faculties. (V)

Navtā (नवता) (*f*) Freshness, novelty.

Nayah (नयः) (*m*) The controlling and regulating factor of the world order. (V)

Nayan (नयन) (*m*) Eye, leading, directing.

Nayandip/Nayanadipā (नयनदीप/नयनदीपा) (*m/f*) Light of the eye.

Nayanatārā (नयनतारा) (*f*) Star of the eyes.

Nāyika (नायिका) (*f*) Woman, heroine,

Neh (नेह) (*m*) Affection. Tadbhav (Sanskrit word used in a slightly changed form) form of Sanskrit. See Sneh.

Nemchandra (नेमचन्द्र) (*m*) Half moon. Name of a prince.

Neyah (नेयह) (*m*) Comprehensibvle by superior knowledge (V)

Neta (नेता) (*m*) The driver of the world in the form of a vehicle. (V)

Nayachandrikā (नयचन्द्रीका) (*f*) Moonshine, anything looking bright to the eyes.

Nayaga (नयग) (*m/f*) Behaving properly or prudently.

Nayapriti (नयप्रीति) (*f*) Eye delight, lovely sight.

Nayapriya (नयप्रीया) (*m/f*) Favourable to mankind.

Nayasiddhi (नयसिद्धी) (*f*) Political success.

Nemchandra (नेमचन्द्र) (*m*) Half moon. Name of a prince.

Nepathya (नेपथय) (*n*) An ornament, decorating, costume.

Neti (नेती) (*f*) A Sanskrit expression meaning "there is no end", used by philosophers to underline the view that He (God) defers all description.

Netri (नेत्री) (*m/f*) Leading, guiding, a leader.

Neyah (नेयह) (*m*) Comprehensive by superior knowledge. (V)

Nibhā (निभा) (*f*) Resembling, like, smilar.

Nichandra (निचन्द्र) (*m*) Leading moon. Leader.

Nidhā (निधां) (*n*) To put or lay down, deposit, preserve.

Nidhi (निधि) (*m*) Abode, a store house, a treasure, the ocean. Nine treasures belonging to the god Kuvera, each of them is personified or has a guardian spirit which is an object of worship among the Tantrikas.

Nidhirvyayāh (निधिर्व्याह) (*m*) Th imperishable embodiment of the bodily form surviving through the dissolution. (V)

Nidish (निदीष) (*n*) Direct, order, point out.

Nidisvaram (निदीश्वरम) (*m*) Master of all kinds of treasures. (G)

Nigaraha (निगरहा) (*m*) All restraint personified (V)

Nighantu (निघन्तु) (*n*) A glossary of Vedic hymns.

Nihitā (निहिता) (*m/f/n*) Laid, deoposited, bestowed.

Niket (निकेत) (*m*) A house, residence, abode.

Nikhil (निखिल) (*m/f*) Complete, all, entire, whole, totally.

Nīl (नील) (*n*) Dark blue, the blue colour, saphire.

Nilābh (नीलाभ) (*m*) Moon. Bluish hue.

Nilābja (नीलाब्ज) (*n*) Blue lotus.

Nilachandra (नीलचन्द्र) (*m*) Blue moon.

Nilam (नीलम) (*m*) Saphire.

Nilay (निलय) (*m*) Abode, habitat, dwelling place.

Nilibh (निलीभ) (*m*) Moon. Bluish hue, bee.

Nilkanth (नीलकंठ) (*m*) Blue throat. An epithet of Lord Shiva.

Nilotpal (नीलोत्पल) (*m*) Blue lotus.

Nilpadma (नीलपदम्) (*m/f*) Blue water-lily.

Nilpushpa (नीलपुष्प) (*m*) Blue flowered.

Nilsarasvati (नीलसरस्वती) (*f*) Name of a Goddess

Niman (निमन) (*n*) Healthy, hale and hearty.

Nimi (निमि) (*m/f*) Twinkling of the eyes. To perceive, notice, understand, name of a prince.

Nimish (निमिष) (*m*) Twinkling of an eye, blink. Time taken in the twinkling of an eye.

Nimithā (निमीथा) (*f*) Cause, motive, reason, ground, the state of being.

Nimittā (निमित्ता) (*f*) Auspicious sign, omens

Nimittam (निमित्तम) (*m*) The son of Dandapāni and father of Kshemaka.

Ninishā (निनीषा) (*m/f*) Desire of bringing or carrying or taking away.

Nipa (निप) (*n*) To guard or protect from, observe, watch (from Rig Veda). Also it Means to drink, or suck or kiss.

Nipuna (निपुण) (*m*) Skilful, proficient, kindly, complete, clever, sharp, efficient.

Nirā (नीरा) (*m/f*) Water, juice, liquor.

Niraj (नीरज) (*m*) Lotus, a pearl.

Nirajākshi (नीरजाक्षी) (*f*) Lotus eyed, beautiful.

Nirājan (नीराजन) (*f*) Brilliance, renown. Waving of lights before an idol—one way of honouring a deity.

Niranjan (निरंजन) (*m*) God who is beyond the spell of Maya (illusion) or the range of worldly flaws and defects. A name of Lord Shiva.

Nirav (नीरव) (*a*) Quiet, calm, still.

Nirbhayā (निर्भया) (*f*) A mind-born mother.

Nirek/Nirekā (नीरेक/नीरेका) (*m/f*) Prominence, superiority, pre-eminence over.

Nirgunah (निर्गुणः) (*m*) The Attributeless (V).

Niriksha (निरीक्षा) (*m/f*) Behold, regard, to look at or perceive.

Nirji (नीरजी) (*m/f*) To conquer, win, acquire, subdue, vanquish.

Nirjitā (नीर्जिता) (*f*) Conquered, subdued, gained, won.

Nirmā (निरमा) (*f*) To buid, to make out. Value, measure, equivalent.

Nirmamiti (निरमामिती) (*f*) Formation, creation, making, adding, addition.

Nirmātri (निरमात्री) (*m*) Maker, builder, creator, author.

Nirmil (निर्मिल) (*a*) Clean, clear, pure, unsullied, spotless, stainless.

Nirmiti (निर्मिति) (*f*) Formation, creation, making, addition.

Nirmitra (निर्मित्र) (*m*) Son of Nakul (Pandava prince) and Karenmati. Also a name of a son of the king of Trigarta. In the Mahabharata war he fought on the side of Kauravas

Nirmitsu (निर्मित्सु) (*m/f*) Wishing to create, desire of creating.

Nirmol (निरमोल) (*a*) Priceless, rare, very valuable.

Nirmucha̅ (निरमुचा) (*f*) To liberate, free from, loosen

Nirti (नीर्ति) (*f*) Great love.

Niruj (निरुज) (*m/f*) Healthy, wholesome.

Nirukta (निरुक्त) (*m*) Uttered, pronounced, expressed, explained, defined. defined. Declared, explicitly mentioned - containing the name of God.

Nirukti̅ (निरूक्ति) (*f*) Etymological interpretation of a word. Same as Nirukta.

Nirup (निरुप) (*n*) To perform, represent on the stage, act, to perceive, notice.

Nirupadhi (निरुपधी) A guileless, honest.

Nirupam (निरुपम) (*a*) Peerless, matchless.

Nirvanam (निरवनम) (*m*) The Abode of the liberated soul. (V)

Niryukta (निर्युक्त) (*m/f/n*) Constructed, built, directed towards, in music limited as to metre and measure.

Nisha̅ (निशा) (*f*) Night, turmeric. Nisha̅ also means Sita̅ (wife of Lord Ra̅m).

Nisha̅di (निशादि) (*m*) Beginning of twilight.

Nisha̅ka̅nt (निशाकांत) (*m*) Beloved of the night (name of the moon).

Nishchal (निश्चल) (*a*) Steady, unwavering, quiet, immoveable.

Nishesh (निशेष) (*m*) Shining at.

Nishi (निशि) (*f*) Night.

Nishka̅ (निष्का) (*f*) Pure, honest, golden necklace.

Nishna̅shna̅ (निश्नाश्ना) (*m/f*) Clever, skilful, versed or experienced in composition.

Nishna̅t (निष्णात) (*a*) Adept, expert, skilled.

Nishtha (निष्ठा) (*m*) Honest. The object of every body's loyalty (V)

Nita (नित) (*m/f/n*) Guided, brought, gained, obtained, wealth, well behaved, correct.

Nitandra̅ (नितन्द्रा) (*m*) A deity on the Yantra of Vishukra.

Ni̅ti (नीति) (*f*) Guidance, virtue, moral behaviour, polity, ethics, political science, public good, good conduct.

Nitin (नीतिन) (*m*) Having knowledge of law, moralist, policy maker.

Nitya (नित्य) (*m/f*) Innate, native, continual, perpetual, eternal, constant or indispensable rite or act, constantly, regularly. Another name of goddess Durga (D)

Nitya̅cha̅r (नित्याचार) (*m*) Constant good conduct.

Nityānand (नित्यानन्द) (*m*) Eteranal happiness.

Nityashri (नित्यश्री) (*f*) With eternal happiness.

Nityapushta (नित्यपुष्ट) (*f*) Gaining strength day bay day. Name of goddess Lakshmi (L)

Nityasundar (नित्यसुन्दर) (*m*) Ever beautiful (S)

Nivratātm (निव्रतात्म) (*m*) He who has discharged His Duties (V)

Nivrittatma (निव्रित्तात्म) (*m*) The Released Soul (V)

Niyamah (नियामः) (*m*) The One Who Brings Order in Creator (V)

Niyanta (नियन्ता) (*m*) He who defines every being's duty (V)

Nrdeva (नरदेव) See Naradeva.

Nrivattātma (नरिवात्तात्मा) (*m*) The Relaxed Soul (V)

Nupur (नूपुर) (*m*) An anklet.

Nutan (नूतन) (*m/f*) New, fresh, young, strange.

Nuti (नूती) (*f*) Praise, worship, reverence.

Nyagrodha (नयग्रोधा) (*m*) The Grand Banyan (V)

Nyayah (नय्यह) (*m*) The argument in logic proved by facts. (V)

O (ओ, औ)

Ochitya (औचित्य) (*m*) Rightness, suitableness, propriety, aptness.

Odatī (ओदती) (*f*) Sprinkling or refreshing. Name of Ushas or the dawn. (mythologically it means daughter of heavem).

Oha (ओहा) (*m/f*) True, knowledge,

Ojal/Ojala (ओजल/ओजला) (*m/f*) Vision, splendour

Ojajs (ओजज्स) (*m/f*) Bodily strength, vigour, power, ability, energy, manifestation, appearance.

Ojasīv (ओजसिव) (*m/f*) Strong, powerful.

Ojasvat (ओजस्वत) (*m/f*) Same as Ojas.

Ojasvī (ओजस्वी) (*a*) Ability, power, strenght, vigorous, splendour, brilliance.

Ojasvin (ओजसविन्) (*m/f*) Name of a son of Manu Bhautya. Very powerful, energetic, or emphatic manner of expression or style.

Ojasvitā (ओस्विता) (*f*) Splendour, briliance.

Ojasyā (ओजस्या) (*m/f*) Vigorous, powerful.

Ojati (ओजति) (*f*) To be strong, or to increase vital power.

Ojayati (ओजयति) (*f*) Same as Ojati.

Ojāyit (ओजायित) (*m*) Stout-heartedness, courageous behaviour.

Ojāyita (ओजायित) (*m/f*) Stout-heartedness, courageous behaviour.

Ojishtha (ओजिष्ठ) (*m*) Best, powerful, vigorous, very strong, name of a sage.

Ojo (ओजो) (*m/f*) Granting power, strengthening.

Om/Omkār (ओम/ओंकार) (*m*) The most sacred word prefixed to Vedic mantras (hymns) symbolising God Almighty. A combination of letters invested by Hindu mysticism with peculiar sanctity. In the Vedas it is said to comprehend all the gods; and in the Puranas it is directed to be prefixed to many sacred formulas. A word of solemn invocation, affirmation, benediction, and consent—a very sacred word. The word is used at the commencement of prayers and religious ceremonies, and is generally placed at the beginning of books. A whole chapter of the Vayu Puran is devoted to this term. It is a compound of the three letters A. U. M. which are typical of the three Vedas; and it is declared in the Upanishads, where it first appears, to have a mystic power and to be worthy of the deepest meditation. In later times the monosyllable represents the Hindu triad or union of three gods, A. being Vishnu, U, Shiva, and M, Brahma. This monosyllable is called Udgitha. It is also said to typify the three spheres of the world, the three holy fires, the three steps of Vishnu. Some people believe that in ancient times the word AUM stood for A Agni (fire); the U Varuna (water); and the M Marut (wind).

Omān (ओमान) (*m*) Help, protection, favour, kindness.

Omānvat (ओमान्वत) (*m/f*) Helping, useful, favourable, propitious.

Omkār (ओमकार) (*m*) The sacred monosyllable Om. Name of one of the twelve great lingas (the symbol under which Shiva is universally worshipped). See Om.

Omesh (ओमेश) (*m*) Lord of the sacred word Om. See also Om.

Omisha (ओमीश) (*f*) Goddess of the sacred word Om. Goddess of birth, life and death. See also Om.

Omkārnāth (ओमकारनाथ) (*m*) Lord of the Om. See Om.

Onī (ओनी) (*m/f*) Protection from misfortunes. The two protectors (heaven and earth).

Opash (ओपश) (*m*) A support, stay, pillar.

Oshadhi (ओषधि) (*f*) Light-containing. herbs, any medicinal plant.

Oshadhipati (ओषधिपति) (*m*) Lord of herbs. the moon.

Oshthya (ओष्ठ्य) (*m/f*) Labial sound. Being at lips, belonging to lips.

P (प, पा)

Padadi (पदादि) (*f*) Begining of a verse.

Padam (पद्म) (*m*) Lotus flower and its plant. A name of Brahmā (the first member of the Hīndu triad).

Padmā (पद्मा) (*f*) Lotus, the wife of Vishnu. Also means Lakshmi as the earth-lotus.

Padmabālā (पद्मबाला) (*m*) Daughter of lotus.

Padmabandhu (पद्मबंधु) (*m*) Friend of lotus. Another name of sun.

Padmabhāsa (पद्मभाषा) (*m*) With the brilliance of the lotus. (V)

Padmadi (पद्मदी) (*m/f*) A lotus flower.

Padmagandhi (पद्मगंधी) (*f*) Having the fragrance of the lotus-goddess Lakshmi. (L)

Padmagrabha (पद्मग्रभ) (*m*) Worth concentrating in the lotus of heart. (V)

Padma-griha (पद्म-गृह) (*f*) Name of Goddess Lakshmi. Lotus housed.

Padmahas (पद्महास) (*m*) Smiling like lotus.

Padama-hasana (पद्म-हसन) (*n*) Smiling like lotus.

Padam-hasta (पद्म-हस्त) (*m*) Lotus handed. Lord Krishna holds a lotus in His upper left hand. The lotus is the symbol of causal power of illusion from which the universe emerges. (K)

Padamajā (पद्मजा) (*f*) Born of a lotus. (L)

Padma-kānt (पद्म-कांत) (*n*) Beloved of a lotus.

Padmakshyā (पद्माक्ष) (*f*) Lotus eyed - goddess Lakshmi. (L)

Padmalayā (पद्मालय) (*f*) Residing on the lotus. Emerging from ocean goddess Lakshmi has her abode in the lotus, which is a shelter of bliss and happiness. (L)

Padmalini (पद्मलिनी) (*f*) Garland with lotuses. (L)

Padma-lochan (पद्म-लोचन) (*m/f*) Lotus-eyed.

Padma-mālā (पद्म-माला) (*f*) Garland of lotus.

Padam-mālini (पद्म-मालिनी) (*f*) Name of Goddess Lakshmi (see also Lakshmi) Garlanded with lotus flowers.

Padmanā (पद्मना) (*f*) Lotus faced. (L)

Padma-mukhi (पद्म-मुखी) (*f*) Beautiful face like water-lily or lotus. Alhagi maurorum.

Padma-nābh (पद्म-नाभ) (*m*) One having a lotus in His navel. Name of Lord Vishnu from whose navel sprang the lotus which contained Brahma, the future creator. (V)

Padma-nābhah (पद्म-नाभा) (*m*) Having lotus in the Navel from which oiriginated Creation. (V)

Padmanābhahpriya (पद्मनाभाप्रिय) (*f*) Beloved of Padmanabh (Lord Vishnu). Name of goddess Lakshmi. (L)

Padmānandana (पद्मानन्दन) (*m*) Arisen from lotus. Another name of Brahma.

Padma-netra (पद्म-नेत्र) (*m/f*) Lotus eyed, a species of bird.

Padma-nibhekshan (पद्म-निभेक्षन) (*m*) Having a sight as soft as the stalk of lotus. (V)

Padma-nuttamam (पद्म-नुतमम) (*m*) The Highest state (aspired by the nobles). (V)

Padma-patrakshi (पद्म-पत्राक्षी) (*f*) Eyes like the lotus leaf - Goddess Durga's eyes sparkle like the colourful lotus petals, giving knowledge of Shiva to her devotees. (D)

Padma-prabhā (पद्म-प्रभा) (*n*) Shining like lotus.

Padma-priya (पद्म-प्रिय) (*f*) Lover of lotus - goddess Lakshmi. (L)

Padmaratan (पद्मरत्न) (*m*) Lotus jewelled. A Buddhist patriarch.

Padma-rekhā (पद्म-रेखा) (*f*) A line in the palm of a hand indicating the acquisition of great wealth.

Padma Shri (पद्मश्री) (*f*) Beautiful as the lotus.

Padam Sundari (पद्म सुन्दरी) (*f*) Beautiful like the lotus-goddess Lakshmi. (L)

Padmāvatī (पद्मावती) (*f*) A name of Lakshmi.

Padmesh/Padmesha (पद्मेश) (*m/f*) Dressed in lotus flowers.

Padmi (पद्मी) (*m*) Wielder of lotus in his hand. (V)

Padminī (पद्मिनी) (*f*) An exceptionally charming woman (the first of the kinds specified by ancient Indians. A lotus.

Padminishā (पद्मिनिषा) (*m*) Lord of lotus flowers.

Padmodbhāv (पद्मोद्भाव) (*f*) One who emerged out of the lotus - goddess Lakshmi. (L)

Pakshila (पक्षील) (*m*) Saintly person. Name of a saint.

Paila (पैल) (*m*) A learned man who was appointed in ancient days to collect the hymns of Rig Veda. He arranged in two parts and must have been a co-adjutor of Ved Vyās.

Pājas (पाजस) (*m/f*) Firmness, strength, brightness, glitter.

Pakshila (पक्षिल) (*m*) Saintly person. Name of a saint.

Pakshina (पाक्षिन) (*m/f/n*) Winged, taking the side of, the bird Garuda as one of the 18 attendants of the Sun.

Paktha (पकथ) (*m*) Name of a man protected by the Ashvins.

Pālak (पालक) (*m*) King, sovereign, protector.

Pallav (पल्लव) (*m*) A new tender leaf. Sprout, shoot.

Pallavi (पल्लवी) (*f*) Bud, a young shoot, sprouting.

Pallavit (पल्लवित) (*a*) Having growing new leaves, flourishing, thriving, prospered.

Pampā (पम्पा) (*f*) Name of a river in the south India.

Pamrā (पमरा) (*f*) A kind of fragrant substance.

Panah (पनाह) (*m*) He whose behaviour is ideal. With all; worldwise. (V)

Panchajanya (पंचजन्य) (*n*) The conch of Krishna, blown by him at the siege of Mathura by Jarasandha.

Panchāksha (पंचाक्ष) (*m*) Five-eyed. An attendant of Lord Shiva.

Panchāli (पंचाली) (*f*) Another name of Darupadi, wife of Pandavas, as princess of Panchal (name of a country from Mahabharata).

Panchavakra (पंचावक्र) (*m*) Five-faced. Another name Hanuman. Taking any form at will, He is five-faced at times (all-knowing, all-seeing, and fully aware of everything). (H)

Panchavati (पंचवटी) (*f*) A place in great southern forest near Godavari, where Rāma passed a long period of his banishment.

Panchyudha (पंचयुद्ध) (*n*) Armed with five weapons.

Pandā (पण्डा) (*f*) Wisdom, knowledge, learning.

Pāndu (पण्डु) (*m*) The pale. Brother of Dhritarashtra, king of Hastinapur and father of the Pandavas or Pandu princes. He was born to king Vichitravirya's widow queen Ambalika through the grace of Krishnadwaipayana Vyas.

Pānini (पाणिनी) (*m*) Name of the most eminent of Sanskrit grammarians. Born about four centuries BC. Author of Ashtdhyayi and several other works.

Panit (पनित) (*m*) Praise, admire.

Pankaj (पंकज) (*m*) A lotus flower.

Pankaj-lochan (पंकज-लोचन) (*m*) Lotus-eyed. (K)

Pannā (पन्ना) (*f*) Diamond, emerald.

Panu (पनु) (*f*) Admiration.

Panya (पन्य) (*m/f/n*) To be praised or commended, to be bought or sold.

Panyatā (पन्यता) (*f*) A praise worthy person.

Pāpanāshan (पापनाशन) (*m*) The destoyer of sin. (V)

Parāg (पराग) (*m*) The pollen of a flower, fame, celebrity, and eclipse of the sun or moon.

Paraj (परज) (*m*) Gold.

Paraksha (परक्ष) (*m*) A son of Anu (son of kking Yayāti by his wife Sarmishth a, a Daitya princess.)

Param/Parama (परम) (*m/f*) Most distant, extreme, chief, most prominent or conspicuous, most excellent.

Paramānand (परमानन्द) (*m*) The supreme bliss, blessedness, god, the ultimate pleasure.

Paramāni (परमाणि) (*m/f*) A beautiful or excellent jewel.

Paramapurusha (परमपुरुष) (*m*) Supreme being. (R)

Paramātmā (परमात्मा) (*m*) The Suspreme Spirit. (V)

Parāmbika (पराम्बिका) (*f*) A Shakti (See goddess Durga).

Parameshvara (परमेश्वर) (*m*) Lord Shiva, also an epithet of Vishnu.

Parameshvari (परमेश्वरी) (*f*) The Chief Shakti (goddes Durga).

Paramikā (परमिका) (*f*) One who fulfills desires, best, greatest.

Pāras (पारस) (*m*) The mythical philosopher's stone which is said to convert iron into gold by mere touch; an object of unusual merits.

Paramspashta (परमसपष्ट) (*m*) Crystal clear about everything. (V)

Paramjyotishi (परमजयोतिशी) (*m*) Divine radiance. Lord Kirshna radiate divine love and eternal brilliance to all. (K)

Parardhi (पररधि) (*m*) One with great glory. (V)

Parāsara/Parāshar (पाराशर) (*m*) A Vedic Rishi to who some hymns of the Rig Veda are attributed, He was a disciple of Kapila, and he received the Vishnu Puran from Pulastya and taught it to Maitreya. He was also a writer on Dharm Shastra, and tests of his are often in the law books. By an amour with Satyavati he was father of Krishna Dwaipayana, the Vyas or arranger of the Vedas.

Parashuchi (परशुची) (*m*) Very pure, sacred, holy.

Parasu-Rām (परशू-राम) (*m*) Rām with the axe. Born in the Tretā or second age, son of the Brahman Jamadagni. He was the first Rām and sixth incarnation of Vishnu.

Parāyānam (परायाणम) (*m*) The final abode of the salvation seekers. (V)

Parayus (परायुस) (*m*) Another name of Lord Brahma. See also Brahma.

Paresa (परेस) (*m*) Highest Lord. Another name of Brahma.

Pareshti (परेश्ति) (*m*) With great worship.

Paribhash (परिभेष) (*m/f*) To speak to, address, admonish, declare, teach, persuade, encourage.

Paribhu (परिभु) (*m/f*) Surround, enclose, superior, surpass, conquer.

Parigai (परिगई) (*m/f*) Sing or celebrate everywhere.

Parijā (परिजा) (*f*) Place of origin, source of everything.

Parijanya (परिजन्य) (*m*) A Vedic deity, the rain god or rain personified. The three hymns in the Rig Veda are addressed to this deity.

Pārijāt (परिजात) (*m*) The tree produced at the churning of the ocean, "and the delight of the nymphs of heaven, perfuming the world with its blossoms." Name of one of the five trees said to exist in paradise.

Parikshit (परीक्षित) (*m*) Son of Abhimanyu by his wife Uttarā, grandson of Arjuna. When Yudhishtra retired from the world, Parikshit succeeded him on the throne of Hastinapur.

Parilasa (परीलस) (*f*) To shine all around.

Parilash (परीलेश) (*m/f*) To desire, long for.

Parimā (परिमा) (*f*) Periphery, rim, magnitude.

Pariman (परिमन) (*m/f*) Quality, bounty, too much.

Parimohan (परिमोहन) (*m/f*) Extremely fascinating.

Parimoksha (परिमोक्षा) (*m/f*) To set free, liberate, deliverance, final beautitude.

Parinand (परिनन्द) (*m/f*) To rejoice greatly, give great pleasure to (from Mahabharata).

Parinandan (परिनंदन) (*n*) Gratified, presented.

Parinut (परिणु) (*m/f*) Praised, celebrated.

Paripalya (परीपल्य) (*n*) Governorship.

Paripasha (परीपशा) (*m/f*) To look over, survey, to perceive, behold, learn recognise (from Atharva Veda).

Paripsā (परीप्सा) (*f*) Desire of obtaining or preserving, haste, hurry

Paripsu (परीप्सु) (*m/f*) Wishing to obtain or preserve.

Paripuj (परीपुज) (*m/f*) To honour greatly, adore, worship.

Parirama (परीरम) (*m/f*) To take pleasure in, be delighted with.

Parisatya (परिसत्या) (*m/f*) Full of pure truth.

Parishil (परिशील) (*m*. To practise, use frequently, to treat well, cherish.

Parishobhit (परिशोभित) (*f*) Adorned, beautiful.

Paritan (परितन) (*n*) To stretch round, embrace, surround (from Rig Veda).

Paritush (परितुश) (*m/f*) Satisfied, pleased, delight.

Parmārath (परमार्थ) (*m*) The highest, the wholle truth, spiritual knowledge, any excellent or important thing.

Parmatmikā (परमतमिका) (*f*) Omnipresence - supreme goddess Lakshmi of three worlds who gives shelter to distressed and destitute. (L)

Parmaya (परमय) (*m*) Wielder of the great maya. (S)

Parmeshthi (परमेष्ठी) (*m*) Excelling in His great glory. (V)

Parmeshvarah (परमेशवर) (*m*) Supreme Lord, Almighty. (V)

Paramjyoti (परमज्योति) (*m*) Greatest splendour. (S)

Parnād (परनाद) (*m*) A Brahman in the court of king Bhim of Vidarbha. He was the one who found Nala and brought him to Damayanti. His story is mentioned in the Mahabharata.

Parnasa (परनस) (*f*) Mother of Shrutayudha. She had pleased god Varuna by her austerities and had obtained from him a divine mace for her son which made him invicibel.

Parshād/Parshāda (परशाद) (*m*) Any treatise on the Vedas produced in a Vedic college.

Pārshati (पारशती) (*f*) Draupadi, Durga. See under both the names.

Parshu (परशु) (*m*) A hatchet, axe, thunderbolt.

Parshuchi (परशुची) (*m*) Very pure, sacred, holy.

Parshu-rām (परशु-राम) (*m*) Rām with an axe (son of Jamad-agni and sixth incarnation of Vishnu).

Pārtha (पारथा) (*m*) A son of Prithā or Kuntī. A title applicable to the three elder Pāndavas, but especially used for Arjuna.

Pārthasārthi (पारथासार्थी) (*m*) Means Lord Krishna.

Pārthiv (पार्थिव) (*a*) Terrestrial, earthly, material, worldly.

Pāru (पारू) (*m*) The sun.

Parvani (परवनी) (*m*) A judge, a year.

Parvata (पर्वत) (*m*) Mountain, Parvata sage and Narada sage were great friends and their story is mentioned in the Mahabharata.

Pārvati (पार्वती) The mountaineer. A name of the wife of Shiva. See Devi.

Pārvatimāyā (पार्वतीमाया) (*f*) Meaning the same as Devi and Māyā. See Devi and Māyā.

Pārvatipriya (पार्वतीप्रिय) (*m*) Lord Shiva

Paryapta (पर्याप्त) (*m/f/n*) Obtained, gained, extensive, spacious.

Paryās (प्रयास) The earth equal to sky or heaven in size.

Paryatan (प्रयत्न) (*m*) Circuit, circumference, edge, limit border, adjoining, extending in all directions.

Pashadhārini (पशधारिनी) (*f*) Holder of rope. Goddess Durga, holding a rope in one hand, is the power behind all creation, the only supporet for all in the universe. (D)

Pashin (पशीन) (*m*) One who sits like a rock-Lord Ganesha who is unshakeable, invincible, seat of infinite power, the pure essence of fuminous kind. (G)

Pashupata (पशुप्त) (*m/f*) Relating or sacred to or coming from Lord Shiva. A follower or worshipper of Lord Shiva.

Paspasha (पसपश) (*m/f*) Preface, introductory matter. Name of the introduction of the Mahabhashya of Patanjali.

Pastya (पसत्य) (*f*) Homestead, dwelling, household, the goddess of domestic affairs, a wealthy person.

Patākin (पटाकिन) (*m/f*) Having or bearing a flag, adorned with flag.

Patanjal (पतंजल) The Yoga philosophy.

Pātanjali (पतांजली) (*m*) The founder of the Yoga philosophy. The author of Mahā-bhāshya, (142 BC), a celebrated commentary on the grammar of Pānini.

Pathaṣpati (पथस्पति) (*m*) Lord of water. Another name of Varuna.

Pāthin (पाथीन) (*m/f*) One who has read or studied any subject.

Patishtha (पतिष्ठ) (*m/f*) Very sharp, skilful, clever.

Patmāvati (पदमावती) (*f*) Having a lotus. As Padmāvati (epithet of lakshmi). See Lakshmi.

Pātri (पात्रि) (*m/f*) Protector, defending.

Paulomī (पौलोमी) (*f*) Wife of Indra and mother of Jayanta. Also a name of Bhrigu Rishi's wife.

Pauravi (पौरवी) (*f*) A queen of Yudhishtra and mother of Devak.

Paurush (पौरुष) (*m/f*) Manly, human, belonging or sacred to Purush (human being).

Paurtikā (पौर्तिका) (*m/f/n*) Relating to a charitable or meritorious work.

Pavaka (पावक) (*m/f*) Pure, clear, bright, shining.

Pavaki (पवकी) (*f*) Purifying, Another name of Goddess Saraswati.

Pavan (पवन) (*m*) Air, breeze, the god of Wind (Hanuman).

Pavani (पावनी) (*f*) Holy, pure. Another name of Ganges.

Pāvanī-Nandā (पावनी-नन्दा) (*f*) One of three branches of the river Ganges going to the east.

Pavit (पवित) (*m/f*) Purified, cleansed.

Pavitra (पवित्र) (*a*) Holy, sacred, pure.

Pavitram (पवित्रम) (*m*) All purifier. (V)

Pavitri (पवित्री) (*a/f*) Meaning the same as Pavitra.

Pāyal (पायल) (*m*) An anklet.

Payoshini (पायोशिनी) (*a*) A sacred hill visited by Balrām.

Pelava (पेलव) (*f*) A delicate, fine, soft, tender.

Perā (पेरा) (*f*) A kind of musical instrument.

Perani (पेरनी) (*f*) A kind of dance in music.

Peshal (पेशल) (*m*) Beautiful, charming, decorated, charming.

Peshana (पेशन) (*f*) Well formed, beautiful (from Rig Veda).

Phanindra (फणीन्द्र) (*m*) An epithet of Sheshnāg (the mythological serpent king).

Phānish (फाणीश) (*m*) Same as Phanindra.

Phānishvar (फाणीश्वर) (*m*) Same as Phanindra.

Pidari (पीदरी) (*f*) Name of a mother or female deity.

Pinākin (पिनाकिन) (*m*) An epithet of Lord Shiva.

Pita (पीत) (*m/f*) Yellow colour of butter and oil. Name of several plants (Curcuma Longa and Aromatica, a species of Dalbergia Sisoo. In Hindu mythology - yellow colour of gold is a sign of good luck and prosperity.

Pitamani (पितामणि) (*m*) Yellow gem.

Pītāmbar (पीताम्बर) (*m*) Yellow silk cloth (Dhoti) worn by men and women during worship. A name of Vishnu who is clothed in yellow garments.

Pitāmbaram (पीताम्बरम) (*m*) Yellow cloth worn by Buddha at birth.

Pitikā (पितीका) (*f*) Yellow Jasmine, saffron, honey, turmeric.

Pitrabhakta (पित्रभक्त) (*m*) Devoterd to father. Another name of Lord Rama. (R)

Piyush (पीयूष) (*m*) Nector, ambrosia.

Poshita (पाषित) (*m/f*) Nourished, cherished, supported.

Poshya (पोष्य) (*m/f/n*) Thriving, well fed, abundant, copious, causing wealth or prosperity.

Prabālakā (प्रबालका) (*f*) Strong, mighty, powerful.

Prabandhari (प्रबन्धरी) (*m/f*) One who connects together, composer, author, interpreter.

Prabhā (प्रभा) (*f*) Lustre, radiance, light, splendour, goddess Durga. Circle of rays which surrounds Lord Shiva-to symbolize the dance of nature.

Prabhaj (प्रभज) (*n*) To honour, to divide, to accomplish.

Prabhākar (प्रभाकर) (*m*) The sun, moon.

Prabhānu (प्रभानु) (*m*) The brightest sun, name of a son of Krishna and Satyabhama.

Prabhāt (प्रभात) (*m*) The morning, dawn, day-break.

Prabhātā (प्रभाता) (*f*) Goddess of dawn.

Prabhāsh (प्रभाश) (*n*) To speak, tell, disclose, manifedst (from Mahabharata).

Prabhāhita (प्रभाहित) (*m/f*) Spoken, uttered, declared (from Mahabharata).

Prabhāshin (प्रभाशिन) (*m/f*) Saying, speaking (from Mahabharata).

Prabhāv (प्रभाव) (*m/f*) Prominent, excelling, distinguished.

Prabhāvat (प्रभावत) (*m/f*) Luminous, splendid, radiant. Name of a daughter of a king.

Prabhāvati (प्रभावती) (*f*) Same as Prabhā. Also name of wife of Pradyumma (son of Krishna).

Prabhāve (प्रभावे) (*m*) Popular Lord Hanuman's sincere devotion to Lord Ram make Him divinely lovable and worthy of worship. (H)

Prabhāvah (प्रभावाः) (*m*) The Special divine existence. (V)

Prabhu (प्रभु) (*a*) Mighty, abundant, Lord owner. All powerful. Lord Vishnu, Lord Indra.

Prabhutah (प्रभुताः) (*m*) Well endowed with knowledge, opulence and virtues. (V)

Prabodh (प्रबोध) (*m*) Awakening, consciousness, enlightenment, vigilance, wisdom.

Prabudh (प्रबुध) (*m/f*) Awake, develop, open, bloom, enlightened, clever.

Prabhudhitā (प्रभुधिता) (*f*) Intelligence, wisdom.

Prabhuti (प्रभूति) (*f*) Source, origin, mighty.

Prāchi (प्राची) (*f*) The east, the eastern quarter, the orient.

Prachipati (प्रचीपति) (*f*) Lord of the east, Name of Lord Indra

Prachita (प्रचित) (*n*) To know or make known (from Rig Veda). To become visible or manifest.

Prachur (प्रचुर) (*m/f*) Much, many, abundant, plentiful, frequent.

Prada (प्रद) (*n*) To give offer, present, grant, bestow (from Rig Veda) To give in marriage.

Pradan (प्रदन) (*n*) Giving, bestowing, presentation (esp. of an offering in the fire), also náme of a sacred text recited at this occasion. Gift, aonation.

Pradarsha (प्रदर्श) (*m*) Look, appearance, showing, indicating, foretelling, proclaiming.

Pradarshana (प्रदर्शन) (*m/f*) Look, appearance, showing, teaching, explaining, taught, mentioned, specified prophesying.

Pradhā (प्रधा) (*f*) Eminent, distinguished, supreme. A daughter of Daksha and mother of Gandharvas and Asparas.

Pradhan purusheshwar (प्रधान पुषेश्वर) (*m*) The master of nature and being. (V)

Pradhi (प्रधी) (*m/f*) To continue to study, advance in studies. Well read, learned.

Pradīp (प्रदीप) (*m*) A lamp, an instrument of illumintion.

Pradipkā (प्रदीपका) (*f*) One that illuminate, light.

Pradīpati (प्रदीप्ति) (*f*) Lustre, splendour.

Pradish (प्रदीश) (*f*) Pointing to or out, indicate, declare, appoint, command dominion, region of the sky.

Pradiv (प्रदीव) (*f*) Heaven, the third of the highest heaven.

Pradul (प्रदुल) (*a*) Beautiful.

Pradyumna (प्रद्युम्न) (*m*) Wealthiest, the pre-eminently mighty one, an aspect of Lord Vishnu. In most cases Pradyumna is regarded as son of Krishna and Rukmini.

Prāg (प्राग) (*m*) Dust, pollen of a flower, fragrant powder, fame, sandal, an eclipse, strong willed.

Pragnya (प्रागन्य) (*m*) Scholar. Hanuman is verily a limitless fount of divine knowledge. (H)

Pragti (प्रगति) (*f*) Progress, development.

Praggya (प्रग्य) (*f*) Prudence, intellect.

Pragraha (प्रग्रह) (*m*) He who accepts offerings of His Devotees. (V)

Praguna (प्रगुन) (*m*) Full of qualtities, honest, efficient.

Pragvansha (प्राग्वंश) (*m*) The origin of all families. (V)

Prahlād (प्रलहाद) (*m*) A Daitya, son of Hiranyaksipu and father of Bali. After the death of Hiranyaksipu, he became the King and was raised by Vishnu to the rank of Indra for life, and finally united with Vishnu.

Prajābhāvah (प्रजाभावा) (*m*) The progenitor of All Beings. (V)

Prajāgarah (प्रजाग्रह) (*m*) He who is ever conscious and awakened. (V)

Prajakta (प्रजाकता) (*f*) Mother of the people, goddess of creation.

Prajāpatī (प्रजक्त) (*m*) The sustainer of all being, the progenitor, Lord of all creation. (V)

Prajāpatya (प्रजापत्या) (*m/f*) Coming or derived from Prajpati, relating or sacred to him. (from Atharva Veda).

Prajesh (प्रजेष) (*m/f*) Intelligent, wise, clever, wisdom.

Prajyoti (प्रज्योति) (*m*) An Amitābha god (a deity in the Buddhist Pantheon).

Prakāsh (प्रकाश) (*m*) Light, shine, lustre.

Prakāshan (प्रकाशन) (*m*) One who illuminates everything. (V)

Prakāshātma (प्रकाशात्मा) (*m*) The enlightened soul. (V)

Prakāshikā (प्रकाशिका) (*f*) One who elinghtens, illuminates, bright, shining, renowned.

Prakāshinī (प्रकाशिनी) (*f*) To enlighten, making visible, shining.

Prakāshya (प्रकाश्य) (*m/f*) Manifestation, celebrity, renown (from Mahabharata).

Prakhyā (प्राख्या) (*m/f*) Visible, clear, bright, announce, proclaim.

Prakriti (प्रकृति) (*f*) Nature. The personified will of the supreme in the creation, indentified with Māyā. The Shakti or female energy of any deity. Temperament, disposition, habit, genius.

Prakruti (प्राकृती) (*f*) Nature. Goddess Lakshmi is nature, the centre of all, the manifested and the unmanifested. (L) See also Prakriti.

Pramā (प्रमा) (*f*) Consciousness, correct knowledge, beauty.

Pramād (प्रमाद) (*m*) Joy, pleasure, delight (from Mahabharata).

Pramadā (प्रमदा) (*f*) A young and beautiful woman. Any woman.

Pramadvara (प्रमदवर) (*f*) Daughter of apsara Menaka and Gandharava Vishvavasu. She was married to Ruru and they had a son called Shunaka.

Pramanam (प्रमनम) (*m*) The evidence or self evident. (V)

Pramāni (प्रमाणी) (*a*) Reliable, authoriative.

Pramānina (प्रमाणिना) (*v*) To consider rightly, to accept an authority, to prove

Pramārthi (प्रमार्थी) (*a*) One is search of the highest truth. Philosopher.

Pramata (प्रमत) (*m*) One possessing true knowledge, on looker.

Pramati (प्रमति) (*m*) Son of Chyavana Rishi and Sukanya. Father of Ruru

Pramīlā (प्रमिला) (*f*) Lassitude, enervation, exhaustion from fatigue. Soverign of a kingdom of women.

Pramita (प्रमिता) (*m/f/n*) Meted out, measured, known, understood, proved, established.

Pramlocha (प्रमलोच) (*f*) A celestial nymph sent by Indra to beguile the sage Kandu from his devotion and austerities and she gave birth to a lovely nymph Marisha.

Pramod (प्रमोद) (*m*) Entertainment, mirth, joy delight, gladness, perfume.

Pramodanah (प्रमोदनः) (*m*) He who delights merely by rememering Him. (V)

Pramuchi (प्रमुचि) (*m*) A sage of Tamil Nadu. Liberated person.

Prān (प्राण) (*m*) Breath of life. In the Atharvaveda it is personified and a hymn is addressed to it. Vital breath, soul, spirit, sweet heart.

Prānad/Pranadah (प्राणद/प्राणदः) (*m*) The giver of life. (V)

Prānanātha (प्राणनाथ) (*m*) Lord of life. Another name of Yama.

Prānanilaya (प्राणनिलय) (*m*) The basis of life. (V)

Pranav (प्रणव) (*m*) The sacred and mystical syllable Om. God Almighty.

Prānesh (प्राणेश) (*m*) Lod of life, breath.

Prāneshvari (प्राणेश्वरी) (*f*) Goddess of life, breath. Very dear.

Prāni (प्राणी) (*m/f*) Lader or guide, guidance, devotion.

Prāniti (प्रणिति) (*f*) Guidance, leading, conduct.

Prānjivan (प्राणजीवन) (*m*) The vital air to keep all being alive. (V)

Prānmani (प्राणमणि) (*m*) Leading jewel, jewel among leaders.

Prannati (प्रन्नति) (*f*) Salution, bowing.

Pranshu (प्रंशु) (*m/f*) High, strong, intense, name of a Manu. See Manu.

Prapā (प्रपा) (*n*) To protect, defend from.

Prapad (प्रपद) (*f*) A way, sacred texts.

Prapana (प्रपन) (*m/f*) Appearance, occurrence, attainable, to be reached.

Prāpanch (प्रपंच) (*m/f*) Expansion, develpment, manifestation, phenomenon, expansion of the universe, the visible world.

Prapatti (प्रपत्ति) (*f*) Ardent devotion

Prāpattikā (प्रपत्तिका) (*f*) Young shoot or sprout.

Praphulat (प्रफुलत) (*a*) Blooming, smiling.

Prāphulati (प्रफूलति) (*f*) Blooming, blossoming.

Prāpitāmah (प्रापितामह) (*m*) The Sire of the Grand Deity Brahma. (V)

Prāpti (प्राप्ति) (*f*) Power of obtaining everything, saving, rescue or deliverance, fortune, luck.

Prasadabhimukhi (प्रसादभिमुखी) (*f*) Emerging to grant boons-goddess Lakshmi. (L)

Prasanna (प्रसन्न) (*f*) Cheerful. Goddess Durga is the abode of cheer and bliss being the great power. (D)

Prasannākshi (प्रसन्नाक्षी) (*f*) Lively eyed-goddess Lakshmi. (L)

Prasanātma (प्रसन्नात्मा) (*m*) Delighted soul. (V)

Prasena (प्रसेन) (*m*) Son of Nighna and brother of Satrajit. Also a name of a son of Karna. Both are mentioned in Mahabharata.

Prasenjit (प्रसनजित) (*m*) Father of Parshuram's mother Renuka.

Prāshā (प्राशा) (*f*) Ardent desire or longing.

Prashami (प्रशमी) (*m*) Calm, tranquil. An apsara (from Mahabharata).

Prashānt (प्रशांत) (*a*) Pacific, tranquil, quiet, calm.

Prashasti (प्रशस्ति) (*f*) Praise, fame, glorification (from Rig Veda).

Prashu (प्रशु) (*m/f*) Very quick or speedy, rapidly victorious.

Prashubh (प्रशुभ) (*m/f*) To be bright, sparkle (from Rig Veda).

Prashuch (प्रशुच) (*m/f*) To glow, beam, radiate (from Rig Veda).

Prashuchi (प्रशूचि) (*m/f*) Perfectly pure.

Prashudhi (प्रशुद्धि) (*f*) Purity, clearness (from Mahabharata).

Prasna (प्रस्न) (*m/f*) Name of an Upanishad.

Prastāv (प्रस्ताव) (*m*) Hymn of praise, chant, song, a favourable moment.

Prastāvanā (प्रस्तावना) (*f*) Sounding forth hymn of praise, begining, commencement.

Prasū (प्रसू) (*m/f/n*) Fruitful, bringing forth, bearing, productive (from Rig Veda).

Prasuti (प्रसूति) (*f*) A daughter of Manu and wife of Daksha (son of Brahma).

Pratāp (प्रताप) (*m*) Glorious, dignified, dignity, glorious, renown, influence, overwhelming

Pratapan (प्रतपन) (*m*) Providing heat to all luminaries like sun and fire. (V)

Pratapavate (प्रतपवति) (*m*) Known for valour-Hanuman. (H)

Pratardanah (प्रतर्दनः) (*m*) Destroyer of Beings at the time of Dissolution. (V)

Prathameshvar (प्रथमेश्वर) (*m*) One who holds the first place. Lord Ganesh, the eternal spirit, is the god of auspiciousness, holding the first place. (G)

Prathu (प्रथु) (*m*) Spreading in large billows. (V)

Prati (प्रति) (*n*) Name of a son of Kusha and father of Sanjay.

Pratibhā (प्रतिभा) (*f*) Genius, brilliance, intellect, Characteristics of education, poetry, art etc.

Pratibhānu (प्रतिभानु) (*a*) Son of Krishna and Satyabhāmā.

Pratibhāvati (प्रतिभावती) (*m/f*) Full of understanding, bright, intelligent, bold.

Pratibudh (प्रतिबुद्ध) (*m/f*) Awakened, to learn, perceive, made prosperous, illuminated, enlightened.

Pratigyā (प्रतिज्ञा) (*f*) A pledge, vow, promise, enunication.

Pratikriti (प्रतिकृति) (*f*) Likeness, Image of a deity.

Pratikshā (प्रतीक्षा) (*f*) Admission, promise, a vow, assertion.

Pratilābh (प्रतिलाभ) (*m/f*) Receive, obtain, learn, understand.

Pratimā (प्रतिमा) (*f*) An image, reflection, a measure, a symbol, a statue, effigy.

Pratimān (प्रतिमान) (*m*) Resemblance, imge, idol, model.

Pratinand (प्रतिनन्द) (*m*) Name of a poet. Great, welcome, cheerful, salute, favour, friendly, very happy.

Pratip (प्रतिप) (*m*) King of Hastinapur and husband of queen Sunanda. Father of king Shantanu and grandfather of Bhishma.

Pratipāl (प्रतिपाल) (*m*) To protect, defend, guard.

Pratipuj (प्रतिपुज) (*m*) To return a salutation, reverence, salute, honour, praise, commend, approve.

Pratirupā (प्रतिरूपा) (*m*) Grandfather of king Shantanu. Father of king Pratip.

Pratishrutī (प्रतिश्रुति) (*f*) Promise, assent.

Pratishtha (प्रतिष्ठा) (*f*) A Shakti (wife or female energy of Lord Shiva).

Pratitā (प्रतिता) (*m/f/n*) Acknowledged, recognized, known.

Pratitī (प्रतीति) (*f*) Going towards, approaching (from Rig Veda), being clever or intelligible by itself, Vedants. Clear apprehension or insight into anything, complete understanding.

Pratta (प्रत्त) (*m/f/n*) Giving, offering, granting, give away (also in marriage).

Pratti (प्रत्ति) (*f*) Giving away, giving gift.

Pratulya (प्रतुल्य) (*m*) Unique, uncomp arable. Another name of. Kartikeya

Pratush (प्रतुष) (*m*) Delighted. Very happy.

Pratyaksha (प्रत्यक्ष) (*m/f*) Present before the eyes, visible, perceptible, clear, distinct.

Pratyani (प्रत्यनी) (*n*) To lead, restore, to recover again.

Pratyaya (प्रत्यय) (*m*) Comprehensible only to the best brain. (V)

Pravin (प्रवीण) (*a*) Proficient, adept, expert.

Pravīr (प्रवीर) (*m/f*) Surpassing heroes. Chief, prince.

Prayāg (प्रयाग) (*m*) Meeting place, the confluence of the three holy rivers (Ganga, Jamuna and Sarasvati).

Prayās (प्रयास) (*m/f*) Pleasure, enjoyment, delight (from Rig Veda), valuable, precious, object of food and delight.

Prayog (प्रयोग) (*m*) Joining together, connection, position, addition of a word.

Preksha (प्रेक्षा) (*m/f*) Seeing, viewing, beholding, regarding, looking on.

Prem (प्रेम) (*m*) Love, affection, attachment.

Premāmrit (प्रेमामृत) (*m*) Nectar of love.

Premendra (प्रेमेन्द्र) (*m*) Lord of love. Another name of Kama.

Premin (प्रेमीन) (*m/f*) Loving, affectionate.

Premlatā (प्रेमलता) (*f*) Vine of love.

Premnidhi (प्रेमनिधि) (*m/f*) Treasure of love.

Premsāgar (प्रेमसागर) (*m*) Ocean of love.

Preyas (प्रेयस) (*m/f*) Dear friend, dearer, more agreeable.

Prisha/Prishdhar (प्रिश/प्रिशधर) (*m*) Name of a man in Rig Veda. Name of a son of the Manus.

Prishāni/Prshāni (प्रीशानी/प्रशानी) (*f*) Tender, gentle

Prisni (प्रीसनी) (*f*) In the Vedas and Puranas, the earth, the mother of the Maruts (the storm god who hold a very prominent place in the Vedas).

Prītam (प्रीतम) (*m*) A lover, beloved.

Prithā (प्रिथा) (*f*) A name of Kunti (mother of Pandavas). Se Prutha.

Prithi, Prithu, Prithi-Vainya (प्रिथी, प्रिथु, प्रिथी-वैन्य) (*m*) Prithi or Prithi-vainya, i.e. Prithi, son of Vena, is mentioned in the Rig Veda, and he is the decalred sage and author of one of the hymns. He was called the first king, and from him the earth received her name Prithvi. It is mentioned in Satapatha Brahmana.

Prithikā (प्रिथिका) (*f*) Jasmine.

Prithisha (प्रीतिषा) (*m*) Lord of the world.

Prithu (प्रिथु) (*m*) A king of the Solar race-a descendant of Ikshwāku (son of the Manu Vaivaswat).

Prithushri (प्रिथुश्री) (*m*) A person of great wealth and fortune.

Prithvi (पृथ्वी) (*m*) The earth, ground, terrestial. In Vedas the Prithvi is personified as the mother of all beings, and is invoked together with the sky.

Pritī (प्रीति) (*f*) Pleasure, joy, love affectin. Also a name of the wife of the God Love.

Pritivardhan (प्रीतिवर्धन) (*m*) He who enriches affection for Him in His Dearest votaries. (V)

Priya (प्रिय) (*a*) Dear, agreeable, fond, expensive, usual, a lover, favour.

Priyā (प्रिया) (*a/f*) Beloved, darling, sweetheart, wife.

Priyabhakta (प्रियभक्त) (*m*) Favourite of the devotees. Epithet of Lord Shiva. (S)

Priyadarshan (प्रियदर्शन) (*a*) Lovely, pleasant to the sight.

Priyadarshani (प्रियदर्शनी) (*a/f*) Same as Priyadarshan.

Priyadarshi (प्रियदर्शी) (*a*) Beautiful, beloved of the gods. Another name of king Ashok.

Priyakam (प्रियकम) (*m/f*) Desirous of showing kindness, friendly disposed.

Priyakarin (प्रियकरीन) (*m/f*) Showing kindness.

Priyakrita (प्रियकृत) (*m*) He Who Does what is good for his devotees. (V)

Priyam (प्रियम्) (*m/f*) Very dear, beloved.

Priyankara/ Priyamkara (प्रियम्कर/प्रियंकर) (*m/f*) Showing kindness, acting kindly.

Priya-ranjana (प्रिय-रंजन) (*m/f*) Good looking, pleasant, loving.

Priyārtha (प्रियार्थ) (*m*) He who deserves to be offered one's dearest object or thing. (V)

Priyatā (प्रियता) (*f*) Very dear person, loving.

Priyātman (प्रियात्मन) (*m/f*) Dear to soul, pleasant, agreeable.

Promilā (प्रोमिला) See Pramilā.

Prutha/Pritha (परुथा/पृथा) (*f*) Name by which Kunti (mother of Pandavas) was known before she was given by her father Shura to Kuntibhoj.

Pujā (पूजा) (*f*) Worship, adoration, veneration, honour.

Pujak (पूजक) (*m/f*) Honour, respect, worship.

Pukhrāj (पुखराज) (*m*) King of jewels.

Pulaha (पुलह) Name of one of the prajapatis (creator) and great sage. His wife was Kshama, and he had three sons, Kardama, Arvarivat, and Sahishnu.

Pulastya (पुलस्त्य) (*m*) One of the Prajāpatis or mind born sons of Brahmā and Prītī.

Punan (पूनन) (*m/f*) Clear, bright, purified.

Punarvasu (पुनर्व) (*m*) The spirit which repeatedly comes back to the body. (V)

Pundarīka (पुण्डरीक) (*m*) White lotus.

Punderikākshah (पुण्डरीकाक्ष) (*m*) The one having lotus like eyes. (V)

Punisha (पुनीश) (*m*) Lord of the pious.

Punīt (पुनीत) (*a*) Holy, pious, sacred.

Punitā (पुनीता) (*a*) Purified.

Punjarāj (पुंजराज) (*m*) Lor of multitude.

Punya (पुण्य) (*m/f*) Auspicious, virtuous, meritorious, purity, sacred. Punya-Sloka are holy verses in holy books. Punya Sloka is also an appellation applied to Krishna. Yudhishthira, Nala, Draupadi and Sita.

Punyabālā (पुण्याबाला) (*m*) Meritorious, virtuous, pious, holy.

Punyagandha (पुण्यागन्ध) (*f*) Having divine perfume-goddess Lakshmi. (L)

Punyajit (पुन्यजीत) (*m*) Gained by virtue.

Punyakirti (पुण्यकीर्ति) (*m*) One noble renown. (V)

Punyanidhi (पुण्यानिधि) (*m/f*) Treasure of virtue.

Punyashravan Kirtan (पुण्यश्रवन कीर्तन) (*m*) He-listening to whose glories and singing his hymns grant all merit. (V)

Punyodaya (पुण्योदय) (*m*) Granter of immortality. (R)

Puralā (पुरला) (*f*) Name of goddess Durga.

Puran (पूरन) (*m/f*) Filling, completing, satisfying. A deity.

Purān (पुराण) (*m/f*) Ancient, old, name of a Rishi (sage). Name of a class of sacred books of Hindus, compiled by the poet Vyās.

Puranjaya (पूरंजय) (*m*) Conqueror of city. Son of Sanjay-whose glory is sun in the heaven.

Puraritvam (पुरारित्वम) (*m*) An incarnation of Lord Shiva.

Purin (पूरिन) (*m/f/n*) Filling, making full.

Purishi (पुरीशि) (*n*) Produced by Brahmā.

Puriyata (पूरीयत) (*m*) He who makes His devotee devoid of want. (V)

Purnachandra (पूर्णचन्द्र) (*m*) Full moon. A boddhisattva.

Purnah (पूर्णः) (*m*) Perfect in every way. (V)

Purnamā/Purnimā (पूर्णमा/पूर्णिमा) (*f*) Full moon-day.

Purnāmrit (पूर्णामृत) (*m*) Full of nectar.

Purnmukhī (पूर्णमुखी) (*f*) Most beautiful and perfect face.

Purnī (पूर्णि) (*f*) Fulfilling, completely satisfying.

Purnimā (पूर्णिमा) (*f*) A day of the full moon.

Puru (पुरु) (*m*) A son of Chakshushā Manu.

Purujit (पुरुजीत) (*m*) Conquering many. Brother of Kunti. He succeeded Kuntibhoj to the throne and fought on the Pandava side in Mahabharata war.

Purukutsa (पुरुकुत्स) (*m*) A son of Mandhatri, into whose person Vishnu entered for the purpose of destroying the subterranean Gandharvas, called Mauneyas.

Purumantu (पुरुमन्तु) (*m*) Full of wisdom.

Puru-Ravas (पुरु-रवस) (*m*) In the Vedas, a mythical personage connected with the sun and the dawn, and existing in the middle region of the universe.

Purushotam (पुरुषोत्तम) (*m*) Literally "best of men", but it also means the "supreme soul". It is a title of Lord Vishnu and asserts his right to be considered the Supreme God.

Purvachī (पूर्वची) (*f*) Apsaras (heavenly nymphs).

Purvi (पूर्वी) (*a*) Eastern.

Pushan (पूशन) (*m*) A deity frequently mentioned in the Vedas. Many hymns are addressed to him. The word comes from the root and the primary idea is that of "nourisher" of Providence. Taittiriya Brahmana says that when Prajapti formed living creatures, Pushan nourished them.

Pushanā (पूशना) (*f*) Nourisher, protector.

Pusharaksha (पुष्रक्ष) (*m*) The lotus eyed. (V)

Pushkal (पुष्कल) (*a*) Plenty, abundant, in abundance.

Pushkar (पुष्कर) (*m*) Lake, pond, tank, lotus. Also means Lord Krishna.

Pushkara (पुष्कर) (*m/f*) Blue lotus-flower.

Pushkarin (पुष्करिन) (*m/f*) Abounding in lotuses.

Pushpa (पुष्प) (*n*) Flower, blossom, politeness.

Pushpa-giri (पुष्प-गिरि) (*m*) Flower mountains. Name of a mythical mountain.

Pushpaka (पुष्पक) (*n*) A self-moving aerial car of large dimensions, which contained within it a palace or city. Kuvera obtained it by gift from Brahma, but it was carried off by Ravana. After Rama killed Ravana, he made use of this capacious car and after that he returned it to its owner Kuvera.

Pushpalochan (पुष्पलोचन) (*m*) Flowery-eyed. (S)

Pushpavatī (पुष्पवती) (*f*) A woman in her flower gardens. Flower garden.

Pushpāya (पुष्पाया) (*a*) To become a flower.

Pushpit (पुष्पित) A blossomed, flower garden.

Pushp-mālā (पुष्प-माला) (*f*) A garland of flowers.

Pusharaksha (पुषारक्षा) (*m*) The louts eyed. (V)

Push-Sari (पुष-सारी) (*f*) Having the essence of the lotus. A kind of writing.

Pushti (पुष्टि) (*f*) Well nourished, comfort, prosperity, wealth. A daughter of Daksha and wife of Dharma.

Putātma (पूतात्म) (*m*) The soul purified. (V)

Purātan (पुरातन) (*m*) The ancient being. (V)

Purjanya (पुरजन्य) (*m*) He who showers all desired objects. (V)

Purnendu (पूर्णेन्दु) (*m*) Full moon.

Purujit (पुरुजीत) (*m*) Victorious of many battles. (V)

Purupriya (पुरुप्रिय) (*f*) Dear to many.

Purusha/Purushah (पुरुषा/पुरुष) (*m*) The Primal person. (V)

Purushotam (पुरुषोत्तम) (*m*) The best universal form. (V)

Pushkala (पुष्कल) (*m/f*) Much many, abundant, complete, strong, powerful.

Pushkārakshā (पुषकारक्षा) (*m*) The lotus eyed. (V)

Pushkarin (पुष्करीन) (*m/f/n*) Abounding in lotus, a lotus pool.

Pushpabhuti (पुष्पभूति) (*f*) Essence of flowers.

Pushpahas (पुष्पहास) (*m*) He whose laughter is like the blooming flower. (V)

Pushpāmbu (पुष्पाम्बु) (*m/f*) Water of flowers, honey, nectar.

Pushpāngi (पुष्पांगी) (*f*) Delicate, flower bodied.

Pushpāveni (पुष्पावेणी) (*f*) Garland of flowers. A river's name in Mahabharata.

Pushpendra (पुष्पेन्द्र) (*m*) Lord of flowers.

Pushpendu (पुष्पेन्दु) (*m*) Lord of flowers.

Pushpi (पुष्पी) (*f*) Flower like.

Pushpin (पुष्पिन्) (*f*) Full of flowers. Full blossom.

Pushta (पुष्ट) (*m*) Fully healthy, nourished, cherished, complete. (V)

Pushya (पुष्य) (*m/f*) Nourishment, the blossom or flower.

Putamali (पुतमली) (*m*) Pure minded. Another name of Shiva. (S)

R (र, रा)

Rabhas (रभस) (*m/f*) Shining, zeal, rapid, fierce, strong, wild.

Rabhod (रभोद) (*m*) Bestowing strength.

Rabhya (रभ्य) (*m/f*) Agreeable, kind, aesthetic in music. Justice.

Rachanā (रचना) (*f*) Composition, artistic, creation, structure, to make or form, arrangement, performance.

Rādhā (राधा) (*f*) Prosperity, lighting. Wife of Adhiratha and foster-mother of Karna. The legendary favourite beloved of Lord Krishna. While he lived as Gopal among the cowherds in Vrindavan. She was actualy wife of Ayana-ghosha, a cowherd. Considered by some to be incarnation of Lakshmi, and worshipped accordingly. Some have disocvered a mystical character in Radha, and consider her as the type of the Human soul drawn to the ineffable god, Krishna, or as that pure divine love to which the fickle lover returns.

Rādhākānt (राधाकांत) (*m*) Another name of Krishna. Beloved of Radha. (K)

Rādhanā (राधना) (*m/f*) Proppitiating, conciliating.

Rādhāraman (राधारमन) (*m*) Lover of Radha. Name of Lord Krishna. (K)

Radhesh (राधेश) (*m*) Lord of Rādhā, another name of Lord Krishna.

Radhi (राधी) (*f*) Accomplishment, perfection, success, good fortune.

Rādhikā (राधिका) (*f*) A diminutive and endearing form of the name of Rādhā.

Rāghav (राघव) (*m*) Descendant of Raghu, a name of Lord Rāṁ.

Raghu (रघु) (*m/f*) Hastening, going speedily. Name of an ancient king and ancestor of Lord Rāma.

Raghumani (रघुमणि) (*m*) Jewel of Raghu. See also Raghu. Name of Lord Ram.

Raghunandan (रघुनन्दन) (*m*) An epithet of Vishnu.

Raghunāth (रघुनाथ) (*m*) Another name of Lord Ṛam. Lord of Raghu. (R)

Raghupunghav (रघुपुंघव) (*m*) Scion of Raghukul dynasty - Lord Ram. (R)

Raghuvir (रघुवीर) (*m*) Hero of Raghu. Lord Ram.

Rāgini (रागिनी) (*f*) The Rāgas (*m*) They are musical modes or melodies personified, six or more in number, and the Rāginis are their consorts. R¯ agini means a modification of a musical mode.

Rāglatā (रागलता) (*f*) Another name of Rati. Passion creeper. See also Rati.

Rāgmālā (रागमाला) (*f*) Series of musical Ragas (Indian calssical music).

Rāhul (राहुल) (*m*) Name of the son of Gautama Buddha and Yashodharā.

Raibhya (रैभ्य) (*m*) A sage who was the friend of Bhardwaj sage. He was a great scholar of Vedas.

Raivata (रैवत) (*m*) Son of Reva or Revat. He had a very beautiful daughter named Revati.

Rāj (राज) (*m*) A kingdom, realm, sate, reign.

Rājā (राजा) (*m*) A king, monarch, prince, darling.

Rājādhidevi (राजाधिदेवी) (*f*) Kunti's younger sister. Wife of king Jayasena of Avanti.

Rājamannār (राजामन्नार) (*m*) In South India an epithet of Krishna.

Rājan (राजन्) (*m*) King, Lord Indra, Moon.

Rājanvati (राजनवती) (*f*) The good earth abode of the kings.

Rajanī (रजनी) (*f*) Night, turmeric.

Rajanipati (रजनीपति) (*m*) Lord of night, the moon.

Rājanya (राजन्य) (*m/f*) Kingly, princely, royal (from Rigveda).

Rājapushpa (राजपुष्प) (*f*) Royal flower (Mesua roxburghii-tree).

Rājārām (राजाराम) (*m*) King of Ram.

Rājarājeshvari (राजेश्वरी) (*f*) Royal lady. Name of Pārvati. See Parvati.

Rājarishi (राजऋषि) (*m*) A Rishi or saint of the regal origin; a Kshatriya who, through pure and holy life on earth has been raised as a saint or demi-god to Indra's heaven, as Vishwāmitra, Puru-ravas etc.

Rājashri (राजश्री) (*m/f*) Belonging to royalty, grandeur, a Gandharv.

Rājasī (राजसी) (*f*) Another name of Goddess Durga. Passionate.

Rājatā (राजता) (*f*) Royalty, sovereignty, kingship.

Rājavat (राजवत) (*m*) Royal fragrace.

Rājaya (राजय) (*m*) To act or behave like a king.

Rājbandhu (राजबन्धु) (*m*) Relation of a king.

Rājdip (राजदीप) (*m*) Light of the king.

Rājduhitri (राजदुहित्रि) (*f*) Princess, king's daughter.

Rājendra (राजेन्द्र) (*m*) A supreme sovereign, a lord of kings. Lord of, the Lords. Another name of Lord Rama. (R)

Rājeshvar (राजेश्वर) (*m*) Lord of Kings.

Rājgiri (राजगिरि) (*m*) King's hill.

Rāj-hans (राज-हंस) (*m*) A white goose.

Rājin (राजिन) (*m*) Moonlight. Light considered as a vehicle of the moon.

Rājindu (राजिन्दु) (*m*) An excellent king.

Rājit (राजीत) (*m/f*) Illuminated, resplendent, brilliant.

Rājiv (राजीव) (*m*) A blue lotus. Living at King's expense.

Rājivini (राजीविनी) (*f*) The lotus plant or a group of lotuses.

Rājivalochana (राजीवलोचन) (*m*) Lotus-eyed. Another name of Lord Rama. Everpleasant-faced Rama has eyes like a full-blown lotus. (R)

Rājiv-netra (राजीव-नेत्र) (*m/f/n*) Lotus eyed.

Rājiv-mukha (राजीव-मुख) (*m/f*) Lotus faced.

Rājkalā (राजकला) (*f*) The sixteenth part of the moon's disk. See also Raj and Kala.

Rājkanyā (राजकन्या) (*f*) Peincess.

Rājkul (राजकुल) (*m/f*) King's race, royal family.

Rājkumār (राजकुमार) (*m*) Prince. Son of a king.

Rājkumāri (राजकुमारी) (*f*) Daughter of a king. Princess.

Rājlakshmi (राजलक्ष्मी) (*f*) The fortune or prosperity of a king (personified as a Goddess).

Rājmani (राजमणि) (*m*) Precious jem or royal diamond.

Rājmukhī (राजमुखी) (*f*) Beautiful, shining face. With a king's face.

Rājnī (राजनी) (*f*) The queen, princess, the wife of the Sun.

Rājnikānt (रजनीकांत) (*m*) Another name of moon. Beloved of the night.

Rajnikar (रजनीकर) (*m*) Name of the moon. Night maker.

Rajnīsh (रजनीष) (*m/f*) The moon.

Rājpāl (राजपाल) (*m*) King, from royl family. Protector of kingdom.

Rājpati (राजपति) (*m*) Lord of kings.

Rājpriya (राजप्रिया) (*f*) Favourite of the Kings. King's favourite wife.

Rājrishi (राजऋषि) (*m*) The same as Rājarishi.

Rājshekhar (राजशेखर) (*m*) Crown of a king. Name of a renowned Sanskrit dramatist.

Rājyadā (राज्यदा) (*f*) Bestower of kingdom - goddess Durga. (D)

Rājvidyā (राजविद्या) (*f*) Royal science, state policy, statesmenship.

Rājyalakshmi (राज्यलक्ष्मी) (*f*) Goddess/fortune of the king or state.

Rājyashri (राज्यश्री) (*f*) Goddess of the state. Royal grace.

Rājyavardhana (राज्यवर्धन) (*m*) Enchancing the glory of the king.

Rājyavati (राज्यवती) (*f*) Princess. Queen.

Rākā (राका) (*f*) The Goddess presiding over the actual day of the full moon. Moon's consort.

Rākesh (राकेश) (*m*) The moon.

Rākhi (राखी) (*f*) A sacred thread tied by a sister on the wrist of her brother as a mark of affection that binds the brother to protect her in the time of crisis.

Rakshā (रक्षा) (*f*) Defence, protection, guarding, safe keeping, custody, an amulet, preservation.

Rakshana/Rakshanaḥ (रक्षण/रक्षणः) (*m*) Protector, guarding. He who protects the noble by all means. (V)

Rakta (रक्त) (*m*) Red coloured. Lord Ganesha's body hue is compared to the red lotus and his tusk to the vermilion blood marks when it is thrust into his enemies for destruction. (G)

Raktapushpa (रक्तपुष्प) (*f*) The blossom of pomegranate, red flower.

Rām (राम) (*m.*) Rāma/Rāma-Chandra. Eldest son of Dasarath, a king of the Solar race, reigning at Ayodhya. He is the seventh incarnation of the Vishnu, and made his appearance in the world at the end of the Tretā or second age. His story is given in full length as the grand subject of the Rāmayana.

Ramā (रमा) (*f*) Another name of Lakshmi (the goddes of wealth and prosperity).

Rāmabhadra (रामभद्रा) (*m*) Auspicious Rama. Another name of Lord Rama. (R)

Ramā-kānt (रमा-कांत) (*m*) Husband of Lakshmi (Lord Vishnu).

Raman (रमन) (*m*) Sporting, amorous, erotic, playfulness, merriment.

Ramanāni (रमनाणी) (*f*) A charming woman, a mistress.

Ramanī (रमण) (*f*) A pretty woman, young woman.

Rāmanikā (रमणिका) (*m*) Worth loving, pleasing, attractive.

Rāmaniya (रमणीय) (*m/f*) Pleasant, delightful, agreeable, charming, to be enjoyed.

Rāmānujā (रामनुजा) (*m*) Means Younger brother of Rām. Name of a celebrated Vaishnava reformer.

Rāmāyi (रामायी) (*f*) Pleaser of the Lord. Goddess Lakshmi roams the three worlds and showers grace and blessings on her devotees.

Rambhā (रम्भा) (*f*) Name of gracious aspect of Pārvati who grants all the desires of her votaries. Also it means an Apsara or nymph produced at the churning of the ocean, and pupularly the type of female beauty.

Rāmbhakta (रामभक्त) (*m*) Devoted to Lord Ram. Another name of Hanuman. (H)

Rāmbhapriya (रम्भाप्रिया) (*m*) Another name of Lord Krishna.

Ramachandra (रामचन्द्र) (*m*) See Ram.

Ramesh (रमेश) (*m*) Ramesh/Rameshvar. Name of Lord Vishnu. Also it means Lord of Ram. Name of one of the twelve great Lingas (Rameshwar) set up as is said by Rām at Rāeshwaram, which is a celebrated place of pilgrimage, and contains a most magnificent temple. Rameshvara also means

Lord Krishna.

Rāmeshwaram (रामेश्वरम्) A sacred place. See Ramesh.

Rāmgitā (रामगीता) (*f*) Name of the chapter of Adhyatma-Ramayana, in which spiritual knowledge is shown to be better than ritualistic observances.

Rāmgopāl (रामगोपाल) (*m*) Ram and Krishna conjoined.

Ramit (रामित) (*a*) Attracted, enticed, bewitched.

Rāmmurti (राममूर्ति) (*m*) Idol of Lord Ram.

Rāmnāth (रामनाथ) (*m*) Ram's Lord.

Rāmyā (राम्या) (*m/f*) Pleasing, delightful, beautiful, enjoyable.

Rāmya-rūp (राम्य-रूप) (*m/f/n*) Having a lovely form, beautiful.

Rāmya-shri (राम्य-श्री) (*m*) Pleasing to Vishnu. Name of Vishnu. (V)

Ranajit (रणजीत) (*m*) Victorious in battle.

Ranajitā (रणजीता) (*f*) Victorious in battle.

Ranapriya (रणप्रिया) (*m*) He who loves wars. (V)

Ranesh (रणेश) (*m*) Lord Shiva, Lord of War.

Ranjan/Ranjanā (रंजन/रंजना) (*m/f*) Colouring, pleasing, charming, rejoicing, entertainment, recreation.

Ranjani/Ranjini (रंजनी/रंजिनी) (*f*) Same as Ranjan. Also name of various plants e.g. Indigo, Rubia Munjista.

Ranjidev (रंजिदेव) (*m*) Lord of entertainment. A king descendant of King Bharata.

Ranjikā (रंजिका) (*f*) Red Sandalwood. Pleasing, charming, exciting.

Ranjit (रणजीत) (*a*) Coloured, dyed, delighted.

Ranti (रंती) (*f*) Loving to stay, abiding gladly with, pleasure, delight.

Rantibhar (रंतिभर) (*m*) An early ancestor of the Kauravas and Pandavas. Father of Kanva Rishi and great grandfather of Dushyant.

Rantidev (रंतीदेव) (*m*) A pious and benevolent king of the Lunar race, sixth in descent from Bhārat. He is mentioned in the Mahābhārata and Puranas as being enormously rich and charitable person.

Rantrī (रंत्री) (*m/f/n*) Gladly abiding with, delighting in.

Rasendra (रसेन्द्र) (*m*) Mercury.

Raseshvar (रसेश्वर) (*m*) Lord Krishna, Lord of Ras.

Rāshi (राशि) (*f*) A head, collection, fund, a sign of the zodiac. Three fold, as Brahmā, Rudra and Vishnu.

Rashmi (रश्मि) (*f*) A ray, sun ray, a rein.

Rashmikā (रश्मिका) (*f*) A ray of light.

Rashmimālin (रश्मिमालिन) (*f*) Gartland of rays.

Rashmin (रश्मिन) (*m*) Bearer of rays (Sun or Moon).

Rasik (रसिक) (*m/f*) Tasteful, elegant, aesthetic.

Rasikā (रसिका) (*f*) An emotional wife, the juice of sugar-cane. molasses

Rasishvari (रसीश्वरी) (*f*) Radha, goddess of Ras.

Rasmani (रसमणि) (*m*) Jewel of the Ras, Lord Krishna.

Ratan (रतन) (*n*) A jewel, anything excellent, precious stone, most outstanding individual of a class.

Ratanā (रतना) (*f*) Same as Ratan. name of a daughter of Shaibya, queen of Akrur.

Ratan Chandra (रतन चन्द्र) (*m*) Name of God. Guardian of jewel mines.

Ratan-dip (रतन-दीप) (*m*) Jewel lamp (Gem serving as lamp).

Ratan-ketu (रतन-केतु) (*m*) Name of Buddha. Name common to 2000 future Buddhas.

Ratan-mālā (रतन-माला) (*f*) A jewek necklace.

Ratan-mālin (रतन-मलिन) (*f*) Adorned with a necklace of jewels.

Ratan-māyā (रतन-माया) (*m/f*) Made or consisting of jewels.

Ratan-rāshi (रतन-राशि) (*n*) A heap of precious stones. Collection of pearls.

Ratan-dhipti (रतन-धीप्ति) (*m*) Superintendent of jewels.

Ratansu (रतंसु) (*m/f*) Producing jewels. (the good earth).

Ratanvarā (रतन्वरा) (*m/f*) Best of precious stones.

Rathāngpāni (रथांगपाणि) (*m*) He who wielded the wheel of the chariot as his discus to challenge Bhishampitamah in the Mahabharata. (V)

Rathika (रथिक) (*m*) One who rides a chariot.

Rāthindra (राथीन्द्र) (*m*) Lord of the chariot.

Rati (रति) (*f*) Love, desire, daughter of Daksha. She also called Revā, wife of Kām (god of love), and Kāmi, Prītī, Priya (beloved), Rāg-latā (vine of love), Māvatī (deceiver), Kelikilā (wanton), Subhāngrī (fair limbed).

Ratipriyā (रतिप्रिया) (*f*) Same as Rati. Also the goddess enshrined at Ganādvār.

Ratna (रत्न) (*m*) Same as Ratan.

Ratnagarbh (रत्नगर्भ) (*m*) Hiding gems inside his person. (V)

Ratnābh (रत्नाभ) (*m*) Having navel as beautiful as a gem. (V)

Ratnakalā (रत्नकला) (*f*) Tiny piece of jewel.

Ratnākar (रत्नाकर) (*m*) An ocean.

Ratnaketu (रत्नकेतु) (*m*) Jewel bannered.

Ratnam (रत्नम) (*m*) Jewel, precious object.

Ratnanidhi (रत्ननिधि) (*m/f*) Treasure of jerwels.

Ratnaprabhā (रत्नप्रभा) (*f*) Shine of jewels. A not her name good earth.

Ratnarāj (रत्नराज) (*m*) King of jewels, the ruby.

Ratnarāshi/Ratna-rāshi (रत्नराशि/रत्न-राशि) (*f*) Collection of jewels.

Ratnashekhra (रत्नशेखर) (*m*) Jewelled crown.

Ratnāsū (रत्नासु) (*f*) Producing jewels, the good earth.

Ratnāvalī (रत्नावली) (*f*) "The necklace". A drama ascribed to a king of Kashmir, named Shri Harsh Dev. It is written about AD 1123.

Ratnavati (रत्नवती) (*f*) Good earth, with too many jewels.

Ratnesh (रत्नेश) (*m*) Lord of the jewels.

Ratneshvar (रत्नेश्वर) (*m*) Lord of jewels. Name of various men.

Ratnin (रत्निन) (*m/f/n*) Possessing or receiving gifts (from Rig Veda)

Rauhina (रौहीन) (*m/f*) Connected with the Nakshatra (heavenly body).

Raukma (रौक्म) (*m/f*) Golden, adorned with gold.

Ravi (रवि) (*m*) The Sun as a planet.

Ravidās (रविदास) (*m*) Devotee of the sun.

Ravidev (रविदेव) (*m*) Lord of the sun.

Ravi-dīpta (रवि-दीप्त) (*m/f*) Lighted or illuminated by the sun.

Ravija (रविज) (*m/f*) Born of the sun. Another name of planet Saturn and Karna.

Ravikānt (रविकांत) (*m*) The sun-stone.

Ravikiran (रविकिरण) (*m/f*) Ray of the sun.

Ravikirti (रविकीर्ति) (*f*) As famous as the sun. Renowned.

Ravi-Kiran (रवि-किरण) (*m/f*) Sunbeam.

Ravilochana (रविलोचन) (*m*) He who has the Sun as His eye. (V&S)

Ravinandan (रविनन्दन) (*m*) A name of Manu. See Manu.

Ravind/Arvind (रविन्द/अरविन्द) (*m/f*) Lotus flower.

Ravindra (रवीन्द्र) (*m*) Sun plus Lord Indra. Lord of the sun.

Ravirāj (रविराज) (*m*) King of the sun.

Ravi ratna (रवि रत्न) (*m*) Sun jewel.

Ravishankar (रविशंकर) (*m*) Lord of the sun.

Ravishta (रविष्ट) (*m*) Loved by the Sun.

Rāyishin (राइशिन) (*m/f/n*) Desiring treasures.

Rebhā (रेभा) (*m/f*) Singer of praise.

Rechaka (रेचक) (*m/f*) Rotation, spinning, circular movement of limbs in Kathak dance.

Rechita (रेचित) (*m/f*) Moving the limbs separately in a Kathak dance. Meaning the same as Rechaka.

Rekhā (रेखा) (*f*) A Shakti (wife of Lord Shiva) See Devi.

Rekhā (रेखा) (*f*) A line, fullness drawing, a small portion, a mark.

Renu (रेणु) (*m/f*) Dust, pollen of flower, a small particle, an atom, sand, soil.

Renukā (रेणुका) (*f*) Same as Renu. Name of the mother of Parshurām.

Renumati (रेणुमती) (*f*) Same aa Renu. One of the queens of Nakula, mother of Niramitra.

Revā (रेवा) (*f*) Epithet of Rati. See Rati. Also an epithet of river Narmadā.

Revati (रेवती) (*f*) The most beautiful woman. Daughter of king Raivat and wife of Balrām.

Ribhu (रिभु) (*m*) Clever, skilful. An epithet used for Indra, Agni, and the Adityas. In Puranas, Ribhu is a son of the supreme Brahma, who, from his innate disposition, was of a holy character and acquainted with true wisdom.

Richā (रिचा) (*f*) A vedic hymn.

Rīchīka (रिचिका) (*m*) Rishi descended from Bhrigu and husband of Satyavati, son of Urva and son of Jamad-agni.

Riddhā (रिद्ध) (*m*) Excelling in all match. Well versed in Dharma, knowledge etc. (V)

Riddhi (रिद्धि) (*f*) Prospperity. The wife of Kuvera, god of wealth. The name is also used for Parvati, the wife of Shiva.

Riddhiman (रिद्धिमन) (*m*) Prosperous, successful.

Riju (रिजु) (*a*) Straight, simple.

Rijula (रिजुल) (*m/f*) Simple. honest, innocent.

Rishabha (रिषभ) (*m*) Son of Nabhi and Meru, and father of a hundred sons, the eldest of whom was Bhārata. Also the name of the first jain Tirthakara or saint was Rishabha.

Rishi (ऋषि) (*m*) A sage, seer, preceptor. An inspired poet or person to whom the hymns of the Vedas were revealed. There are seven Rishis often referred to in the Satapatha Brahmana and their names are given as Gotama, Bhardwaj, Vishwamitra, Jamad-agni, Vashishtha, Kashyap and Atri.

Riti (रीति) (*m*) A head of Shiv gana (troops of deities).

Ritu Parna (रितु पर्ण) (*m*) A king of Ayodhya, and son of Sarvakama, into whose service Nala entered after he had lost his kingdom.

Riyā (रीया) (*f*) Singer.

Rocha (रोच) (*m/f*) Shining. One who make bright.

Rochaka (रोचक) (*m/f*) Brightning, enlightening. Pleasing.

Rochaman (रोचमन) (*m*) A pleasing mind. A name of a king who fought on Pandava side in the Mahabharata war.

Rochanā (रोचना) (*f*) The bright sky or luminous sphere, beautiful woman, red lotus flower.

Rochani (रोचनी) (*f*) Delighting, agreeable.

Rochi (रोची) (*f*) Ray, light, beam.

Rochish (रोचिष) (*m/f*) Light, lustre, brightness, grace, loveliness (from Rig Veda).

Rochishnu (रोचिष्णु) (*m/f/n*) Shining, bright, brilliant, splendid.

Rochuka (रोचुक) (*f*) Bringing pleasure or delight.

Rohan (रोहन) (*m*) Climbing, ascending, mounting.

Rohinī (रोहणी) (*f*) A young girl, lightining, mother of Balrām, name of a constellation. A red cow. A daughter of Valmiki. A wife of Vasudev.

Rohit (रोहित) (*m*) A red coloured horse of the sun or of fire gods. Name of a son of king Harish Chandra.

Rūchā (रूचा) (*f*) Light, speldnour, brightness, good, beautiful.

Ruchi (रुचि) (*f*) Interest, liking, taste, rellish, fancy, light, beauty, desire, passion. Beautiful wife of sage Devasharma.

Ruchikā (रुचिका) (*m/f*) Meaning the same as Ruchi. Also the name of grand-father of Parshuram.

Rūchiparva (रुचिपर्व) (*m*) Festival of lights, filled with beauty.

Rūchipati (रूचिपति) (*m*) Lord of light, master of desire.

Rūchirangadah (रूचिरंगदः) (*m*) He who wears auspicious armelts. (V)

Rūchira (रूचिरा) (*m/f*) Bright, brilliant, radiant, splendour, pleasant, charm-ing, agreeable (from Mahabharata).

Rūchita (रूचित) (*m/f/n*) Bright, brilliant, glittering, pleasant, sweet, delicate, dainty.

Rūchya (रूच्यि) (*m/f*) Bright, brilliant, radiant, beautiful, pleasing.

Rudhi (रूधि) (*f*) Rise, ascent, increase, growth, development, fame, celebrity.

Rudra (रुद्र) (*m*) A howler or roarer. In the Vedas Rudra has many attributes and many names. He is the god of storms. Rudra/Shiva is first called Mahadev in the White Yajurveda. Other names of Rudra/Shiva are: Bhava, Sarva, Isana, Pasupati, Bhim, Ugra and Mahadev.

Rudra Gita (रुद्र गीता) (*f*) A song of Rudra/Shiva.

Rudra-Kati (रुद्र कटि) (*f*) A form of Durga. See Devi.

Rūdrapriya (रुद्राप्रिया) (*m*) Beloved of Shiva-revered and noble son. (G)

Rukmā (रुक्मा) (*n*) What is bright or radiant.

Rukmāvati (रुक्मावती) (*f*) Daughter of Rukmi. Wife of Krishna's son Pradyumna.

Rukmi (रुक्मी) (*f*) Same as Rukmini.

Rukmini (रुक्मिणी) (*f*) Wearing golden ornaments. Daughter of Bhishmaka, king of Vidarbh, and wife of Krishna.

Rumā (रूमा) Wife of king Sugriv, and daughter of Panasa.

Rup/Rupā (रूप/रूपा) (*n*) Form, beauty, quality, natural state, figure, sign symbol.

Rupak (रूपक) (*n*) Metaphor drama. One who is beautiful.

Rūpali (रूपाली) (*f*) Most beautiful, excellent in shape.

Rupasharman (रूपश्रमन) (*m*) Rupa means form, figure, beautiful. Here it means beautiful. We have similar names, e.g. Rupalāl, Sundarlāl, Rupachand etc. In modern times, the first part of the names is based on a virtue i.e. beauty, it would mean 'one who is beautiful.'

Rūpāsharya (रूपाश्रय) (*m/f*) Exceedingly handsome, a repository of beauty.

Rūpasvin (रूपास्विन) (*m/f*) Handsome, beautiful.

Rūpavan (रूपवान) (*m/f*) Possessed with beauty. Most beautiful.

Rupavati (रूपवती) (*f*) The most beautiful. Daughter of Kashyap.

Rūpbhaj/Rup-bhaj (रूपभज/रूप-भज) (*m/f*) Endowed with beauty.

Rūpendra (रूपेन्द्र) (*m*) Lord of form, form of Indra, another name for an eye.

Rūpeshvara (रूपेश्वर) (*m/f*) Name of a God, Goddess, Devi (image of God). Most beautiful.

Rūpeshvari (रूपेश्वरी) (*m/f*) Name of Goddess of beauty.

Rūpguna (रूपगुण) (*m/f/n*) Beauty of form. Possessing the quality of colour/beauty.

Rūpin (रूपिन) (*m/f*) Having or assuming a particular form or figure well shaped, handsome, beautiful.

Rupini (रूपिणी) (*f*) The most beautiful. A Varna Shakti (female energy of a deity).

Rūpita (रूपित) (*m/f/n*) Beautifully formed, represented, exhibited, imagined.

Rūp Kalpanā (रूप कल्पना) (*f*) The assuming of a shape/beautiful body.

Rūpkar (रूपकर) (*m*) Sculptor, maker of images.

Rūpmālā (रूपमाला) (*f*) Garland of beauty/beautiful forms. Name of a grammatical work. Name of metre.

Rūppati/Rūppati (रूपपति/रूपपति) (*m*) Lord of forms. Most beautiful.

Rūpsampati/Rūp-Sampati (रूपसम्पति/रूप-सम्पति) (*f*) Perfection or excellence of form, beauty (From Mahabharata).

Rūpshalin/Rūp-Shalin (रूपशालीन/रूप-शालीन) (*m/f/n*) Handsome, beautiful, possessed of beauty.

Rupya (रूप्य) (*m/f/n*) Well shaped, beautiful.

S (स, सा)

Sabhā (सभा) (*f*) Congregation, meeting.

Sabhāgya (सभाग्य) (*m/f*) Fortunate, having a good fortune.

Sabhāj (सभाज) (*n*) Praise, honour, worship.

Sabhājana (सभाजन) (*m/f*) Service, honour, courteousy, politeness, civility.

Sabhājita (सभाजीत) (*m/f/n*) Served, honoured, gratified, pleased, praised, celebrated.

Sabhāpati (सभापति) (*m*) President of an assembly. Chairman. Name of King Bhutakarma.

Sabhāratā (सभारता) (*f*) Fulness, abundance, great prosperity.

Sabhāvanā (सभावना) (*m*) Name of Shiva.

Sabhikam (साभिकम) (*m/f*) Having affection, loving, affectionate.

Sabhilāsh (सभिलाष) (*m/f*) Having desire or longing for.

Sachi (सची) (*f*) Wife of Indra. See Indrāni.

Sachchidānanda (सच्चिदानन्द) (*m*) Endless bliss. (K)

Sachin (सचिन) (*m*) Pure existence and thought. Another name of Lord Shiva.

Sachinta (सचिंत) (*m/f*) Thoughtful.

Sachit (सचित) (*m*) Pure existence and thought. Another name of Brahma.

Sachiv/Sachiva (सचिव/सचिवा) (*m/f*) An associate, companion, friend, a king's friend or attendant, counsellor, minister.

Sadāchār (सदाचार) (*m*) Of noble conduct. (S)

Sadājit (सदाजीत) (*m*) Always victorious. Name of a Bharat dynasty king.

Sadāmārshi (सदामार्षि) (*m*) He who always forgives the noble and others. (V)

Sadan (सदन) (*n*) A house.

Sadānand (सदानन्द) (*m*) Perpetual bliss.

Sadāpriya (सदाप्रिय) (*f*) Always dear, lovely, beloved.

Sadāshish (सदाशीश) (*f*) A good blessing.

Sadāshiv (सदाशिव) (*m*) Name of god Shiv.

Sadāvir (सदावीर) (*m*) Always brave.

Sadāyogi (सद्योगी) (*m*) Ever reposing in the Yoga. (V)

Sadbhuti (सद्भूति) (*m*) Visible in many forms. (V)

Sadgati (सद्गति) (*m*) The final stage of the noble. (V)

Sadhaka (सधक) (*f*) Effective, efficient, productive, magical, another name for goddess Durga.

Sādhanā (साधना) (*f*) Worship, devotion, mental training, spiritual endeavour, practice.

Sadhani (साधनी) (*m*) Companion, comrade.

Sadhimān (साधिमान) (*m*) Full of intelligence, goodness, perfection.

Sādhita (साधिता) (*m/f/n*) Brought about, accomplished, perfected, mastered, subdued, proved.

Sādhu (साधु) (*m*) One who make the devotes achieve their aim. (M)

Sadhumati (साधुमती) (*f*) Virtuous minded. A Tantra deity.

Sādhvī (साध्वी) (*f*) Chaste, virtuous, faithful, honest, righteous, pious, noble, peaceful.

Sāgar (सागर) (*m*) The ocean. Son of Shakti. Lord of rivers. King of Ayodhya, of the Solar race.

Sagarottaraka (सागरोत्तरक) (*m*) Leapt across the ocean-Lord Hanuman. (H)

Sāh (साह) (*m*) Tolerating every afflication for the benefit of his devotees. (V)

Sāhas (साहस) (*m/f*) Powerful, mighty, victorious.

Sahasarjit (सहस्रजित) (*m*) Conqueror of thousands.

Sahastramurdhā (साहस्रमूर्धा) (*m*) A thousand headed. (V)

Sahastrānshu (सहस्रांशु) (*m*) Like a sun with thousand rays. (V)

Sahastrārchi (सहस्त्रार्चि) (*m*) Having infinite rays. (V)

Sahastrapāda (सहस्रपाद) (*m*) One with thousand feet. (V)

Sahāsya (सहास्य) (*m*) Mighty, strong.

Sahdev (सहदेव) (*m*) With the Gods. The youngest of the five Pandu princes, twin son of Madri, the second wife of Pandu. He was learned in the science of astronomy, and also well acquainted with the management of cattle.

Sahdevi (सहदेवी) (*f*) Together with the deities.

Sahendra (सहेन्द्रा) (*f*) With Lord Indra or resembling Indra in power.

Sāhishnu (साहिष्णु) (*m*) Capable of bearing all the opposites' effect simultaneously. Tolerant. (V)

Sahmān (सहमान) (*m/f/n*) Conquering, victorious (from Atharva Veda).

Sahojit (सहोजित) (*m*) Victorious in strength.

Sāhuri (साहुरी) (*f*) Mighty, strong, victorious, the good earth.

Sairanddhri (सैरन्ध्री) (*f*) A maid-servant in the women's apartment. It was under this name that Draupadi spent the thirteenth year of banishment in the court of king Virata. Also assumed name under which Damyanti while in search of her husband king Nala, worked as the attendant of princess Sunanda of Chedi.

Sajīv (सजीव) (*a*) Living, alive, lively, vivacious.

Sākheya (साखेय) (*m/f*) Frienfly, amicable.

Sākshi (साक्षी) (*m*) An eye witness, testimonial, evidence.

Sālagrām (सालग्राम) (*m*) A stone held sacred and worshiped by the Vaishnavas, because its spirals are supposed to be typical of Vishnu.

Salit (सलित) (*m*) Water.

Salonā (सलोना) (*m/f*) Beautiful.

Saloṇi (सालोनी) (*f*) Beautiful.

Salya (सल्य) (*m*) King of the Madras, and brother of Madri, second wife of Pandu.

Sām (साम) (*m*) Embodiment of Sām Veda. (V)

Samah (समाह) (*m*) Equinamous. (V)

Samakhyā (समाख्या) (*f*) Name, appelation, explanation, interpretation, celebrity.

Samaksha (समक्ष) (*f*) Fame.

Samam (समम) (*f*) The eyes of personified Veda.

Samanj (समंज) (*m*) A Pārāvata god.

Samāntā (समानता) (*f*) Equality with, community of kind or quality.

Sāmānya (सामान्य) (*m/f*) Equally, jointly together, whole, entire, universal, general.

Samāpti (समाप्ति) (*f*) Completion. Complete acquisition of knowledge, learning, perfection, accomplishment.

Samatā (समता) (*f*) Equality, sameness, fairness, benevolence, peaceful.

Samātma (समात्मा) (*m*) The spirit dwelling evenly among all beings. (V)

Samāvarta (समावर्त) (*m*) He who keeps the world moving with even pace. (V)

Samayāgya (समयाज्ञ) (*m*) The even reward of all the sacrifices. (V)

Samba (सम्ब) (*m*) To relate or to tell. Name of a son of Krishna and Jambavati. It is also one of the eighteen Upa Puranas.

Sambhā (सम्भा) (*m*) Shine, to be bright, visible.

Sambhāvah (सम्भावः) (*m*) Emerging at will. (V)

Sambhu/Shambhu (सम्भु/शम्भु) (*m*) A name of Shiva.

Sambhuti (सम्भूति) (*f*) Birth, manifestation of power, fitness personified as the daughter of Daksha and wife of Marichi.

Sambodh (सम्बोध) (*m*) Perfect knowledge or understanding.

Sambodhi (सम्बोधि) (*f*) Perfect knowledge or enlightenment according to Buddhism.

Samedh (समेध) (*m/f*) To prosper greatly, thrive, increase.

Samgah (समगाः) (*m*) He who sings Sam Veda. (V)

Samgayanah (समज्ञाना) (*m*) He who chants the hymns of Sam Veda. (V)

Samihanāh (समीहनाः) (*m*) Making conscious efforts for creation. (V)

Samikshā (समीक्षा) (*m/f*) Name of Sankhys system of philosophy, investigation, thorough inspection, beholding, deep understanding, intellect, understanding.

Samiptā (समीप्ता) (*f*) Nearness, proximity, continuity.

Samjiv/Sanjiv (सम्जीव/संजीव) (*n*) To live together.

Samīr (समीर) (*m*) Air, breeze, wind, the god of wind. To create, accomplish.

Samiran (समिरन) (*m*) Permeating the whole world like air. (V)

Samit (समीत) (*m/f*) Measured, meted out, continually, always, united, Storm gods (Maruts) who hold very prominent place in the Vedas, and are friends of Indra.

Samiti (समिति) (*f*) A sacred verse beginning with sam.

Samitinjayah (समीतिन्जयः) (*m*) Victor in every war. (V)

Samitra (समित्र) (*m/f*) Attended by friends, along with friends.

Samjanā (सम्जना) (*f*) A Shakti. See Devi.

Samjneya (सम्ज्नेय) (*m*) A son of Kunti.

Sammata (सम्मत) (*m/f/n*) Thinking together, being of the same opinion.

Sammati (सम्माति) (*f*) Harmony, agreement, evenminded, wish, desire, self knowledge, love, order.

Sammishlā (समिशला) (*m*) Name of Indra, Mingling together (from Rig Veda).

Samishra (समिश्र) (*m/f*) Mixed together, joined, connected, furnished.

Sammita (समित) (*m/f*) Measured, symmetrical.

Samni (सम्नी) (*m/f*) To lead or bring or put together, connect, unite.

Sampāti (सम्पाति) (*m*) A mythical bird in the Ramayana as son of Vishnu's bird Garuda and brother of Jatayu.

Samprabhā (समप्रभा) (*m/f*) To shine forth clearly, be conspicuous, appear (from Mahabharat).

Sampramardan (संप्रमर्दन) (*m*) Crushing every one is His Rudra form. (V)

Sampriti (समप्रीति) (*f*) Complete satisfaction, joy, delight.

Sampriya (समप्रिया) (*f*) Beloved, dear, wife of Vidur and mother of Anashva (from Mahabharata).

Sampujā (समपूजा) (*f*) Reverence, great respect.

Sampuran (सम्पूर्ण) (*adj*) Completed, total, whole, solid, universal, integral, entire.

Sampushti (संपुष्टि) (*f*) Prosperity, perfection.

Samriddh (समृद्ध) (*a*) Prosperous, flourishing, affluent, rich.

Samsār-vairini (समसार-वैरिनि) (*m*) Destroyer of evil. (K)

Samupchi (समूप्चि) (*n*) To grow, to increase.

Samvarn (सम्वर) (*m*) Son of Riksha, fourth in descent from Ikshwaku, and father of Kuru.

Samvarta (सम्वर्त) (*m*) Son of rishi Angira. Younger brother of Brihaspati.

Samvatsarah (सम्वत्सरः) (*m*) The beginning of the cycle. Setter of time cycle. (V)

Samvrat (सम्वर्त) (*m*) Enveloped by His own illusion. (V)

Sanak, Sanad, Sanātan, Sanat Kumar (सनक, सनद, सन्तान, सनत कुमार) (*m*) The four Kumaras or spiritual sons of Brahma.

Sanand (सन्नद) (*m/f*) Having joy or happiness, joyful, glad, delighted. A form of Lakshmi.

Sanat (सनत) (*m*) The form at the final hour. (V)

Sanātan/Sanātana (सनातन/सनातन) (*m/f*) Eternal, perpetual, permanent, everlasting. (S)

Sanatantamah (सनातनतमह) (*m*) The cause and root of all the oldest being. (V)

Sandhātā (सन्धाता) (*m*) One who brings efforts and rewards together. (V)

Sandhimān (सन्धिमान) (*m*) One who fills the gap between the effort and the result. (V)

Sandhyā (सन्ध्या) (*f*) Twilight. It is personified as the daughter of Brahmā and wife of Shiva.

Sandīp/Samdīp (संदीप/सम्दीप) (*m*) Flame, burn, glow, animate, kindle.

Sandipak (संदीपक) (*m/f*) Inflaming, exciting, arousing.

Sandipan (संदीपन) (*n*) Exciting. Same as Sandipak.

Sandipani (संदीपनी) (*m*) A master-at-arms who gave instruction to Balram and Krishna.

Sandipani (संदीपनी) (*m/f*) Illuminator, perceptor of Krishna and Balbhadrarām.

Sangit/Sangita (संगीत/संगीता) (*m/f*) Chorus, concert, symphany. Music.

Sangiti (संगीती) (*f*) Concert, symphony.

Sangrah (संग्रह) (*m*) One who collects everythings at the time of dissolution (Pralaya). (V)

Saniya (सनीय) (*f*) Beyond comparison.

Sanjanā (संजना) (*f*) Creator, to join.

Sanjaya (संजय) (*m*) A charioteer and a minister of Dhritrashtra who related to him the account of war during the Mahabharat.

Sanjit (संजीत) (*m*) Victorious.

Sanjiti (संजीती) (*f*) Complete victory.

Sanjnā (संजना) (*f*) Conscience. According to Purānas, she was daughter of Vishvakarma and wife of Sun. She is also called Dayumayī (the brilliant) and Mahāvīryā (the very powerful).

Sanjīvan (संजीवन) (*m*) Restoring to life, revival.

Sanjivanī (संजीवनी) (*f*) A kind of medicine which is supposed to restore a dead man to life.

Sanjobal (संजोबल) (*a*) Arranged, arrayed, careful.

Sankara (संकर) (*m*) Auspicious. A name of Shiva in his creative character or as chief of Rudras.

Sankarāchārya (शंकराचार्य) (*m*) The great religious reformer and teacher of the Vedanta philosophy (AD 800).

Sankarshanoachhyut (शंकरशनोच्युत) (*m*) Infallible by any attraction. (V)

Sankara-vijaya (शंकर-विजय) (*m*) The triumph of Sankara. A biography of Sankarāchārya relating his controversies with heretical sects and his refutation of their doctrines and superstitions.

Sankarshana (संकर्षण) (*m*) A name of Balrām.

Sankha (शंख) (*m*) Writer of a Dharma-sāstra or law-book bearing his name.

Sānkhāyan (संखायन) (*m*) Name of a writer who was the author of the Sānkhāyan Brahmanā of the Rig-Veda. He is also the author of the work called Sānkhāyan Kām-sutra.

Sankirat (संकीर्त) (*m/f*) To mention or relate fully, celebrate, praise (from Mahabharata).

Sankshepta (सक्षिप्त) (*m*) He who condenses the world is a trice. (V)

Sannivas (संनिवास) (*m*) The abode of the noble. (V)

Sanojā (सनोजा) (*f*) Eternal.

Sanrāj (सनराज) (*m*) To reign in the whole universe.

Sansrisht (संसृशत) (*f*) Union.

Sansthān (संसथान) (*m*) The abodes of dissolution. (V)

Sant (संत) (*m*) He who spreads education and humility by his action and voice. (V)

Sāntanu (सांतनु) (*m*) A king of Lunar race. Father of Bhishma, and in a way the grandfather of Dhritrashtra and Pandu. Regarding him it is said "every decrepit man whom he touches with his hands become young".

Santas-krit (संतस-कृत) (*m*) He who ordained sanyas ashram for the aspirant desiring salvation. (V)

Santosh (सन्तोष) (*m*) Satisfaction, gratification, contentment.

Sanyuktā (संयुक्त) (*f*) Relating to, united, a kind of metre.

Saparyā (सपर्या) (*f*) Worship, homage, adoration, to perform, worship.

Saparyu (सपर्यु) (*m/f*) Serving, honouring, devoted, faithful (from Rig Veda).

Saptadha (सप्तधा) (*m*) The fire with seven radiances. (V)

Saptajivah (सप्तजीवः) (*m*) The seven tongued flame. (V)

Saptavahan (सप्तवहन) (*m*) The Sun having vehicle with seven horses. (V)

Saraja (सरज) (*m/f*) Lotus, born in water.

Saralā (सरल) (*a/m/f*) Simple, straight, direct, light, ingenous.

Saralāya (सरलया) (*a*) To advance well.

Sarali (सरली) (*f*) Simple, straight, making straight.

Saralitā (सरलिता) (*a*) Straight, straightened.

Sarang (सरंग) (*m*) Variegated colour a lion, an elephant, spotted deer, the bow of Lord Vishnu, a gold ornament, beauty.

Saraswati (सरस्वती) (*f*) The goddess of learning, speech, name of the river. In the Vedas Saraswati is primarily a river, but is celebrated in the hymns both as river and a deity.

Sārath (सारथ) (*a*) Significant, a collection, a caravan.

Sarava (सरव) (*m*) A Vedic deity. Afterwards a name of Shiva and one of the Rudras.

Saravan (सरवन) (*m*) Son of the sage Andhak.

Sarāyu (सरायु) (*f*) The Sarju river.

Sargah (सर्गः) (*m*) The cause of creation. (V)

Sārikā (सारिका) (*f*) A kind of Indian bird famous for its melodious notes.

Saritā (सरिता) (*f*) A river, stream.

Sarlā (सरला) See Sarala.

Sarmishthā (सरमिष्ठा) (*f*) Daughter of Vrisha Parvan the Dānava (descendents of the sage Kashyap).

Sarni (सरनी) (*f*) A way, arrangements, a straight line.

Saroj (सरोज) (*m*) A lotus flower.

Sarojini (सरोजिनी) (*f*) A pond abounding in lotuses.

Sārthi (सारथि) (*m*) A charioteer.

Sarūpā (सरूपा) (*m/f*) Having the same shape or form, uniform, similar, like, resembling beautiful, handsome.

Sarupin (सरूपिन) (*m/f*) Equally shaped or formed, beautiful.

Sarvachārya (सर्वचार्य) (*m*) Proeceptor of all. (S)

Sarvadarshanah (सर्वदर्शनाः) (*m*) The sear of all. (V)

Sarvadarshi (सर्वदर्शी) (*m*) One who looks at all. (V)

Sarvadevastuta (सर्वदेवस्तुत) (*m*) Worshipped by all celestial beings. (R)

Sarvadevātma (सर्वदेवात्मा) (*m*) God of Gods-as the source of all beings. (K)

Sarvadevātmika (सर्वदेवात्मिका) (*m*) Dweller in all gods. Another name of Lord Rama. (R)

Sarvadevtam (सर्वदेवतम) (*m*) Acceptor of celestial offerings. (G)

Sarvadih (सर्वदीह) (*m*) The root cause of all beings. (V)

Sarvadrika (सर्वद्रिका) (*m*) One who sees all. (V)

Sarvadukhhara (सर्वदुखड़ा) (*m*) Reliever of all agonies-Hanuman. (H)

Sarvaga (सर्वग) (*m*) Son of Bhim and Balandhara.

Sarvagah (सर्वज्ञ) (*m*) The all pervading cause. (V)

Sarva-graha-rupini (सर्व-ग्रह-रूपिणी) (*m*) Lord of all the planets. Lord Krishna is the beginning, the middle and the end of all things. (K)

Sarvagya (सर्वज्ञ) (*m*) Omniscient. All knowing. (V)

Sarvah (सर्वः) (*m*) All in all. (V)

Sarvakamad (सर्वकामद) (*m*) Fulfiller of all desires. (V)

Sarvakar (सर्वकर) (*m/f*) In all forms, in every way, casting one's eyes in everywhere.

Sarvakaryasiddhi (सर्वकार्यसिद्धि) (*f*) Granter of success in every attempt-goddess Durga. (D)

Sarvalakshan (सर्वलक्षण) (*m*) Having all comely features. (V)

Sarvani (सरवानी) (*f*) Durga, name of Lord Shiva's wife.

Sarvapāl (सर्वपाल) (*m*) Protector of all-Lord Krishna. (K)

Sarvarāj (सर्वराज) (*m*) King of all

Sarvarūp/Sarvarūpā (सर्वरूप/सर्वरूपा) (*m/f*) Having or assuming all forms.

Sarvasaha (सर्वसह) (*m*) Having capacity to tolerate everything. (V)

Sarvashakti (सर्वशक्ति) (*f*) Entire strength, power of accomplishing all.

Sarvashastrabhritam Varah (सर्वशस्त्रभृतम् वरः) (*m*) The best among all the weapons welders. (V)

Sarvasidhant (सर्वसिद्धांत) (*m*) Provider of adeptness/success to his disciples. (G)

Sarvasunilaya (सर्वसुनीलय) (*m*) The beautiful home for the noble. (V)

Sarvatashchakshu (सर्वतश्चक्षु) (*m*) He who can see everything in all directions at all times. (V)

Sarvātman (सर्वात्मन) (*m*) Blesser of the universe. (G)

Sarvātomukh (सर्वतोमुख) (*m*) Having face in every direction. (V)

Sarvavagishvar (सर्ववागीश्वर) (*m*) The lord of all sounds. (V)

Sarvavas (सर्ववेस) (*m*) All-abiding (Lord Shiva).

Sarvayogvinihstratah (सर्वयोगविनिःस्रतः) (*m*) Comprehensible by scores of means ordained by the scriptures.

Sarvavidhanu (सर्वविधानु) (*m*) The all knowing elightenment. (V)

Sarvavijayi (सर्वविजयी) (*m/n*) Victor of all. (V)

Sarvesh (सर्वेष) (*m*) Lord of all, supreme being.

Sarvesha (सर्वेषा) (*f*) Goddess of all.

Sarveshvar/Sarveshvarah (सर्वेश्वर/सर्वेश्वराह) (*m*) The god of all gods. (V&S)

Sasmitā (सस्मिता) (*f*) Smiling, full of smile, happiness.

Sat (सत) (*m*) The true being. (V)

Satangatih (सतंगतिः) (*m*) The ultimate destination of the nobles. The final refuge of the noble. (V)

Satkarta (सत्कार्ता) (*m*) Hospitable to his devotees. (V)

Satkirti (सत्कीर्ति) (*m*) One with real glory. (V)

Satkrita (सत्कृत) (*m*) Adorable by those worshipped. (V)

Satparāyan (सत्परायण) (*m*) The desirted destination of the noble. (V)

Satpathāchar (सतपथाचर) (*m*) He who ever moves on the righteous path. (V)

Satrajit (सत्रजित) (*m*) Son of Nighna. In return for praise rendered to the Sun he beheld the luminary in his proper form, and received from him the wonderful Syamantaka gem.

Satru-ghan/Satrughna (शत्रु-घन/शत्रुघना) (*m*) Foe destroyer. Twin borther of Lakshmana and half brother of Rām in whom an eighth part of the divinity of Vishnu was incarnate. His wife was Sruta-kirti, cousin of Sītā.

Satrupā (शत्रुपा) (*f*) The hundred-formed. The first woman-the daughter of Brahmā.

Satsom (सत्सोम) (*m*) Son of Bhim and Draupadi. Real moon.

Satta (सत्ता) (*m*) The authority. (V)

Sattva (सत्त्व) (*n*) Existance, reality, true, essence, nature, spiritual, vital breath, life, energy, resolution.

Sattvan (सत्त्वन) (*m/f/n*) Loving, breathing, strong, powerful.

Sattvik (सात्त्विक) (*m*) Of noble demeanour. (V)

Satvastha (सत्वस्थ) (*m*) Omnipresent: knowing truth of every heart. (V)

Satvatā (सत्वता) (*m/f*) Relating to the Satvats or the Satvatas. Sacred to Lord krishna. Worshipper of Lord Krishna.

Satvatam-pati (सत्वतम-पति) (*m*) The leader of the Yadavas and the Lord of his devotees. (V)

Satvavan (सत्ववंन) (*m*) Having all puissance. (V)

Satvati (सत्वती) (*f*) Princes of the Satvats. Name of the mother of Shishupal. One of the four divisions of dramatic style (expression of bravery, generosity, happiness etc.)

Satya/Satyah (सत्य/सत्यः) (*m*) The truth of faith. (V)

Satya (सत्य) (*a*) True, truth, an oath, the first of the four Yugas. One of the heavenly worlds.

Satyā-bhāmā (सत्या-भामा) (*f*) Daughter of Satrājita and one of the four chief wives of Krishna.

Satyadev (सत्यदेव) (*m*) A kaurava king mentioned in Mahabharata.

Satyādharma (सत्याधर्म) (*m*) The truth of faith. (V)

Satyādharmap-arayanah (सत्याधर्मप-अरण्यः) (*m*) He who adheres to the righteous path, the Dharma, truthfully. (V)

Satyādharma parat kramah (सत्याधर्म परतक्रमः) (*m*) The manifestation of the strength of truth and dharma. (V)

Satyajit (सत्यजीत) (*m*) A king who ruled for 83 years.

Satyajiti (सत्यजीती) (*f*) True victory

Satyajyoti (सत्यज्योति) (*m*) Having a real beauty or splendour.

Satyaketu (सत्यकेतु) (*m*) One whose banner is truth. Honest/truthful person.

Satyaki (सात्यिक) A great Yadav who was a lifelong friend of Arjuna and Krishna.

Satya-kriyā (सत्य-क्रिया) (*f*) Promise, oath.

Satyamedha (सत्यमेधा) (*m*) Having only truth carrying wisdom. (V)

Satyamoti (सत्यमोती) (*m*) The pearl. Jewel among the truthful.

Satyamurti (सत्यमूर्ति) (*m*) Symbol of truth.

Satyapāl (सत्यपाल) (*m*) A religious counsellor in the court of King Yudhishthira.

Satyapān (सत्यपान) (*m/f*) Verification, speaking or observing the truth.

Satya prākaram (सत्य पराक्रम) (*m*) One who performs real feats. (V)

Satyarām (सत्यराम) (*m*) Protector of the noble. (V)

Satyarūp (सत्यरूप) (*m/f*) Having true appearance.

Satyasandha (सत्यसन्ध) (*m*) Truthful, vendicious. (V)

Satyashil (सत्यशील) (*m*) Virtuous, pious.

Satyavāche (सत्यवाची) (*m*) Speaker of truth-Lord Ram. (R)

Satyavat (सत्यवत) (*m/f*) Truthful, veracious.

Satyavati (सत्यावती) (*f*) A wife of Rishi Parāshara and mother of Vyās. Also the name of the queen of king Santanu, mother of Vichitra-viryā and Chitr¯angada and grandmother of the Kauravas and Pandavas.

Satyavikrama (सत्यविक्रम) (*m*) Truthfully powerful. Lord Ram is the truth in the beginning, middle and the end. (R)

Satyavrat (सत्यव्रत) (*m*) Name of the seventh Manu.

Saubhā (सौभा) (*f*) A magical city, first mentioned in the Yajur-veda.

Saubhadrā (सौभद्र) (*f*) Mother of Abhimanyu.

Saubhāgini (सौभागिनी) (*f*) A fortunate woman.

Saubhāgya (सौभाग्य) (*f*) Fortunate, richness of style or composition.

Saubhāri (सौभारी) (*m*) A devout sage and adevotee of Vishnu.

Saudamanī (सौदामनी) (*f*) Lightning.

Saudamatī (सौदमती) (*f*) Light.

Saudās (सौदास) (*m*) Son of king Sudās, a king of the Solar race. His legend is told in the Mahabharata. Also name of King Kalmashpada.

Saujanya (सौजन्य) (*m/f*) Goodness, kindness, benevolence, friendliness.

Saukhyadaye (सौख्यदई) (*f*) Bestower of well being-goddess Durga. (D)

Saumitra (सौमित्र) (*m*) An epithet of Lakshman (son of Sumitra) brother of Ram.

Saumya (सौम्य) (*m*) Calm. Another name of Lord Rama. (R)

Saunanda (सौनन्द) (*n*) A club shaped like a pestle, which was one of the weapons of Balrām.

Sauparna (सौपर्ण) (*m/f*) Relating or belonging to bird Suparna. Sauparna hymn in Rig Veda-relating to transformation of the metres into birds that they might fetch the Soma from heaven.

Sauparni (सौपर्णि) (*f*) A mind-born mother.

Saurabh/Sorabh (सौरभ/सोरभ) (*m*) Fragrance, aroma. See also Surabhi.

Saurabhi/Surabhi (सौरभि/सुरभि) (*f*) The 'cow of plenty', produced at the churning of the ocean, who granted every desire, and is reverenced as the fountain of milk and curds.

Saurājya (सौराज्य) (*m/f*) Good sovereignty, enjoying good government.

Saurikā (सौरिका) (*m/f/n*) Heavenly, celestial. The planet saturn.

Sauti (सौती) A name of a Rishi who repeated the Mahabharata to other Rishis in the Naimaisha forest.

Savah (सवह) (*m*) The receptacle which holds the sap of the herb soma. (V)

Sāvan (सावन) (*m*) The fifth month of the Hindu calendar. Rainy season.

Savan (सवन) (*m*) The moon. A sacrifice.

Savarnā (सवर्ण) (*f*) Wife of Sun. Manu was the offspring of Savarna.

Savarni (सावर्णि) (*m*) The name of eighth Manu.

Sāvasti (सावस्ती) (*f*) A city founded by King Shāva or Shavasta.

Savitā (सविता) (*m*) The begetter of the entire universe, deity causing birth of every being, the Sun. (V)

Savitar (सवितर) (*m/f*) Like the sun.

Savitra (सवित्र) (*m/f*) Relating to or belonging to the sun, derived from the sun, belonging to the solar dynasty.

Savitta (सवित्त) (*m/f*) Together with the property.

Savitri (सावित्री) (*f*) The holy verse of the Veda, commonly called Gayatri. A name of Satarupa, the daughter of Brahma who is regarded as a personification of the holy verse. Aslo name of a daughter of King Aswapati, and wife of Satyavan.

Savradrigvyas (सव्रादिग्व्यास) (*m*) The all seeing Vyas. (V)

Savyasachi/Savyasachin (सव्यसाची/सव्यसाचीन) (*m*) Who pulls a bow with either hand. Another name of Arjuna.

Sāyan/Sāyanachārya (सायन/सायनाचार्य) (*m*) The celebrated commentator on the Rig Veda.

Sendra (सेन्द्र) (*m/f/n*) Accompanied by or together with Indra.

Setu (सेतु) (*m/f/n*) Binding, Rama's bridge, land mark, boundary.

Setukrite (सेतुकृति) (*m*) Builder of the Bridge, over the ocean, cemented with divine powers-Lord Rama. (R)

Sevati (सेवती) (*f*) Indian white rose (Rosa Alba).

Shabd-pati (शब्द-पति) (*m*) Word lord. Nominal leader.

Shabdasah (शब्दसः) (*m*) He whose glory is described by the scriptures. (V)

Shabdatigah (शब्दातिमः) (*m*) He who is beyond the range of voice or sound. (V)

Shabnam (शबनम) (*f*) Dew, a very fine quality of muslin.

Shabari (शबरी) (*f*) Variegated, belonging to the Sahbara tribe, a Gandhari who was changed into a forest woman and then saved by Rama (Kumbha Ramayana).

Shachi (शची) (*f*) Very beautiful. The name of Indra's wife.

Shachi-pati (शची-पति) (*m*) Lord of might or help (applied to Lord Indra).

Shachisa (शचीसा) (*m*) Lord of Sachi (might).

Shachishtha (शचिष्ठा) (*m/f*) Most powerful or helpful (from Rig Veda).

Shagun (शगुन) (*n*) A good omen, a bird.

Shaguni (शगुनी) (*f*) Auspicious, lucky omen, virtuous.

Shaibya (शैब्या) (*f*) Relating or belonging to Shibis. Wife of Harish Candra; wife of Jyamagha; wife of Sata-dhanu; mother of Satyavan.

Shailadi (शैलादि) (*m*) Patriarchical of Nandin (one of Lord Shiva's attend ants).

Shailjā (शैलजा) (*f*) Another name of Parvati (wife of Lord Shiva). Daughter of the mountain.

Shailendra (शैलेन्द्र) (*m*) The Himalayas.

Shaileya (शैलेय) (*m/f*) Rocky, stony, mountain like, hard.

Shailī (शैली) (*f*) Carved in rock, style, custom, visage, habit.

Shaivā (शैवा) (*m/f*) Relating or belonging or sacred to Lord Shiva. Derived from Shiva.

Shaivya (शैव्य) (*m/f*) Relating or belonging to Shiva.

Shakhya (शैख्य) (*m/f*) Able, possible practicable.

Shakti (शक्ति) (*f*) Ability, strength, a missile, a female deity. Divine power, wife of Shiva. See Devi.

Shaktijā (शक्तिजा) (*m*) A worshipper of Shakti.

Shakuntalā (शकुन्तला) (*f*) The daughter of Vishvamitra and Menakā.

Shalesh (शैलेष) (*n*) Smoothness, polish.

Shālinī (शालिनी) (*f*) A mistress of the house, hous-holder.

Shamā (शमा) (*f*) A candle, lamp.

Shamastha (शमस्थ) (*m/f/n*) Being in prosperity, happy, prosperous.

Shākin (शाकिन) (*m/f/n*) Helpful or powerful, mighty (from Rig Veda).

Shākini (शाकिनी) (*f*) Another name of Parvati as goddess of plants and herbs. Helpful, powerful, an attendant of goddeass Durga.

Shaktikā (शक्तिका) (*m*) Able, powerful, another name of Kartikkeya.

Shaktimat (शक्तिमत) (*m/f/n*) Possessed of ability, powerful, might, able, one who has gained fortune.

ShaktimātanShreshta (शक्तिमातन श्रेष्ठ) (*m*) Mighty than the mightiest. (V)

Shaktimati (शक्तिमती) (*f*) Powerful.

Shaktipujā (शक्तिपूजा) (*f*) Shakti worship. See also Shakti and Puja.

Shaktivat (शक्तिवत) (*m/f*) Powerful or helpful (from Rig Veda).

Shalalu (शललु) (*m/f*) Sort of perfume or fragrant substance.

Shālin (शालीन) (*m/f/n*) Possessing a house, full of possessed of, distinguished, praiseworthy.

Shamah (शमह) (*m*) The queller of the disturbance caused by the wicked. (V)

Shamaka (शमक) (*m/f/n*) Pacifying, pacifier, peace-maker.

Shamani (शमनी) (*f*) Tranquility, peace.

Shāmatha (शमथ) (*m*) Quiet, tranquility, minister, counsellor.

Shāmbhav (शम्भव) (*m/f*) Coming or derived from Lord Shiva.

Shāmbhavi (शाम्भवी) (*m/f*) Name of Goddess Durga, Tantras. A kind of blue flowering Dhruva grass. Also the name of Lord Ganesha.

Shāmbhāvya (शम्भाव्य) (*m/f/n*) Relating or belonging to Lord Shiva.

Shambhu (शम्भु) (*m*) A name of Shiva.

Shambhu-kānt (शम्भु-कांत) (*f*) Lord Shiva's wife. Name of Goddess Durga.

Shambhu-priya (शम्भु-प्रिया) (*f*) Dear to Lord Shiva (Parvati-his wife) Name of Durga.

Shāmbrī (शांबरी) (*f*) An illusion.

Shami (शमी) (*f*) Effort, labour, toil (from Rig Veda).

Shamika (शमिक) (*m*) Peaceful, self restrained, a Rishi was the father of Shringi, a son of Sura and brother of Vasudeva.

Shamilā (शमीला) (*m/f*) Made of the wood of Shami tree (Prosopis Spicigera).

Shamsā/Shansā (शामसा/शांसा) (*m/f*) Recitation, praise (from Rig Veda) Wishing well, blessing or a curse.

Shāmya (शाम्य) (*m/f/n*) Relating to peace, peaceful (from Mahabharata).

Shāmyu (शाम्यु) (*m/f/n*) Benevolent, benficient (from Rig Veda), happy, fortunate, name of a son of Brihaspati

Shāndili (शांदिली) (*f*) An extremely pious and ascetic woman who lived on top of the mount Rishabha.

Shankar (शंकर) (*m*) Lord Shiva. Name of a great Indian philosopher who flourished during the quarter of the eighth and first quarter of 9th centruy.

Shankar-Acharya (शंकर-आचार्य) See Sankarāchārya.

Shankaralaya (शंकरलय) (*m*) Lord Shiva's abode (the mountain Kailash).

Shankardev (शंकरदेव) (*m*) Name of a form of Lord Shiva.

Shankari (शंकरी) (*f*) Wife of Lord Shiva.

Shankar-priyā (शंकर-प्रिया) (*f*) Dear to Shankara. (Shiva's wife Parvati).

Shankar-Vijaya (शंकर-विजय) See Saṇkara-vijaya.

Shankhābhrita (शंखाभृत) (*m*) The weilder of the conch-shell called Panchajanya. (V)

Shansana (शंसना) (*m/f*) Reciting, praisd, announcement, communication.

Shansita (शंसिता) (*m/f/n*) Praised, celebrated, told, praiseworthy, wished, desired.

Shansitva (शंसित्व) (*m/f*) Having praised.

Shāntā (शांता) (*f*) Spiritual, serenity, calm. Peace.

Shāntah (शांतः) (*m*) Embodiment of quietude. (V)

Shāntanav (शांतनव) (*m/f*) Written or composed by Shantanau (father of Bhishma).

Shantanu (शांतनु) (*m*) See Santanu.

Shānti (शांति) (*f*) Peace, calmness, quiet, tranquility, silence.

Shāntidah (शांतिदः) (*m*) He who gives peace. (V)

Shāntidevi (शांतिदेवी) (*f*) Goddedss of peace.

Shāntih (शांतिः) (*m*) Peace personified. (V)

Shāntika (शांतिक) (*m/f/n*) Propitiatory, expiatory, averting evil.

Shāntikar (शांतिकर) (*m/f/n*) Causing peace or prosperity.

Shāntikrit (शांतिकृत) (*m/f/n*) Removing evil or causing alleviation by reciting texts.

Shāntinā (शांतिना) (*f*) Name of a deity.

Shāntipriya (शांतिप्रिया) (*f*) Beloved of peace.

Shāntiyukta (शांतियुक्त) (*m/f/n*) Connected with welfare or prosperity.

Shāntmoh (शांतमोह) (*n*) Having delusion dispelled. According to Jainism-name of the 11th of the 14th steps towards supreme happiness.

Shanyu (शन्यु) (*m/f*) Happy, fortunate, benevolent, beneficient.

Sharabh (शरभ) (*m*) Illumining bodies in orderly manner. (V)

Sharachchandra (शरच्चन्द्र) (*m*) The moon, moonshine, moonlight.

Sharad (शरद) (*m*) Autumn, wintry, the full moon day of the month of Ashwin (September).

Sharad-chandra (शरद-चन्द्र) (*m*) The full moon of autumn.

Sharadvat (शरदवत) (*m*) Name of an ancient sage.

Sharadwān (शरदवान) (*m*) Father of Kripacharya and Kripi. Descendant of Gautama Rishi. He was a great archer and an expert in the use of weapons. He taught Kripa the art of warfare.

Sharanam (शरणम्) (*m*) The shleter of all. (V)

Sharani (शरणि) (*f*) Protecting, guarding, defending, name of good earth.

Sharat (शरत) (*m*) A mind-born son of Brahmā in the 16th Kalpa.

Sharava/Sharvah (शरव/शरवह) (*m/f*) Relating or belonging or sacred to Shiva. (V)

Sharbhā (शरभा) (*m*) Brother of Shishupala's son Dhrishtaketu. He fought on the side of Pandavas in the Mahabharata war.

Shārdā (शारदा) (*f*) Saraswati (the godess of learning). Name of an ancient Indian script prevalent in the 10th century AD in Kashmir and Punjab.

Shrirbhrita (श्रीर्भरीत) (*m*) Nourishing every body with food. (V)

Shrirbhubhrita (श्रीर्भुभरीत) (*m*) The nourisher of the five basic elemnts of the body. (V)

Shāringa/Shārnga (शरिंग/शारंग) (*m/f*) The bow of Hari, reached Krishna during Jarāsandha's siege of Mathurā

Sharmin (शार्मिन) (*m/f/n*) Possessing happiness, lucky, auspicious (from Mahabharata).

Sharmishtha (शर्मिष्ठा) (*f*) Most fortunate. Name of the wife of Yayati (she was daughter of Virsh-parvan and mother of Druhyu.

Shārngadhanī/Sharangī (शारंगधनी/शारंगी) (*m*) An epithet of Vishnu.

Shārvānī (शार्वणी) (*f*) An epithet of Umā (light), consort of Shiva.

Sharvarī (शार्वरी) (*f*) A night.

Shās/Shāsa (शास/शासा) (*m/f*) Order, command, commander, ruler, chastiser, name of a hymn (from Atharva Veda).

Shashabindu (शशबिन्दु) (*m*) A great king of ancient times whose story is mentioned in the Mahabharata.

Shashānk (शशांक) (*m*) The moon.

Shashanka (शशांक) (*m/f*) Hare-marked, the moon, camphor, lovely as the moon, shining like the moon, resembling a ray of th moon

Shashi (शशि) (*m*) The moon.

Shashi-bhushan (शशि-भूषण) (*n*) Moon decorated. Name of Lord Shiva.

Shashideve (शशिदेव) (*m*) Lord of the moon.

Shashikalā (शशिकला) (*f*) A digit of the moon.

Shashi-kānt (शशि-कांत) (*m*) Moon loved, the moon stone. A white lotus flower opening by night.

Shashi-mani (शशि-मणी) (*m*) The moon stone.

Shashi-mat (शशि-मत) (*m/f*) Possessing the moon.

Shashi-mauli (शशि-मौली) (*n*) Having the moon as diadem. Name of Lord Shiva.

Shashini (शशिनी) (*f*) A digit of the moon.

Shashiprabhā (शशिप्रभा) (*f*) A Shakti (female energy of Shiva) see Devi.

Shashi-priya (शशि-प्रिया) (*m/f*) A pearl. Loved of the moon.

Shashirashmi (शशिरश्मि) (*f*) Beam of the moon.

Shashi-rekhā (शशि-रेखा) (*f*) Moon-streak, digit of the moon.

Shashisā (शशिसा) (*m*) Eternal. Lord Rama an incarnation of Lord Vishnu is Narayan, the eternal divinty. (R)

Shashvata (शाश्वत) (*m*) Eternal. Lord Rama an incarnation of Lord Vishnu is Narayan, the eternal divinity. (R)

Shāshvati (शाश्वती) (*f*) A Shakti. See Devi. Shāshvati also means the earth.

Shasta (शस्त) (*m/f/n*) Recited, repeated, praised, commended, approved (from Rig Veda).

Shasti (शस्ति) (*f*) Praise, a hymn from Rig Veda.

Shatābji (शताब्जि) (*m/f/n*) Having a hundred lotus flowers.

Shatadhriti (शतधृकम) (*m*) A name of Indra or Brahmā.

Shatakirti (शतकीर्ति) (*f*) With the fame of hundreds.

Shatajit (शतजित) (*m*) A son of Krishna and Jāmbavatī.

Shatākshi (शताक्षी) (*f*) Another name of goddess Durga. Hundred eyed.

Shatananda (शतानन्द) (*m*) Bestower of a hundred kinds of happiness and bliss. (V)

Shatananah (शतानन्ह) (*m*) Having hundreds of faces. (V)

Shatānik (शतानीक) (*m*) Son of Draupadi and Nakula.

Shatāyup (शतायुप) (*m*) A former king of Kekaya. He became a sage and it was in his hermitage that Dhritarashtra, Gandhari and Kunti stayed for the last three years of their lives.

Shatmurti (शतमुर्ति) (*m*) Having hundreds of images. (V)

Shatrughan (शत्रुघन) Same as Satru-ghan. See Satrughan.

Shatrujita (शत्रुजीत) (*m*) Vanquisher of the enemy. (V)

Shatrupā/Satrupā (शत्रुपा/सत्रुपा) (*f*) The hundred-formed. The first woman. Wife of Brahma's son Manu. Mother of Ahuti, Devhuti and Prasuti. She is also called Savitri.

Shatrutapan (शत्रुतपन) (*m*) Scorcher of the foe. (V)

Shat-tejas (शत-तेजस) (*m/f/n*) Having a hundred-fold vital power.

Shattrunjay (शत्रुन्जय) (*m*) Conqueror of the enemy.

Shatval (शत्वल) (*m*) Name of Shakha (branch) of Vedic shcool.

Shaunak/Saunak (शौनक/सौनक) (*m*) A sage, the son of Sunaka and grandson of Grits-mada. He was the author of the Brihad-devata, an Anukramani, and other works, and he was a teacher of the Atharya Veda.

Shauri (शौरी) (*m*) Son of chivalrous Vasudeva (in Krishna's form). Born in the family of gallants (Shri Krishna). (V)

Shaurya (शौर्य) (*m/f*) Heroism, valour, prowess, might, courageous.

Shayichi (शईची) (*m*) Name of Lord Indra.

Shchandra (शचेन्द्र) (*m/f*) Shining, brilliant.

Shemushi (शेमुशी) (*f*) Understanding, intellect, wisdom, resolve, purpose.

Sheva (शेव) (*f*) Prosperity, happiness, homage.

Shibham (शिभम्) (*m/f*) Quickly, swiftly, speedily (from Rig Veda and Atharva Veda).

Shibhya (शिभय) (*m/f/n*) Moving quickly. Name of Lord Shiva.

Shibika (शिबिक) (*m*) Name of a king. Name of people in the South India.

Shibira (शिबिरा) *(m/f)* A royal camp or residence.

Sheikar (शेखर) *(m)* The top or crown of the head.

Shibi (शिबी) *(m)* Name of a Rishi. Also a name of a very righteous king in ancient time. He was a son of king Ushinara and queen Madhavi.

Shikhā (शिखा) *(f)* Top, a flame, a crest. A tuft or distinc tive lock of hair on the crown of head, traditionally worn by Hindus. One of the four vedic Brahman disciples of Shveta.

Shikhādevi (शिखादेवी) *(f)* A Shakti (female energy of Shiva) See Devi.

Shikshā (शिक्षा) *(f)* Learning, study, wish to accomplish, skilfully, artistically, training in higher moreality, thought.

Shīl/Shilā (शील/शिला) *(m/f)* Modesty, piety, virtue, moral conduct, chastity.

Shilam (शिलम) *(n)* Repeated practice, constant study of Shastras.

Shilin/Shilini (शिलिन/शिलिनी) *(m/f/n)* Virtuous, moral, honest (from Mahabharata).

Shilpā (शिल्पा) *(m)* The science of mechanics; it includes architecture. It also means Vishvakarma (the great architect of the universe).

Shilpavat (शिल्पवत) *(m/f)* Skilled in art.

Shilpikā (शिल्पिका) *(m/f/n)* Skilled in art (applied to Lord Shiva).

Shilpin (शिल्पिन) *(m/f/n)* Belonging to or skilled in art, artist, craftsman.

Shimi/Simi (शिमी/सिमी) *(f)* Effort, labour, work, industry.

Shimyu (शिम्यु) *(m/f/n)* Strenuous, vigorous, aggressive (from Rig Veda).

Shini (शिनी) *(m)* Grandfather of the great Yadava Satyaki.

Shipavishtah (शिपविष्टः) *(m)* The radiance in the sun rays. (V)

Shiphaka (शिफक) *(m/f)* The root of a water lily.

Shiphara (शिफर) *(m/f/n)* Charming, delightful.

Shipi (शिपी) *(m/f)* A ray of light.

Shipi-vishtha (शिपी-विष्ठ) *(m/f/n)* Pervaded by rays (applied to Lord Shiva and Vishnu).

Shiprā/Siprā (शिप्रा/सिप्रा) The river on which the city of Ujjayini stands.

Shirodevi (शिरोदेवी) *(f)* A Shakti (female energy of Shiva). See Devi.

Shish (शिश) *(m)* Lord of Lakshmi. (V)

Shishirah (शिशिरः) *(m)* The cool image for those afflicted by the oppressive heat of three kinds (the physical, the mental and the spiritual). (V)

Shishtha (शिष्ठा) *(m/f/n)* Taught, directed, ordered, wise, eminent, superior.

Shishthi (शिष्ठ) *(f)* Direction, instruction, command.

Shivadevi (शिवदेवी) *(f)* Goddess of grace.

Shistakrita (**शिष्टकृत**) (*m*) Wo controls all. (V)

Shītal (**शीतल**) (*a*) Cool, cold, frigid.

Shitānshu/Sitānshu (**शीतांशु/सीतांशु**) (*m/f*) White rays, another name of moon.

Shiv/Siva (**शिव/सिवा**) (*m*) The third deity in the Hindu triad. Shiva is the same as Vishnu in the character of destroyer of creation. He also personifies reproduction, as Hindu philosophy excludes the idea of total annihilation without subsequent regeneration. Hence he is sometimes identified with Brahmā the first person in the triad. Other names or epithets of Shiv are Aghora (horrible), Babhru, Bhagavat (divine), Chandrasekhar (moon-crested), Gandhar (bearer of the Ganges), Girish (mountain Lord), hara (seizer), Ishana (ruler), Jatā-dhar (wearing matted hair), Jal-murti (whose form is water), Kāl (time), Kālangara, Kapāla-mālin, Mahākāl (great time), Mahesh (great lord), Mrityunjaya (vanquisher of death), Pasu-pati (lord of animals), Shankar, Sarva, Sadāshiv or Sambhu (the auspicious), Sthānu (the firm), Tryambak (three-eyed), Ugra (fierce), Virupaksha (of mis-formed eyes), Vishwanāth (lord of all).

The name Shiv is unknown to the Vedas, but Rudra, another name of Shiv occurs in the Veda both in the singular and plural, and from these the great deity Shiv and his manifestations, the Rudras have been developed. In the Rig Veda the word Rudra is used for Agni, and the Maruts are called his sons. He is lauded; as the lord of songs, the lord of sacrifices, who heals remedies, is brilliant as the sun, the best and most beautiful of gods, who grants prosperity and welfare to every one in this universe. He is without beginning, middle or end; the one, the prevading, the spiritual and blessed, the wonderful, the consort of Uma, the supreme lord, the three-eyed, the blue throated, the tranquil.

Shitānshu/Sitānshu (**शीतांशु/सीतांशु**) (*m/f*) White rays, another name of moon.

Shivadevi (**शिवदेवी**) (*f*) Goddess of grace.

Shivaduti (**शिवदूती**) (*f*) Shiva's messenger. A form of Durga, A Yogini.

Shivah (**शिवह**) (*m*) The auspicious form, beyond the three attributes. (V)

Shivak (**शिवक**) (*m*) An idol or image of Lord Shiva.

Shivam (**शिवम्**) (*m*) Of Lord Shiva. Prosperous, auspicious, graceful.

Shivāngī (**शिवांगी**) (*f*) A part of Lord Shiva.

Shivasundari (**शिवसुन्दरी**) (*f*) Wife of Lord Shiva. Another name of Parvati.

Shivānandin (**शिवानन्दिनी**) (*m*) The first part is Shiva and the second nandin, the whole literally meaning 'an attendant of Lord Shiva.'

Shivanārāyana (**शिवनारायण**) (*m*) An image of a deity; on the left Mādhava (Krishna or Vishnu) and on the right Shiv. It may mean Trimurti. The Hindu traid (Brahma, Vishnu, Shiv).

Shivāni (शिवानी) (*f*) Pārvati (wife of Shiva) See Devi.

Shivatā (शिवत्ता) (*f*) The good, well being.

Shiv-bhāskara (शिव्-भास्कर) (*m*) Shiva compared with the Sun.

Shivdatta (शिवदत्त) (*m*) Given by or presented to Lord Shiva.

Shivdhātu (शिवधातु) (*m*) Lord Shiva's essence.

Shivdish (शिवदिश) (*f*) Lord Shiva's quarter.

Shivdūti (शिवदूती) (*f*) Lord Shiva's messenger.

Shiveshta (शिवेष्ट) (*m/f*) Loved by Shiva.

Shivgitā (शिवगीता) (*f*) Name of a chapter of Padma-Puran (propounding the doctrine of Shaivas)

Shivkāntā (शिवकांता) (*f*) Beloved of Shiva (Name of Goddess Durga).

Shivkārini (शिवकारिणी) (*f*) Name of a form of Durga. One of the Matris (divine mother).

Shivkaryi (शिवकर्यी) (*f*) Source of auspicious things-goddess Lakshmi. (L)

Shivkeshav (शिवकेशव) (*m*) Name of Lord Shiva and Krishna together.

Shivmālā (शिवमाला) (*f*) Rosary of Shiva.

Shivmāyā (शिवमाया) (*m/f*) Full of prosperity.

Shivpriya (शिवप्रिया) (*m/f*) Dear to or esteemed by Lord Shiva.

Shivrūpa (शिवरूपा) (*m/f*) The form or image of Lord Shiva.

Shivshakti (शिवशक्ति) (*f*) Lord Shiv and his female energy Parvati.

Shivtā (शिवता) (*f*) The state or condition of a person absorbed in Shiva.

Shobhā (शोभा) (*f*) Grace, elegance, beauty, glamour, splendour, brilliance, lustre.

Shobhanā (शोभना) (*m/f*) Brilliant, splendid, beautiful, excellent, glorious, auspicious, welfare, prosperity.

Shobhaniya (शोभनीय) (*m/f*) To be beautified or adornped, beautiful, splendid.

Shivrūpa (शिवरूपा) (*m/f*) The form or image of Lord Shiva.

Shivshakti (शिवशक्ति) (*f*) Lord Shiv and his female energy Parvati.

Shivta (शिवता) (*f*) The state or condition of a person absorbed in Shiva.

Shobhniya (शोभनीय) (*m/f*) To be beautified or adornbed, beautiful, splendid.

Shobhikā (शोभिका) (*f*) Brilliant, beautiful.

Shibhini (शिभीनी) (*f*) Graceful, splendid, beautiful.

Shobhishtha (शोभिश्ठ) (*m/f*) Most brilliant or splendid (from Rig Veda).

Shobhita (शोभित) (*m/f*) Splendid, beautiful, adorned or embellished.

Shobhin (शोभिन) (*m/f*) Brilliant, splendid, beautiful.

Shobhishtha (शोभिष्ठ) (*m/f*) Most brilliant or splendid.

Shodhana (शोधन) (*m/f/n*) Cleaning, purifying, cleansing (from Mahabharata).

Shodhita (शोधित) (*m/f*) Cleansed, purified, refined, corrected or improved.

Shokanashanah (शोकनाशनः) (*m*) Destroyer of sorrow. (V)

Shona (शोण) (*m/f*) Red, crimson, purple (from Rig Veda).

Shona-mani (शोण-मणि) (*f*) Ruby.

Shona-ratna (शोण-रत्न) (*m/f*) Red gem, ruby.

Shradhā (श्राद्धा) (*f*) Faith, respect, strong desire, veneration, reverence. Faith, personified in the Vedas and lauded in a few-hymns. Daughter of sage Daksha, wife of the god Dharma and reputed mother of Kāma-deva (the god/ love).

Shraman (श्रमन) (*m*) The scourge of the wicked. (V)

Shravā (श्रवा) (*m*) Son of Bhrigu.

Shravan (श्रवण) (*m*) The fifth month of the year (July) according to the Hindu calendar.

Shravani (श्रवणी) (*f*) The day of full moon in the month of Shravan (July/ August)

Shravasya (श्रवस्य) (*m/f*) Fame, glory, renown, glorious deed (from Rig Veda).

Shravishtha (श्रविष्ठ) (*m*) The best among the storms.

Shreshta (श्रेष्ठ) (*m*) A Sudhāmāna god.

Shreshth (श्रेष्ठ) (*m*) The best. (V)

Shrey (श्रेय) (*m*) The good, credit, bliss, worldly achievements.

Shreyah (श्रेयः) (*m*) Auspiciousness personified. (V)

Shravani (श्रावणी) (*f*) The day of full moon in the month fo Shravan (July/ August).

Shravasya (श्रवस्र) (*m/f*) Fame, glory, renown, glorious deed (from Rig Veda).

Shreshthin (श्रेष्ठीन) (*m/f*) Having the best, chief, a distinguihed man.

Shreyah (श्रेयह) (*m*) Auspiciousness personified. (V)

Shri/Sri (श्री/श्री) (*f*) Fortune, prosperity. Wife of Vishnu. An honorific prefix to the names of gods, kings, heroes, men and women, and books of high estimation (Shri/Srimad Bhagvat Gita).

Shribālā (श्रीबाला) (*f*) Divine maiden.

Shribandhu (श्रीबन्धु) (*m*) Brother of goddess Lakshmi. Another name of moon.

Shribhadra (श्रीभद्र) (*f*) Shri is the name of the goddess of wealth, fortune and prosperity (wife of Vishnu) and bhadra means blessed. Thus the whole literally means-blessed by goddess of wealth.

Shribhānu (श्रीभानु) (*m*) A son of Krishna and Satyabhāmā (one of the four wives of Krishna).

Shribindu (श्रीबिन्दु) (*m/f*) Sing of fortune.

Shridhara (श्रीधर) (*m*) A name of Vishnu.

Shrigarbha (श्रीगर्भ) (*m*) Preserving every wealth of world inside his stomach (at the time of dissolution). (V)

Shrikānt (श्रीकांत) (*m*) An epithet of Vishnu.

Shrikanth (श्रीकंठ) (*m*) An epithet of Shiva.

Shrikanthikā (श्रीकंठिका) (*f*) In music a particular kind of Rag. See also Shri Kanth.

Shrikarah (श्रीकरः) (*m*) He who gives all opulence and peace to his devotees. (V)

Shrikirti (श्रीकीर्ति) (*f*) In music a kind of measure.

Shri Krishna (श्रीकृष्ण) (*m*) The divine Krishna.

Shrila (श्रीला) (*m/f*) Prosperous, happy, wealthy, beautiful, eminent.

Shrilakshmi (श्रीलक्ष्मी) (*f*) Divine Lakshmi.

Shrimālā (श्रीमाला) (*f*) Divine rosary. A kind of shrub.

Shriman (श्रीमान) (*m*) One endowed with oppulence. Having all sorts of riches. (V)

Shrimani (श्रीमणि) (*f*) Best among the jewels. Name of a Rag.

Shrimatam Varah (श्रीमात्म वराह) (*m*) The best groom. (V)

Shrimate (श्रीमते) (*m*) Revered. Another name of Lord Hanuman who is most adorable and popular among His devotees. (H)

Shrinandini (श्रीनन्दिनी) (*f*) Daughter of prosperity. Good fortunes.

Shrināth (श्रीनाथ) (*m*) Husband of Shri (Name of Vishnu).

Shringi (श्रृंगी) (*m*) Having a thorn (in his fish incarnation). (V)

Shrinidhi (श्रीनिधि) (*m*) Fount of all wealth. Receptacle of beauty. (V)

Shrinivās (श्रीनिवास) (*m*) Abode of Lakshmi. (V)

Shripadi (श्रीपदी) (*f*) A kind of Jasmine flower.

Shripadma (श्रीपद्मा) (*m*) Name of Lord Krishna.

Shripāl (श्रीपाल) (*m*) Protector of prosperity, good fortune and good luck. (V)

Shripati (श्रीपति) (*m*) A king, Vishnu, Krishna.

Shripriya (श्रीप्रिया) (*m/f*) Divine lover, divine favour.

Shri-rang (श्री-रंग) (*m*) An epithet of Vishnu.

Shrirūpā (श्रीरूपा) (*f*) Divine form (applied to Radha).

Shrivāni (श्रीवाणी) (*f*) Divine speech.

Shrivasah (श्रीवसह) (*m*) The abode of Lakshmi. (V)

Shrivatsa (श्रीवत्स) (*m*) Favourite of divine.

Shrivatsal (श्रीवत्सल) (*m*) Darling of the goddess of glory. (S)

Shrivibhavan (श्रीविभवन) (*m*) Granter of the desired fruit according to devotees efforts. (V)

Shrividyā (श्रीविद्या) (*f*) Divine knowledge. Form of Durga.

Shri Visal (श्री विसाल) (*m/f*) Abounding in good fortune.

Shriya (श्रीया) (*f*) Prosperity, happiness, (personified as the wife of Vishnu).

Shroddhatri (श्रोद्धात्री) (*m/f*) One who has belief or is faithful.

Shrushti (श्रुष्टि) (*f*) Obedience, complaisance, willing service.

Shruta (श्रुत) (*m/f*) Heard, listened to, orally transmitted or communicated from age to age.

Shrutakirti (श्रुतकीर्ति) (*m*) Son of Arjun and Draupadi.

Shrutasen (श्रुतसेन) (*m*) Son of Sahdev and Draupadi.

Shrutavati (श्रुतवती) (*f*) Daughter of sage Bhardwaj. Shw was extremely pious and devoted to Indra.

Shruti (श्रुति) (*f*) Direct revelation of Vedas by hearing. What was heard. The Mantras and Brahmanas of the Vedas are always included in the term, and the Upanishads are generally classed with them. See also Smriti.

Shrutiprakāsh (श्रुतिप्रकाश) (*m*) Illuminator of the Vedas. (S)

Shrutisāgar (श्रुतिसागर) (*m*) An ocean of Vedic knowledge. (V)

Shubh (शुभ) (*a*) Auspicious, good, the good, well being.

Shubhāksha (शुभाक्ष) (*m*) Auspicious eyed. Name of Lord Shiva.

Shubhan (शुभन) (*m/f/n*) Shining, bright, brilliant. One who is auspicious (Name of Lord Ganesh) (R.V.)

Shubhānan (शुभानन) (*m/f*) Handsome faced, good looking.

Shubhangah (शुभंगः) (*m*) He who has beautiful organs and body. (V)

Shubhanvita (शुभन्वित) (*m/f/n*) Endowed with prosperity or good fortune.

Shubhpradā (शुभप्रदा) (*f*) Granter of auspicious things-goddess Lakshmi. (L)

Shubhātmak (शुभात्मक) (*m/f/n*) Pleasant, charming, benevolent, kind.

Shubhavah (शुभवः) (*m/f*) Causing prosperity.

Shubhekshana (शुभेक्षण) (*m*) He who ensures welfare merely by His Darshan. (V)

Shubhgunkanan (शुभगुंकनान) (*m*) Mine of all virtues. (G)

Subhikā (शुभिका) (*f*) Auspicious, garland formed of flowers.

Shubhlakshana (शुभलक्षण) (*m/f*) Having auspicious marks.

Shubhmaya (शुभमय) (*m/f*) Splendid, beautiful.

Shubhnandā (शुभनन्दा) (*f*) Name of goddess, said to be a form of Dakshayani.

Shubhrā (शुभ्रा) (*f*) Radiant, shining, beautiful, splendid, spotless (from Rig Veda).

Shubh-suchani (शुभ-सूचनी) (*f*) Indication good. Name of a female deity (worshipped by women in times of calamity (She is also called Suvachini).

Shubhr (शुभ्र) (*a*) Radiant, shining, clear, spotless.

Shuchaye (शूचये) (*m*) Chaste. Another name of Lord Hanuman. (H)

Shuchi (शूची) (*m*) Indra of the epoch of the fourteenth Manu. The five with sun, has 1,000 streams, taking water from rivers, mountains and pools, of these 400 pour out rain, 300 dew, 300 heat-all for the benefit of men and gods.

Shuchikā (शूचिका) (*f*) An Apsara (heavenly nymphs).

Shuchindra (शूचीन्द्रा) (*m*) Lord of purity.

Shuchimani (शूचीमणि) (*m/f*) Pure jewel, crystal.

Shuchishrava (शूचीश्रवा) (*m*) The one with noble glory. (V)

Shuddhi (शुद्धि) (*f*) Purity, cleansing, purification, holiness.

Shuddhrupin (शुद्धरूपिन) (*m/f*) Having the pure or true form.

Shuddhvigraha (शुद्धविग्रह) (*m*) Of pure body. (S)

Shudhatā (शुद्धता) (*f*) Purity, correctness, faultlessness.

Shudhātma (शुद्धात्मा) (*m/f*) Pure soul or spirit. Pure minded. Name of Lord Shiva.

Shuki (शुकी) (*f*) Mother Vyasa's son Shukadeva.

Shukla (शुक्ला) (*m*) A name of Hari (Vishnu). A name of one of the sons of Vashishtha.

Shukti (शूक्ति) (*f*) Shining, bright, pearl-oyster or oyster shell.

Shukti-vadhu (शुक्ति-वधु) (*f*) Mother of pearls.

Shulin (शूलिन) (*m*) Having a trident. (S)

Shunya (शून्य) (*m*) Beyond all definitions. (V)

Shur (शूर) (*m*) Valiant. (V)

Shura (शूरा) (*m*) Grandfather of Krishna. Father of Kunti and Vasudeva.

Shurjaneshvar (शूर्जनेश्वर) (*m*) The chosen Lord, owing to his powers, for Indra and other gods. (V)

Shursen (शूरसेन) (*m*) The commander of the army of valiants in His Ram incarnation. (V)

Shushi (शूशी) (*f*) Strength, power.

Shushmā (शुषमा) (*f*) Hissing, roarng, strong, bold, fragrance, courage, valour.

Shushman (शुषमान) (*m/f*) Strength, vigour, energy, courage.

Shushmaya (शुषमय) (*m/f*) Strengthening, encouraging.

Shushmin (शुषमिन) (*m/f*) Roaring, strong, vigorous, courageous.

Shushrusha (शुश्रूषा) (*f*) Desire or wish to hear, reverence, obedience.

Shushrushu (शुश्रूशु) (*m/f*) Desirous of hearing or learning, obedient, eager to obey.

Shveta (श्वेत) (*m*) A sage. An incarnation of Shiva. Also a name of a son of king Virat of matsya. He was a great warrior and is mentioned in Mahabharata.

Shvetaki (श्वेतकी) (*m*) A very religious and righteous king. His story is mentioned in the Mahabharata.

Shvetanshu (श्वेतांशु) (*m*) White rayed, another name of the moon.

Shyām (श्याम) (*m*) Black, cloud. A name of Krishna.

Shyāmā (श्यामा) (*f*) A small singing black bird, a woman. Name of **Rādhā**.

Shyāmangā (श्यामांगा) (*m*) Dark coloured. Anothr name of Lord Rama. (R)

Shyāmāntak-priya (श्यामांतक-प्रिया) (*m*) Lover of diamond jewel. (K)

Shyāmā-pujā (श्यामा-पूजा) (*f*) The worship of Shyam or Durga (on the new moon of the month of Kartik (October-November).

Shyāmsundar (श्यामसुन्दर) (*m*) Dark and beautiful (Name of Lord Krishna).

Siddha (सिद्ध) (*m*) Ever evident. (V)

Siddānt/Sidhānta (सिद्धांत/सिद्धांता) (*m/f*) Any scientific work on astronomy or mathematics.

Siddhārath (सिद्धार्थ) (*a/m*) Whose wishes have been fulfilled, enlightenment, Name of Buddha.

Siddhasankalpah (सिद्धसंकल्प) (*m*) One with resolute determination. (V)

Siddhesh (सिद्धेश) (*m*) The prediction of a seer, one whose predictions are fulfilled. Prophet, soothsayer, fortune teller.

Siddheshvar (सिद्धेश्वर) (*m*) An epithet of Lord Shiva.

Siddhi (सिद्धि) (*f*) Accomplishment, proof, truth, preparation, success, super-human power, readiness. Wealth and prosperity.

Sikshā (शिक्षा) (*f*) Phonetics; one of the Vedangas (the science which teaches the proper pronunciation and manner of reciting the Vedas).

Siddhidah (सिद्धिदाह) (*m*) Bestower rewards according to the doers efforts. (V)

Siddhidhatra (सिद्धिधात्र) (*m*) Bestower of success. (G)

Siddhipriya (सिद्धिप्रिया) (*m*) Bestower of boons. (G)

Siddhisadhan (सिद्धिसाधन) (*m*) He who provides means for accomplishment. (V)

Siddhivinayak (सिद्धिविनायक) (*m*) Bestower of success. (G)

Sidhyā (सिध्या) (*f*) Auspicious. Name of the asterism Pushya.

Sidupriyā (सिदुप्रिया) (*f*) Goddess Durga fond of divine nectar. When She is in trance, Her steps become unbalanced and eyes roll under the influence of the divine nectar, and Her movements indicate that she is engrossed in Her feelings for the love of Her devotees. (D)

Sīmā (सीमा) (*f*) A border, boundary, bunds, range, limit, extent, verge. A landmark, last degree.

Simi (सीमी) See Shimi.

Simtā (सिमता) (*n*) Smile.

Sindhur (सिंदूर) (*n*) Red lead.

Sisu Pal (शिशु पाल) (*m*) Son of Dama-Ghosh, king of Chedi; a cousin of Krishna.

Sīta (सीता) (*f*) 'A furrow'. In the Veda, Sītā is the furrow, or husbandry personified, and worshipped as a deity presiding over agriculture and furits. In the Ramayana and later works she is daughter of king of Videha (Mithila) and wife of Rama.

Sitābja (सीताब्ज) (*m/f*) White lotus.

Sitavallabh (सीतावल्लभ) (*m*) Lord of Sita. Lord Krishna, who was Lord Rama in His previous incarnation, is the Lord of all. (K)

Sitikanth (सितीकांथ) (*m*) Shiva. See Shiva.

Sitavallabh (सीतावल्लभ) (*m*) Lor of Sita. Lord Krishna, who was Lord Rama in His previous incarnation, is the Lord of all. (K)

Sitrāshmi (सित्राश्मि) (*m/f*) White rayed, the moon.

Sitruchi (सित्रुचि) (*m/f*) Bright coloured, the moon.

Siva (सिव) Shiv/Siva

Sivi/Shivi (सिवी/शिवी) (*m*) Son of Usinara, and king of the country also called Usinara, near Gandhara. The great charity and devotion of Sivi are extolled in the Mahabharata by the sage Markendeya.

Skambha (स्कम्भ) (*m*) The supporter. A name sometimes used in the Rig Veda to designate the supreme deity.

Skandaguru (स्कन्दगुरु) (*m*) Preceptor of Skanda. (S)

Skandpurvaj (स्कन्दपूर्वज) (*m*) Older than Skanda (Karik). (G)

Smar (स्मर) (*m*) Cupid-the god of love.

Smaran (स्मरण) (*m*) Recollection, memory, recognition.

Smayin (स्मयीन) (*m/f/n*) Smiling, laughing.

Smer (स्मेर) (*a*) Smiling, blooming.

Smerā (स्मेरा) (*f*) Smiling, friendly, blossomed, evident, apparent.

Smitā (स्मिता) (*m*) Noiseless smile.

Smiti (स्मिति) (*f*) smile.

Smritā (स्मृता) (*m/f/n*) Remembered, recollected, called to mind, enjoined by smriti or traditional law.

Smriti (स्मृति) (*f*) Memory, a law book. What was remembered; inspiration, as distinguished from Shruti (direct revelation). What has been remembered and handed down by tradition. Manu says that by Shruti is meant the Veda, and by Smriti the institutes of law. The code of traditional Hindu law.

Sneh (स्नेह) (*m*) Love, affection.

Sobhanā (सोभना) (*v*) To appear, impressive.

Som (सोम) (*m*) The moon. A creeper (milky white plant) yielding and intoxicating juice which was drunk at sacrifices.

Somadatta (सोमदत्त) (*m*) Som means moon and Datta means-assigned, given, one of the Jaina gods. Somadatta-son of Shantanu's brother Bahalika.

Somadeva Bhatt (सोमदेव भट्ट) (*m*) Some (moon), Deva (god). The name of celebrated lingam or emblem of Shiva at the city of Somnāth (Gujrat).

Sombhu (सोम्भु) (*m/f*) Belonging to the family of the moon.

Somendra (सोमेन्द्र) (*m/f*) Belonging to Soma and Indra.

Somepah (सोमेपह) (*m*) The partaker of 'Soma' offered to him in the Yagyas. (V)

Somesh (समेश) (*f*) Lord of the moon.

Somlatā (सोमलता) (*f*) Soma plant.

Somprabhā (सोमप्रभा) (*m/f/n*) Having the splendour of the moon.

Sonā (सोना) (*m*) Gold, an excellent thing.

Sotkarsha (सोत्कर्ष) (*m/f/n*) Having eminence, excellent.

Smayin (स्मयीन) (*m/f/n*) Smiling, laughing.

Spashtakshar (स्पष्टाक्षर) (*m*) With well defined letter (word) like 'AUM'. (V)

Spriha (स्पृहा) (*f*) Eager, dedsire, wished for, longed for.

Sprihita (स्पृहिता) (*m/f/n*) Eager, desire, wished for, longed for.

Sprihiya (स्पृहिया) (*m/f/n*) Eager, dec sire, wished for, longed for.

Sragvi (श्रागवी) (*m*) One who dons Vaijayanti garland. (V)

Srashta (स्रष्टा) (*m*) The creator. (V)

Sridevi (श्रीदेवी) (*f*) Sri. Shri and for Devi, see Devi. Name of a daughter of Devaka and one of the wives of Vasudeva. Also it means born of milk ocean.

Srishta (सृष्ट) (*m*) Procreator of all realms: the cause of existence. (V)

Srivatsavaksha (श्रीवत्सवाक्ष) (*m*) Having Shri Vatsas mark upon his bosom. (V)

Srishti (सृष्टि) (*f*) Creation, nature.

Srutakirti (स्रुतकीर्ति) (*m*) A son of Arjuna and Draupadi.

Stavapriya (स्तवप्रिया) (*m*) One who gets propitiated by chanting hymns. (V)

Stavya (स्तव्य) (*m*) Adorable for every one. (V)

Sthanadah (स्थानदः) (*m*) He who granted firm position to His devotees like Dhruva and Prahlad. (V)

Sthānu (स्थानु) (*m*) A name of Shiva.

Sthavartsthanu (स्थवर्तस्थनु) (*m*) Though Himself stable yet keeping the world at move. (V)

Sthaviro Dhruvah (स्थाविरो ध्रुवः) (*m*) Very ancient and very stable. (V)

Sthavishtha (स्थाविष्ठ) (*m*) Reposing everywhere. Huge-bodied. (V)

Sthir (स्थिर) (*m*) Immutable. (V)

Sthira (स्थिरा) (*m/f*) Firm, hard, solid.

Sthula (स्थूल) (*m*) The heavy (Huge) bodied. (V)

Stoma (स्तोम) (*m*) Praise, eulogium, a hymn. (V)

Stomya (स्तोम्य) (*m/f*) Worthy of a hymn of praise laudable (from Rig Veda).

Stotā (स्तोता) (*m*) He who creates hymns. (V)

Strotram (स्त्रोत्रम) (*m*) The hymn (for singing glory). (V)

Stubhā (स्तुभा) (*m/f*) Humming, making joyful exclamations, hurrahing.

Stuta (स्तुत) (*m/f/n*) Praised, eulogised, glorified, celebrated. (RV)

Stuti (स्तूति) (*m*) Praise, eulogy, Name of Durga and Vishnu. The object of orisons. (V)

Stuti priya (स्तुति प्रिया) (*f*) Found of praise. See also Stuti.

Stuvi (स्तुवी) (*m*) Praiser, worshipper.

Subāhu (सुबाहु) (*m*) Five armed. A son of Shatrughan and king of Mathura.

Subhā (सुभा) (*f*) Nectar, beauty. Wife of sage Angira and mother of Brahaspati.

Subhadrā (सुभद्रा) (*f*) Daughter of Vasudeva, sister of Krishna and wife of Arjuna. She was mother of Abhimanyu.

Subhāg (सुभाग) (*a*) Beautiful, fortunate, lucky, beloved, giving delight, pretty.

Subhāga (सुभाग) (*f*) A beautiful and fortunate woman who is very dear to her husband.

Subhalakshmi (शुभलक्ष्मी) (*f*) Radiant goddess Lakshmi.

Subhalochana (सुभलोचन) (*f*) Beautiful eyes.

Subhāmā (सुभामा) (*f*) A queen of Krishna.

Subhamālā (शुभमाला) (*f*) With a splendid garland.

Subhangi (शुभांगी) (*f*) Fair-limbed. Most beautiful woman.

Subhānu (सुभानु) (*m*) Most beautiful son of Krishna and Satya-bhāmā.

Subhāsh (सुभाष) (*m*) Well spoken and eloquent speaker.

Subhāshī (सुभाषी) (*m*) An elegant or eloquent speaker.

Subhikshā (सुभीक्षा) (*m*) Time of plenty and prosperity.

Subhitā (सुभीता) (*m*) Opportunity, convenience, leisure, comfort.

Subhotī (सुभोति) (*f*) Beauty, excellence.

Subhujah (सुभुजः) (*m*) Of well formed arms (for protectrin the world). (V)

Subodh (सुबोध) (*a*) Intelligent, intelligible. easily understood.

Subodhini (सुबोधिनी) A commentary of Visveshvara Bhatt on the law-book called Mitakshara.

Subrahmanya (सुब्रह्मण्य) (*m*) Shiv, Vishnu.

Suchandra (सुचन्द्र) (*m*) Beautiful moon.

Suchāru (सुचारु) (*m*) A son of Krishna and Rukmini.

Suchendra (सुचेन्द्र) (*m*) Lord of piousness.

Suchetna (सुचेतन) (*m*) Very conscious, notable, distinguished.

Suchitra (सुचित्र) (*m*) Purity. A kin who fought on the side of Pandavas in the Mahabharata war.

Sudāmā (सुदामा) (*m*) A poor Brahman who was a great friend of Krishna. A name of a maternal grandfather of Damyanti. King of Dashrna.

Sudāman (सुदामन) (*m*) A cloud. Sea. One of Krishna's friends.

Sudāmini (सुदामिनी) (*f*) Wife of Shamika.

Sudan (सूदन) A Sanskrit suffix used to denote a destroyer or killer, or conqueror of-as Repusudan or Madhusudan.

Sudāntā (सुदांता) (*f*) Apsaras (heavenly nymphs).

Sudarshan (सुदर्शन) (*m*) Good looking, elegant. The name of mythological discus wielded by Krishna.

Sudās (सुदास) (*m*) Name of an ancient country, the son of Devadas. A king who is frequently mentioned in the Rig Veda.

Sudatī (सुदति) (*f*) Apsaras (heavenly nymphs).

Sudershan (सुदर्शन) (*m*) Having auspicious appearance good at look at. (V)

Sudesh (सुदेश) (*m/f*) A beautiful country.

Sudeshna (सुदेशना) (*m/f*) Wife of king Virat of Matsya. Mother of Shankha and Uttara. Also a name of a wife of king Baliraja. Also a name of a song of Krishna and Rukmini.

Sudev (सुदेव) (*m*) A name of a diety. Also a name of brahman in the court of king Bhima. He found king's daughter Damyanti when she was working in the household of king Virabahu of Chedi under the assumed name of Sairandhri. He was given one thousand cow as a reward for bringing Damyanti. Later Damyanti sent him to Ayodhya to arrange for the return of Nala (Damyanti's husband).

Sudevi (सुदेवी) (*f*) A Devi, consort of Krishna, name of wife of Dharma.

Sudhā (सुधा) (*f*) Nectar, water, juice, whitewash.

Sudhābhuj (सुधाभुज) (*m*) Feeding on nectar, a god, deity.

Subhābhuji (सुधाभुजी) (*f*) Same as Sudhabhuj.

Sudhāmāyā (सुधामाया) (*f*) Consisting of nectar.

Sudhāmukhi (सुधामुखी) (*f*) Nectar faced. Name of a heavenly nymph.

Sudhānshu (सुधांशु) (*m*) The moon.

Sudhanva (सुधन्वा) (*m*) Wielder of a beautiful bow. (V)

Sudharma (सुधर्मा) (*m*) Pious, virtuous, piety.

Sudharmi (सुधर्मी) (*f*) Pious, virtuous, piety.

Sudhā Sār (सुधा सार) (*n*) A shower of nectar.

Sudhā Sindhu (सुधा सिंधु) (*m*) Ocean of nectar.

Sudhā Sutī (सुधा सुती) (*f*) Producing nectar, the moon, a lotus flower.

Sudhāvās (सुधावास) (*m*) Nectar-abode, the moon.

Sudhī (सुधी) (*a/f*) Remembrance, learned, pious, wise.

Sudhmā (सुधमा) (*f*) Exceptional beauty, charm.

Sudipā (सुदीपा) (*f*) Very bright, shining brightly.

Sudiptā (सुदीप्ता) (*f*) Very bright, shining brightly.

Sudití (सुदिति) (*f*) Brightness, bright flame.

Sugandh (सुगन्ध) (*m*) Fragrance.

Sugandhā (सुगन्धा) (*f*) Apsåras (heavenly nymph).

Sugandhi (सुगन्धि) (*f*) Same as Sugandh.

Sugati (सुगति) (*f*) A good or happy condition, welfare, happiness, bliss.

Sugatrā (सुगत्रा) (*f*) Fair limbed, beautiful, graceful.

Sughoshah (सुघोषः) (*m*) Having sweet and deep voice. (V)

Suguna (सुगुन) (*m/f/n*) Very virtuous, or excellent.

Suhrita (सुहृत) (*m*) Kind to all being without any selfish desire. (V)

Sujān (सुजान) (*a*) Intelligent, wise, clever, learned, polite.

Sujātā (सुजाता) (*a*) Brahmavādinī, Born in a good family.

Sukānt/Sukāntā (सुकांत/सुकांता) (*m/f*) Very beautiful.

Sukānti (सुकांति) (*f*) Full of beauty, glory.

Sukanyā (सुकन्या) (*f*) Beautiful maiden. Also the name of the daughter of Sharyati and wife of Rshi Chavana.

Sukartu (सुकर्तु) (*m*) One who does virtuous deeds.

Suketu (सुकेतु) (*m*) A son of Uttama Manu.

Sukhada (सुखद) (*m*) Bestower of happiness to his devotee. (V&S)

Sukheshtha (सुखेष्ठ) (*m*) Living in joy. Applied to Lord Shiva.

Sukhgandha (सुखगन्ध) (*f*) Sweet smelling, fragrant.

Sukhkar (सुखकर) (*m/f*) Causing pleasure or happiness.

Sukhbhuj (सुखभुज) (*m/f*) Enjoying happiness, happy, lucky.

Sukhin (सुखीन) (*m/f*) Possessing or causing happiness, or pleasure, happy, joyful.

Sukhitā (सुखीता) (*f*) Comfort, happiness.

Sukhkriyā (सुखक्रिया) (*f*) The act of causing delight or happiness.

Sukhnāth (सुखनाथ) (*m*) Name of a deity worshipped in Mathura.

Sukhtā (सुखता) (*f*) Ease, comfort, delight, happiness, prosperity.

Sukirti (सुकीर्ति) (*a*) Reputation, renown, reputed.

Suksham (सूक्ष्म) (*a*) Minute, sharp, exact, subtle.

Sukshmā (सूक्ष्मा) (*f*) A Shakti. See Devi.

Sukta (सूक्त) (*f*) A vedic hymn.

Sukumār (सुकुमार) (*m*) A tender child, delicate, gentle, soft, youthful.

Sukti (सूक्ति) (*f*) A good or friendly speech, wise saying, beautiful verse.

Sukul/Sukulā (सुकुल/सुकुला) (*m/f*) From a noble family.

Sukumār (सुकुमार) (*m*) Very tender, delicate.

Sukumari (सुकुमारी) (*f*) Very tender and delicate.

Sulabh (सुलभ) (*a*) Attainable, easily, feasible, obtainable.

Sulakshan (सुलक्षण) (*a*) Gifted with laudable ways, having auspicious features, characteristic, fortunate, lucky.

Sulakshanā/Sulakshni (सुलक्षणा/सुलक्षणी) (*f*) Same as Sulakshan.

Sulekha (सुलेख) (*f*) Having or forming auspicious lines.

Sulochanā (सुलोचना) (*f*) Beautiful eyed woman, having charming eyes.

Suman (सुमन) (*m*) A flower, favourably disposed, happy.

Sumangal (सुमंगल) (*m*) Auspicious, bringing good fortune.

Sumangalā/Sumangali (सुमंगला/सुमंगली) (*f*) Auspiciousa, Another name of goddess Parvati.

Sumanī (सुमणि) (*f*) A beautiful jewel, adorned with jewels.

Sumantra (सुमंत्र) (*m*) The chief counsellor of king Dasrath and a friend of Rām.

Sumantu (सुमंतु) (*m*) The collector of the hymns of the Atharva-Veda; a pupil of Ved-Vyāsa.

Sumanya (सुमान्या) (*m/f*) Piously, devoutly, kindly, graciously.

Sumati (सुमति) (*f*) Wise, kind, benevolent.

Sumedha (सुमेधा) (*m*) Having noble brilliance. (V)

Sumit (सुमित) (*m/f*) Well pleased.

Sumitrā (सुमित्र) (*f*) Wife of Dasrath and mother of Lakshman and Shatrughan.

Sumna (सुम्न) (*m/f*) Benevolent, kind, gracious, favourable (from Rig Veda).

Sumukha (सुमुख) (*m*) Handsome face. This epithet is used for Garuda and for the son of Garuda (a mythical bird on which Vishnu rides).

Sunāmī (सुनामी) (*f*) Beautiful name. A daughter of Devas and wife of Vasudev.

Sunanda (सुनन्द) (*f*) A princess of Chedi who befriended Damyanti when she was deserted by her husband. See Nala.

Sunandana (सुनन्दन) (*m*) A son of Krishna.

Sunār (सुनार) (*m/f*) Glad, joyous, merry, delightful. Sunar word is from Sundar.

Sunda/Sundah (सुन्द/सुन्दह) (*m*) Extremely kind. (V)

Sunāti (सुनाती) (*f*) Beautiful, well-bred, good family, born in a good family.

Sundar (सुन्दर) (*a*) Beautiful, handsome, pretty, fine, good.

Sundarah (सुन्दरः) (*m*) Beautiful. (V)

Sundari (सुन्दरी) (*f*) Beautiful woman.

Sunitā (सुनीता) (*f*) Well behaved, polite.

Suniti (सुनीति) (*f*) Equity.

Sunrita (सूनृता) (*m/f*) Joyful, glad, pleasant and true.

Supadma (सुपद्म) (*m*) Beautiful as lotus.

Suparna (सुपर्णा) (*m*) A Sudhāmana god.

Suparsād (सुप्रसाद) (*m*) Gracious to even the wicked (by granting space in His Abode after slaying their bodies. (V)

Suprabhā (सुप्रभा) (*f*) Beautiful, very bright, splendid.

Suprabhāt (सुप्रभात) (*f*) The beautiful and earliest dawn.

Suprasidh (सुप्रसिद्ध) (*a*) Very famous.

Suprasnna (सुप्रसन्न) (*f*) Ever cheerful and beaming-goddess Lakshmi. (L)

Supratimā (सुप्रतिमा) (*m/f*) Beautiful idol. Name of a king in Mahabharata.

Suprita (सुप्रिता) (*m*) Well pleased. (S)

Supriya (सुप्रिया) (*f*) Very dear. Chief of the Gandharas. An Apsaras (heavenly nymph).

Supushpā (सुपुष्पा) (*f*) Beautiful. flowers.

Surabhav (सुरभव) (*m/f*) The dignity of god.

Surabhi (सुरभि) (*f*) Fragrance, aroma, perfume, scent. Also the name of the *Cow of plenty*, produced at the churning of the ocean, who granted every desire, and is reverenced as the fountain of milk and curds.

Surachirta (सुरचित्र) (*m*) Worshiped by celestials. Another name of Lord Hanuman. (H)

Surādhās (सुराधास) (*m/f*) Granting good gifts and receiving good gifts, rich, wealthy. Name of a sage in the Rig Veda.

Suradhyaksha (सुरध्यक्ष) (*m*) The head of gods. (V)

Suraj (सूरज) (*m*) The sun.

Surājan (सुराजन) (*m*) A good king.

Surajmukhi (सूरजमुखी) (*f*) The sun-flower.

Surakshā (सुरक्षा) (*m*) The 4th Vyās, Gautama (incarnation of Vishnu).

Surānanda (सूरानन्द) (*m*) The delighter of gods. (V)

Surārchana (सुरार्चन) (*m/f*) The act of worshipping the gods.

Surariha (सुररिह) (*m*) Slayer of the god's enemies. (V)

Surasā (सुरसा) (*f*) Apsaras (heavenly nymphs).

Surashmi (सुरश्मि) (*f*) Having the rays of the sun. Most beautiful.

Surāsu (सुरासु) (*m/f*) Father of gods, mother of gods.

Surat (सूरत) (*f*) Reflection, memory, recollection, amorous pleasures.

Survānī (सूरवानी) (*f*) The earth a mother of the gods or Aditi.

Suravi (सुरवी) (*m*) Beautiful sun. Divine sun.

Surekh (सुरेख) (*a*) Beautiful, shapely, with symmetrical lines.

Surendra (सुरेन्द्र) (*m*) God Indra-the chief gods. See Indra.

Suresh (सुरेश) (*m*) Lord of gods. (V&S)

Sureshi (सुरेशी) (*f*) Durga, supreme goddess.

Sureshtha (सुरेष्ठ) (*m/f*) Beloved or desired by gods. (A kind of plant=Brahmi).

Sureshvaram (सुरेश्वरम) (*f*) Lord of all the gods. (G)

Sureshwar (सुरेश्वर) (*m*) A god, the sun, literary person, learned man, a sage.

Surshreshtha (सुरश्रेष्ठ) (*f*) Supreme among the celestials. Manifested as energy in every matter, Goddess Durga is the almighty power, the ruler of the unsiverse, and supreme among the celestials. (G)

Surin (सुरीन) (*m*) A wise or learned man or scholar.

Surottama (सुरोत्तम) (*m*) Chief of the gods.

Suruchi (सुरुचि) (*f*) A great delight, happiness. Name of a wife of Dhruv and mother of Uttama.

Suruchih (सुरुचिः) (*m*) Having comely grace and choicest taste. (V)

Surukmā (सुरुक्मा) (*m/f*) Beautifully shining or adored.

Surupā (सुरूपा) (*f*) Most beautiful, wise, learned.

Surupakā (सूरूपका) (*f*) Well-formed, most beautiful, wise, learned.

Surya (सूर्य) (*m*) The sun. He is one of the three chief deities in the Vedas, as great source of light and warmth.

Suryabhā (सूर्यभा) (*m/f/n*) Bright as the Sun.

Suryadev (सूर्यदेव) (*m*) God Surya (the Sun).

Surya-kānt (सूर्य-कांत) (*m*) A sun-gem. A crystal supposed to be formed of condensed rays of the sun.

Suryakānti (सूर्याकांति) (*f*) Sunlight, sunshine. The flower of sesamum.

Suryamani (सूर्यमणि) (*m*) The sun-stone, sun-gem. A kind of flower (Hibiscus Phoeniceus).

Suryānı (सूर्यानी) (*f*) Wife of the Sun.

Suryarashmi (सूर्यरश्मि) (*m/f*) Sun-beam, having the rays of the sun.

Surya Siddhānt (सूर्य सिद्धान्त) (*m*) A celebrated work on astronomy, said to have been revealed by the sun (Surya).

Sushansa (सुशंस) (*m/f/n*) Saying or wishing good things.

Sushansa Shobhana (सूशांसा शोभना) (*m/f*) Very handsome or beautiful, splendid, excellent (from Mahabharata).

Sushen (सुषेन) (*m*) Vishnu, son of Parikshit, son of Varuna. Name of older brother of Parshuram.

Sushenah (सुषेण) (*m*) Well attended by an army of lieutenants. (V)

Sushīl (सुशील) (*a*) Courteous, gentle, modest.

Sushīlā (सुशीला) (*f*) A Devi. See Devi.

Sushmā (सुषमा) (*m/f*) Very beautiful, charming. Splendour.

Sushansa (सुशंस) (*m*) Blessing, saying good things.

Sushsva (सुश्व) (*m/f*) Very dear, kind, favourable, auspicious.

Sushrī (सुश्री) (*a*) An honorific prefixed to the name of a woman-married or umarried.

Sushubha (सुशुभ) (*f*) Auspicious, very beautiful.

Sutantu (सुतांतु) (*m*) Having beautiful bond to bind the world in one body. (V)

Sutapah (सुतपः) (*m*) One who performs right penances. (V)

Sutejas (सुतेजस) (*m/f*) Very bright, mighty, splendid.

Sutikshna (सुतीक्षण) (*m*) A hermit sage who dwelt in the Dandaka forest and was visited by Rām and Sītā.

Suvāch (सुवाच) (*m/f*) Praiseworthy, worth mentioning. Sounding beautiful.

Suvāchinni (सुवाचिनी) (*f*) Indicating good. Female deity. See Shub-Suchani.

Suvandan (सुवन्दन) (*m/f*) Having handsome or beautiful face.

Suwarn (सुवर्ण) (*n*) Gold, money, beautiful.

Suvarnabindu (सुवर्णबिन्दु) (*m*) Having golden pointed name (the word OM) (V)

Suvarnalekhā (सुवर्णलेखा) (*f*) Streak of gold on a touch-stone.

Suvarnāmaya (सवर्णमय) (*m/f*) Made or consisting of gold.

Suvarnavarna (सुवर्णवर्ण) (*m*) Having aureate Body Hue. (V)

Suvarni (सुवर्णि) (*f*) To become gold.

Suvibhāt (सुविभात) (*m/f*) Shining splendidly, very bright.

Suvihita (सुविहित) (*m/f*) Well done or performed or arranged or carried out. Richly provided with.

Suvipra (सुविप्र) (*m/f/n*) Very learned especially in sacred knowledge (from Rig Veda).

Suvirah (सुविरः) (*m*) He who inspires faith in the devotees' heart. (V)

Suvishishtha (सुविशिष्ठ) (*m/f*) Most distinguished or excellent.

Suvratah (सुव्रतः) (*m*) Of nobel resolve. (V)

Suyamunah (सूयमुनः) (*m*) Whose presence conseacrated the river Yamuna bank (Shri Krishna). (V)

Sumukhah (सुमुखः) (*m*) Of beautiful visage. (V)

Suraksha (सुरक्षा) (*m/f*) A good protector.

Suratna (सुरत्न) (*m/f*) Possessing good jewels.

Surup/Surupā (सुरूप/सुरूपा) (*m/f*) Well formed, beautiful, wise, learned. Name of Lord Shiva.

Surupakā (सुरूपका) (*f*) Well formed, beautiful, wise.

Suvartā (सुवर्ता) (*f*) Good news, one who brings good news. Name of wife of Lord Krishna.

Suvimal/Suvimalā (सुविमल/सुविमला) (*m/f*) Perfectly pure.

Suyog (सुयोग) (*m/f*) Good opportunity, a favourable juncture.

Svabhāvya (स्वभाव्य) (*m*) Owing to the self-evidence of the existence, the need of whose birth does not arise. (V)

Svābhishti (स्वाभिष्टि) (*f*) Helpful, favourable. (RV)

Svadhā (स्वधा) (*f*) Self-position, self-power, inherent power.

Svādhipatya (स्वाधिपत्य) (*n*) Own supremacy, supreme sway, sovereign.

Svangah (स्वंगः) (*m*) Self supporting. Having beautiful organs. (V)

Svapan (स्वपन) (*m*) He who throws everyone in the stupor during the dissolution (Paralaya). (V)

Svarāj (स्वराज) (*m*) Lord Indra, king of heaven. Supreme being (Brahma, Vishnu, Indra).

Svaran (स्वर्ण) (*n*) Same as Suvarn. Svarnā (*f*) Same as Suvarn.

Svarjita (स्वरजीतं) (*m/f/n*) Self acquired.

Svarup (स्वरूप) (*m*) Shape, form, appearance, identity, beautiful, alike.

Svarupamān (स्वरूपमान) (*m*) Beautiful, handsome.

Svarupi (स्वरूपी) (*a*) Having an identical form or shape.

Svaruptā (स्वरूपता) (*f*) Most beautiful.

Svaryu (स्वर्यु) (*m/f/n*) Desirous of light or splendour. (RV)

Svasti (स्वस्ति) (*m/f*) Well being, success, prosperity (personified as goddess). The embodiment of all that is auspicious. (V)

Svastibhuk (स्वस्तिभुक) (*m*) He who protects welfare of His devotees. (V)

Svastidah (स्वस्तिदः) (*m*) He who ensures welfare of all. (V)

Svastidakshinah (स्वस्तिदक्षिण) (*m*) The Right Hand ensuring Welfare to His devotees. (V)

Svastikritah (स्वस्तिकृत) (*m*) The auspicious Refuge of the noble. (V)

Svasya (स्वस्य) (*m*) Of beautiful visage. (V)

Svavash (स्ववश) (*m*) Self dependent. (V)

Svāti (स्वाति) (*f*) The fifteenth lunar asterism.

Svayambhu (स्वयम्भू) (*m*) The self-created Lord. (V)

Svayamjatah (स्वयम्जतः) (*m*) He who creates Himself at His will. (V)

Svecha (स्वेच्छ) (*f*) Own wish or will. At pleasure of one own's wish.

Svyamprabhā (स्वयंप्रभा) (*f*) Self shining, an aspara.

Swadhā (स्वधा) (*f*) Oblation.

Swaran (स्वर्ण) (*n*) Gold. Same as Suwarn.

Swaranā (स्वर्णा) (*f*) Same as Swaran.

Swāti (स्वाति) (*f*) Same as Svāti.

Swayambhu (स्वयम्भू) (*m*) The self-existent. A name of Brahmā, the creator.

Syāmā/Shyāmā (स्यामा/श्यामा) (*f*) The black. A name of Shiva's consort. See Devi.

Syamantaka (स्यमन्तक) (*n*) A celebrated gem given by the Sun god to Satrajit. It yielded daily eight loads of gold, and dispelled all fear of portents, wild beasts, fire, robbers and famine.

T (त, ता)

Taditprabhā (तदित्प्रभा) (*f*) Flash of lightning.

Tālam (तालम) (*n*) The throne of goddess Durgā.

Tālikā (तालिका) (*f*) Nightingale, palm of a hand.

Tālita (तालित) (*m/f*) A musical instrument.

Taluni (तलुनी) (*f*) Maiden.

Tālvali (ताल्वली) (*f*) A kind of musical composition.

Tamaharani (तमहरणी) (*f*) Remover of darkness, a deity who destroys darkness.

Tāmarasā (तामरसा) (*f*) Wife of sage 'Atri (author of many vedic hymns).

Tāmasi (तामसी) (*f*) Night, sleep, another name for Durga. (D)

Tamishvar (तमीश्वर) (*m*) Lord of darkness i.e. moon.

Tāmrā (तामरा) (*f*) A daughter of Daksha and wife of Kashyap.

Tamu (तमु) (*m*) A praiser.

Tāndi (तांडी) (*m*) Art of dancing. A sage who repeated to Brahma thousand names of Shiva.

Tandu (तांडू) (*m*) One of Shiva's attendants. He was skilled in music, and invented the dance called Tandavā.

Tansu (तांसू) (*m*) A prinnce of a lunar race. Decorator.

Tantipāl (तंतिपाल) (*m*) Tanti means a cord, line, string especially a long line to which many calves are fastened by smaller cords. Pal mean look after. Tantipal is a name under which Sahdev spent the thriteenth year of banishment looking after cows of king Virat of Matsya.

Tantuvardhan (तंतुवर्धन) (*m*) The enricher of the mortal bonds. (V)

Tanu (तनु) (*a/f*) Thin, small, delicate the body, form.

Tanuj (तनुज) (*m*) A son.

Tanujā (तनुजा) (*f*) A daughter.

Tanulatā (तनुलता) (*f*) With a vine like body, slender, flexible, elastic.

Tanusatya (तनुसत्य) (*m/f*) Simple truth.

Tanushri (तनुश्री) (*f*) With a divine body

Tanya (तन्य) (*f*) A daughter. Propagating a family, belonging to a good family.

Tapan/Tapanā (तपन/तपना) (*m/f*) Warming, shining, the sun. A panchal chief who fought on the side of Pandavas in the Mahabharata war.

Tapandyuti (तपन्दुति) (*m/f*) Brilliant like the sun.

Tapankar (तपंकर) (*f*) Sun-beam.

Tapanmani (तपन्मणि) (*m*) Sun-stone.

Tapansutā (तपन्सुता) (*f*) Sun daughter.

Tapashri (तपश्री) (*f*) A queen of Shishira.

Tapasnidhi (तपसनिधि) (*m*) Store of ascetism, the su preme spirit.

Tapati (तपती) (*f*) A daughter of Surya (Sun god and Chāyā). Married Samvarna, and became mother of Kuru.

Tapita (तपित) (*m/f*) REfined gold.

Tapiyas (तपियास) (*m/f*) Most devoted to austerities. Pious person.

Tapasomurti (तपासोमूर्ति) (*m*) A sage an example of austerity.

Tapasrāj (तपसराज) (*m*) Lord of ascetics.

Tapesh (तपेश) (*m*) Lord of penances. (Brahma, Vishnu and Mahesh).

Tapita (तपिता) (*m/f*) Refined gold.

Tapiyas (तपीयस) (*m/f*) Most devoted to austerities.

Tārā (तारा) (*f*) A star, a planet, the pupil of the eye, a pearl. Name of a goddess.

Tārādhipati (ताराधिपति) (*m*) Lord of stars i.e. Moon

Tārādhish (ताराधीश) (*m*) Lord of the stars (moon).

Tarah (तरः) (*m*) He who makes one (his devotee) transcend the sea of life and dealth. (V)

Tārāmati (तारामती) (*f*) Wife of king Harishchandra of Ayodhya. Mother of Rohit.

Tārambā (तारम्बा) (*f*) Mother of star (from Pranas).

Tarang (तरंग) (*f*) A wave, ripple, whim. A section of a book.

Tarangini (तरंगिनी) (*f*) A river flows through the Uttarakuru country and falls into the north ocean.

Tarani (तरणी) (*m*) The sun, a ray of light, a boat.

Tārāpati (तारापति) (*m*) Lord of the stars, the moon.

Tārāupa (तारूपा) (*f*) A form of Durga. Star shaped, beautiful. See Devi.

Tarasvi (तरस्वी) (*m*) A Yādava, a son of Sāmbā.

Tārāvati (तारावती) (*f*) A form of Durga. See

Tārāvākya (तारावाक्य) (*f*) A speech of goddess Tara

Tārkshya (तारक्ष्य) (*m*) An ancient mythological personification of the sun in the form of a horse or bird. In later times the name is applied to Garuda. Aslo a name of a sage who received from goddess Saraswati some knowledge concerning the proper mode of behaviour for Brahman.

Tarpita (तर्पित) (*m/f* Satisfied person.

Tarsha (तर्श) (*m*) Thrist, wish, desire, eagerly desirous of.

Taru (तरु) (*m/f*) Quick, speediness.

Tarun (तरुण) (*a/m*) Young, youthful, a youth, youngman. A newly born.

Taruni (तरुणी) (*f*) A newly born girl, youthful woman.

Tathāguna (तथागुण) (*m/f*) Endowed with such qualaities.

Tattvam (तत्त्वम) (*m*) The essence of the reality. (V)

Tattvavita (तत्त्वत) (*m*) He who knows the reality. (V)

Tavas (तवस) (*m/f*) Strong, energetic, courageous.

Tāvish (तावश) (*m*) The ocean, heaven, gold.

Tavishi (तावेशी) (*f*) Power, strength, courage heavenly virgin, name of a daughter of Indra.

Tavishya (तविश्य) (*m*) Power, strength, courage.

Tej (तेज) (*m*) Glow, splendour, brilliance, refulgence.

Tejaschandra (तेजसचन्द्र) (*m*) Very bright, powerful moon.

Tejashri (तेजश्री) (*f*) With divine power and grace.

Tejasvi (तेजस्वी) (*a*) Lustrous, glorious, magnificent, skilled, splendid, noble spirited, illustrious, lordly, luminous.

Tejasvin (तेजस्विन) (*m*) Brilliant, bright, heroic, famous, noble, respectful.

Tejasvitā (तेजस्विता) (*f*) Radiance, nobility, lordliness, lustre.

Tejavant (तेजवन्त) (*a*) Glorious, energetic, strong, brilliant, powerful, shining.

Tejavati (तेजवती) (*f*) A Shakti. See Devi.

Tejindra (तेजीन्द्र) (*m*) Glorious chief.

Tejonidhi (तेजोनिधि) (*m*) Abounding in glory and wealth.

Tejovrashā (तेजोव्रषा) (*m*) He who showers brilliance upon his devotees. (V)

Tijila (तिजिल) (*m*) The moon.

Tilak (तिलक) (*m*) An ornamental or religious mark over the forehead.

Tilottamā (तिलोत्तमा) (*f*) Name of an Apsara (heavenly nymphs).

Timilā (तिमिला) (*f*) Name of a musical instrument.

Tirath (तीरथ) (*m/f*) A passage, place of pilgrimage, an object of veneration.

Tirthadev (तीर्थदेव) (*m*) Lord of Pilgrimage. (S)

Tirthākarah (तीर्थाकरः) (*m*) Creator of all knowledge and its interpreter. (V)

Toshana (तोशण) (*m/f*) Pleasing, satisfying, gratifying.

Toyesh (तोएश) (*m*) Lord of water, another name of Varuna.

Traibkyamohini (त्रैब्क्यमोहिनी) (*f*) A goddess created by Nrsimha; a follower of Vāgisha.

Triāksha (त्रिअक्षा) (*m*) Three eyed. (S)

Triambika (त्रिअम्बिका) (*f*) Consort of Shiva (Parvati).

Tribandhu (त्रिबन्धु) (*m*) Friend of the three worlds (Indra).

Tribhānu (त्रिभानु) (*m*) The sun of the three Vedas and morning, noon and sun.

Tribhuvana/Trilok (त्रिभुवन/त्रिलोक) The three worlds' Swarga (heaven), Bhumi (earth), Patāl (hell).

Tribhuvneshvari (त्रिभुवनेश्वरी) (*f*) Goddess of the three worlds. (D)

Tridashādhyaksha (त्रिदशाध्यक्ष) (*m*) Lord of all gods, demons and men. (V)

Tridaspujitā (त्रिदसपूजिता) (*f*) Goddess Durga the goddedss of the celestials. (D)

Tridev (त्रिदेव) (*m*) Trimurty (Brahma, Vishnu and Mahesh). Three gods in one and one in three.

Tridhām (त्रिधाम) (*m*) Shining in three worlds. (S)

Tridhārā (त्रिधारा) (*f*) Three streams. Another name of Ganges river.

Tridip (त्रिदीप) (*m*) Consisting of three lights (Gyan, karam and Bhakti).

Tridivā (त्रिदीवा) (*f*) Heaven, cardamoms. Name of a river in Mahabharata.

Trijati (त्रिजती) (*f*) A mind-born mother.

Trikarmanirata (त्रिकर्मणि) (*m*) A name of Shiva.

Trilalubah dadham (त्रिलालुबः दधम) (*m*) The support of top, middle and bottom quarters (directions). (V)

Trilochan (त्रिलोचन) (*m*) Three eyed i.e. god Shiva. The Mahabhārata relates that the third eye burst from Shiva's forehead with a great flame when his wife playfully placed her hands over his eyes after he had been engaged in austerities in the Himalaya. This eye has been very destructive. It reduced Kāma, the god of love, to ashes.

Trilok/Triloki/Trilokya (त्रिलोक/त्रिलोकी/त्रिलोक्य) (*a*) Pertaining to the three worlds. See Tribhuvana.

Trilokatman (त्रिलोकत्मान) (*m*) Soul of the three worlds. (S)

Trilokchandra (त्रिलोकचन्द्र) (*m*) Moon of the three worlds.

Trilokesh (त्रिलोकेश) (*m*) Lord of the three worlds.

Triloknāth (त्रिलोकनाथ) (*m*) Lord of the three worlds. A name of Indra and Shiva. (S)

Trilok-rakshaka (त्रिलोक-रक्षक) (*m*) Protector of the three worlds (Ram). **(R)**

Trilokātmā (त्रिलोकात्मा) (*m*) The spirit pervading the three realms. (V)

Trilokātmane (त्रिलोकात्मने) (*m*) Lord of the three worlds - Lord Rama. **(R)**

Trilokdhrik (त्रिलोकध्रिक) (*m*) The lone support for the three world (heaven, earth and patal). (V)

Trilokesha (त्रिलोकेक्ष) (*m*) The Lord of the three realms. (V)

Trilokināth (त्रिलोकीनाथ) (*m*) Lord of the three worlds. (V)

Trilokyarakshini (त्रिलोक्यरक्षिणी) (*f*) Protector of the three worlds. (D)

Tripadhā (तृपधा) (*m*) He who measured al the realms in three steps. (V)

Tripan (तृपन) (*m*) Follower of three types of knowledge.

Triptā (तृप्ता) (*f*) Satisfaction, contentment.

Tripti (तृप्ति) (*f*) Same as Triptā.

Tripurte (त्रिपूर्ति) (*m*) Having the forms of trinity (Brahma, Vishnu & Mahesh). Another name of Lord Ram. (R)

Trisama (तृसम) (*m*) Whose glory is sung by the three Vedas. (V)

Trishani (तृशनी) (*m*) Desire of the trinity (Brahma, Vishnu and Mahesh).

Trishti (तृष्टि) (*f*) Satisfaction, pleasure.

Trividya (त्रिविद्या) (*m*) One who knows three Vedas.

Tri-Vikrama (त्रि-विक्रम) (*m*) A name of Vishnu used in the Rig-Veda.

Turkram (तुरक्रम) (*m*) Youthful Ram. Name of a saint and poet of 17th century.

Tulsi (तुलसी) (*f*) The holy basil plant.

Tulsidam Bhushan (तुलसीदाम् भूषण) (*m*) Lover of Tulsi (basil plant) garland. (K)

Tungeshvar (तुंगेश्वर) (*m*) Lord of Mountains (Shiva), a temple of Shiva.

Tungish (तुंगीश) (*m*) The moon, Shiva, Krishna.

Tushta (तुष्ट) (*m*) Fully satiate (God). (V)

Tushār (तुशार) (*m*) The Himalayas.

Tushta (तुष्टा) (*m/f*) Satisfied, pleased.

Tushti (तुष्टि) (*f*) Satisfaction, contentment.

Tushya (तुश्य) (*m*) Very happy, satisfied. (S)

Tuvideshna (तुविदेश्न) (*m*) Giving much. Another name of Indra.

Tvashta (त्वष्टा) (*m*) The cause of decay in all beings at the time of Pralaya or dissolution. (V)

Twashtri (त्वश्त्री) (*m*) In the Rig-Veda this deity is the ideal artist, the divine artisan, the most skilful of workmen. He is the beautiful and imparts generative power and bestows offspring. He is the shaper of all form, human and animal.

U (उ, ऊ)

Ubhyavidya (**उभयविद्या**) (*f*) The two-fold science. (religious knowledge and acquaintance with worldly affairs).

Uchathā (**उचथा**) (*m/f/n*) Delightful, pleasureable, agreeable.

Uchitā (**उचिता**) (*m/f/n*) Deligtful, pleasurable, agreeable, known, accurate, understood, suitable. (R.V)

Udakshaya (**उदाक्षय**) (*m*) The son of Bhim.

Udanda (**उदण्ड**) (*m*) Punisher of evil-Lord Ganesha. (G)

Udant (**उदन्त**) (*m*) Good virtuous, rest, news, message.

Udantaka (**उदन्तक**) (*m/f*) News, intelligence.

Udapi (**उदपी**) (*m*) A successful person.

Udāratā (**उदारता**) (*f*) Generosity, charity, liberality, gentleness.

Udārthi (**उदार्थी**) (*m*) Rising. (V)

Uday (**उदय**) (*m*) Rising, rise, ascent, emergence.

Udayan (**उदयन**) (*m/f/n*) Rise, rising of the sun, outcome, result, conclusion.

Udayantā (**उदयन्ता**) (*m/f/n*) Ending with sun rise.

Udayāsat (**उदयास्त**) (*a*) From sunrise to sun-set from east to west.

Udayati (**उदयती**) (*f*) Of Uday. See also Uday. Daughter of the mountains.

Udayvat (**उदयवत**) (*m/f/n*) Risen as the moon.

Udbhav (**उद्भव**) (*m*) Birth, production, prosperity.

Udbhodan (**उद्भोदन**) (*m*) Awakening.

Udbhodhak (**उद्भोधक**) (*m*) A teacher, one who awakens through one's teaching.

Uddesh (**उद्देश**) (*m*) Illustration, exemplification.

Uddish (**उद्दीश**) (*m*) Lord of the divines. (S)

Uddhav (**ऊधव**) (*m*) Creation, source.

Uddyām (**उद्याम**) (*m*) Enterprise, venture, exertion.

Udgatri (**उद्गात्री**) (*m*) A priest whose duty is to chant the prayers or hymns from the Sama Veda.

Udirna (**उदीर्ण**) (*m*) Best among all beings. (V)

Udit (**उदित**) (*a*) Emerged, ascended, risen.

Udumbar (**उदुम्बर**) (*m*) He who stays beyond the skies. (V)

Uditi (**उदीति**) (*f*) Ascending or rising of the sun, apparent, visible.

Udipiti (**उदीप्ति**) (*f*) A place for drinking water.

Udyati (**उद्यती**) (*f*) Elevation aised.

Ugra (उग्र) (*m*) Hot, sharp, strong, the sun, epithet of god Shiva.

Ugracharini (उग्रचरिणी) (*f*) Moving impetuously. (D)

Ugradev (उग्रदेव) (*m*) Worshipping mighty deities. Name of a sage.

Ugra-kāli (उग्र-काली) (*f*) A form of Durga.

Ugrasen (उग्रसेन) (*m*) A king of Mathura, husband of Karni, and father of Kans and Devakka. He was deposed by Kans, but Krishna after killing Kans, restored Ugrasen to throne.

Ugrashakti (उग्रशक्ति) (*m/f*) Very powerful.

Ujjal (उज्जल) (*a*) Towards the upstream, bright, splendid, clear, radiant.

Ujjaval (उज्जवल) (*m/f*) Luminous, splendid, lovely, beautiful, glorious.

Ujjesha (उज्जेश) (*m/f*) Victorious.

Ujji (उज्जी) (*n*) To win, conquer, acquire by conquest, to be victorious.

Ujjiti (उज्जिती) (*f*) Victory, name of the verse.

Ujjiv (उजीव) (*n*) To restore to life, animate.

Uksha (उक्ष) (*n*) Watery, fluid, becoming strong (from Rig Veda).

Ukta (उक्त) (*m/f*) Uttered, name of a divine being, a stanza of 4 lines.

Uktha (उक्थ) (*n*) Saying, word, eulogy, verse, praise, a kind of recitation from religious books. Divine being belonging to Visve Deva.

Ukthavi (उक्थवी) (*m/f/n*) Fond of verses.

Ukthavid (उक्थविद) (*m/f/n*) Conversant with hymns of praise.

Ukthin (उक्थीन) (*f*) Uttering verses.

Ukthya (उक्थ्य) (*m/f/n*) Consisting of praise, accompanied by verse or praise.

Ulkā (उल्का) (*f*) Falling from heaven, firebrand. Meteor.

Ullās/Ullasa (उल्लास/उल्लासा) (*m/f*) Shining, bright, radiate, brilliant, joyful.

Ullāsita (उल्लासिता) (*m/f/n*) Shining, bright, brilliant, rising, appearing, merry, happy, joyful.

Ulupi (उलूपी) (*f*) A daughter of Kauravya, Raja of the Nagas, with whom Arjuna contracted a kind of marriage. She was nurse to her step-son, Babhruvāhana, and had great influence over him. According to the Vishnu Puran, she has a son named Iravat.

Ulupya (उलूप्य) (*m*) Charming face. (S)

Umā (उमा) (*f*) Light, splendour, tranquility. Uma also known as Ambikā, Rudrāni, and Garui (consort of Shiva). She is also identified with Vāch (goddess of speech).

Umākānt (उमाकांत) (*m*) Uma's loved one (name of Shiva).

Umāmani (उमामणि) (*f*) Gem of Umā, gem of fame.

Umā-nāth (उमा–नाथ) (*m*) Uma's husband (name of Shiva).

Umang (उमंग) (*f*) Aspiration, gusto, zeal.

Umāpati (उमापति) (*m*) Husband of Uma (god Shiva).

Umesh (उमेश) (*m*) Uma's lord (name of Shiva). Also name of an idol representing Shiva joined with Uma.

Unmād (उमाद) (*m*) A son of Nārāyan and Shri.

Unmādanātha (उन्मादनाथ) (*m*) Shiva as the Lord of Unmādas.

Unmādini (उन्मादिनी) (*f*) A mudrā Shakti. See Devi.

Unmani (उन्मानी) (*m*) A superior gem.

Unmesh (उन्मेष) (*m*) Visible, blossoming of a flower, flashing.

Unnāt (उन्नत) (*a*) Elevated, high, developed, lofty, improved.

Unnati (उन्नति) (*f*) Increase, promotion, improvement, prominence. Name of a daughter of Daksha and wife of Dharma.

Unnatkirti (उन्नतकीर्ति) (*m*) Of lofty fame, respected by sages, gods and other celestials. (S)

Upachiti (उपाचिती) (*f*) A daughter of Marichi (one of the seven great Rishis (sages).

Upadesh (उपदेश) (*m*) Counsel, advice, lesson, lecture, enlightenment, instruction. One of the ten Lakshanas of the Brahmanas.

Upadevi (उपदेवी) (*f*) One of the wives of Vasudev, and mother of four sons. It means great goddess.

Upaguru (उपगुरु) (*m*) Great guru. Name of a son of Satyaratha and father of Gupta.

Upajas (उपजस) (*m*) A deity, produced.

Upal (उपल) (*m*) A rock, stone, jewel, precious stone.

Upalābhdi (उपलब्धी) (*f*) Gain, obtainment, acquisition, mind, knowledge, understanding.

Upalakshana (उपलक्षण) (*n*) Observe, designation.

Upali (उपाली) (*m*) Name of one of the Buddha's most eminent pupil.

Upanishad (उपनिशद) (*f*) Esoteric doctrine (6th century BC). The third division of the Vedas attached to the Brahmana portion, and forming part of the Shruti/Sruti (revealed word). They ascertain the mystic sense of the text of the Vedas.

Upanshu (उपांशु) (*m/f*) A prayer uttered in a low voice.

Upant (उपांत) (*m/f/n*) Near to the end, border, nearness.

Upantika (उपांतिका) (*n*) Vicinity, proximity, neighbourhood.

Uparichar (उपरिचर) (*m*) A Vasu or demigod, who, according to the

Mahabharata, became king of Chedi by command of Indra. He had five sons and a daughter, Staya-vati, who was the mother of Vyas, and second wife of king Shantanu of Hastinapur.

Upāsak (उपासक) (*m/f*) Serving, worshipping, attendance, respect.

Upāsanā (उपासना) (*f*) Service, attendance, respect, adoration, worship.

Upashanta (उपशांत) (*m/f/n*) Calmed, appeared, pacified.

Upashikshā (उपशिक्षा) (*f*) Learning, acquisition.

Upashobhā (उपशोभा) (*f*) Very beautiful, graceful, Ornaments of decoration. See also Shobha.

Upashruti (उपश्रुति) (*f*) Listening attentively, hearing, supernatural voice answering questions about future.

Upāsit (उपासित) (*m/f*) Honoured, worshipped.

Upasruti (उपश्रुती) A supernatural voice which is heard at night revealing the secrets of the future.

Upasthā (उपास्था) (*n*) Present, friendly, copnciliate, middle part, sheltered place, secure place (from Rig Veda).

Upasya (उपास्य) (*n*) Having served or worshipped.

Upaved (उपवेद) (*m*) Class of writings appended to four Vedas.

Upayāja (उपयाज) (*m*) A sage who performed a Yajna for the benefit of king Drupad (king of Panchal and son of Prishata) and obtained two children, a son and a daughter, who were called 'the altar-born'. These better known by her patronymic Draupadi.

Updesh (उपदेश) Same as Upadesh.

Updeshak (उपदेशक) (*m*) A preceptor, sermoniser.

Updev (उपदेव) (*m*) A demi-god.

Updish (उपदिश्) (*n*) To indicate, specify, explain, inform, instruct, command, govern.

Upendra (उपेन्द्र) (*m*) A title given to Krishna by Indra. A manifestation of Hari (Vishnu).

Updish (उपदिश) (*m/f*) Indicate, inform, instruct, command, govern. Name of a son of Vasudev.

Upgā (उपगा) (*f*) Accompaniment of a song.

Upkānta (उपकांत) (*m*) A benefactor. One who does a good turn to a person.

Upkār (उपकार) (*m*) Beneficience, benefaction, good.

Upkāri (उपकारी) (*a*) Beneficial, favourable, helping.

Upkārin (उपकारिन्) (*m/f*) Helping, assistance, doing a favour.

Upkarna (उपकरण) (*n*) Doing a service, favour, helping, assisting, benefitting.

Upkāsh (उपकाश) (*m*) Dawn, aurora, aspect, appearance

Upkosh (उपकोश) (*f*) A treasure.

Uplabdh (उपलब्ध) (*a*) Available, acquired.

Uplaksh (उपलक्ष) (*m/f*) Distinction, distinguishing, to observe, behold.

Upmā (उपमा) (*f*) Smile, resemblance, a figure of speech, the standard of comparison. The goddess in Brahmakshetra.

Upmatā (उपमता) (*f*) To support.

Upmati (उपमती) (*f*) Comparison, simlarity (from Rig Veda).

Upmey (उपमेय) (*m*) That which is compared, comparable.

Upananda (उपनन्द) (*m*) A son of Vasudev and Madirā.

Upanidhi/Upanidhi (उपनिधी/उपानिधी) (*m*) A son of Bhadrā and Vasudev.

Upmit (उपमित) (*a*) Compared, illustrated by comparison.

Upoditi (उपोदिति) (*m*) Name of Rishi. Son of Gopal.

Uppati (उप्पति) (*f*) Happiness, occurring, becoming, visible, fitness, propriety, possibility.

Upraman (उपरमण) (*n*) Vedantas. Abstaining from worldly desires and actions.

Uprānt (उपरांत) (*a*) Afterwards.

Upsad (उपसाद) (*m/f/n*) Approaching, worshipping, serving.

Upsadana (उपसदन) (*n*) Respectful salutation, setting about, undertaking, respect.

Upsatu (उपसतु) (*n*) Praise, celebrate in song, to invoke (from Rig Veda).

Upstuti (उपस्तुति) (*f*) Celebrating, praising, invoking.

Uragāriketana (उरगरिकेतन) (*m*) A name of Krishna.

Urdhvagah (ऊर्ध्वगः) (*m*) He-who dwells at the top. (V)

Urjā (ऊर्जा) (*f*) Energy, vigour and vitality.

Urjani (ऊर्जनी) (*f*) Strength, power.

Urjassvi (ऊर्जस्वी) (*a*) Energetic, vigorous, full fit vilality. Name of a son of a Manu.

Urjitā (ऊर्जिता) (*m/f*) Powerful, excellent, great, important.

Urjitashāsan (ऊर्जितशासन) (*m*) Whose administration, as ordained through the scriptures, is the best. (V)

Urmi (ऊर्मि) (*f*) Wave, speed, velocity, desire, ripple.

Urmil (उर्मिल) (*a*) Wavy, undulating, undulatory.

Urmilā (उर्मिला) (*f*) Daughter of king Janak, sister of Sitā, wife of Lakshman, and mother of Gandharvi.

Urmimālā (ऊर्मिमाला) (*f*) A garland of waves. Undulation, a series of waves.

Urukrama (उरुक्रम) (*m*) A surname of Hari (Vishnu).

Uruta (उरुता) (*f*) Wideness, spacious, excellent.

Urva (ऊर्व) (*m*) A rishi (sage). Father of Richika and grandfather of Jamadagni. See also Aurva.

Urvashi (उर्वशी) (*f*) A celestial nymph, mentioned first in the Rig Veda. She was extremely beautiful and the story of her love with Puru-ravas is first told in Satapatha Brahmana. The loves of Puru-ravas, the Vikrama or hero, and of Urvashi are the subject of Kalidasa's drama called Vikramorvasi.

Urvi (उर्वी) (*f*) The good earth and heaven. Also it means, day, night, water and vegetation.

Ushā (ऊषा) (*f*) Dawn, early morning. A princess, daughter of Bāna and grand-daughter of Bali. She is also called Priti Jushā. She fell in love with a prince whom she saw in a dream, and was anxious to know if there was such a person. Her favourite companion, Chitra-lekha, drew the portraits of many gods and men, but Usha's choice fell upon Anirudh, son of Pradyumna and grandson of Krishna. They got married and lived in Dwarka.

Ushasya (ऊषास्य) (*m/f*) Sacred to the dawn, light.

Ushimay (ऊषीमय) (*a*) Thermal.

Ushinik (ऊषिनीक) A poetic metre, a horse of the sun's chariot.

Ushmā (ऊष्मा) (*f*) Heat, warmth.

Ushnih (ऊष्णिः) (*f*) Name of a Vedic meter.

Usrā/Usri (ऊसरा/ऊसरी) (*f*) Morning light, day-break, brightness.

Utkalā (उत्कला) (*f*) A queen of Samrāt, and mother of Marichi.

Utkalikā (उत्कलिका) (*f*) A bud, a wave, dalliance.

Utkanth (उत्कंठ) (*a*) Anxious, eager.

Utkanti (उत्कंठी) (*f*) Excessive splendour.

Utkashana (उत्कशन) (*f*) Giving order. Superior person.

Utkanthā (उत्कण्ठ) (*f*) Longing, anxiety.

Utkarsha (उत्कर्ष) (*m/f*) Superior, eminent, attractive. Exaltation, excellence, eminence.

Utkhalā (उत्खला) (*f*) A kind of perfume.

Utkhali (उत्खली) (*f*) Name of a Buddhist goddess.

Utpada (उत्पद) (*n*) Coming forth, orith, production.

Utpal (उत्पल) (*m*) A blue lotus. Any water lily.

Utpana (उत्पन) (*m/f/n*) Risen, gone up, born, produced.

Utpara (उत्परा) (*n*) Endless, boundless.

Utpatti (उत्पत्ति) (*f*) Creation described.

Utpavan (उत्पवन) (*n*) Cleaning, cleansing, act of sprinkling clarified butter or other fluids on the sacrificial fire.

Utpaviti (उत्पविति) (*m/f*) Purifying, purifier.

Utsāh (उत्साह) (*m*) A son of Nārāyana and Shri. Power, strength of will, to encourage, energy, firmness.

Utsāhin (उत्साहीन) (*m/f*) Powerful, mighty, active, energetic.

Utsarga (उत्सर्ग) (*m*) A son of Mitra and Revati.

Utsav (उत्सव) (*m*) Enterprise, beginning, festival, jubilee, joy, gladness, merriment.

Utsuka (उत्सुक) (*m*) A son of Balrām (brother of Krishna).

Uttālatā labhettā (उत्तालता लभीता) (*m*) A name of god Krishna.

Uttam (उत्तम) (*a*) Handsome, preferable, eminent, excellent, chief, best.

Uttamā (उत्तमा) (*f*) An excellent woman.

Uttambālā (उत्तमबाला) (*f*) Excellent young woman.

Uttammani (उत्तममणि) (*m*) Excellent gem.

Uttanka (उत्तंक) (*m*) Disciple of Gautama Rishi.

Uttar (उत्तर) (*m*) Name of anasterism. The son of king of Virāt of Matsya.

Uttara (उत्तरा) (*m*) The name of an asterism. Name of a daughter of king of Virata, she married Abhimanyu, son of Arjuna.

Uttarah (उत्तरः) (*m*) The other bank of the ocean of metempsychosis. (V)

Uttaramālikā (उत्तरामालिका) (*f*) A goddess following Revati.

Uttarana (उत्तरन) (*m*) He who takes (the soul) across the ocean of matempsychosis. (V)

Uttarayān (उत्तरयान) (*m*) When the sun is on the north equator.

Uttareshvara (उत्तरेश्वर) (*m*) The name of the god enshrined and worshiped by the Bādavas.

Uttejak (उत्तेजक) (*m/f*) Incitement, encouragement, stimulation, exciting, inspiring.

Uttejana (उत्तेजना) (*f*) Same as Uttejak.

Utthapana (उत्थापना) (*n*) Causing to rise or get up, concluding verse.

V (व, वा)

Vāchā (वाचा) (*f*) Speech, voice, sacred text.

Vachan/Vachana (वचन/वचना) (*m/f*) Speaking, speaker, statement, declaration.

Vāchāspati (वाचास्पति) (*m*) Lord of speech. (S)

Vāchāspati Rudaradhi (वाचास्पति रुद्राधि) (*m*) The master of all knowledge that reveals the reality. (V)

Vāchāspatiryonijah (वाचास्पतिर्योनिजः) (*m*) Master of knowledge and not born. (i.e. self created. (V)

Vāchi (वाची) (*f*) Nectar like speech-goddess Lakshmi. (L)

Vād (वाद) (*m*) Discourse, disputation, discussion, an exposition of the holy text.

Vādak (वादक) (*m/f*) A speaker, musician.

Vādan (वादन) (*m*) A player of any musical instrument.

Vādānya (वादन्य) (*m*) Bountiful, liberal, munificent, speaking kindly.

Vāduli (वादूलि) (*m*) Orator. Name of a son of Vishvamitra in Ramayana.

Vāgalā (वागला) (*f*) A goddess worshipped by Tantrikas.

Vāgami (वागमी) (*m*) Eloquent and orator, a learned man.

Vāgbhatt (वागभट्ट) (*m*) An ancient sage who had composed several works on medical science.

Vāgdevi (वागदेवी) (*f*) The power of speech, the goddess Sarasvati.

Vāgdhiksha (वागधिक्षा) (*m*) Lord of spokesmen. Another name of Lord Hanuman. Hanuman as a young boy swallowed the sun and released it at the requesst of gods. As a boon the Sun-God blessed Him with intelligence and divine knowledge, making Him the Lord' spokesmen. (H)

Vāgish (वागीश) (*m*) Lord of speech. A name of Brahspati.

Vāgishvar (वागीश्वर) (*m*) Lord of speech. A name of Brahma.

Vāgishvari (वागीश्वरी) (*m*) Goddess of speech.

Vāgmi (वाग्मी) (*m*) The originator of the Vedic speech. (V)

Vāgmine (वाग्मिने) (*m*) Spokesmen. Another name of Lord Hanuman. (H)

Vāgya (वाग्य) (*m*) Embodiment of all sacrifices. (V)

Vāhni (वाहनी) (*m*) The fire which accepts all offering (in a sacrifice). (V)

Vaibhav (वैभव) (*n*) Might, power, high position, greatness, superhuman power.

Vaibhrāj/Vibhrāj (वैभराज/विभराज) (*m*) Name of a powerful country, celestial grove, name of a mountain.

Vaidarbhī (वैदर्भि) (*f*) Pertaining to Vidarbha country. Name of Damayanti and

Rukamani.

Vaidya (**वैद्य**) (*m*) Well versed in all knowledge. (V)

Vaijayanti (**वैजयन्ती**) (*f*) The necklance of Vishnu, composed of five precious gems (pearl, ruby, emealed, sapphire and diamond). It also means a shield or banner, a garland.

Vaikhan/Vaikhanah (**वैखन/वैखनः**) (*m*) The digger of earth (Lord Vishnu dug earth in His Boar Incarnation to slay Hiranyaksha who dwelled inside the bowels of the earth. (V)

Vaikuntha (**वैकुण्ठ**) (*m*) A name of Hari. The abode of Vishnu, established by him at the request of Shri in his manifestation as Vaikuntha.

Vaikuntha-Nāth (**वैकुण्ठ-नाथ**) (*m*) Lord of Vaikunth (paradise). Name of Vishnu

Vaimitra (**वैमित्र**) (*f*) Friend of the universe. Very popular person.

Vairāj (**वैराज**) (*m*) Manu the son of Virāj. Also a name of Brahmā.

Vairochan (**वैरोचन**) (*m*) Belonging to the sun, name of a son of Vishnu and father of Boddhisattva.

Vairupam (**वैरुपम**) (*m*) Reated from the west face of Brahmā.

Vaishāli (**वैशाली**) (*f*) One of Vasudev's queen and mother of Kaushik. Name of an ancient city of the time of Gautama Buddha.

Vaishanavi (**वैष्णवी**) (*m*) Worshipper of Vishnu, the Shakti of Vishnu.

Vāj (**वाज**) (*m*) Strength, vigour, energy, speech.

Vājasanah (**वाजसनः**) (*m*) Bestower of good to the hungry. (V)

Vājijit (**वाजीजीत**) (*m*) A Marichi god (Prajāpati or creator).

Vājin (**वाजीन**) (*m/f*) Heroic, warlike, swift, impetuous, spirited.

Vājit (**वाजीत**) (*m/f*) Conquering in a contest, winning.

Vajra (**वज्र**) (*m*) The thunderbolt of Indra. Name of great grandson of Krishna who was appointed as the regent of Indraprastha. under the guidance of Subhandra.

Vajrakāyā (**वज्रकाया**) (*m*) Strudy like metal. Another name of Lord Hanuman. (H)

Vajrashri (**वज्रश्री**) (*f*) Divine diamond.

Vajrendra (**वज्रेन्द्र**) (*m*) Lord of the thunderbot, i.e. Indra.

Vallabh (**वल्लभ**) (*a/m*) Dear one, beloved, a lover.

Vallabhā (**वल्लभा**) (*f*) Dear one, beloved, wife.

Vālmiki (**वाल्मीकि**) (*m*) A sage and bard, famous as the author of the Ramayana; he lived at Chitra Kuta (a hill in Bundelkhund). It was in this hill that Ram. Sita and Lakshman stayed when exiled from Ayodhya.

Vālukeshvara (**वालुकेश्वर**) (*m*) A name of Shiva.

Vāmā (वामा) (*f*) A Shakti. See Devi

Vāmadeva (वामदेव) (*m*) A name of Shiva. A Vedic Rishi, author of many hymns. Also a name of a Vedic Rishi mentioned in the Mahabharata as possessor of two horses of marvellous speed called Vāmyas.

Vāmakī (वामकी) (*f*) A deity worshiped by magicians.

Vāmākshi (वामाक्षी) (*f*) A name of Lalitā. See Lalitā and Devi.

Vāmana (वामन) (*m*) The dwarf incarnation of Vishnu. See Avtār.

Vāmikā (वामिका) (*f*) Most beautiful. of Durga. (D)

Vandan (वन्दन) (*m*) Adoration, obeisance, vermilion.

Vandanā (वन्दना) (*f*) Deferential saluation, obesiance, worship.

Vandit (वन्दि) (*a*) Worshipped, revered.

Vandya (वन्द्य) (*a*) Adorable, venerable, fit to be reverenced.

Vānī (वाणी) (*f*) The goddess of speech. Speech, eloquence, praise.

Vānichī (वाणीचि) (*f*) Musical instrument.

Vanitā (वनिता) (*f*) Wife, a beloved woman.

Vanlakshmi (वनलक्ष्मी) (*f*) Goddess of a forest. Beauty of a forest.

Vanmālī (वनमाली) (*m*) A gardener of woods. An epithet of Krishna.

Vanshidhar (वंशीधर) (*m*) A flute-player-an epithet of Krishna.

Vanshikā/Vānshikī (वंशिका/वांशिकी) (*f*) Flute.

Vanshvardhan (वंशवर्धन) (*m*) He who augments families. (V)

Vapush (वपुश) (*m*) Wonderful, admirable, embodied.

Vapushi (वपुषि) (*f*) Wonderful, admirable, embodied. Beauty personified as a daughter of Daksha.

Varad/Varadā (वरद/वरदा) (*m/f*) Granter of boons. (S&D)

Varalakshmi (वरलक्ष्मी) (*f*) Granter of bounty-goddess Lakshmi. (L)

Vārahamukhī (वारहमुखी) (*f*) A Shakti. See Devi.

Varaṇ (वर्ण) (*m*) Selecting or choosing. reverence.

Varanā (वर्णा) (*f*) Same as Varan.

Varānana (वरानन) (*f*) A daughter of the Gandharvas. See Gandharva.

Varanga (वरांग) (*m*) Having an exalted physique. (V)

Varanī (वर्णी) (*f*) Same as Varan.

Varanlīlā (वर्णलीला) (*m*) In music a kind of measure.

Varapradā (वरप्रदा) (*m*) Responsive to all prayers. Another name of Lord Rama. (R)

Vararohā (वररोहा) (*m/f*) The high rider. Ready to offer boons. Name of Lord Vishnu and goddess Lakshmi. (V&L)

Vararuchi (वररुचि) (*m*) A celebrated Rishi/Brahman, the son of Somadatta, distinguished for a wonderful memory, which enabled him to recite perfectly and discuo rse he had once heard. He was a great writer on philological topics.

Vardāni (वरदानी) (*m/f*) One who confers a boon.

Vardavināyak (वरदविनायक) (*m*) Bestower of bounty and success. (G)

Vardhamān (वर्द्धमान) (*m*) He who grows life in the world. (V)

Vardhana (वर्द्धन) (*m*) Son of Krishna and Mitravindā.

Vārendra (वारेन्द्र) (*m*) The name of a country in India, chief, sovereign, Indra.

Varenyā (वरेणय) (*f*) Apsara (heavenly nymph).

Varga (वर्ग) (*f*) An Apsara living in the forest of the gods. Var means choosing, bridegroom, most excellent.

Varganpati (वर्गपति) (*m*) Bestower of boons. (G)

Vargātra (वगात्र) (*m/f*) Beautiful person, fair-limbed.

Vārij (वारिज) (*m*) Lotus, conch, purified gold.

Varimán (वरीमन) (*m*) The best, excellent, superior, worthy.

Vārindra (वारीन्द्र) (*m*) Sea, ocean. See also Virindra.

Varishtā (वरिष्ठ) (*m*) An Apsara (heavenly nymphs).

Varishtha (वरिष्ठा) (*m/f*) The most excellent or best.

Varkshi (वरक्षी) (*f*) Daughter of a sage, who is instanced in the Mahabharata as being a virtuous woman.

Varnaka (वर्णक) (*m/f*) Painting, picture, fragrant ointment.

Varnāri (वरनारी) (*f*) The best woman, most excellent woman.

Varnyāti (वरण्यती) (*f*) In music a kind of measure.

Varpradā (वरप्रदा) (*m*) Granter of boons. (G)

Varshā (वर्षा) (*f*) Rain, rainfall.

Vartā (वार्ता) (*f*) News, tiding, intelligence, business, information, discourse.

Vārtali (वार्तली) (*f*) A name of Lalitā; a Shakti. See Lalita and Devi.

Vartikā (वर्तिका) (*f*) Wick/glow of a lamp (from Kalika Puran); a paint brush, colour, paint.

Varun/Varuna (वरुण/वरुणा) (*m*) The universal encompasser, the all-embracer. One of the oldest of the Vedic deities, a personification of the all-investing sky, the maker and up-holder of heaven and earth. As such he is king of the universe. In later times he became a sort of Neptune, a god of the seas and rivers.

Varunāni (वरुणानी) (*f*) Varuna's wife. See Varun.

Varunavi (वरुणवी) (*f*) Name of Lakshmi.

Varuni (वरुणी) (*f*) Devi, the goddess. See Devi.

Varyuvati (वर्युवती) (*f*) A beautiful young woman.

Vāsanā (वासना) (*f*) Imagination, fancy, knowledge, longing, impression, desire, wish, trust.

Vasant (वसन्त) (*m*) The spring season. A kind of rāg in Indian classical music sung during the spring.

Vasanti (वसन्ती) (*a/f*) Pertaining to Vasant (spring), light yellow colour. A kind of sweet smelling creeper.

Vasavā (वसवा) (*m*) Name of Indra. See Indra.

Vashatkar (वशत्कर) (*m*) The object of the Vashat worship in the Yagya. (V)

Vashilā (वशीला) (*f*) A Siddhi Devi. See Devi.

Vashisht (वशिष्ठ) (*m*) One of the stars in the Great Bear, the name of an ancient sage. See also Vishisht.

Vasordhārā (वसोर्धारा) (*f*) A wife of Agni (one of the chief deities of the Vedas).

Vastri (वस्त्री) (*m/f*) Shining, illuminating.

Vasu (वसु) (*m/f*) Excellent, good, beneficient. Wealth, jewel, gold, water, a class of demi-gods.

Vasuda/Vasudha, Vasundhar, Vasumati (वसुदा/वसुधा, वसुंधर, वासुमती) (*f*) The mother earth. Granting wealth or treasure.

Vasudev (वसुदेव) (*m*) Son of Sura, of the Yādava branch of the Lunar race. He was father of Krishna, and Kunti, the mother of the Pandava princes, was his sister. Vasudev is also an epithet of god Krishna.

Vasudevasutam (वसुदेवसुत) (*m*) Son of Vasudeva. (K)

Vasudevbhāgini (वसुदेवभागिनी) (*f*) Sister of Vasudev. Goddess Durga is the female counterpart of Vishnu, bearing the Shank, Chakra and Gada. She is Mahalakshmi the power of Vishnu, and sister Vaishnavi of Vasudeva, whı is incarnation of Vishnu. (D)

Vasudhā (वसुधा) (*m/f*) Producing wealth, prince, king, liberal, the earth, a name of Lakshmi (goddess of wealth).

Vasudhān (वसुधान्) (*m/f*) Containing or keeping wealth.

Vasudhār (वसुधार) (*m/f*) Holding wealth or treasure.

Vasudharini (वसुधारिणी) (*f*) Treasure holding, the earth.

Vasuh (वसुः) (*m*) The abode of all beings. (V)

Vasu-karan (वसु-कर्ण) (*m*) Name of a Rishi (sage).

Vasumana/Vasumanah (वसुमन/वसुमनः) (*m*) The dweller in all hearts. Large hearted. (V)

Vasumati (वासुमती) (*f*) Possessing treasure, the good earth, name of various women.

Vasundharā (वसुंधरा) (*f*) The mother earth, from which the whole world springs and ends.

Vasupāl (वसुपाल) (*m*) Protector of wealth. A king.

Vasupati (वसुपति) (*m*) Lord of wealth.

Vasupradā/Vasupradāh (वसुप्रदा/वसुप्रदः) (*m/f*) Bestower of great wealth in the form of Moksha (final release). Also the name of goddess Lakshmi who is personification of benevolence and bestows lavishly. (V&L)

Vasu-prān (वसु-प्राण) (*m*) Breath of Vasu.

Vasurā (वसुरा) (*m/f*) Valuable, rich.

Vasureta (वसुरेत) (*m*) The seed of existence. (V)

Vasuruchi (वसुरुचि) (*f*) An Apsara (heavenly nymph).

Vasurup (वसुरूप) (*m/f*) Having the nature of Vasus (said of Shiva).

Vasushakti (वसुशक्ति) (*m/f*) Divine power.

Vatsal (वतसल) (*a*) Parental affection.

Vatsar (वत्सर) (*m*) Ultimate abode of all. (V)

Vatsy (वत्स्य) (*m*) Rearing up the heifer (in Vrindavan as Krishna). (V)

Vayās (व्यास) (*m*) A name of Hari (Vishnu) See Vishnu.

Vāyu (वायु) (*m*) The god of wind.

Vāyuvahan (वायुवाहन) (*m*) He who imparts wind the capacity to move. (V)

Ved/Veda (वेद/वेदा) (*m*) Divine knowledge. The Vedas are the holy books which are the foundation of the Hindu religion. Vedic hymns were composed about 1500 BC. There are four Vedas (Rig, Yajur, Sāma and Atharva). Each Veda is divided into two parts: Mantra (consists of prayer and praise) and Brahmana (contains liturgical and ritualistic glosses, explanations, and application of Vedic hymns illustrated by various legends).

Vedagya (वेदज्ञ) (*m*) The knower of the Vedas. (V)

Vedah (वेदः) (*m*) The manifested learning (the Veda-form). (V)

Vedakarta (वेदकर्ता) (*m*) Originator of the Vedas. (S)

Vedanā (वेदना) (*f*) Knowledge, perception.

Vedāng (वेदांग) (*m*) The six subordinate branches of Vedas.

Vedangah (वेदांगः) (*m*) Who has Vedas as His body parts (i.e. the ultimate fount of knowledge). (V)

Vedantasara (वेदांतसार) (*m*) Essence of philosoplhy. Another name of Lord Ram. (R)

Vedānti (वेदान्ती) (*m*) Theologian, a follower of the Vedanta philosophy.

Vedapati (वेदपति) (*f*) Acquisition of the Vedic knowledge.

Vedashruti (वेदश्रुति) (*f*) Hearing the Vedas. Name of a river in Puranas.

Vedātmane (वेदात्मने) (*m*) Spirit of the Vedas. Another name of Lord Ram. (R)

Vedavati (वेदवती) (*f*) An Apsara (heavenly nymph). Also the vocal daughter of Rishi Kusa Dhwaja, who was born again as Sita (wife of Lord Rāma).

Vedavita (वेदवित) (*m*) One who knows the real meaning of the Vedas. (V)

Ved-dip (वेद-दीप) (*m*) Lamp of knowledge or of the Vedas.

Vedeshvar (वेदेश्वर) (*m*) Lord of the Vedas.

Vedgupta (वेदगुप्ता) (*m/f*) One who has preserved the Vedas. Name of Krishna.

Vedhah (वेधाह) (*m*) One who constitutes everything. (V)

Vedi (वेदी) (*m/f*) Wise person, Pandit, Name of Sarasvati. Marriage altar.

Vedish (वेढीश) (*m*) Lord of the wise (Brahma).

Vedkār (वेदकार) (*m*) The composer of the Vedas. Extremely knowledgeable person.

Vedmātri (वेदमात्री) (*f*) Mother of the Vedas. Name of Sarasvati, Savitri and Gayatri.

Ved-murti (वेद-मूर्ति) (*f*) Embodiment of the Vedas (applied to the Sun).

Ved Vedya (वेद वेद्या) (*m*) Exponent of the four Vedas (K)

Ved&Vidyā (विद्या) (*f*) Knowledge of the Vedas, Master of Vedic lore.

Vedya (वेद्य) (*m*) Approachable by those who seek their welfare (V)

Vegavān (वेगवान) (*m*) Very fast moving (V)

Venimādhava (वेणीमाधव) (*m*) Vishnu at Prayāga. See Vishnu.

Venkatesha (वेंकटेश) (*m*) Lord of Venkata. Name of Krishna.

Venkateshvara (वेंकटेश्वर) (*m*) Help Same as Venkatesha.

Venu (वेणु) (*m*) A flute, bamboo.

Venuganpriya (वेणुगणप्रिय) (*m*) Lover of flute (K)

Vibhā (विभा) (*f*) Shine, glow, brilliance, lustre, light, beauty.

Vibhās (विभास) (*f*) Same as Vibhā

Vibhāsana (विभासन) (*f*) Same as Vibha.

Vibhav (विभव) (*m*) Wealth, riches, dignity, splendour.

Vibhrāj (विभराज) (*m/f*) Shining, splendid, luminous. Name of the author of Rig Veda.

Vibhu (विभु) (*m*) Help God—the all pervading, omnipresent, mighty, powerful, omnipoten. Supreme being, a king

Vibhush (विभूश) (*m/f*) Brilliant, adorn, decorate.

Vibhushā (विभूशा) (*f*) Same as Vibhush.

Vibhushan (विभूषण) (*m/f*) Same as Vibhush

Vibhushanā (विभूषणा) (*f*) To beautify, to decorate with ornaments.

Vibhushat (विभूशत) (*a*) Same as Vibhushanā

Vibhuti (विभूति) (*f*) Ash, majesty, magnificence, an outstanding personality, welfare, superhuman power. Also a name of Lakshmi (goddess of wealth and prosperity.)

Vibodh (विबोध) (*m*) perception, intelligence.

Vibudh (विबुध) (*m/f*) Wide awake, skilful, clever, learned man, the moon, wisom.

Vichitra (विचित्र) (*m*) Many coloured, fantastic, uprising, singular, wonderful.

Vichitravirya (विचित्रवीर्य) (*m*) Younger son of king Shantanu and Satyavati.

Vidarbha (विदर्भ) A kingdom to which the Yadus migrated, its capital Kundina, visited by Krishna.

Vidaranah (विदर्णः) (*m*) Tearing apart the wicked (V)

Viddrum (विद्रुम) (*m*) Coral, the coral tree.

Videha (विदेह) (*m*) A name of Janak. He had realized by Yoga the power of Hari (Vishnu). See Vishnu.

Vidhātā (विधाता) (*m*) The special carrier of the whole world. The creator of deeds and their fruits (V)

Vidhātri (विधात्री) (*m*) Creator. A name of Brahma, of Vishnu, and of Vishwa karmā.

Vidhi (विधि) (*f*) An order, a command, manner, process, behaviour, ceremony.

Vidhu (विधु) (*m*) The moon shone in ten directions having got the overlordship of the seven worlds by penance.

Vidip (विदीप) (*m*) Shining, illuminated, bright.

Vidishah (विदीशः) (*v*) He who gives each what is due on the basis of the deed performed (V)

Vidrāvini (विद्राविनी) (*f*) A Mudrā Devi. See Devi.

Vidulā (विदूला) (*f*) The good earth.

Vidur (विदूर) (*m*) A learned man. Younger brother of Pandavas. He enjoyed the character of the wisest of the wise. He was also a chief minister of the Pandavas.

Vidush (विदुष) (*m*) A learned man.

Vidushi (विदुष) (*f*) A learned woman.

Vidvāttamah (विद्वत्तमः) (*m*) The most learned scholar.

Vidyā (विद्या) (*f*) Learning, knowledge, education.

Vidyādhara (विद्याधर) (*m*) Identified with Bhagvān (God). Possessor of knowledge. A class of demigods.

Vidyāvati (विद्यावती) (*f*) Knowledgeable woman. Name of a daughter of Gandharvas.

Vidyudvarnā (विद्युद्वर्णा) (*f*) An Apsara (heavenly nymph).

Vidyavaridhi (विद्यावारिधि) (*m*) Repository of knowledge (G)

Vidyotā (विद्योता) (*f*) Lightning, shining, glittering. Name of an heavenly nymph in Mahabharata.

Vidyunmālin (विद्युन्मालिन) (*f*) A Shakti. See Devi.

Vidyut (विद्युत) (*m/f*) Flashing, shining, glittering.

Vidyutparnā (विद्युतपर्णा) (*f*) An Apsara (heavenly nymph).

Vignahara (विग्नहर) (*m*) Destroyer of evil (G)

Vihayasagatih (विहायशगतिः) (*m*) He who moves in the skies.

Vijay (विजय) (*a*) Conquered, won over.

Vijayā (विजया) (*f*) Name of goddess Durga. See Devi.

Vijayalakshmi (विजयलक्ष्मी) (*f*) Goddess of victory. One of the eight Lakshmi's who keeps the treasure of Brahma.

Vijayantā (विजयन्ता) The palace or the banner of Indra.

Vijetā (विजेता) (*m*) Conqueror.

Vijit (विजित) (*a*) Conquered, won over.

Vijitātma (विजितात्मा) (*m*) He who has his mind under his control (V)

Vijitendriya (विजितेन्द्रिय) (*m*) Controller of the senses, Another name of Lord Hanuman (H)

Vikarna (विकर्ण) (*m*) A son of Dhritrastra.

Vikarta (विकर्त) (*m*) The special creator of the realms (V)

Vikās (विकास) (*m*) Evolution, development, growth, bloom.

Vikāsh (विकाश) (*m*) Brightness, light, lustre.

Vikāshini (विकाशिनी) (*f*) Shining, radiant, illuminating.

Vikatā (वीकता) (*f*) A Shakti, See Devi.

Vikatodara (विकतोद्रा) (*n*) HelpA follower of Shiva.

Vikesā (विकेसा) (*m*) A son of Damana, an Avtār of the Lord in the third dvāpara.

Vikeshi (विकेशी) (*f*) The mother of the planet Angaraka and the wife of Agni.

Vikram (विक्रम) (*m*) Heroism, valience, valour. Name of an ancient great king of Ujjain, founder of an era which commenced earlier than the Christian era. It commenced on 23 February, 57 BC.

Vikramaditya (विक्रमादित्य) (*m*) A celebrated Hindu king who reigned at Ujjain. Same as Vikram.

Vikramah (विक्रमः) (*m*) Fast mover (on his vehicle Garuda) (V)

Vikramī (विक्रमी) (*m*) Heroic, strong, pertaining to Vikramaditya (king of India). A name of Vishnu.

Vikrānt (विक्रांत) (*m*) A prajapati (Lord of creatures, a progenitor, creator.) In the Vedas Prajapati means many deities.

Vikrānti (विक्रांति) (*f*) All pervading power, heroism, courage, strength.

Vikruti (विकृति) (*f*) Multi-faceted nature - Goddess Lakshmi (L)

Vikshar (वीक्षर) (*m*) Decayless (V)

Vikukshi (विकुक्षि) (*m*) A king of the solar race, who succeeded his father Ikshwaku.

Vikuntha (विकुंठ) (*m*) A name of Hari (Vishnu).

Vimal (विमल) (*a*) Clear, clean, spotless, flawless, pure.

Vimarsh (विमर्श) (*m*) Investigation, examination, consideration, consultation, deliberation.

Vimlā (विमला) (*f*) A Rahasya yogini Devi. The goddess enshrined at Purushottama.

Vimlayi (विमलयी) (*f*) Pure. Goddess Lakshmi is the mine of all virtues, as pure as the best gems. (L)

Vīnā (वीना) (*f*) Indian lute. An instrument of the guitar kind supposed to have been invented by Narad Muni, usually having seven strings raised upon nineteen frets, towards the ends of which are tow large gourds. It has many varieties.

Vinatā (वीनता) (*f*) A daughter of Daksha, one of the wives of Kashyap, and mother of Garuda.

Vinati (विनती) (*f*) Humility, modesty, request, prayer.

Vinava (विनव) (*m*) The punisher of the wicked (V)

Vinay (विनय) (*f*) Modesty, politeness, humbleness, humility, discipline.

Vināyak (विनायक) (*m*) The God Ganesh.

Vinayitasakshi (विनयितसाक्षी) (*m*) He who discerns the humility of his devotees quickly (V)

Vindhyavasini (विन्ध्यवासिनी) (*f*) Resident of the Vindhyas (mountains) (D)

Vindu/Bindu (विन्दु/बिन्दु) (*m/f*) A drop of water, a point, dot, zero, a small particle, finding, acquiring, procuring.

Vindu-mādhav (विन्दु-माधव) (*m*) The name of an idol of Vishnu in Banaras.

Vindusār (विन्दुसार) (*m*) The name of the father of Emperor Ashok.

Vinetri (विनेत्री) (*m*) Leader, guide, instructor, prince, king.

Vinīta (विनीता) (*m/f*) Led or taken away, educated, lovely, handsome.

Vinod (विनोद) (*m*) Diversion, pleasure, humour, amusement, recreation.

Vinodī (विनोदी) (*a*) Jovial, witty, jolly, humorous.

Vipan (विपन) See Vipin.

Vipās (विपास) (*m/f*) Without harm or injury.

Vipāsā (विपासा) (*f*) The river Vyas or Bias.

Vipin (विपिन) (*n*) A forest, garden, stirring or waving in the wind.

Vipul (विपुल) (*a*) Large, big, abundant, copious, extensive, mammoth. Name of a son of Vasudev and Rohini.

Vipulā (विपुला) (*f*) The goddess enshrined at Viputa.

Vīr (वीर) (*a*) Heroic, brave, valiant, gallant.

Vīrabhadra (वीरभद्र) (*m*) One of Shiva's attendants; the head of a Shivagana.

Virah (विरह) (*m*) Slayer of the demons for protectting Dharma (V)

Virahā (विरहा) (*m*) He who gallantly alters the course of his devotees destiny (V)

Virāj (विराज) (*m*) Another name of Manu. See Manu.

Virāj (विराज) (*f*) A Shakti. See Devi.

Virām (विराम) (*m*) The final resting place of all beings (V)

Virāt (विराट) (*a*) Colossal, gigantic, enormous, huge. Name of a king of Matsya near the present Jaipur.

Virbahu (वीरबाहु) (*m*) Mighty armed (V)

Virbhadra (वीरभद्र) (*m*) Supreme leader of three worlds. (S)

Virendra (वीरेन्द्र) (*m*) A chief of heroes, Lord Indra—a great warrior.

Viresh (वीरेश) (*m*) Lord of heroes. (S)

Virganpati (वीरगणपति) (*m*) The valliant warrior. Lord Ganesha is sometimes attributed with eight pairs of arms, holding a bow, arrow, goblin, spear, hammer, mace, pick-exe, serpent, banner, trident, discus, goad, noose, battle-axe, sword and shield - all signs of valiant warrior (G)

Virincha/Virinchi (विरिंच/विरिंचि) (*m*) a name of Brahma. See Brahma.

Virindra (विरेन्द्रा) (*m*) Vir means brave and Indira is a god. See Indra.

Virochan (विरोचन) (*m*) Shining, glittering, sun, moon, Vishnu, name of the son of Prahalad.

Vishad (विशाद) (*a*) Spotless, clean, clear, evident, white, beautiful.

Vishadarbha (विशदार्भ) (*m*) A very pious and generous king.

Vishāl (विशाल) (*a*) Huge, large, big, spacious, grand, extensive, vast, great, gigantic, colossal. A name of the city of Ujjayini.

Vishālāksha (विशालाक्ष) (*m*) Wide-eyed. The wide-eyed Lord's three eyes are the sun, the moon and the fire, representing infinite vision. (S)

Visham (विशम) (*m*) The only one (having none like him) (V)

Vishambhar/Vishambharā (विशम्भर/विशम्भरा) (*m/f*) The good earth which covers the whole universe etc. Its manifestations are Dhriti, Stithiti,, Kshamā, Kshigni, Prithvi, Vasumati and Rasā.

Visheshana (विशेषण) (*m/f*) Distinguishing, surpassing, individuality.

Vishisht/Vishishta (विशिष्ट/विशिष्टा) (*n*) Great, particular, superb, superior, respective, sublime, prominent.

Vishnuh (विष्णुः) (*m*) The Lord of the trinity who preserve the world. All pervading. Embodiment of nobility (V)

Vishodhanah (विशोधानः) (*m*) He who purifies all (V)

Vishok (विशोक) (*m*) Exemption from grief, free from sorrow. Name of a prince. One of Bhim's charioteer.

Vishokā (विशोका) (*f*) Name of one of the perfections which are obtained by Yoga. One who has no sorrow or grief.

Vishnu (विष्णु) (*m*) Root, vish, 'To pervade'. The second god of the Hindu triad. He is a manifestation of the solar energy, and is described as striding through the seven regions of the universe in three steps, and enveloping all things with the dust (of his beams). Vishnu's preserving and restoring power has been manifested to the world in a variety of forms called Avatars (incarnations). See Avtar. As preserve and restorer, Vishnu is a very popular deity. His wife is Lakshmi or Shri, the goddess of fortune, 'wealth and prosperity. He has a thousand names, the repetition of which is a meritorious act of devotion. Of the thousand names of Vishnu the following are some of the most common:- Achyuta (imperishable); Ananta (the endless); Janardhana (whom men worship); Keshav (the radiant, the hairy); Lakshmipati (lord of Lakshmi); Madhusudan (destroyer of Madhu); Madhav (descendant of Madhusudan); Makunda (deliverer);Murari (the foe of Mura); Narayan (who moves in the waters);Panchyudha (armed with weapons); Purushottama (the highest of men, the supreme spirit); Vasudev (Krishna), Varshaneya (descendant Vrishni); Vaikuntha-nath (lord of Vaikunth—paradise).

Vishrutātma (विश्रुतात्म) (*m*) Renowned in the scriptures (V)

Vishu (विशु) (*m*) A man.

Vishubh (विशुभ) (*a*) To shine brightly, be beautiful.

Vishudh (विशुद्ध) (*m*) Pure, genuine, true, holiness, virtue, removal of error.

Vishuddhatma (विशुद्धात्मा) (*m*) Pure soul (V)

Vishudhi (विशुद्धि) (*f*) Same as Vishudh.

Vishva (विश्व) (*m*) The world, universe. A name of Hari (Vishnu).

Vishva-bandhu (विश्व-बन्धु) (*m*) A friend of the whole world.

Vishvabhuk (विश्वभुक) (*m*) The nourisher of the world. (V)

Vishvadakshin (विश्वादक्षिण) (*m*) The receiver of all 'Dakshina' in the sacrifice arranged by Bali (V)

Vishvadev (विश्वदेव) (*m*) All the gods. In the Vedas they are preservers of men and bestowers of rewards.

Vishvadhrik (विश्वधृक) (*m*) The support of the world. (V)

Vishva-dip (विश्व-दीप) (*m*) All-awakening, all-enlightening.

Vishva-dipi (विश्व-दीपी) (*m*) Light of the universe.

Vishva-jit (विश्व-जीत) (*m/f*) All conquering, the cord or noose of Varuna, all honoured.

Vishvajanani (विश्वजननी) (*f*) Mother of the universe - goddess Lakshmi (L)

Vishvakarma (विश्वकर्म) (*m*) Omnificent. God of creative power, architect of the universe. In Rig Veda it is all-seeing god, who has on every side eyes, faces, arms and feet, who, when producing heaven and earth, shapes them with his arms and wings. He is the Lord of arts, executor of a thousand handicrafts, the carpenter of the gods and maker of their weapons, ornaments, and inventor of the celestial chariots of the deities.

Vishvakeshna (विश्वकेशना) (*m*) A name of Krishna.

Vishvakaya (विश्वकय) (*m*) Universal form.

Vishvam (विश्वम) (*m*) The cause of the happening of the world. (V)

Vishvambhreshvar (विश्वम्भरेश्वर) (*m*) Lord of the earth (S)

Vishvāmitra (विश्वामित्र) (*m*) A celebrated sage who was born a Kshatriya, but by intense austerities raises himself to the Brahman caste, and became one of the seven great Rishis.

Vishvamitrapriya (विश्वामित्रप्रिया) (*m*) Belova of Vishvamitra. Lord Rama is greatly revered by the great sage Vishvamitra for His uprighteousness and just nature. (R) ,

Vishvamohini (विश्वमोहिनी) (*f*) The form which Vishnu assumed and embraced by Shiva, resulting in the birth of Mahāshasta.

Vishvamukh (विश्वमुख) (*m*) Lord of the universe (G)

Vishva-murti (विश्वमूर्ति) (*m/f*) Having all forms or one whose body is the universe.

Vishvananda (विश्वनन्दा) (*m*) A disciple of Brahma.

Vishva-nāth (विश्व-नाथ) (*m*) Lord of the universe.

Vishva-rāj (विश्व-राज) (*m/f*) All-ruling.

Vishvaretā (विश्वरेता) (*m*) The cause of the world.

Vishvarupā (विश्वरूपा) (*f*) Wife of Dharma and motho of Dharmavratā.

Vishvarupa (विश्वरूप) (*m*) Wearing all forms, omnipresent, universal, a title of Vishnu.

Vishvās (विश्वास) (*m*) Belief, trust, faith, reliance, confidence, assurance.

Vishva-Shri (विश्व-श्री) (*m/f*) Useful to all (said of Agni). Shri also means Lakshmi.

Vishvātmā (विश्वत्मा) (*m*) The spirit of the world (V)

Vishvesh/Vishveshvar (विश्वेश/विश्वेश्वर) (*m*) God, the master of the universe. A name of Shiva.

Vishveshwar (विश्वेश्वर) (*m*) Same as Vishvesh. The celebrated Linga or emblem of Shiva at Benares.

Vishvakarma (विश्वकर्मा) (*m*) The creator of the whole world (V)

Vistar (विस्तर) (*m*) The cause of expansion of the universe. (V)

Vitavhayah (वित्वहाया) (*m*) Free from all fright. (V)

Vitatha (वितथा) (*m*) A name of Bharadvāj after adoption by Bharat. A god to be worshipped in house building, before building a palace or house.

Vithal (विट्ठल) (*m*) Name of god to be worshipped at Pandharpur in Deccan. He is stated to be incarnation of Vishnu.

Vitolā (विटोला) (*f*) Very calm. Name of a river mentioned in Rajatarangini (Kashmir's history)

Vittadā (वित्तदा) (*f*) Wealth giver.

Vittaka (वित्तक) (*m*) Wealthy and famous.

Vittesh (वित्तेश) (*m*) Lord of wealth (Kubera)

Vitushan (वितुशन) (*a*) Content, satisfied, competent, wealthy.

Vivakshā (विवक्षा) (*f*) Wish, desire, significance, meaning.

Vivaktah (विवक्तः) (*m*) One who remains aloof from the world (V)

Vivek (विवेक) (*m*) Reasoning, wisdom intelligence, judgement.

Vivitsā (विवित्सा) (*f*) Desire of knowing or learning.

Vivitsu (विवित्सु) (*m/f*) Same as Vivitsā.

Vrageshvaras (व्रगेश्वरस) (*m*) Lord of Nagas.

Vrajesh (व्रजेश) (*m*) Lord of Vrindaban (K)

Vratdhara (व्रतधारा) (*m*) Practising penance (R)

Vribatah (वृबतः) (*m*) Huge (V)

Vriddhātma (वृद्धात्मा) (*m*) The ancient soul. (V)

Vrihadrupah (वृहद्रुपः) (*m*) The universal form (V)

Vrikādipti (वृकादिपति) (*m/f*) Shining like lightning, name of a son of Krishna.

Vriksha (वृक्ष) (*m*) The tree of Ashwattha (The Pipal tree) (V)

Vrishabhah (वृषभः) (*m*) One who showers choicest gifts for his devotees (V)

Vrishabh-āksha (वृषभ-आक्ष) (*m*) Having gracious look for all (V)

Vrishabha-priya (वृशभ-प्रिया) (*m*) The lover of dharma (V)

Vrishahi (वृशाही) (*m*) Reposing the effects of the sacrifice (Yagya) like Dvadasha and others within his control. (V)

Vrishakapi (वृषकपि) (*m*) Like the bull and monkey or the dharma and its tenets; also like the bull and boar. (V)

Vrishakarmā (वृषकर्मा) (*m*) The doer of the deeds to sustain dharma (V)

Vrishakriti (वृषकृति) (*m*) The bull like form (of Dharma) (V)

Vrishaparva (वृषपर्व) (*m*) The stairs of dharma to seek salvation for the aspirants (V)

Vrishni (वृष्णि) (*m/f*) Strong, powerful, mighty. Name of Shiva, Vishnu, Krishna and Indra.

Vrishodar (वृशोदर) (*m*) Holding the Dharma close to heart (V)

Vrishvāhan (वृषवाहन) (*m*) With bull (Nandi) as vehicle. (s)

Vriti (वृति) (*f*) Selecting, choosing, choice or boon.

Vyadīp (व्यादीप) (*n*) Illuminate thoroughly.

Vyāpana/Vyāpin (व्यापन/वयापिन) (*m/f*) Spreading through, pervading, filling, comprehensive.

Vyādishah (व्यादिशः) (*m*) He who gives appropriate orders to all (or who assigns every being's duty). (V)

Vyakta (व्यक्त) (*m*) Wise, distringuished, beautiful, one of the main disciples of Mahavira.

Vyalah (व्यलह) (*m*) He-like a serpent-no body could hold him. (V)

Vyapta (व्याप्त) (*m*) All round spreading. (V)

Vyās (व्यास) (*m*) An arranger. This title is common to many ancient authors and compilers, but it is especially applied to Veda-Vyas the arranger of the Vedas, who is also called Saswatās (the immortal). The name is also given to the compiler of the Mahabharata, the founder of the Vedanta philosophy, and the arranger of the Puranas; all these persons being held to be identical with Ved-Vyas. Ved Vyas Was the son of the Rishi Parasara and Satyavati, and was brought forth on an island (dwipa) in the Yamuna. The Puranas mention about twenty-eight Vyasas, incarnation of Vishnu, who descended to the earth in different ages to arrange and promulgate the vedas.

Vyavasāya (व्यवसाय) (*m*) The very source of knowledge (V)

Vyavasthān (व्यवस्थान) (*m*) One who ordains order in the creation (V)

Y (य, या)

Yādava (यादव) (*m*) A descendant of Yadu. The Yādavas were the celebrated race in which Krishna was born.

Yādavi (यादवी) (*f*) The wife of Bāhu and mother of Sagar.

Yadukumār (यदुकुमार) (*m*) Prince of Yadav tribe. (K)

Yadumani (यदुमणि) (*m*) Jewel of the Yadus.

Yadunandan/Yadupati/Yadurāj/Yadunāth (यदुनन्दन/यदुपति/यदुराज/यदुनाथ) (*m*) The leading luminary of the Yadu clan i.e. Krishna.

Yadupati (यदुषति) (*m*) Ord of Yadus. (K)

Yadurāj (यदुराज) (*m*) Lord of Yadus. (K)

Yaduvir (यदुवीर) (*m*) Hero of the Yadus.

Yadushreshtha (यदुश्रेष्ठा) (*m*) The best among the family of Yadu (as Krishna). (V)

Yādvendra (यादवेन्द्र) (*m*) Leader of the Yadavas. (K)

Yāgayatā (याज्ञता) (*f*) State or condition or worship.

Yagnaseni (यज्ञसेनी) (*f*) Another name of Draupadi who was born from fire of the Yajna/Yagna performed by her father king Drupada of Panchal.

Yagneshvar (यग्नेश्वर) (*m*) Lord of the sacrtifice. (V)

Yagneshvari (यगनेश्वरी) (*m*) Goddess of the scrtifice. (L)

Yagya/Yajan (यज्ञ/यजन) (*m*) Worship, devotion, prayer, praise, act of worshipping or devotion, sacrifice.

Yagyabhrit (यज्ञाभृत) (*m*) He who nourishes every activity. (V)

Yagyabhuk (यज्ञभुक) (*m*) He who enjoys the outcome of every Yagya. (V)

Yagyaguhyām (यज्ञगुह्यम) (*m*) The imperceptible manifestation of knowledge trhough Yagya. (V)

Yagyah (यज्ञः) (*m*) The cause of all catıvities in the world. (V)

Yagyā Kām (यज्ञा काम) (*m/f*) Desirous of worhsip.

Yagyakāyā (यज्ञकाया) (*m*) Accepter of sacrificial fires. (G)

Ygyakrita (यज्ञकृत) (*m*) The performer of the Yagya or who makes every Yagya an accomplishment. (V)

Yagyangah (यज्ञांगः) (*m*) The embodiment of all organs of a Yagya or the one who decides every activity in a Yagya. (V)

Yagyantakrita (यज्ञन्तकृत) (*m*) He who ends every Yagya or who bestows the reward of every Yagya. (V)

Yagyapatih (यज्ञपतिः) (*m*) The Lord of all Yagya or the decider of all activities. (V)

Yagya-rup (यज्ञ-रूप) (*m/f*) A form of worship. Name of Krishna.

Yagyasadhana (यज्ञसाधना) (*m*) The deity or the ultimate aim for which the Yagyas are performed. (V)

Yagyai (याज्ञी) (*m*) The ultimate goal of every Yagya or the final outcome of every activity. (V)

Yajantā (यजन्ता) (*m/f*) Worshipper of good things.

Yāji (याजी) (*m/f*) Sacrificing, worshipping.

Yajishnu (यजीश्णु) (*m/f*) Worshipping the gods.

Yajishthā (याजीश्था) (*m/f*) Worshipping very much.

Yajtā/Yajatā (यजता/यजता) (*m/f*) Worthy of worship, adorable, holy, sublime.

Yajtrā (याजत्रा) (*m/f*) Same as Yajtā.

Yājvā (याजवा) (*m*) He who is also the host of the Yagya or sacrifice. (V)

Yājvane (याज्वने) (*m*) One who performs Yagnas. Another name of Lord Rama. (R)

Yaksha (यक्ष) (*m*) Protector of the forest-a semi-divine being, quick, fast.

Aksharāj (यक्षराज) (*m*) King of the Yakshas.

Yākshī (याक्षी) (*f*) A female Yakshi. See also Yaksha.

Yamah (यमः) (*m*) The controlling deity inside every being. (V)

Yāminī (यामिनी) (*f*) One of the wives of Tārkshya. A Shakti. See Devi. Yāmini also means night.

Yamuna/Jamuna (यमुना/जमुना) (*f*) The river Yamuna rises in a mountain called Kalinda (Sun). The river is personified as the daughter of the Sun by his wife Sanjanā. The river is also called Kalindi. One of the most important rivers sacred to the Hindus.

Yash (यश) (*m*) Fame, reputation, renown, glory.

Yashaskarama (यशकर्म) (*m*) Giver of fame and glory. (G)

Yashasvani (यशस्वनी) (*f*) Beautiful, famous, illustrious. Reputed to the embodiument of highest knowledge and ultimate reality. Name of goddess Lakshmi. (L)

Yashchandra (यशचन्द्र) (*m*) Glorified, famous like the moon.

Yashobhadrā (यशोभद्र) (*m*) Famous as a gentle person.

Yashodā/Yashodhā (यशोदा/यशोधा) (*f*) Wife of cowherd Nanda, an foster-mother of Krishna.

Yashodānandan (यशोदानन्दन) (*m*) A name of Krishna.

Yashodāvatsala (यशोदावत्सल) (*m*) A name of Krishna.

Yashodevi (यशोदेवी) (*f*) A queen and mother of Jayadratha.

Yashodhagarbā (यशोधगर्बा) (*f*) Emerging from Yashoda's womb. Goddess Durga is believed to the daughter of Yashoda, and hence, the sister of Lord Krishna. (D)

Yashodhaman (यशोधमन) (*m*) Abode of glory.

Yashodhan (यशोधन) (*m*) Whose wealth is glory/fame.

Yashomati (यशोमति) (*f*) Having fame. Name of a foster mother of Krishna.

Yashonidhi (यशोनिधि) (*m*) Whose wealth is glory/fame.

Yashodhārī (यशोधरी) (*f*) Mother of Kāmadeva.

Yashovati (यशोवती) (*f*) Bright, lustrous gold.

Yashtikā (यशतिका) (*f*) String of pearls.

Yashvasin (यश्वसिन) (*m*) The popular, auspicious and beloved of all - Lord Ganesha. (G)

Yat (यत) (*m*) Self evident. (V)

Yathārup (यथारूप) (*m/f*) Extremely beautiful.

Yati (यति) (*m/f*) Restraint, control, guidance, stopping, a pause in music. Eldest of the six sons of king Nahush. He gave up worldly life to became a sage.

Yatirāj (यतिराज) (*m*) King of ascetics, name of Ramanuja.

Yog/Yoga (योग/योगा) (*m*) Joining, union, application, performance, supernatural means, meditation, contemplation, concentration of thoughts.

Yogadhip (योगधीप) (*m*) Lover of meditation. Lord Ganesha's name is chanted at the beginning and end of meditation at all times. (G)

Yogah (योगः) (*m*) The summit combination of mind and body. (V)

Yogānand (योगानन्द) (*m*) Delightring in meditation.

Yoganāth (योगनाथ) (*m*) Lord of Yoga.

Yogati (योगती) (*f*) State of union, the being united together.

Yogātman (योगात्मन) (*m*) One whose essence is Yoga.

Yogavidan (योगविदान) (*m*) The leader who knows Yoga Neta. (V)

Yogendra (योगेन्द्रा) (*m*) A master or adept in the Yoga.

Yogesh (योगेश) (*m*) Same as Yogish.

Yogeshvari (योगेश्वरी) (*m*) Goddess of all Yogis. (D)

Yogi (योगी) (*m*) Ever in communion (with His World). (V)

Yogine (योगीन) (*m*) Saint. Another name of saintly appearance-Lord Hanuman. (H)

Yogiraj (योगीराज) (*m*) The greatest ascetic. As an ascetic-Lord Shiva teaches mankind to mortify the body and suppress emotions and passions so that the loftiest spiritual knowledge may be attained. (S)

Yogish/Yogishvar (योगीश/योगीश्वर) (*m*) The most outstanding of the Yogis. An epithet of Lord Krishna.

Yudhishthira/Yudhishtra (युधिष्ठिर/युधिष्ट्र) The eldest of the five Pandu princes, mythologically the son of Dharma, the god of justice.

Yugal/Jugal (युगल/जुगल) (*n*) Yoke, team, a pair, couple.

Yugandhara (युगंधरा) (*m*) A great warrior who fought on the side of Pandavas in the Mahabharata war. He was a son of Satyaki.

Yukti (युक्ति) (*f*) Joined, united, union, connection.

Yukta (युक्त) (*m/f*) Joined, united, connected, combined, fit, suitable.

Yukta-rup (युक्त-रूप) (*m/f*) Suitably formed, fit, proper.

Yuti (युति) (*f*) Uniting, junction, union or meeting.

Yuvak (युवक) (*m*) A young man.

Yuvan (युवन) (*m/f*) Young, youthful, god, healthy. In Vedas it means some gods especially Indra, Agni and Maruts.

Yavati (युवती) (*f*) Young girl. In Rig Veda applied to night, morning, heaven and earth.

Yuvrāj (युवराज) (*m*) Young king, crown prince.